BILL STANFORD

*Aboriginal readers are advised that this book contains
photographs and information of people who have passed away*

First published in Australia 2021
This edition published 2023
Copyright © Bill Stanford 2021
Cover design, typesetting: WorkingType (www.workingtype.com.au)

The right of Bill Stanford to be identified as the Author of the Work has been asserted in accordance with the Copyright, Designs and Patents Act 1988.

All rights reserved. No part of this publication may be reproduced, stored in a retrieval system, or transmitted, in any form or by any means without the prior written permission of the author, nor be otherwise circulated in any form of binding or cover other than that in which it is published and without a similar condition being imposed on the subsequent purchaser.

Stanford, Bill, *Skirmish Hill*,
ISBN: 978-0-6453347-0-8
pp526

The man on the front cover is Arrai-iga, an Aborigine of the Arrernte tribe, of the Alice Springs area of the Northern Territory. The original photograph was taken in 1897 by Baldwin Spencer and Francis Gillen when Arrai-iga was the ceremonial leader of the emu totem. The body-scarring indicates his ritual status. Today that image is courtesy of Dr. Philip Jones, Senior Curator of Anthropology with the South Australia Museum, as published in his book, *The Images of Australia*.

Here, Arrai-iga stands in front of the Alice Springs waterhole as discovered and named by surveyor William Whitfield Mills on 11th March, 1871.

About the Author

Bill Stanford was born in Orange, New South Wales and educated in Moss Vale and Sydney. He started work with a stock and station agency in Mudgee, before being a jackaroo at Wingadee, Coonamble, and Ebor, east of Armidale, NSW, and then a driller in a mining camp in the Kimberley of Western Australia. The latter exposure to men from a great variety of lands encouraged him to buy a one-way ticket to Europe on a Russian ship. For two years he travelled, with stops in Italy, working on a Chianti vineyard; Germany, where he was a civilian assistant to a four-star General at an American Army base and England as a tour guide before accepting the position of a club manager. Along the way he was unfortunately stoned by a crowd of Muslims at the main mosque in Mashad, Persia, stopped by the police in Kandahar, Afghanistan, for speeding in a horse-drawn cart, chased on foot by four Afghans, two of whom were wielding their knives over an economic mis-understanding in Kabul, mugged twice in Brazil and detained for five days by the KGB in Russia.

Next, he met and married Janice, settled down and they raised their family at Dubbo, NSW. Then, over 14 consecutive years he and Janice explored at ground level but first-hand the lands, cultures and histories of peoples around the globe, in total more than one hundred and twenty countries. They undertook camping trips from Alaska to Mexico, Buenos Aires to Rio de Janeiro, Istanbul to Cairo, overland journeys from St Petersburg to Shanghai, five visits to the African continent, to the Americas and Asia, to North Korea, Moldova, Cuba, Syria, Bhutan and others along with a horse-riding expedition across western Mongolia. The highlight has most likely been aboard a Dutch Tall Ship, a three-masted, square-rigged barquentine constructed in 1911, working as voyage crew on five adventures including from Argentina to Antarctica and onto South Africa and later sailing 5,163 nautical miles non-stop from northern Brazil to go around Cape Horn from east to west, the first such rounding in a barquentine since 1939, to celebrate the 400th anniversary of the first rounding of the Horn.

Having seen something of the history of other lands Bill has now traversed those of his own country and wishes to pass on as best he can, some of the happenings and characteristics of our colonial era forebears that made Australians who they are today, wherever they originally came from.

A Dedication

This book is dedicated to the memory of William Whitfield Mills and others who went the extra mile for themselves, their fellow men, women and children, their country and, even if it didn't occur to them, for the likes of us today.

Bill Stanford, author.

Janice Stanford, author's wife.

Acknowledgements

To most modern day Australians much of remote inland Australia is a complete enigma, shrouded in mystery. Few travel there. Even fewer make it to Skirmish Hill but, fortunately, my travels have taken me there and other similarly distant places mentioned in this book.

I am very much indebted to the Ngatjatjatjarra, the traditional owners of the Blackstone-Wingellina area in the south-east of Western Australia that includes Skirmish Hill, and the Anangu Pitjantjatjarra Yankunytjatjarra, of the north-west of South Australia, who so kindly granted me permission to access their lands. But for their consideration some of the key information set out in this book would of necessity have fallen into the category of hearsay.

In that context I thank David and Margaret Hewitt of Alice Springs who helped me in gaining such approval and in guiding Roger and myself to Skirmish Hill. Since 1964 David and Margaret have lived and worked amongst many of the remote Aboriginal communities of the Northern Territory, Western Australia and South Australia. In 2009 they were both awarded the OAM for their efforts and are still going strong. David has constructed and maintained more than one hundred houses and other structures whilst also managing the community stores. In 1972 he built the first shop and service station at Uluru (Ayers Rock). As a nurse Margaret has devoted her career to Aborigines of many outback communities.

I am sincerely and eternally grateful for the considered encouragement, input and inspiration I received from the following people to make this narrative possible.

Dorothy Grimm, formerly of Alice Springs, now of Honolulu, Hawaii.

Janet Loneragan, formerly of Mudgee, now of Washington D.C., USA.

Barbara Ivusic, formerly of Sydney, now of Berlin, Germany.

Rawdon Stanford, of Peregian Springs, Queensland, technical support.

Roger Anonymous, fellow student of colonial Australia, my travelling companion to Skirmish Hill and likewise another long-term resident of Dubbo, Australia.

Janice Stanford, my eternal and understanding wife, who since 11th October, 1973, has always maintained the joy of my fortunate life.

This map features places named in the book. Those highlighted in large print are of more significance to the author. Graphic created by Deborah Dawson, of Wongarbon, via Dubbo.

Contents

About the Author		iii
A Dedication		iv
Acknowledgements		v
Introduction		xi
1	Shipwreck	1
2	Corroboree and Victoria Cross	20
3	Coming to Australia	47
4	The Royal Flying Doctor Service and The Overland Telegraph Line	61
5	Gold and Copper	74
6	Kapunda	97
7	Smoke Signals	108
8	Wonnaminta Station	140
9	Cattle Theft	161
10	Sidney Kidman & the Broken Hill	178
11	Cobb and Co. and first car Adelaide to Darwin	192
12	Aboriginal Maps and Outback Water	222
13	Waltzing Matilda	247
14	The Boer War	266
15	James 'Hungry' Tyson	284
16	Islamic attack and Railways.	295
17	Woomera and Coober Pedy	325
18	Ways of the Aborigines	337
19	Skirmish Hill	349
20	Alice Springs	379
21	Birdsville Races and Bloods Creek	395
22	Beltana and Wingadee	415
23	Dubbo to Manjimup	453
24	Convoy of the First Anzacs	460
25	Hardy Norseman	469
26	Coolgardie and the Afghans	478
27	Vale W.W. Mills	490
Bibliography		505
Index		506

Preface

The Battle of Melrose was waged between supporters and opponents of the 14-year old boy King James V, at verdant Skirmish Hill, Scotland, in 1526.

This book is named in honour of Australia's Skirmish Hill and the locations could hardly be more diverse for the latter resides in the region of Western Australia's Great Victoria Desert. In Australia's period of white settlement of the 19th century, no more than a handful of inquisitive and relentless explorers passed that way. Since then it has been asleep for it is distant, uninhabited and of no apparent interest to today's society.

Skirmish Hill may be seen as two books in one for the first half is a tale of some of the more interesting people, who, along with the policies and places of the day, made and left their mark in this great country. The storyline wanders at times as there are characters of interest that do not move and live in tandem but as fate dictates, and they are difficult to deny. Some, who sailed here in the Second Fleet, were prison guards and convicts, others were explorers, cattlemen, bushrangers, gold prospectors, stagecoach drivers, amateur doctors, soldiers, rabbit trappers, writers, Afghan cameleers and drovers. Many of them were to encounter the Aborigines who amazed the newcomers with the skills of their culture that enabled them to survive and live via their age-old ways of finding water with their maps, utilising a superior signalling system and adhering to their centuries-old social structures.

The book's central character, William Whitfield Mills, is called upon to connect some of the dots as he was a man who rode and worked far and wide in this unique and ancient land. In some instances the story includes family history as it is hard to ignore and easy to use the exploits of forebears when they also lived adventurous lives in challenging times, in the days when physical demands on men and women were infinitely more so than they are today.

William Whitfield Mills and other explorers arrived at Skirmish Hill by camel train, where they blazed a tree, as was the custom of the day, that proved they were there. The second part of the book jumps to the 21st century and a modern-day journey by the author and his friend to find the Skirmish Hill tree for themselves, after a ten-month quest to obtain permission from an Aboriginal tribe. During their 3,000 km return journey, they take a different route when they are exceedingly fortunate to be allowed to pass through the sacred lands of the Pitjantjatjara people in the north-west of South Australia.

The outcome of that modern day exploration leads the author, this time with wife Janice, to then search for the final resting place of William Whitfield Mills, said to be an unmarked grave on an island in a salt lake amongst the century-old goldfields of Western Australia.

"A people which no longer remembers
has lost its history and its soul"
Aleksandr Solzhenitsyn
The Gulag Archipelago

In 2002 I joined four farmers from Mudgee, Gilgandra, Gulargambone and Coonamble along with a fearless motorbike-riding butcher from Greystanes, Sydney, on an 11,175 km, forty day camping trip around the interior of Australia, camping out each night in a swag. Our journey included traversing the 1,900 km Canning Stock Route with its 900 sand dunes. That section began at Wiluna, an Aboriginal community of 200 to 600 people, according to traditional ways. As I entered the Wiluna store I passed four Aboriginal men, full blood, each holding a kangaroo tail. I asked the lady inside what the men do with the tails and she replied, word for word, 'Fighting. Today is pay day. They'll be fighting tonight and they'll be fighting tomorrow night.' Like a few remote outback stores she keeps 'roo tails in the freezer. Having made kangaroo tail soup I know kangaroo tails consist of bone and pure muscle, that strength enables the 'roo to sit on its tail to do its own fighting and also to be used as a powerful club. Greystanes was the site of the first land granted to emancipated convicts in 1791. In the 20th century a Maltese migrant, Frank Cefai, was famous for building thousands of Greystanes homes.

This is the route we took from the Docker River to Kalgoorlie.

Modern day nomads on the track.

Some 400 km north of Wiluna we turned off the CSR and drove east for 2 hours and 37 km to the Calvert Range with its cave paintings and startling red rock gorges where three descending layers of fresh water rock pools give life to magnificent snow-white gum trees.

Explorer John Forrest and his men were following the Murchison River, seeking pastoral country. These rocks are the remnants of a rock fort they built after being attacked by 40 to 60 Martu men —all plumed up and armed with spears and shields---at Weld Springs, CSR, June, 1874.

Happy and friendly adults.

Kids being kids, the world over.

Introduction

A Chinese proverb says 'past ignored, future ignoble'; another way of saying that if you don't know where you have come from, how can you hope to ensure that you make the most of where you are going? However, many non-indigenous people who came to Australia were all too happy to forget where they had come from. The majority of them knew only a life of poverty, despair, crime and discrimination and for decades, they outnumbered those who came of their own free will. Either way, they soon found they had the opportunity to shed the shackles of the past and that a person, man or woman, could, not easily but readily, make a fresh start in the great southern land.

With that in mind, I set out to uncover segments of Australian history, from the time of the Second Fleet to that of Adelaide-born Sir Sidney Kidman, who passed away in 1935, owning more land than any private individual ever has on this planet. I write this story via the life and times of W.W. Mills, my central figure, who is in turn a surveyor, an explorer and a gold prospector, a man of varied success along with much hardship and determination as shared by those he knew and whose paths he crossed. Mills is worthy of study because he was an authentic individual in a harsh land, as evidenced when in the employ of the management of the Overland Telegraph Line, whose superiors placed him in a leadership role, in the field. In later years, when fending for himself in the then unknown deserts of both Central and Western Australia, he displayed not only gritty determination and resolve to succeed, but consideration for Afghan cameleers and the Indigenous Australians.

At times, the reader may query the abrupt appearance of certain figures or why I seemingly change horses mid-stream. These moments are deemed necessary to connectively transmit how Mills and many other pioneering men, women and children were lightly touched by, or, deeply immersed in, the challenges of colonial Australia. You will also discover that several of the historical sites referred to in the first half of the story, are brought to life in the second segment when my travelling companion and I set out to physically meld the past with the present.

Cattle Muster — Tobias Keller.

1
Shipwreck

Who is to know when and where they will die? Personally I don't wish to know but on reflection perhaps I do, leastways the day and the month. My father died on 3 January, 2000, and his mother on 3 January, 1967, while an earlier relative expired on 3 January, 1836. Before I leave the known world, I would like to acknowledge the men and women who preceded us and perhaps one in particular, a man named William Whitfield Mills, who blazed a track or two through the genuine Australian outback and like thousands of others of a similar ilk, who endured a life of hardship in an untamed environment, helped to set up this great country for those who came after them. He died on 18th August, 1916 and, as I will in due course explain, I set out to honour his life on 18th August, 2016, the 100th anniversary of his death and burial.

When I selected Mr. Mills to represent many, I had good intentions of pursuing that sole course, but I have since discovered there is historical need to utilise some of my forebears as I now see justification for their inclusion. Apart from any unintended inclination on my part, they were also instrumental in setting the scene that was changing Australia in the 19th century. I may be biased but for the most part I shall only be relating their more interesting and challenging times. After all, the blood that freely courses through my veins today is derived from the combinations of those I never encountered. I have a third cousin, once removed, who is a keen student of family history and genealogy. Over time, she has determined that she is related to no less than 128,132 people. Obviously most of them are deceased. It seems a huge number but she says that once one can trace one's history back to royalty, the task becomes much easier as the lineage preceding kings and queens was generally well documented. I know a young English woman who can trace her family line back to William the Conqueror. This story is much more than family history, it is Australian history.

I ask you bear with me as the road ahead twists and turns with the events and the years, and so to keep this narrative in chronological order, where possible, I must start at the beginning. Due to there being so many people involved it is unavoidable that at times my characters come and go, as did their times and their individual activities.

My earliest ancestor to arrive in Australia was Andrew Hamilton Hume, born in County Down, Ireland, in 1762. His mother was Ann Hamilton of Scotland and Andrew was proud of his Scottish lineage. He was a descendant of Sir Patrick Hume, 5th Baron Polwarth, Gentleman of the Bedchamber and a Scottish courtier to King James VI and, after 1589, of the household of Queen Anne. By the time Andrew was twenty-one, he had a working knowledge of growing and processing flax, a plant grown for its seed, as in linseed, and the thread that comes from flax to make linen. At age twenty-four, he was in the army when he fell into an argument with a senior officer in his regiment, whom he felt had made a most disparaging remark. After he had thrown his superior out of his saddle and to the ground, the two men embarked upon a duel, with Hume having a general and a captain as his seconds. Hume was a big man with a quick and ready temper and he severely wounded his opponent, following which he quickly left the army. A friend, who would later be Earl Moira, arranged a suitable position for Hume but he ruined that by having an affair with the gentleman's daughter. He may have been unlucky when a rich uncle, believing Andrew to have died, then omitted him from his will.

From there he must have found life somewhat difficult as the next we know of Andrew Hume is as a prison guard on one of His Majesty's hulks at Woolwich, London. His Majesty then was King George III who ruled from 1760 to 1820, a remarkably long reign. The hulks were old, dismasted warship hulls, destined to be broken up and burned. In their day they had been some of the Royal Navy's most renowned ships. They were then used to house prisoners of war and convicts awaiting transportation to the colonies. Initially such hulks were to be utilised as a temporary measure, for just two years. Despite those people who rightly deplored the diseases, despair and death that heavily infiltrated the prison hulks and called for them to be banned, the reality is that the authorities used those wretched hulks for eighty years. As housing convicts was an expensive exercise, even in the atrocious hulks, the convicts were put to work, hard labour in fact, to pay their way. They had to dredge the River Thames, build the Arsenal and the nearby docks and do the pile-driving. In summer they worked ten hours a day and in the winter for seven hours.

The prisoners were chained up at night and at other times wore fetters or shackles on each leg, with a chain in between that tied up around their waist or else it went right up to their neck. Some prisoners were chained together in pairs and the worst villains had the heaviest fetters. Either six or seven guards with drawn cutlasses constantly walked among them to prevent escape or laziness. Andrew Hume was such a guard at the Woolwich prison hulks.

When prisoners were convicted in England and sentenced to transportation to Australia, it was for seven or fourteen years or for the length of their life. Anticipating the long, if not permanent separation from their family or other loved ones, many of the condemned gave convict love coins to those they left behind. Using copper coins, which were soft, they smoothed the surface of the popular coins, which was a criminal act in itself. The 1797 cartwheel penny and the 1827 halfpenny were the most popular coins on account of their size as a good working platform. Some convicts such as silversmiths and metal workers had enough ability to design their own love tokens while others strove to make their own. As few survived, the better coins nowadays have a good degree of value.

In 1789, Andrew Hume was selected as one of eight Superintendents of Convicts. Hume was also assigned as an agricultural instructor to convicts, on account of his experience with growing flax, and no doubt his proven ability to control prisoners, at £40 per year. This position gained him a berth on the 44-gun frigate *Guardian* which was to support the First Fleet in taking convicts to the fledgling colony at Sydney, Australia. Half of the ship's armaments were removed and the regular crew of ninety-three sailors along with the eight instructors, twenty-five convicts and 1,003 tons of cargo set sail on 10th September, 1789. The cargo included two years of stores and food that were intended for the colonists in Sydney as it was anticipated they would be essentially starving until they could grow their own produce.

The *Guardian*, under the command of then Lieutenant but later Captain, Edward Riou, sailed without incident to Cape Town where it dropped anchor to take on board salted beef and pork for the voyage ahead. Edward Riou had gone to sea at the age of twelve and later sailed on *HMS Resolution* with Captain James Cook. After Captain Cook was killed in Hawaii and Captain Clerke left the HMS *Discovery* to take command of the *Resolution*, Riou sailed with Captain Clerke aboard the *Resolution*. In Cape Town, Captain Riou oversaw the loading of trees and plants for the new colony along with fresh water. Cattle, sheep, pigs, geese, horses, ducks and rabbits were also brought onto the ship. Rabbits!

Cape Town was full of French and, new to the commercial world, American, trading ships. Their captains constantly enquired of Captain Riou about trade prospects at the new colony. Some did not know of its precise location but he endeavoured to dissuade them, one and all, as such possible foreign intervention would not yet be welcome and the convicts would likely try to escape via trading vessels, which more than a few would later do.

After weighing anchor and leaving Cape Town in her wake, the *Guardian* continued her long journey. On 11th December, the *Guardian* was 2,080 kilometres (km), further to the south, at 43 degrees south and not far from the Crozet Islands, which are a sub-Antarctic archipelago and part of the French Southern and Antarctic Lands. We shall return to the Crozet Islands later.

The Captain intended to reach 44 degrees south, at which point he could expect to pick up the strong westerly winds which should carry him across the Indian Ocean to Tasmania. As there were icebergs in the vicinity he hove to and put the jolly boat and the two cutters over the side to collect ice so the livestock could have fresh water. Captain Riou kept his ship well back, two kilometres or more, from those icebergs and when the work was done moved off. Not much later, the *Guardian* was nicely underway at some six or seven knots, when a heavy and totally unexpected fog suddenly closed in on the *Guardian*. This was followed by a savage grating sound and a ship's shudder which told one and all that there was a problem. The ship had gone onto a slightly submerged section of an iceberg. The crew managed to move the ship off the iceberg but water poured in through the hull.

The four pumps were called into action and all were found to be in good working order but water continued to rise in the hull, up to two metres. All believed the sinking ship had no chance of surviving but Captain Riou refused to leave his ship and he called for volunteers who would stay with him nonetheless to not give up whatever chance they may have. Many, perhaps trusting in his calm and controlled manner, stayed with him. Andrew Hume, the rogue, was one who supported his Captain. Half the ship's company, as many as could fit, lowered and then set off in the small boats, carrying as many provisions as was by then possible. One boat was immediately lost when it capsized on hitting the water.

The other two boats were soon lost to sight and between them those on board continued pumping water non-stop, for every minute of every day. They rigged a studding sail under the ship to try to seal off some of the water from entering the hull. The exercise was not initially successful but after several attempts, they managed to place eight ropes on either side of the underwater sail and lash it to both sides of the ship. This certainly helped but with bursts of bad weather including southern-ocean storms the men were tested to the limit to eventually hold their own. As it happens I have experienced two Force 10 storms in the Great Southern Ocean whilst sailing aboard the Dutch three-masted, square-rigged, barquentine *Europa*, from Antarctica to South Africa, and can in some small measure comprehend the weather conditions they encountered.

The remaining crew of the *Guardian*, including the convicts, who before leaving England had been advised by Captain Riou that if they behaved on the voyage, he would ensure their good conduct was suitably rewarded, toiled away non-stop for an extraordinary sixty-one days. The convicts performed as well as the freemen and somehow the *Guardian* limped into Cape Town. Captain Riou was true to his word and petitioned the Lords Commissioners to grant the convicts a pardon and fourteen of them received such a reward. Of the sixty-five men who had deserted the ship and taken to the boats, ten survived but only after fortuitously being picked up by a passing French merchant ship, the *Viscountess* of Brittany. Of the sixty-one men who stayed with Captain Riou all survived. Family records report Andrew Hume lost all his hair due to exposure and later family members made a wig that he then wore continually.

The wrecked *Guardian* was beached near Cape Town and Captain Riou was lauded as a hero throughout England for his illustrious command throughout the harrowing sixty-one days in which he kept his men alive. He later worked closely with Vice-Admiral Horatio Nelson who observed his death at the Battle of Copenhagen and called the loss irreparable. If one day you visit St. Paul's Cathedral, London, you may find the monument to Captain Edward Riou and of course that of Horatio Nelson.

Before we sail on, there are a few surprising coincidences amongst the above names. Captain William Bligh was married to the niece of Duncan Campbell who was the contractor in charge of the convict hulks at Woolwich, where Andrew Hume was a guard. Captain Bligh was sailing master for Captain Cook on the *Resolution* and Edward Riou was also then on the *Resolution*. When Bligh was Captain of the *Bounty*, his sailing master was John Fryer, who accompanied Bligh in his epic voyage in the open longboat. Fryer was also appointed to that position by Captain Riou when he was trying to salvage the *Guardian* in Cape Town. Andrew Hume knew Riou and Fryer. The previous year, 1788, Captain Bligh had dinner in Cape Town with a man by the name of Lachlan Macquarie, who twenty-two years later would replace Bligh as Governor of NSW.

We will now return to the Crozet Islands, near where the *Guardian* struck the iceberg. The Crozets were discovered a mere seven years before the *Guardian* came their way, by the French explorer Marion du Fresne. He commanded the ship, *Le Mascarin*, and his second-in-command was Julien-Marie Crozet, who landed on the island of Isle de la Possession and claimed the archipelago for France. After that, *Le Mascarin* sailed on to New Zealand where Captain du Fresne and most of his crew were killed and eaten by the Maori. Crozet escaped the massacre and brought the survivors back to Cape Town, where in 1776 he met Captain James Cook, at the start of his famous third voyage.

As time went on the Crozet Islands became infamous for the high number of shipwrecks on their coasts, sealing and whaling attracting scores of hunters. In

1887 the French ship, *Tamaris*, was wrecked and the crew stranded on the Isle de Cochons, the isle of pigs. The Frenchmen caught an albatross and fastened a small piece of metal around its neck. According to the *Bendigo Advertiser* newspaper, on it were scratched the French words, 'Thirteen shipwrecked men took refuge upon the Crozet Islands. August 4th 1887'. Seven months later the albatross, still wearing that dramatic message, was discovered, dead, on the beach at Fremantle, Western Australia.

France and England both then sent rescue ships to the Crozets and a French transport ship, *Meurthe*, reached the Isle de Cochons. On the shore the crew found a pile of stones, heaped up to attract attention. On a piece of paper therein and written in French with a lead pencil was the following message, 'The iron ship, *Tamaris*, of Bordeaux, with thirteen men in the crew, went ashore on the island of Cochons during a heavy fog. Some time after that she got clear and floated off, but three hours later she filled and sank. The crew escaped in two small boats to the island, taking with them 100 kilograms of biscuit. The crew has lived on Cochons Island for nine months, and, with their food being exhausted, they are about to set out for Possession Island. September 30, 1887'.

The Crozet Islands receive rain on at least 300 days of the year and usually shipwrecked sailors could exist for some time on seals, eggs, birds and fish. Possession Island is only eight miles from Cochons Island but when the rescue team from *Meurthe* landed there and searched the island they found no trace of the thirteen men and presumed they died whilst making that relatively short but obviously hazardous crossing. The winds thereabouts are remarkably strong, as they would have known, and I wonder if the two boats were capsized. When I sailed from Antarctica to Cape Town on the aforementioned Dutch barquentine, *Europa*, we encountered strong winds for most of the voyage. As we neared the remote but inhabited island of Tristan da Cunha, which is 2,800 kilometres south-west of Cape Town, the winds which had been forceful every day and night since leaving Antarctica, inexplicably eased off as we came to the island. This sudden turn of fortune enabled us to anchor one kilometre offshore and, courtesy of the zodiacs, to be the first visitors to the island for eight months. The winds blow so strong that planes cannot land there. I can envisage the Crozet winds drowning the French sailors. If the noble albatross had flown in a straight line, and at sea I have watched wandering albatrosses fly for long periods of time in circular patterns, but if it had flown direct from La Possession to Fremantle, the shortest straight-line distance is 5,605 kilometres. The great war-bird may well have died of sheer exhaustion, on behalf of the stranded French crew. In the southern hemisphere albatrosses are known to have flown around the world in eighty days.

In 18th century England, children went to work when they were ten years old. While the wealthy adults drank imported and taxed brandy, port, claret and sherry the great unwashed drank gin. This was made from English corn without any restrictions on its distilling, and no matter what effect it had on people, by 1743 they were drinking 8 million gallons of gin per year. From 1750 to 1790 England's population doubled to 12 million. This resulted in mass unemployment and a surfeit of criminals.

There were 223 crimes for which sentencing could incur the death penalty. The list included damaging Westminster Bridge, cutting down trees, splitting someone's nose, and stealing a boat on a navigable river. The trick was to steal the boat from a canal, as that crime did not suffer the death penalty. In the courts it was the magistrate who handed down the sentence and as he was usually a wealthy person of financial means he did not receive payment for his services. Wealthy or not, many magistrates were therefore open to receiving bribes, and Horace Walpole, the noted English historian and playwright, claimed 'the greatest criminals of this town are the officers of justice.'

Court cases lasted only a few minutes so as to get through them all and the courtrooms themselves were sprinkled with fresh flowers and herbs to mask the smell of the prisoners and to hopefully contain the spread of disease. Renowned highwaymen were popular with the common people as evidenced by the supposed crowd of 200,000 which arrived to see Jack Sheppard hanged in 1724, after he had escaped four times from prison. Forgers were hanged because of the increase in paper wealth, via cheques, banknotes, bonds and shares and consequently a decrease in the usual bags of gold. The town of Horsham held its regular 'Horsham Hang Fair' where prisoners arrived in a horse-drawn cart, sitting on their coffin, amidst the cheers of the crowd who were expecting a dramatic farewell speech.

The Industrial Revolution was good for the manufacturers and the bosses and while it gave jobs to many, it also put others on the growing unemployment heap. I sense similarities between the Industrial Revolution and today's globalisation. With machinery taking their place on farms, the displaced workers crowded into the big cities. The increase in crime meant that England was short of prisons and half of the prisons were privately owned. 'The trade of chains' meant that prisoners had to pay for their food, water and straw mattresses. Minor sentences were flogging and branding. For some time, prisoners were branded on the side of the face to indicate their conviction. In later years the British Army branded deserters, at least the ones who were not shot. Prisoners were transported to America for seven or fourteen years. Unscrupulous English gaolers sold them to shipping contractors who in turn sold them to plantation owners in the Caribbean and in America. After the American colonies rebelled and the War of Independence ended in 1783, the English were no longer able to send their prisoners there but the reality was that black African slaves made white convicts redundant. Five years later, England began transporting the surplus convicts to the colony of Australia.

Generally speaking, convicts who had committed violent crimes were put to work by the government in chain gangs, to build roads and public buildings. The government soon found that it was costing too much in scarce funds to maintain so many exiles in the colony so it permitted those men and women who had committed lesser crimes to be assigned to private persons who were then responsible for their maintenance in exchange for labour. It might sound like an improvement but it could be said it was a form of slavery. One convict was granted to a settler for every 100 acres of land the free settler held. Such convicts who were found to be neglectful of duty, losing sheep, absconding, insubordination, stealing and drunkenness were given fifty or one hundred lashes and were then returned, scarred for life, to their masters, where they were made to work in chains for the next twelve months.

In 1530 England introduced the *Whipping Act* which authorised the whipping of thieves, poachers and other offenders, including the insane. The public square of every town had a whipping post, which laid the foundation of a ruthless society. The British Empire was founded on the whip/lash to control the public, slaves, the military and imperial convicts. All were subjected to its horrors in order to conform to certain standards of behaviour. The handle of the whip was connected to a cat o' nine tails, being nine thongs of leather. Every thong had three knots, each of which could puncture a man's skin. Thus there were twenty-seven knots per lash. Eventually the basic punishment was one hundred lashes and they were dispensed over one hour. Convict records show that from 1817 to 1839 in Tasmania alone 1.3 million lashes of the whip were dealt out to convicts.

Here is part of a convict ballad from 1825. 'The very day we landed upon the fatal shore, the planters stood around us full twenty score or more. They ranked us up like horses and sold us out of hand, they chained us up to pull the plough, upon Van Diemen's Land.'

The Dutch explorer Abel Tasman discovered Australia's prominent southern island on 24th November, 1642, and named it Anthoonij van Diemenslandt, in honour of the Governor-General of the Dutch East Indies. In 1855, after the island became independent of NSW, it was re-named as Tasmania.

Many poor immigrants were employed as labourers and shepherds but when the gold rushes began they deserted their employers en masse. As a result, shepherds' wages trebled to £70 to £80 a year. Crops were not harvested, but after the rush subsided, there was an abundance of labour.

Meanwhile the *Lady Juliana*, sailing from England to Australia as part of the dreaded Second Fleet, arrived in Cape Town. The First Fleet had been organised and administered by the British Government but by the time of the Second Fleet, England was once again at war with France and doctors could not now be spared to accompany the Fleet. Additionally the private, non-Naval Captains were in charge of the food they carried for those in Sydney. Consequently they tended to short-change their own passengers so as to have surplus food to sell in Sydney. The Second Fleet carried 1,005 convicts and 25 per cent of them died during the voyage while another 40 per cent died within six months of their arrival. It wasn't known as the Death Fleet for nothing.

Andrew Hume had survived on the *Guardian* and while the *Guardian's* remaining convicts were transferred to the *Neptune* and the *Sphinx*, which took them on to Botany Bay he made sure he gained a berth on the *Lady Juliana*, despite that convict tragedy which was about to unfold. The *Lady Juliana* carried 225 convicts but they were all female and most of them were London prostitutes. When that ship had stopped off at Rio de Janeiro one of her crew, Nicol, poetically reported that 'our Jewesses allowed ashore, set up their tents and did a roaring trade with the local gents'. Nicol says every man on board took unto himself a wife from the 'cargo'. A good time was had by all with no one keen to finally reach Sydney, that last leg taking a leisurely seventy-five days and the entire voyage a staggering 309 days. No wonder the ship was known as a floating brothel. The *Lady Juliana* was the first ship since the First Fleet to reach Sydney and the relief was palpable. The starving population literally wept for joy although most of them sought food rather than wanton women. They were ecstatic when days later the *Justinian* arrived, laden to the gunwales with food and other supplies.

In 1834, the British Parliament passed the South Australia Act which decreed the province lie between 132 degrees east and 141 degrees of east longitude and between the Southern Ocean and 26 degrees south latitude. Amongst a host of other regulations it stated that the sale price of land must not be less than twelve shillings per acre, no matter how worthwhile, or not, the land. The money raised would go into the Emigration Fund that would be used to cover the costs of transporting more migrants. Neither was there to be any form of religious discrimination or unemployment.

That latter ruling did not help the likes of Mary Ann Wade, born in London on the 5th of October, 1777. On 5th October, 1788, when she was having, but probably not celebrating, her 11th birthday, she stole a frock and a scarf, from an eight-year-old child. The frock was sold to a pawnbroker and the police found the scarf in her room. She was a beggar on the streets of London by profession. Mary Wade was tried at the Old Bailey law courts, found guilty and sentenced to death by hanging.

She was detained in London's notorious Newgate Prison, which was in use from 1188 to 1902 and wherein 1,169 inmates were executed. People who stared out of the cell bars were said to be 'polishing the king's iron with their eyebrows'. Prisoners of certain infamy included Casanova, for bigamy; Captain Kidd, pirate; Owen Suffolk, who was transported from England to Australia and was the only convict exiled from Australia back to England for further crimes; Daniel Defoe, the author of *Robinson Crusoe*; William Penn, the Quaker who founded Pennsylvania, Thomas Cream who claimed to be Jack the Ripper and the extraordinary Jorgen Jorgensen, known as the Viking of Van Diemen's Land.

Amongst a myriad of life-time adventures the Danish-born Jorgensen was assistant captain on a whaling ship, the first Dane to sail around the world, fought in sea battles against the British and sailed to Iceland where he declared the country independent from Denmark and himself the new ruler. He was twice interred, for theft, in Newgate Prison where he was the assistant surgeon and after his death sentence in Newgate Prison was commuted he was sent to Van Diemen's Land where he served as a policeman and founded Hobart. He spoke several languages, was a gambler and also a writer whose literary works are in the British Museum.

The Ross Bridge, 78 km south of Launceston, was built by convicts from locally quarried stone. Naturally the convicts did the quarrying. It has to be mentioned because it is not only the third oldest bridge in Australia but possibly the most picturesque, if not the most beautiful bridge in Australia. The bridge, whose three magnificent arches sit astride the Macquarie River, was built by convicts under the guidance of two highly skilled stonemasons, the convicted highwayman, Daniel Herbert, and James Colbeck. The latter, unemployed, was forced into the crime of burglary in an attempt to feed his starving family and sentenced in 1828 to transportation for life in Van Diemen's Land.

The construction of the stone bridge was completed on 14th July, 1836, and to this day the joints in the stonework are of the highest order of accuracy and show no cracks to speak of, such was the quality of the convict labour. The foundations are founded on a rock plate and have not moved. There are 188 carvings in the bridgework, of people, animals, insects, plants and Celtic gods and goddesses. Set amongst them one will find the stone face of Jorgen Jorgensen, the Viking of Van Diemen's Land.

Mary Wade was the youngest ever inmate and during her ninety-three days in that hellhole, which doctors refused to enter, the reigning monarch King George III was seemingly cured of a degenerative mental disease. In celebration of his good fortune the king decreed that all women on death row have their sentences commuted, to transportation to the penal colony in Australia. Mary Wade consequently sailed aboard the notorious *Lady Juliana*, which finally arrived in Sydney in June, 1790.

Barely had Andrew Hume regained his land-legs, than Governor Arthur Phillip, knowing of Hume's farming connections, sent him to Norfolk Island to assist Lieutenant-Governor Philip Gidley King to start up the production of flax on the island. He sailed on the *Surprize* in August, 1790, along with the convict, Mary Wade. I hope he looked after the young girl. I rather gather he did for it became an awful place. Mary Wade had twenty-one children and died at the age of eighty-two in Fairy Meadow, NSW. Her family then numbered more than 300 descendants spread across five generations, one of whom is the former Australian Prime Minister, Mr. Kevin Rudd. Mary Wade was his paternal 5th great grandmother.

I thought the *Guardian* was part of the Second Fleet but I have discovered that the Lords Commission of the Admiralty decreed that it sent the *Guardian* to Botany Bay not only as support to, but as a participant in, the First Fleet. *The Guardian* has been entitled, The Lost Ship of the First Fleet. So I am a descendant of a First Fleeter. Governor Phillip had doubts about the suitability of Botany Bay and attempted to arrive before the rest of the First Fleet. When he decided to see if Port Jackson might be a better site he said he, 'had the satisfaction of finding the finest harbour in the world, in which a thousand sail of the line may ride in the most perfect security.'

On Norfolk Island, Andrew Hume put his flax making skills to work as flax had previously been reported on the island and Captain Cook had endorsed its possible production, hopefully for sailcloth. Hume did produce two yards of cloth which he sent he sent to Governor Phillip along with a letter asking the Governor to supply him with looms, spinning wheels, oil, cat gut, different stays and in particular weaver's brushes. Hume also sent the Governor an 80-litre cask of Norfolk Island flax seeds. These were found to be superior to the flax seeds sent out from England, which were not suitable to the Norfolk Island terrain. The material Hume did make was assessed and found to be adequate for making convict clothes but that was all. It was certainly not good enough for turning into sailcloth. Along with a lack of working materials, Hume and his convicts never had a chance of producing flax products, despite the well-intentioned beliefs of Captain Cook. The project was abandoned but Norfolk Island was then as much a deterrent to French occupation as a penal colony. Historians claim Norfolk Island became a more notorious penal colony than dreaded Port Arthur. Female convicts were forced to dance naked in front of the male convicts. Each woman had a number painted on her back, for judging purposes. That action has arguably mutated to the Melbourne Cricket Ground when crowds of up to 100,000 people now attend international cricket matches. Men in Bay 13 hold up cards numbered from one to ten when young women, foolishly no doubt, choose to walk among them.

On 29th September, 1796, Elizabeth More Kennedy married Andrew Hamilton Hume and they took up a land grant of 14 hectares at Toongabbie, Sydney, not far from Parramatta which at the time was home to Government House. Elizabeth had arrived in Sydney on the *Sovereign* on 5th November, 1795, accompanied by her widower brother and his three daughters who she would be foster mother to. On 19th June, 1797, Andrew and Elizabeth's first son, Hamilton Hume, was born.

Hamilton Hume is regarded by some as being the first child born of free parents in the colony. He is certainly known as an explorer of note and many claim him to be Australia's greatest explorer. He had a natural instinct for the bush and a desire to know its land cover and animals and how they existed. He learned to speak several Aboriginal languages. As a boy he was always roaming far and wide through the bush although he and his brothers, John and Francis Rawdon, known as Rawdon, along with their sister Isabel, were fortunately educated by Elizabeth, their highly intelligent mother.

Andrew Hume had formed connections, and in 1798, Governor Hunter appointed him the government storekeeper at Parramatta, only to be dismissed later by Governor King on a charge of 'malversation of public property', malversation being corrupt behaviour by a person in public office. Essentially Hume had been accused of theft but the reality was that this big man, of strong will but with all-too-quick reactions, had been giving food to those who could not provide enough for themselves. He said of himself, to his wife, Elizabeth, 'Dishonesty. That's what the blackguard called it. If it's stealing to give them poor lags (ex-convicts) a bit more tucker than the regulation says they can have, then a thief I am indeed. And if they take a hog now and again from the government herds and me not looking at the poor devils, then sure I'm lax an' lazy. 'Tis fed up to the teeth with the lot of them I am—(Governor) King an' Johnson an' Foveaux—all of them.'

Philip Gidley King was the third Governor of NSW while Joseph Foveaux was the Lieutenant-Governor who later replaced Major George Johnson as the Colonial Administrator. Hume was not fond of authority where he found fault with it. The trial of Andrew Hume resulted in him being declared not guilty. Knowing that Elizabeth Hume told Andrew that his quick temper was matched by that of Governor King, who may have had it in for his subordinate from the earlier days when both served on Norfolk Island, I rather gain the impression that whilst Andrew Hume may have deserved his reputation in England as a rogue, those dalliances were over once he married Elizabeth in Australia for there is no recorded instance of him stepping out of line, in any direction, from then on. Governor King and Andrew Hume did not get along so when Andrew had the opportunity he signed his name to an address of welcome to the incoming fourth Governor of NSW, Captain William Bligh.

An educated woman, Elizabeth Hume taught orphaned children and she became the Matron of the first Orphan House in Sydney, in George Street. She is regarded as the first public servant in NSW. The institution cared for young girls who otherwise would have little chance then or in later life. Due to her devotion to her young wards Elizabeth was described by a journalist as the Mother of the Colony. By 1804, Elizabeth Hume was tending to the care of 104 girls and more premises were required. To pay for a larger building at Parramatta and to maintain its upkeep, taxes were levied on vessel registrations, permission to sail into Botany Bay, the incorrect use of convict labour, the purchase of coal, a levy on the export of timber, fines for polluting the Tank Stream such as cleaning fish therein, duty on auction sales and imported alcohol and fines imposed by magistrates and judges.

Andrew and the family later moved out to farmland where South Creek flows into the Hawkesbury River but they lost nearly everything when it was flooded in 1809. The man then moved his family to better country near Cowpastures, to the south of the Sydney Basin. Today Cowpastures is known as the town of Camden, 65 km south-west of Sydney, and interestingly Camden Airport will be only 24 km due south of Sydney's now under-construction second airport, less as the crow flies.

Soon after the First Fleet landed, two bulls and four cows had escaped from their new homeland and disappeared. In 1795 wild cattle were found south of the Nepean River and in good condition; they were doing well. When Governor Macquarie later took an interest in the welfare of this rapidly growing herd of cattle, to protect them and also to provide food for the colony, he ordered, 'No person to hunt or travel into the Cowpastures without licence under penalty of death.'

Governor Macquarie gave two grants of 2,270 hectares each, to the sheep and wool supremo and Rum Corps cartel leader, John Macarthur, at the request of the British Government. The land was close to Cowpastures. When Macquarie inspected Cowpastures in 1810 there were 5,000 head of cattle grazing there. When the government eventually realised there were too many cattle at Cowpastures and decided to remove them, the word was spread so quickly that by the time the authorities moved in, the locals and others had all but cleared the cattle out.

Andrew Hume led his family in that direction, to Appin, 16 km south of today's Campbelltown. Specifically he took up a selection of good land on the edge of Cowpastures, and between the Nepean River and the Georges River. Both rivers begin there and the Nepean formed the eastern border of Cowpastures as it flowed north until it joined the Hawkesbury at Richmond. The Georges River begins more to the east and also flows north but only for a while as it then turns completely east and empties into Botany Bay. Hume had chosen well, except for one thing. He was there illegally, on Crown land.

He named it Hume Mount Farm and cleared the tall, thick-butted eucalypt trees by ringbarking them. A year later he dug a trench to the depth of a third of a metre or more around the trees. The lateral roots had to be dug out so as not to interfere with the future ploughing. Then timber was stacked into the trench and the tree burnt until it collapsed on itself. The best branches were saved for winter firewood and the rest added to the burning of the tree. He built a small stone house which exists and is lived in today and grew wheat, corn, potatoes and turnips. From my limited experience it had to be good ground to grow turnips and I am sure it was rewarding. He no doubt felt that way when after just two years his seven-hectare wheat crop prior to harvest was estimated, by other farmers, to yield sixty-six bushels per hectare. That would give him enough money to build a solid new house.

Riding home one evening he was overtaken by an officer, Captain Antill, of the 73rd Regiment. His spirits dropped as he realised he was to be arrested for trespassing on Crown land without due title. He could lose everything. The Captain took him to the riverbank where he was introduced to Governor Lachlan Macquarie, who said to Hume, 'You have a God-given voice, my friend. Too good to be (as previously) heard at a distance. Will you sing for us here by the camp fire?'

The Governor kept Hume singing until he was tired and then talked with him late into the night. Realising Hume's land was outside the nominated area of settlement, Governor Macquarie told Hume he might be able to later extend the boundary, to Hume's benefit. He then asked if he would sing the following morning, at 11 o'clock, for Mrs. Macquarie, in particular with a rendition of Hume's exquisite 'Last Rose of Summer'. Hume duly obliged. The Deputy Surveyor-General, James Meehan, was travelling with the Governor's personal staff and Macquarie sent Mr. Meehan back with Andrew Hume to measure up his selection, with instructions to then draw up a deed of grant. Governor Macquarie granted Andrew Hume 27 hectares in 1812, then 40 at Appin and later, 22 hectares.

When Governor Arthur Philip established the settlement at Sydney, he did so on the basis that the people, settlers and convicts, would produce goods and services that would make the colony self-sufficient. There would be no shops but a myriad of small farms for all to work and live with no money but a utopian socialist barter economy. His military forces being from the Navy were Marines and became known as the NSW Corps. Being sailors, they were conditioned to consuming rum, which had surpassed brandy as the international alcohol. Rum came from Jamaica and India and by controlling its importation and distribution, the NSW Corps ensured rum became the centrepiece of payment in the barter system. Convicts were allowed to work after hours for themselves and wages were paid in rum. When demand required, a ship would go to India to fill its holds with Calcutta rum. The whole economy was based on rum and so the NSW Corps became known as the Rum Corps. With the advent of money they sold bottles of rum to convicts with a 1,200 per cent mark-up.

When Vice-Admiral Horatio Nelson was shot and killed at the Battle of Trafalgar in 1805, his body was placed in a barrel of rum, to be preserved for the journey home. Along the way, a group of sailors drilled holes into the timber barrel and drank the rum and possibly some of the great man himself. Ever since then a popular rum amongst the Navy personnel has been *Nelson's Blood*. A decade ago an English friend who had spent his career in the British Navy aboard submarines presented me with a stone bottle of *Nelson's Blood*, and I kept it. I will mind it a little longer to make sure it matures. I admire people who plan ahead. At the 1798 Battle of the Nile when Nelson had destroyed thirteen of the seventeen French warships he had his coffin constructed from the mast of the vanquished French flagship, *L'Orient*.

For fifteen years, Rum Corps officers controlled the settlement more than the Governor and his officials. The British Government appointed a Lieutenant-Colonel of the Black Watch, Lachlan Macquarie, to be the fifth Governor of NSW and to tame the Rum Corps. Macquarie had joined the army at age fourteen and served in Jamaica and America before becoming the regimental paymaster in India. There he indulged in taking charge of the soldiers' pay before they were due to receive it and investing it, without their knowledge. Despite the risk, he earned a regular six per cent per month, for himself.

Macquarie introduced currency to Australia in the form of Spanish dollars and he convinced the British Government to permit limitless supplies of rum to enter the colony. He applied heavy taxes on it which he used to construct 265 buildings and infrastructure projects. I shall mention one of those as it was well intended, a hospital, soon known as the Rum Hospital, for sick convicts, which initially made sense. The architect designed the largest building in Sydney, a vast, stylish hospital of marble, ornamental pillars and ostentatious latticeworks, for surgeons and convict patients alike.

Due to the architect not including toilets, the hospital was flooded with bedpans whose contents were thrown out the windows, when they were open. Most times they were kept shut otherwise the convicts escaped. The kitchen was used as a morgue, food was cooked in the wards, syphilis was rife, venereal patients were locked in a storeroom, the doors of the male and female rooms were kept locked on the outside in a futile attempt to stop prisoners indulging in sex, the nurses threw warm meat at the patients rather than risk contagion while also selling hospital supplies on the black market. The interior of the building, also known as the 'Sidney Slaughter House' due to the brutal bloodletting and toxic concoctions administered to the patients, was rotten to the core with food and excrement hurled around in tune with petty theft, noxious vapours and diseases, all shielded from the view of the public. Today the northern half of the building, on Macquarie Street, is home to the NSW Parliament, with the southern half known as The Mint. When Macquarie founded Australia's first bank, the Bank of NSW, he boldly appointed ex-convicts with appropriate skills to administer it as he did with business and official government posts such as architects and magistrates, the latter now judging and sentencing those who earlier had judged them.

The bank, established in 1817, may be the oldest business in NSW and only surpassed in Australia in length of service by a few such as the now eighth generation Thompson family who farm their property Summerville in the Derwent Valley of Tasmania. The first owner of that property came to Australia aboard the *Sirius* in the First Fleet as a Marine. Nowadays the farm produces Merino sheep, legumes and poppies, the latter for use in codeine and morphine.

2
Corroboree and Victoria Cross

Hamilton Hume was in his element and he soon made friends with a local Aboriginal boy by the name of Cowpasture Jack. Andrew Hume employed the young man to help out around his farm and also as a sign to the wilder Aborigines that all was well at Hume Mount Farm for at times there were killings on both sides. One evening seventeen-year-old Hamilton was out in the bush when he heard the measured beat of hands on thighs and soft crooning accompanied by drumming.

Noiselessly the young man moved through the trees towards the sounds. Having heard the settlers talk of an anticipated war he was cautious but pressed forward. Up ahead he saw the glow of the fire changing the moonlight-silvered treetops to a shade of reddish gold. He came upon some fifty Aborigines engaged in a corroboree. Young Hamilton Hume knew the pattern of the native dances. First came the principal message, followed by the revelry and the feasting, with the watchers coming in to join the celebrations. As the sentries then closed in, so did he. The warriors were painted with red and white ochre and two bearded medicine men, known as Karakals, sat on their haunches, away from the main group.

The Karakals were listening to a Puntimai and even then, in his teenage years, Hamilton knew about such a person. He recognised his type by the mantle of kangaroo skin the black-bearded man wore over his shoulder and the band of eagle-hawk feathers that encircled his forehead. Today I think most of us would know the eagle-hawk as the wedge-tailed eagle. The kangaroo skin cloak was red and the larger red kangaroos of the western plains and beyond are not found east of the Blue Mountains, so Hamilton knew by this alone that the man was from afar. He leaned back against a tree as he spoke to the two medicine men as Hamilton listened from behind another. The Puntimai were ambassadors with no loyalties except to the spirits who guided them. They were corroboree-makers, the masters of dance and legend. Young Hamilton reported the details direct to Governor Macquarie.

Hamilton Hume came to know the ways of the Aborigines to an extraordinary extent and was held in high regard by many people of both races. He related a story that an Aborigine had told him of their attitude or belief in reincarnation, saying that some departed spirits went to *moroko*, the native heaven, where they remained. Others were held over until removed by the rites of the Karakals to give strength and energy to body and mind before becoming unborn human or animal creatures. When a tribe or clan belonged to an animal totem that held spiritual significance to them, no one could say with certainty whether the departed spirit of that totem person would reinhabit the body of man or beast.

He learned of the Kadaitcha, the professional murderers employed by the Karakals to kill their enemies. They wore kangaroo-skin shoes, padded with the down of young emus. This made it impossible to hear the approach of the Kadaitcha or, if one wished to do so, to track them. They could kill their victims by the black magic method of pointing the bone at the intended victim or directly. At that time the Aborigines of the nearby Illawarra area were regarded as a bloodthirsty lot. They were known to leave their south coast Shoalhaven area below Sydney, climb up and over the Illawarra Escarpment and hunt and plunder in the Southern Highlands districts.

One night Hamilton and his younger brother John were camping out when they were woken by a nearby human cry an hour before sunrise. Somewhat alarmed and decidedly cautious they decided to hold their ground until the light of day. Before that could eventuate, their native friend Cowpasture Jack gave his call and stood up close to them. Jack turned around and, pointing back into the trees, said, 'Him bad blackpfeller, that one. Him Five Islands man. (coastal native man) I catch that pfeller, quick smart. Him dead, prop'ly.'

Hamilton asked Jack why did he kill the intruder and he replied, 'Him get ready all about, Hamilton. Him chop you. My oath!'

The three men inspected the other's body which was no more than 50 metres away. Jack's spear had passed through his chest and alongside his pipeclay and red ochre-painted body was the would-be killer's steel-bladed tomahawk, that he had intended to use on Hamilton. Jack asked, 'You reckon spirit belong that pfeller hang about, p'rhaps?', to which Hamilton replied, 'No Jacky. God has his spirit now.' Jack finished with, 'Illawarra pfeller. Go walkabout longa Toom-boong bime by. Him plurry nearly medicine man, that one.'

I was not aware for some time that Australian Aborigines used drums but it seems they were in regular use in the far north of the country. D.F. Thomson reported that, 'The skin drum, observed in Cape York in the late 1920s, has been associated with the hero cults of the crocodile in the north-east of the Cape York Peninsula and the seagull in the north-west.' Photos from 1966 show Cape York drums. Records also state they worked their way south where lizard or wallaby skin was stretched across the end of a short hollow log, for a drum head, as witnessed by Hamilton Hume.

An item of keen interest was an Aborigine initiation witnessed at Farm Cove, Sydney, by Governor Arthur Phillip in 1795. Farm Cove is the lovely bay in front of the Botanical Gardens, created on orders of Governor Macquarie, adjoining Bennelong Point, on which resides the Sydney Opera House. In the particular ceremony, three young men each had a tooth removed. This was done by way of a sharp and fine bone which was used to lance and prepare the gum. A shortened throwing stick or a spear thrower, presumably a woomera, was placed against the tooth and a large stone was used in the manner of a hammer to strike the back end and force the tooth out. Governor Phillip observed that each person had a front tooth so removed. That initiation was common in the Port Jackson area and in the tribal lands of the Arrernte people of Central Australia, as travelled by our main character yet to come, W.W. Mills.

Arthur Phillip was born in Cheapside, London, in 1738. Cheapside is not as bad as it sounds, being a medieval English word for market and situated close to what is now the centre of London. It must have had a significant appeal to the literary world because those who were born there were John Milton---Paradise Lost, and Robert Herrick---Hesperides, while those who wrote of it include William Shakespeare---Henry IV, Thomas Middleton---A Chaste Maid in Cheapside, Geoffrey Chaucer---Canterbury Tales, William Wordsworth---The Reverie of Poor Susan, Jane Austen---Pride and Prejudice and Charles Dickens Jr---Dickens' Dictionary of London, 1879. The latter wrote that *Cheapside remains now what it was five centuries ago, the greatest thoroughfare in London---and may boast of being the busiest thoroughfare in the world, with the sole exception of London Bridge.*

His father died at a young age but not before he had taught his son to speak German and French. When he was twelve Arthur's mother enrolled him in the Royal Hospital in Greenwich, *a school for the maintenance and education of the children of seamen happening to be disabled or slain.* The school opened in 1712 and today it is still a successful establishment with connections to the Royal Navy. Arthur's language teacher father may not have been a sailor but his mother's first husband had been an English sailor who died of yellow fever in the West Indies while her cousin was Captain William Everett of the Royal Navy. Captain Everett took the boy who would one day be an Admiral of the Royal Navy to sea as a cabin boy at the age of nine to briefly experience a taste of the ocean life. At the school the chaplain noted Arthur's diplomacy and his business-like perfection seeking.

After the mandatory three years fifteen-year old Arthur left the school and went to sea on a whaling ship, for two years. He was obliged to undertake all facets of such a life and that included being a flenser, one of the men who used flenses, three-metre long poles that ended with a long and narrow, razor-shape blade to cut the skin/blubber from the whale. The blubber was cut and boiled down to extract the oil. In Arthur's day the flensing was carried out at sea and there was no provision to bring the whale onboard. The flensers had to precariously stand on a narrow wooden platform known as a cutting stage that was suspended amidships over the water. The men then leaned down over the whale to do the flensing, cutting in parallel lines. Hooks were attached to the whale not only to peel the cut blubber off and haul it up on deck but also to roll the whale over as the flensing progressed while sharks sometimes circled below, attracted by their take-away dinner.

As a boy I spent three days at the Moreton Island whaling station about forty km from Brisbane and the smell of not just one but numerous dead whales was the worst odour I have encountered. Not that it stopped myself and others from enjoying whale steaks each day and sleeping on the whale chasers at night. When I grew up I repented and did volunteer work at sea off the Kimberley coast of north-west Western Australia with marine biologists who annually undertake whale research during the Humpback whale migration from Antarctica to their warm northern calving waters. The biologists give their results to shipping, exploration and oil and gas companies so that today the whales are not disturbed in their traditional migration and calving areas. At Moreton Island I watched the onshore flensers do the work that young Arthur was engaged in and whilst I did not know of him then, I now appreciate the man all the more.

At age seventeen Arthur Phillip signed on with the Royal Navy. The year was 1755, the same year that James Cook also joined up. Young Arthur was initially aboard the 68-gun HMS Buckingham, which one year later was the flagship of the fleet. Due to his worthy characteristics, steadfast beliefs and actions (France, Holland, Spain and the West Indies) he rose through the ranks. After defeating the Spanish forces in Havana, Cuba, where the Royal Navy sailed in with twenty ships carrying sixty to ninety guns each plus smaller vessels, he was mentioned in despatches for meritorious action in the face of the enemy. He was promoted to Lieutenant but with the end of the Seven Years War with France, England was at peace for a while. Like many of the Royal Navy officers he was then retired on half pay before he was seconded to the Portuguese Navy in Brazil. He sailed to Rio de Janeiro to assist Portugal in the conflict with Spain. You might wonder why this would be so but England's oldest ally is not America, Canada, New Zealand, India or Australia but Portugal.

2 Corroboree and Victoria Cross

In 1147 English soldiers who were on their way to the Holy Land during the Second Crusade gave their assistance to King Alfonso Henriques to retake Lisbon from the Muslim Moors. England and Portugal signed the Anglo-Portuguese Treaty in 1373 and it was ratified by King Richard II of England and King John 1 of Portugal in 1386 and on many more occasions. Britain sent its best general, the Duke of Wellington, to Portugal's aid against Napoleon's armies in the Peninsular War and the Treaty has been cited elsewhere when cooperation was requested such as World War Two and the 1982 Falklands War.

Promoted to Captain, Arthur Phillip, though always outnumbered, fought for Portugal against Spain in South America. His ability and determination were shown to one and all when he committed his 26-gun ship *Nossa Senhora do Pilar* and another frigate against the Spanish 74-gun *San Augustin*. Phillip defeated the faster and more powerful Spanish ship of 2,700 tons and 530 officers and men and the Portuguese gave him command of the prize, which was now the largest Portuguese warship. The Spanish crew had seen the *Pilar* approaching but due to its size had thought no ship that small would dare take them on, until Captain Phillip came close enough to fire the first broadside.

The Portuguese then requested Captain Phillip to take troops from Rio de Janeiro to strengthen their fortress at Colonia de Sacramento, which today is in Uruguay but then it was still Brazil. Colonia is in south-west Uruguay across the River de la Plata from Buenos Aires, Argentina. Spain controlled both Buenos Aires and Montevideo, with Colonia in between them. Captain Phillip was posted to Colonia on Portugal's behalf and from there he patrolled the Southern Atlantic to deter Spanish ships.

In 1778 when Arthur Phillip's four years of service to Portugal were completed the Viceroy of Brazil wrote, *Phillip is an officer of education and principle, he gives way to reason and does not before doing so fall into exaggerated and unbearable excesses of temper—he is very clean-handed; is an officer of great truth and very brave; and is no flatterer, saying what he thinks but without temper or want of respect.*

It is believed that the manner of his success for Portugal was instrumental in his being selected to lead the First Fleet to Australia. Although a few people believe Arthur Phillip was Australia's equivalent of America's George Washington I fear most of us have not, individually and as a nation, sufficiently acknowledged the man, the founder of Australia. He detested what he saw of slavery in the West Indies and from then on maintained a strong stance against that evil existence. He made a point of being courteous, interested in and helpful to the Aborigines of Australia despite being attacked on one occasion.

On 17th September, 1790, Governor Phillip was at Manly Cove to meet the Aborigine, Bennelong. The Governor was accompanied by the Judge Advocate, David Collins, who later wrote of, *an Aborigine who lifted a spear from the grass with his foot, and fixing it on his throwing-stick, in an instant darted it at the Governor. The spear entered a little above the collar bone and had been discharged with such force that the barb of it came through on the other side.* Fortunately Arthur Phillip survived.

A few years ago my wife and I were heading for Montevideo. We took the slow ferry from Buenos Aires for the fifty-kilometre trip across the River de la Plata to Colonia and happily walked where 27,000 people live amongst the historic areas of colonial buildings and cobblestone streets. The many original houses are of stone and the streets are narrow due to their one-time military status. The 1995 World Heritage listed town was controlled by either Spain or Portugal seven times during their war-locked years. We were admiring an ancient, rustic house when we knocked on the door and discovered it to be a Portuguese museum. We were invited in and found ourselves in the midst of centuries-old furniture, uniforms, musical instruments, clothing of the 18th century, maps, crockery and battle memorabilia.

The museum building is small but that is because originally it was a private house. As we continued our tour of the rooms we came upon a head and shoulders, oval-shaped painting or picture of a naval officer, with his name beneath it, placed on a wall. It was Captain Arthur Phillip, during his service with the Portuguese Navy. We learned that the house was his residence in Colonia de Sacramento for four years, when he was not hunting Spanish ships.

Bennelong was the Aborigine who acted as interlocutor on behalf of the British Government and Governor Phillip, to open dialogue with the Aborigines and to have them tell him of their thoughts. The current expansive development near the south-western side of the Sydney Harbour Bridge is named after Bennelong's second wife, Barangaroo. Her funeral, also in 1795 and also at Farm Cove, attracted a large gathering of Aborigines from a wide area.

Following his journeys down the New South Wales (NSW) south coast in 1822, Hamilton Hume, in company with William Hovell, undertook a highly acknowledged and successful 1,000 km expedition from Sydney to Corio Bay on Port Phillip, which is all but where Melbourne grandly stands today. This expedition, in 1824, was at the request of Governor Macquarie as he wished to open up more land for settlement and development. The Governor however only contributed £50 towards the undertaking. To finance his share of the costs of the journey, Hamilton Hume sold his most treasured possession, an iron plough. For those ventures, plus his later work with the renowned explorer, Charles Sturt in 1829, Hamilton Hume received numerous land grants. He added to that land bank in his own right and over time he came to own many properties.

In 1825, Hamilton married Elizabeth Dight and a guest at the wedding was a man who had become a close friend to Andrew Hume and his family by the name of Henry 'Black Harry' O'Brien. A big lump of a man from Ireland he had already worked in India, in Calcutta to be precise. When he arrived in Sydney he carried letters of introduction to Governor Macquarie, for like Andrew Hume, he was well connected. He first took up land at Bathurst but as his sheep numbers built up, he started to look further afield. Finding the Lachlan River already occupied, he headed for the Murrumbidgee and established the first sheep run on the Murrumbidgee at Jugiong. In this small but iconic Australian town, the nation's future cricket captain and much loved commentator Richie Benaud would do his early schooling.

Henry O'Brien made his headquarters at the Yass sheep station he named *Douro*, in honour of the Douro River, near Oporto, Portugal. This might sound off the beaten track to us today and in this part of the world but the crossing of the Douro River and the defeat of French troops by a British/Portuguese army was seen as pivotal in the eventual victory of the Duke of Wellington over Napoleon Bonaparte. The beautiful Douro Valley and River is lined with vineyards and olive farms.

Henry lived a full life as a breeder of fine wool sheep, a Commissioner of the Supreme Court, a Member of Parliament and a man determined to rid the colony of disruptive bushrangers. When depression rode the land in the early 1840s it was Henry who galloped to the rescue of the sheep industry, in which sheep and wool prices had fallen into one of their inevitable commodity collapses. He was not the first to do so but he was the best at the technique of boiling sheep down for tallow.

When sheep meat is boiled the resultant product is fat, or tallow. Wethers, being castrated male sheep, when boiled down in Henry's day at 25 kilograms would produce 12 kilograms of tallow, per head. Sheep which at the time were unsaleable, now had a worth of five to eight shillings, a substantial amount. Henry saved many sheep producers from bankruptcy and no doubt the banks from a few more headaches. The tallow was, and still is, used for making soap, high-end shaving soap, candles and crackling which is a component in making wet and dry dog food. Tallow is found in the production of biodiesel, similar to the manner in which oil is derived from plants but more advantageous as it otherwise has little value to the food industry and does not become embroiled in the current food versus fuel debate.

When tallow is combined with bitumen in the printmaking industry it provides metal print plates with resistance to acid etching. The lubricants used in the first steam-driven piston engines were washed away by hot vapours but tallow was regularly resistant to them. Today the steel-rolling industry uses tallow as a lubricant when sheet steel is compressed through steel rollers. Tallow was traditionally used in the deep frying of food before vegetable oils were introduced. Prior to 1990, McDonald's cooked French fries in a mix of 93 per cent beef tallow and seven per cent cottonseed oil.

Tallow is all around, in medicines, woodworking, soldering, biodegradable motor oils and more. We owe a lot to Henry O'Brien and the humble, usually old and castrated male sheep. His own breeding stock were Merino sheep that he crossed with those of Saxon bloodlines. By 1833 he had 12,000 prime sheep and for the next thirty-three years he expanded exponentially in quantity and quality. Hamilton Hume was also regarded as a noted breeder of fine wool sheep and it was said that he received a consignment of Saxon Merino rams from Hamburg, Germany, in 1847.

Hamilton was often at Henry O'Brien's *Douro* property inspecting Merino sheep and discussing the finer points of sheep-breeding. Hamilton, like his father, Andrew Hume, and Henry became firm friends. The explorer Charles Sturt visited both of them on several occasions, once leaving Henry's place with twenty-five lambs from his best flock in tow.

Many convicts served their time or escaped from gaol or their master. After hearing news of the dramatic open-boat voyage of the *Bounty's* Captain Bligh no length of passage, or hazard of navigation seemed above human accomplishment. Bligh and eighteen loyal sailors were cast adrift in a seven-metre long open boat with sixty-five kilos of bread, some rum, four cutlasses, a quadrant and a compass. Bligh could observe latitude but longitude was taken by account i.e. dead reckoning, such as sailing by the stars. The boat had two small sails. Every day the men rowed or bailed water out of the unlikely vessel, which after forty-seven days of relentless mental and physical toil, countered to great extent by Captain Bligh's leadership and brilliant navigation, put 6,700 km of open water behind them to arrive at the Dutch port of Koepang, Timor, and then Batavia (Jakarta).

Of those colonial convicts who had escaped, there were more than a few who believed the story going around that somewhere down on the Yass Plains was a connecting river that would take them the 300 miles to China. Consequently many an escaped convict was seen in that area.

I don't think they found their faith justified, but a group of twenty-one convicts went the other way. They were led to believe the route to China was to be found via a river to the north of Sydney, not to the south. At that time what would be Newcastle was called Coal River. At least they were orientated in the right direction but all they found was more hardship. One convict died of exhaustion and after four of them were speared by Aborigines the remainder returned to the safety of Sydney.

Ex-convicts had been scarred by the brutality of British justice and the sentences imposed on them, all too often for minor offences, certainly by the standards of today. They therefore fell into further crime as a means of support, regularly robbing travellers on the road, bailing up stagecoaches and using their many acquired weapons to raid the larger stations which often carried up to six months provisions such as food, clothes, tools, saddlery, weapons and ammunition, fast horses and money. The profession of bushranger appealed to many a man. Women who informed bushrangers of the approach or presence of the police were known as bush telegraphs. Good horses were invaluable to bushrangers who, where possible, sought out thoroughbred stock, to upgrade as it were, with stamina let alone speed to outrun the police and the vigilantes who sought to put an end to their disturbing ways. One band of four bushrangers was taken alive and all members of the gang were discovered to be policemen from another district, such were the rewards on offer. To aid their existence the bushrangers would invariably pay local land-holders money in return for their silence, meals and for outright harbouring them. Conversely, when the reward on the head of a bushranger grew large enough, some of their saviours then turned them in.

Late one afternoon Hamilton was taking his wife Elizabeth and Cowpasture Jack to visit Henry O'Brien, at *Douro Station*, after the unexpected death of Henry's wife, of fever. They were nearly there, taking a sharp bend through a clump of box trees around the base of a rocky hillock, after which the *Douro* homestead would come into view, when they were ambushed by bushrangers. They shot one of Hamilton's horses but in return fire he killed one of the gang. When Hamilton examined the body the man was shot through the temple, beneath his cabbage-tree hat. Faded broad arrows marked his tattered shirt. Hamilton heard more shots and galloping hooves and over all of that the booming voice of Henry 'Black Harry' O'Brien, cursing alternately in English, Gaelic and Hindustani. He ran to the top of the rise. Half a mile away, on the plain below, he saw a group of horsemen galloping north-west with two riders, O'Brien and Cowpasture Jack's son, Wonga, following.

Hamilton returned to his horses and then found Cowpasture Jack had been shot twice, once through the thigh and also across the forehead. He went down to *Douro* and enlisted the help of O'Brien's convict workmen who, on hearing the news of the shootings, expressed their fears for the safety of the bushrangers, having hardman Black Harry on their trail.

By the time Hamilton had organised men and a wagon made ready to take Cowpasture Jack into Goulburn in search of a doctor, the bushrangers had a significant head start. He was positive they would make for the Weddins, a mountain range between Forbes and Young. Once in there they would not only be damned hard to find but if they arrived there before Black Harry and Wonga they would surely ambush them if they dared continue to follow.

It was said of Hamilton Hume that, 'he knew how to make his way straight to any place, more than the blacks and they know only their own district. He has the same abilities in country he has never seen before.' Thinking it through Hume was adamant the gang would head across the wild country between the Murrumbidgee and the Lachlan Rivers and into the Weddins. He would strike the Lachlan north-west of Gunning, follow that river until it joined the Abercrombie, then swing across country to the Weddins, hoping to cut off not only the bushrangers but Black Harry and Wonga.

Hamilton set off in the dark on a horse borrowed from *Douro*. The moon rose just before midnight and he was on the Lachlan River, moving north and following a track he knew. Before dawn he could smell smoke so he stopped and tied his horse to a tree. Moving carefully forward he came to the embers of a campfire. He approached it cautiously, from the far side, and then saw the figure of a man stretched out on the ground.

Fearful it might be someone he knew, he bent down beside it and then recoiled in horror. 'God help him!' he exclaimed, 'Throat's cut from ear to ear. He's been dead for hours.'

He knew it was the handiwork of Black Harry who had dealt so crudely with the gang's sentry and acknowledged the spoken fears of the Irishman's convict workmen. He rode on, steadily to conserve his horse's energy although he could now see clearly in the rising daylight. Such revelation allowed him to spy a wedge-tailed eagle circling above, before plunging down into the valley ahead of him. He pulled up his horse and listened. There were crows down there. He rode down and on his arrival the massed birds rose in a cloud from the body of a dead horse and a convict with half his face blown away. Black Harry again.

At midday he stopped for a break at a waterhole, found a box tree with possum scratches on the bark and having extracted the possum from a hollowed limb he made a smokeless fire and cooked it for lunch, washing the strong flesh down with water. He heard them before he could see them, Black Harry and Wonga were riding over a ridge. He hailed them and they veered to the waterhole. Bloodstains covered O'Brien's jacket and dried blood matted his long black beard. He acknowledged killing the two bushrangers Hamilton had come across and said they had killed two more who tried to bushwhack them in a forest. In the same breath he bitterly complained of the seven who had escaped Wonga and himself.

In 1862 after Frank Gardiner, Johnny Gilbert, Ben Hall and five other bushrangers, who were mostly disgruntled cattlemen from the Weddins, had robbed the gold escort stagecoach of £14,000 of gold and banknotes at Eugowra Rocks, they rode off to the sanctuary of the Weddin Ranges. However by the time they reached the foothills their pursuers were gaining on them so quickly they had to abandon the packhorse which was carrying all the gold. They escaped with only the banknotes. The stagecoach carrying the gold belonged to Ford and Co, one month before it would be taken over by Cobb and Co. A trooper escorting the gold shipment was unfortunately shot, in the testicles.

Nothing more was heard of the elusive bushrangers for more than a year, when news came that the Weddin men were back on the river.

Small towns were not beyond the bushrangers' boundaries and the day came when Hamilton's brother, John Hume, of *Collingwood*, Gunning, went to call on a friend, a Mr. Cooper, who owned a store in Gunning. When Hume entered the building the staff told him Cooper was away. As John Hume stepped outside a bushranger followed him out and told him to 'stand'. The man asked if he was Cooper, looking to kill him if he was. He replied, 'No,' and was told, 'then throw down your arms.'

When Hume said, 'I will not,' the bushranger cried, 'then take that, my old chap,' and shot him dead, the bullet entering his right temple and passing out above the ear.

While dead on the ground, a second bushranger fired, hitting John Hume at point blank range. That shot took away part of his cheek and jaw bone and the whole of his right ear. Still not satisfied a third bushranger also fired, 'to make sure,' into the right side of Hume's chest. Four men then beat Hume's right side and arm, from the wrist to the ear, until the shoulder was absolutely smashed into small pieces, so that a person could feel the particles of bone with finger and thumb, as reported in the *Sydney Monitor* of 14th February, 1840.

Of all the men who were out looking for the murderers it was Rawdon Hume, my great-great-great grandfather and the brother of my great-great-great granduncle John Hume who came upon the main members of the gang. In similar fashion to Hamilton he calculated where they might have gone. He left word which way he was intending to go, adding that he would leave a clear trail to be followed. He crossed the Crookwell River and picking up the bushrangers' tracks, headed along a well-marked trail to the Abercrombie River. He followed along its cold, clear waters flowing as they do over long reaches of blue-grey slate and believed they were heading for the Abercrombie Caves, a further 20 miles away. As rain began to fall after dark he took refuge himself in a limestone cave. In the morning he came to the top of a ridge which revealed a high valley below, a valley that had a creek running through it and he was certain it had just one way in and the same way out. At the far end, below a limestone cliff, a small log shack was half hidden by box timber. And there were saddle-horses. Even more telling was the big chestnut horse that he recognised as belonging to none other than Thomas Whitton, the notorious leader of the Whitton gang and the man who had killed his brother, John.

Rawdon Hume crept close enough to hear the four men talking, mystified as they were as to why the other six members of the gang, led by McPhail, had not yet arrived.

McPhail and his men had gone to *Humewood*, Hamilton Hume's home, to do away with him before he was on their trail. Only Cowpasture Jack, with his shot-up leg, his wife and another son, Peter, were there. They falsely told the bushrangers the boss had ridden off early that morning but he was expected back that night. Even without that encouragement, the bushrangers moved in and confidently took over the house, not noticing that Peter had slipped away to spread the word bushrangers were at *Humewood*. They were soon helping themselves to Hamilton's supply of brandy and enjoying the comparative luxury of Cowpasture Jack's wife cooking dinner for them. Being suspicious of strychnine in the place for the poisoning of dingoes and crows, McPhail made Jack sip the brandy and his wife taste every plate of food she put on the table. By sunset McPhail and three men were drunk while the two sentries were well on the way to being in that state.

They never knew what happened. Just before midnight Black Harry and Wonga came for them, not with revolvers and rifles but with long-bladed knives. Not even the dogs heard the two men who moved as stealthily as do the Aborigine Kadaitcha. When dawn came the six bushrangers were buried in a mass grave behind the homestead of his friend and then Henry 'Black Harry' O'Brien rode home to *Douro Station*.

About that time Rawdon Hume was observing the four main

bushrangers in their hidden valley when his movement was noticed and he was fired upon. Confidently expecting police troopers to be following his trail by now he ran for the top of a ridge, bullets chasing him and sometimes thudding into protective trees. They couldn't directly follow him on horseback so he made for another ridge where he reasoned he could hold the bushrangers off for some time with his pistol. In their haste and desire the bushrangers failed to see five approaching police troopers and two civilians ahead of and now surrounding them. The police sergeant called on the men to surrender but a bushranger fired at him and struck his horse in the neck. The sergeant landed on his feet and killed the man with his first shot as Rawdon Hume came down from the ridge. Two bushrangers were killed and two taken alive and one of those soon hung himself in gaol, leaving only the leader, Thomas Whitton, to stand trial. Smoke was seen coming from up the valley and it transpired that Hamilton Hume had caught up with the others on a borrowed police horse. Having found the bushrangers' shack he burned it to the ground.

Thomas Whitton, who had proclaimed he would never be taken alive, was nonetheless taken, to Sydney for his trial. One month after he was captured he was sentenced to death by being taken 'to the interior' and there to his hanging in Goulburn. At the same time Henry O'Brien was also in Sydney, staying at the residence he had built in Pitt Street and having just married his second wife, a young Scottish woman. They set off for *Douro Station* and after climbing up the Razorback mountain he reined his horses to a halt to allow his bride to enjoy the view which she said was almost as fine as her homeland Cairngorm Mountains and the River Dee.

Henry O'Brien stirred his horses into their work but before they had gone any great distance he came upon a cavalcade also moving south. Escorted by mounted troopers Thomas Whitton was en route to Goulburn. Not wishing his young wife to have to gaze upon such a sight he whipped his horses into a gallop and with the clatter of iron tyres on stones swept past the rearguard of mounted troopers and then the cart on which the dejected and manacled bushranger sat between two well-armed troopers. The open wagon forward of that contained not only Whitton's coffin but also the gallows on which he would meet his demise. In front of all that rode another detachment of cavalry.

Five days later Hamilton Hume was in Goulburn. It was a Thursday, market day, and he thought the crowd bigger than normal. He soon learned it was the day fixed for the execution of Thomas Whitton, and not wanting to be there, he quickly conducted his business and rode on. Australia saw some 2,000 bushrangers before they died out about the time of Ned Kelly's hanging, in 1880. Hangings of some 1,500 people were carried out from 1820 to 1900. In 1822, thirty-four bushrangers were hanged in Sydney and fifty-six men were hanged in Tasmania in 1826. After Federation in 1901 the number of hangings fell away.

When I was just a boy, some two to twelve years of age, our family lived down south and when my father loaded up his old Plymouth de Soto to drive us to Sydney, once in a while we would come down the Razorback and then he would go via Campbelltown into Sydney. I remember those drives for two things, one being the Razorback Mountain itself on the top of which the Anthony Horden's department store in Sydney had a large advertising board of a lovely tree and underneath it the company words, 'While I live I'll grow'.

The second impression that became ingrained in my memory was that whenever we approached Campbelltown, which then was mostly open country and barely a house to be seen, unlike today, there was always a campsite by the creek, of dark but colourful gypsies. With the same regularity my mother would always tell my father to drive faster, drive faster. Mum was ever fearful of having to stop and then be robbed by the gypsies, whom I always eagerly looked for. One day my father was responding to Mum's exhortations that he drove so fast he was instead stopped by a policeman on a motorbike and fined for speeding.

The Reverend-cum-sheep-breeder, Samuel Marsden, Principal Chaplain of NSW, took his place on the bench. Commissioner J.T. Bigge said the Reverend was very active in the discharge of his duties and 'his sentences are not only more severe than those of other magistrates' and as regards the many prisoners who appeared before him, 'The Lord have mercy on you, for his Reverence will have none'.

There was another interesting crime, at an earlier time. Australia's first bank was the Bank of NSW, founded in 1817. In 1826, a gathering of producers and merchants established the Bank of Australia. It was known as the pure Merino bank as its directors/shareholders included the upper echelon, the aristocracy, or the ruling class whose power was based on their wealth. The Bank of Australia excluded the ex-convicts who had been appointed by Governor Macquarie, to the Bank of NSW, which is nowadays known as Westpac Bank. A cynical person, but not I, might say that following the Hayne Royal Commission into banking 202 years later that some things have not changed.

Amongst the directors of the Bank of Australia was the founder of the Australian wool industry, John Macarthur, and the well-regarded and successful explorer, John Oxley. English-born Oxley joined the Royal Navy and was later in Australia as Master's Mate on the *Buffalo*. In 1809, he was the first lieutenant on HMS *Porpoise* and he conveyed Governor William Bligh to Tasmania, as a passenger. In 1818 as an explorer John Oxley passed through the land where Dubbo would soon be established. He had this to say about it, 'over a very beautiful country, thinly wooded and apparently safe from the highest floods.' Following his explorations John Oxley was appointed Surveyor-General of NSW.

The Bank of Australia had its premises in George Street, Sydney and as its first president was John Macarthur its alternative name was the Squatters Bank, as Mr. Macarthur was squatter extraordinaire. The bank's strongroom was constructed underground, with its walls being a remarkable 2.6 metres thick. On the other side of the street a large drain ran down into Sydney Harbour. A gang of robbers put in play the first bank robbery in Australia. From the drain they dug deep underground, across and under the road and down to the foundations of the bank, part of which they removed before entering the strongroom. They helped themselves to boxes of sovereigns, pound notes and silver but were unable to carry away the sheer weight of all the silver. Just forty boxes of silver weighed one ton. Nonetheless the loot they stole, in September 1828, was to the value of £14,000. That was recently nominated as the largest documented bank theft in Australia, based on relative values and expressed as a proportion of GDP. The thieves were not caught and in 1843 the bank failed. Crime can pay.

At the time of John Hume's murder, his wife Elizabeth was expecting their ninth child. Her brother-in-law, Hamilton Hume, had always settled members of his family on the best of the new-found country around Yass, Goulburn, Gunning and south from there, that he had found on his exploring forays into Victoria. Hamilton took up 85,000 acres of good land, on account of his sister-in-law, along the Victorian side of the Murray River, that being the boundary with NSW, in 1842. It was known as the Yarrawonga Run. The land had a 75 km frontage to the Murray and extended inland for 20 km. The government let him have the land at no cost. That was how the government initially encouraged further settlement. It was the first landholding at Yarrawonga and the beginning of the town.

Fortunate men gained their land courtesy of government grants and there was bias in some of the allocations, such as to the clergy and the English gentry. Others took the law into their own hands and simply squatted on the land as a form of entitlement. To appease the majority who missed out and to put an end to squatting, the government decided on allowing people to take up small allocations of 40 to 320 acres for £1 per acre. Purchasers had to pay a quarter of the price on making their selection and the balance within five years. Using dummy applications care of family members the large landowners took up as much of that land as they could to keep the new prospective neighbours away, plus to enlarge their own holdings. They also took out mining leases and pre-emptive leases to stop the newcomers.

Those who did manage to acquire their heart-desired land also had to make improvements to the value of another £1 per acre, such as clearing the land, erecting fences and growing crops. Additionally they had to show proof of residence and inspectors came around to make sure that had been carried out. Devious men built a portable hut and after it had been inspected at one farm it was then towed to another where the inspector was expected.

Hamilton brought in a team of builders and craftsmen to construct a home for his sister-in-law, one that was originally designed by an Englishman for construction in the heat of India. The house was the first to be constructed in the Yarrawonga district and, with its original 40-centimetre thick walls, today it stands as the oldest homestead in rural Victoria.

The house was built of Murray River pine, a local tree that was then prolific but today is in scarce supply. This is no doubt due to its other name of white cypress pine and its valuable attributes. It contains an oil that makes the wood completely resistant to termites and decay, thus placing it in the Durability Class One category and being the principal reason the house is still in existence. Chemicals are not needed to be added for any form of protection. The other factor is that the bricks are not mud bricks but kiln-fired clay bricks, produced on-site. The Murray River pine is uniquely Australian and it has a naturally low shrinkage rate.

The house was built with an hexagonal shape due its strong emphasis on defence. There is a room, known as the fortress, that occupies the very centre of the homestead and it has an octagonal shape. Around it are the remaining rooms but even so because of the design, the octagonal fortress room provides a 360-degree view of the outside of the building. In this way the household occupants could see any approaching bushrangers or Aborigines as many of both types did attack the then isolated premises. All the windows had wooden shutters, not glass, so that the defenders could shoot through holes in the heavy timber. Originally holes in the strong walls allowed guns to be aimed at enemies outside. Door handles were deliberately kept low so the children could quickly run inside whenever strangers appeared.

At the centre of the front of the building is the main entry door. On either side are reception rooms which are also octagonal. Weapons and other valuables were stored beneath the floorboards in those two rooms while in others the floorboards could be removed to allow the children to be hidden below ground in the enormous cellar, which, along with the verandah that surrounded the entire house, also served to provide cooling in the summer. The builders required twelve months to complete this unique house, which stands today in all its glory, amidst lovely elm trees brought from Gunning to provide further shade. They are the oldest elms in Victoria.

The cook's kitchen is still there. In those times kitchens were outside as they often caught fire and that arrangement kept the heat and the flies from the house. I might be name dropping but when my wife, Janice, and I were staying in Washington D.C. with friends, they took us to visit Mt Vernon, the magnificent family home of former first President of the United States of America, George Washington. The 7,800 acre property overlooking the Potomac River is superb in every detail and not far from the house is the kitchen. It dates from 1753 and is connected by a colonnade for the slave-cooked meals to be carried to the impeccable house dining room. As in Australia the three-workroom kitchen with its fireplace and attached oven was designed to keep fire, heat and cooking aromas from the main house. To tell of its growing popularity 85 million people have visited Mt. Vernon since 1860 and nowadays one million people a year do so.

In Australia the meat room was usually outside but at Yarrawonga Run it was placed inside, as in the early years the family was often under attack and the meat supplies were too tempting to bushrangers. Other outbuildings included a bakery, blacksmith's shed, a dairy, staff quarters, shearing shed, horse stables and of course a convict's camp.

Hamilton managed the farm until 1849 and when the gold rush began shortly after, the government saw those big Runs in another light, a far more enlightening vision of the future. It stated it would resume the land although it could be retained or purchased for a price. Hamilton bought

640 acres or one square mile around the hexagonal house which he then called the Byramine Homestead. The government set the land price at £1 per acre. His sister-in-law, Elizabeth Hume, moved in with her two sons and seven daughters. She had a workforce of farm workers to help her with the sheep and cattle farming and convict women around the house, gardens and other requirements. Over the next few years both of her sons died from farming accidents and a sixteen-year-old daughter drowned. Elizabeth Hume stayed there until she died, in 1864. Her death certificate states that she died of 'Breaking up of the Constitution'.

Today Byramine Homestead consists of 4,700 acres of prime farming land along the banks of the Murray River and in addition to the sheep and cattle, it has a modern brewery and is at the centre of one of Australia's largest vegetable growing operations. There is a staff of sixty to carry out the intensive irrigation and other operations on the land that Hamilton Hume initially brought to life.

So Andrew Hamilton Hume is my great-great-great-great grandfather, one of several of course. In 1856 his son Hamilton Hume sold 10,000 sheep and 100 rams of imported stock. At his death in 1873 he left £12,000 and 18,000 acres of land to his nephews and nieces as he did not have children. Hamilton's younger brother, Rawdon Hume, married Emma Mitchell and of their fourteen children I now refer to two.

The first is their daughter Mary Bozzom Hume. She married Robert Henry Kennedy in 1858 and in 1880 they took up *Wonnaminta Station*, 220 kilometres north-east of Broken Hill, in the Packsaddle district. I gather that name was derived from the fact that the ill-fated Burke and Wills expedition, to cross Australia from south to north, lost a packsaddle thereabouts. The first son of Robert and Mary was also named Robert Henry Kennedy and known as Bob. They were my great-great grandfather and great grandfather. Bob's daughter was my grandmother and her daughter my mother.

Jessie was one of Mary Hume's sisters and she married Albert Middleton. They had five children before the beautiful Jessie, and going by her photo she truly was a beautiful woman, so sadly passed away at age twenty-five. Their son Francis was the father of Flight/Sergeant Rawdon Hume Middleton, 149 Squadron, who was the captain and pilot of a Royal Air Force Stirling bomber in World War Two. On the night of 28 November, 1942, his plane attacked the Fiat Works in Turin, Italy. Such was the darkness Rawdon Hume Middleton flew his plane for three low-level flights over Turin to definitely identify his target. The plane took a hammering from anti-aircraft guns. Gilgandra born but educated at Dubbo High School, Rawdon Middleton's right eye was destroyed, leaving the bone all exposed. He was hard hit across the body and the second pilot was also seriously wounded. Abandoning the aircraft or landing in northern France were options discussed but Middleton stated his intention to ensure his crew returned to England. After flying for four hours the plane reached the English coast and five of the crew parachuted to safety while two remained to assist him but the fuel was gone.

Middleton steered the aircraft out over the sea, off Dymchurch, and ordered his last two crewmen to bail out. They were successful in that but sadly did not survive the night in the English Channel. Rawdon Middleton stayed with his plane to the end, as it crashed into the sea. His body washed up two months later and he was awarded a military funeral with full honours. He received the honoured Victoria Cross, the first awarded to a member of the Royal Australian Air Force. The citation stated: *Flight Sergeant Middleton was determined to attack the target regardless of the consequences and not to allow his crew to fall into enemy hands. His fortitude and strength of will made possible the completion of his mission. His devotion to duty was unsurpassed in the annals of the Royal Air Force.* By the intricacies of marriage lines emanating from Mary Bozzom Kennedy and her sister Jessie, Rawdon Hume Middleton is/was my second cousin, twice removed. A bronze bust of Rawdon was unveiled in Dubbo's Victoria Park by dignitaries of the Royal Australian Air Force, the Dubbo City Council and the Returned Soldiers' League, (RSL). My wife, Janice and I, feeling very humbled, were invited to attend as family.

Rawdon Hume Middleton VC.

Robert Clyde Packer, known as Clyde Packer, born in Tasmania, a journalist who after a big win on a racehorse, in 1902 made his way to the mainland. He joined the Daily Liberal newspaper in Dubbo, where this photo was taken, and after making several headline scoops was appointed editor of the Dubbo paper. That success saw him enticed to Sydney where he was made a one-third partner in the leading Smith's Weekly newspaper, which was read all over Australia. Clyde established the foundations for his son Frank Packer to create the Australian Women's Weekly and for the business and the family dynasty to be followed by his grandson Kerry Packer and his great-grandson James Packer.

Joe Byrne, of the Ned Kelly gang, strung up outside the Benalla gaol the day after his shooting death when and where the Melbourne media took what is thought to be the first commercial press photograph in Australia. 1880.

Four stockmen, horses and dogs quenching their thirst at the Alice Springs waterhole.

Australian Aboriginal cricket team in England 1868. It was the first team in any sport to represent Australia overseas.

Gold prospectors' hut at Upper Dargo, Gippsland, Victoria 1870.

Billy Sing, Australian soldier of Chinese and English descent who served with distinction during World War One as an outstanding sniper at Gallipoli and on the Western Front.

Cobb and Co coach.

3
Coming to Australia

Now we come to the man who rides throughout this story and threads it together.

His name was William Whitfield Mills and that being somewhat of a mouthful, I shall refer to him in brief form but respectfully as Mills. Whilst I went to South Australia (SA) once and Western Australia (WA) twice to further my research into the man, I do acknowledge the previous work and the details of Mills' experiences as regards his Overland Telegraph Line and desert ventures as reported by his descendent Elliott Whitfield Mills. Other contributions such as those from the *Adelaide Advertiser* newspaper, the Mortlock Wing of the State Library, and Peter Taylor's detailed reporting in *An End to Silence* and others as in the Bibliography. Some men may have achieved more but Mills was at the forefront of venturing into little known lands and he had connections to people of interest in rural colonial Australia.

Mills was born in Plymouth, Devon, England on 19th November, 1844 and educated at Heavitree School, which is on the outskirts of nearby Exeter. Upon leaving school Mills entered into and completed an apprenticeship as a printer. Something stirred him to more adventurous climes and on the 23rd January, 1866, at the age of twenty-one, he boarded the American three-masted sailing ship *Atalanta*, of 930 tons. In those days you could pay your way to sail to Australia on a regular commercial vessel or possibly gain a better berth on a ship that carried qualified and selected government passengers under the British Emigration Commissioners' financially approved scheme. The qualifications are interesting as they vary by a country mile from the guidelines of today.

1) *The emigrants must be of those callings which from time to time are most in demand in the colony. They must be sober, industrious, of general good moral character, and have been in the habit of working for wages, and going out to do so*

in the colony, of all of which decisive certificates will be required. They must also be in good health, free from all bodily or mental defects, and the adults must in all respects be capable of going out to work for wages, at the occupation specified on their application forms. The candidates who will receive a preference are respectable young women trained to domestic or farm service, and families in which there is a preponderance of females.

2) The separation of husbands and wives, and of parents from children under 18 will in no case be allowed.

3) Single women under 18 cannot be taken without their parents, unless they go under the immediate care of some near relatives. Single women over 35 years of age are ineligible. Single women with illegitimate children can in no case be taken

4) Single men cannot be taken unless they are sons in eligible families, containing at least a corresponding number of daughters.

Other qualifications were imposed to no doubt ensure a certain standard of persons. As emigrants departing aboard the *Atalanta* and similar ships they were also classified as being in one of the following categories: Assisted Passage, Colonial Nominee, General Emigrant, Passage Paid, General Passenger or Remittance Passenger.

Mills was granted Assisted Passage but of how much I do not know. Agricultural labourers and female domestic and farm servants aged up to forty paid £2 for their fare from England to Australia, the cost rising in stages to £15 if they were over sixty years of age. They must have been more in demand than the blacksmiths, miners, carpenters, bricklayers and gardeners who paid £5 if under forty while other applicants of the working class paid £7 before rising in price commensurate with their age.

Some years later when the convict era had passed and fares were on a commercial basis, an Englishman who made the voyage to the colonies to make a new life for himself wrote back to England to tell his friend that when someone who wishes to migrate is nominated by a person already in Australia, the fare can be bought significantly cheaper in Australia. The friend immediately sent the money for himself and his new wife and never heard from the recipient again.

Some eighty-one days later Mills disembarked in Adelaide, South Australia, on the 15th April, 1866. According to the ship's records he went ashore with £4. While some passengers had as much as £10, many had less than £1 amongst their worldly goods. In 1866, the average weekly earnings of all employees, according to Measuring Worth, in Australia was £.98, or 98 pence. By 1888, when Australia as such reached its Centenary, the average weekly wage had risen to £1.40 but it then dropped and did not exceed that level of income until 1908. Imagine having 20 years of declining or static real income today (2016). It is possible.

Of the 394 immigrants, 182 came from England, 146 from Scotland, sixty-five from Ireland and one other. They consisted of ninety-four labourers, fifty-one domestic servants, fourteen ploughmen, eight bootmakers, seven carpenters, six miners, five blacksmiths, five shepherds and numerous others such as saddlers, coachbuilders, butchers, masons, painters, dressmakers, policemen and tailors.

Mills was a free man and England never transported convicts to Adelaide, which reminds me of an interesting incident. Several years ago an English businessman arrived in Melbourne on his first visit to Australia. At the airport the Immigration officer was looking through the man's passport and the arrival form which all foreigners need to complete. Something in there caught his attention and as he raised his eyes to the visitor, he asked him if he had a criminal record? 'No, I don't,' replied the Englishman, 'I didn't know you still needed one.'

Mills joined the South Australian Government Service, in June, 1866, not as a printer but as a surveyor. At the time, Australia was dependent on Great Britain, not only for people but also for manufactured goods, government and finance. Australia's exports of wool, wheat, gold and other commodities went almost exclusively to Great Britain and the prices they received determined the financial well-being or otherwise of most Australians. The common thread amongst those transactions was communications. Most ships between the two countries took from seventy to ninety days to deliver the goods and that included the mail.

Unlike today letter writing was a prominent activity and people sweated on sending and receiving their long-awaited correspondence. Eventually, land and undersea cables extended from England to Ceylon (Sri Lanka) and for those who could afford the excessive cost that exercise shortened the time delay from three months to one month. Other events unfolded. After Russia's defeat by Great Britain and France in the Crimea, the Russians developed an intense interest in the Pacific Ocean.

Historical evidence confirms that if Russia had to face Great Britain again, she had plans to raid the British colonies in Australia. For that reason Fort Denison was constructed in Sydney Harbour while the South Australian Government decided to build a telegraph line in order to send out warnings of approaching Russian invasions. The cry was, 'The Russians are coming'. The British/Australian fear of the Russians did not abate until the highly trained Navy of Japan utterly destroyed the Russian fleet in the Pacific Ocean, Battle of Tsushima, in 1905. Only three of the Russian fleet of thirty-eight warships returned to their base in Vladivostok. The bigger Japanese ships had more firepower and employed superior wireless telegraphy.

There was little doubt the telegraph line was needed for Australia to join the developing world and three plans were canvassed: a submarine cable from Jakarta to Brisbane and then the Overland Telegraph Line (OTL) landline to Sydney, a submarine cable from Jakarta to Perth and a landline to Adelaide or a submarine cable to Port Darwin with a landline to either Adelaide or Brisbane. The first two options were deleted and then it became a contest between Adelaide and Brisbane. The more practical route was to Brisbane as Queensland said it would bring the submarine cable ashore in the Gulf of Carpentaria and then lay a connecting landline to the telegraph station at Cardwell, on its north coast, a distance of only 650 kilometres (km). South Australia would have to run a 3,000 km landline from Port Augusta to Port Darwin. Against the odds and supported by the most optimistic financial forecasts South Australia won the day, much to the disgust of an outraged Queensland.

Last winter my wife, Janice, and I were in Cairns and from there, we drove 180 km south to Cardwell to look up old friends and to find out what I could about the pygmy Aborigines who lived there. They arranged a meeting between the primary elder, or as he called himself, the chief, of the local Aborigine tribe and myself. We had a good heart-to-heart talk about their pygmy heritage and he kindly referred me to the tribe at Kuranda, on the Atherton Tableland above Cairns. I was also extremely lucky there as I met full-blood Aborigines of three generations, one of whom, the grandmother, still lives at the original Mona Mona Mission station and is definitely a self-proclaimed pygmy of the Djabuganjdji tribe. The younger generations are outgrowing the earlier men and women whose height was no more than four foot six inches or 137 centimetres for the men. They are said to have come from Papua New Guinea a long time ago but that is too big a story for now.

Apart from receiving some 2,200 millimetres of rain in an average year, the town has had another attraction. For several generations the 1,300 citizens of Cardwell have enjoyed the presence of Bismarck, a 4.5-metre long saltwater crocodile who has lived amongst them for most of his 80 to 100 years. A rather friendly croc, Bismarck has never harmed anyone and is quite open about his presence so that people have not had to worry about him sneaking up on them. Recently someone has shot and killed Bismarck. Whilst consideration has been given to holding a memorial service out of respect for the reptilian more people are concerned about the unknown personality of the dominant male crocodile which will now take over Bismarck's territory.

Cardwell has a naturally deep and sheltered harbour and significant government expenditure and infrastructure was invested in the town as it was supported to be the future of development in North Queensland. The mountain range between the harbour and the hinterland obstructed those plans and the town was eventually bypassed in favour of Townsville, 160 km to the south, and which today supports a population of 185,000 people.

Money aside there were two immediate concerns for South Australia. The first was that no one had crossed the continent from south to north and no one knew what lay in the centre, precisely where the Overland Telegraph Line would ideally be placed. In 1859, the South Australian Government offered a reward of £2,000 for the first person to cross the continent. Scottish born John McDouall Stuart set off from Chambers Creek on 2nd March, 1860, with two men and thirteen horses in an attempt to be the first. By the time they reached the MacDonnell Ranges, near the centre, they had succumbed to scurvy. It affected Stuart's right eye so severely he was unable to take observations but on the 23rd April they located the centre of Australia and it is now known as Central Mount Stuart. The men continued on and camped at a good water hole north of Tennant Creek. It was then that they were attacked by a large number of Aborigines wielding their spears and boomerangs.

They fought them off but on the 27th June, worn down by the scurvy and a lack of food, they turned south and headed back to Adelaide. After six months Stuart was ready to go again but now he had to compete for the honour against an expedition from Melbourne, headed by the ill-fated Burke and Wills. The South Australian Government supported Stuart by tipping in £2,500 for his second attempt. This time Stuart had thirteen men and forty-nine horses and he managed to go far further than the first attempt. However after no less than eleven sorties he could not break through extremely harsh country in the far north to reach the Gulf of Carpentaria or the Victoria River and again he was forced to return to Adelaide. Once more with South Australian Government financial support, Stuart saddled up, barely one month later. This time he succeeded, in 1862, and reached the coast, but the reality was that the centre had been found to be a harsh, hot, dry, land with no inland sea. Stuart ended up white-haired, exhausted and all but blind and died in 1866. An achiever nonetheless.

The South Australian Surveyor-General was George Woodroffe Goyder and in 1868 he was selected to lead an expedition north to survey the site of Palmerston, which was to become known as Port Darwin and eventually Darwin. A newspaper contributor wrote: 'All previous pioneers have failed to colonise this country, principally through bad management. It remains to be seen whether South Australia will profit by the errors of our predecessors and bring to a successful conclusion that which has baffled them for so many years.'

Goyder was allowed to hand-pick the 134 men he took with him and Mills, who was now a Second-Class Surveyor, was one of those. There were six First-Class Surveyors and six Second-Class Surveyors. The pay of the latter was £20 per month. According to Measuring Worth, £20 in 1868 equates to £1,623 or approximately Australian $3,500 in 2016. As there was no income tax in those days the men seem to have been well paid although they regularly faced the unknown and they definitely endured living conditions that most of us today could not contemplate let alone overcome.

George Woodroffe Goyder was an exceptional man. Known as 'Little Energy' he was relentless in his application to work and regarded as the ablest administrator and most efficient public servant in South Australia, which no doubt was why he was requested to organise the establishment of Darwin. Prior to that task Goyder had proven himself yet again in another field. South Australia being the driest state in the driest continent, Antarctica excepted, drought has long been an issue. Already with extra duties as Inspector of Mines and Valuer of rural land holdings, Goyder was ordered to determine the demarcation line below which it was considered safe to farm and above which, going north, the likelihood of drought entailed too much risk for pastoral and farming enterprises.

Rather than delegate the work to others Goyder, in just twenty months, rode more than 32,000 km on horseback to make his judgement, visiting eighty-three rural properties and making his assessments, while every night completing his departmental correspondence. Goyder established a line, not a straight line but one that meandered according to rainfall patterns. He determined that above that line, of just 250 millimetres of rainfall, farmers should not attempt to farm. The land to the south of that line generally received sufficient rainfall to do well, as low as the amount of rain was. Some publications of Goyder's work use the figure of 300 millimetres which still appears low to me. Certainly many farmers disputed his results but the reality is that since then Goyder has been proven right on numerous drought occasions as the intervening 148 years have proven. His diligent work made good money for others and helped to set farming up for the future. The line still exists today and is known as 'Goyder's Line of Rainfall' or more simply, 'Goyder's Line'.

For the Darwin expedition, Goyder, Mills and the other 133 men boarded the 627-ton sailing ship, *Moonta*, on the 27th December, 1868, accompanied by their horses, working bullocks, sheep, goats, wagons, stores, tools and tents. A 200-ton schooner, the *Gulnare* brought a steam launch, *The Midge*, which would be used to ferry men and equipment across Darwin harbour.

On the 5th February, 1869, after sailing around the Great Australian Bight and the coast of Western Australia they arrived at Adam Bay, 48 kilometres, east of (Port) Darwin, which Goyder declared would be the capital. For the surveying work the men were split into six groups, each with a First-Class Surveyor in charge. Mills was second-in-command of A.H. Smith's number three section, which like the other five groups also contained two cadets, four axemen, four chainmen, two trenchers and a cook. They slept in four-man tents with their provisions brought by horse from the main camp.

The men were soon into surveying Darwin and future towns of Southport, Virginia and Fred's Pass. In total they surveyed 665,866 acres of land, east to the Adelaide River flood plains and west to the Daly River. It was common for the half acre town blocks to be paired with a 320-acre rural block, for the benefit of wealthy investors back in England. The conditions made work and life uncomfortable. Attacks by wet season mosquitoes and sandflies often resulted in the legs of the men bleeding while they were forever on the alert due to the constant presence of crocodiles. The mosquitoes also bothered the horses and the sheep, the latter being well out of their normal environment.

The Aborigines had a unique way of dealing with crocodiles. They would pole their dugout canoes over a lagoon, prodding the bottom with a harpoon till they felt a crocodile on the bottom. Then they would stab the croc with the harpoon attached to their canoe. The slack would go out of the line as the crocodile took off, taking the canoe with him as he headed straight for the shore and up the bank. There it was not too difficult to club the croc to death, unless he happened to be less than two metres in length. In that case they would slip a noose over his snout and pinion his forelegs up over his back. They repeated the exercise with his hind legs and then inserted a pole between the two sets of legs. The crocodile was then carried back to the tribal camp and roasted, alive, in a cooking pot of hot stones. The stones were covered with earth and then a fire blazed on top of that. Why they did not kill it outright I have no idea unless of course it tasted better that way. The tail was considered the delicacy and when deemed ready it was skinned of its scales. The choice white flesh was firm but tender. I have eaten crocodile but I cannot say it was served up in this fashion.

The lack of fresh vegetables, the mosquito attacks, diarrhoea and the constant loss of sleep contributed to outbreaks of abscesses and boils. For the most part the men existed on flour, rice, oatmeal and tinned meat; that diet being supplemented by snakes, hawks and lizards. Mills gained a reputation as a marksman as he was a particularly good shot with a rifle and fortunately he often returned to the camp with game for the pot. His ability, and that of others, was not enough to provide for all 135 men and the *Gulnare* was sent to Koepang on the island of Timor. It returned with water buffaloes which were slaughtered from time to time to ensure fresh meat. The first water buffalo were brought into Australia about 1830 and 150 years later the country was supporting 350,000 feral water buffaloes. Because they carried brucellosis and tuberculosis a government-organised cull in the 1980s saw the numbers fall away dramatically but they have since climbed back to about 200,000.

It is interesting to realise that the tinned meat the OTL men received contained a fibrous beef from *Booyoolee Station* in South Australia. Initially it was called Booyoolee Beef but soon became Bully Beef, a name that survives in our lexicon today. When a good supply of fresh water was found and a gardener began to grow green vegetables and melons, matters improved but twenty men still developed scurvy. In the dry season up north and for most of the time in the rest of inland Australia health was a major issue. Sandy blight and Barcoo rot often set in. Sandy blight was a painful form of ophthalmia brought on by fly bites, irritation and dirt. Trial and error revealed that the best treatment for the sandy blight eye infection was to rub the open cut end of a potato on the eyelid. Barcoo rot was an unsightly rash of skin ulcers resulting from the infection of scratches in a body deficient in vitamin C.

When I was a jackaroo on *Wingadee Station*, Coonamble, from 1964 to 1966 the cook walked out and no replacement was forthcoming for several months. The station hands refused to cook so the overseer kindly said the jackaroos would do the job. We took it in turn for one week at a time to cook for the seven station hands and six jackaroos. About that time and coincidence or not, a few of us incurred the Barcoo rot, including myself. I had an outbreak of Barcoo on the shins and around the ankles. It looked bad being of a purple shade and it

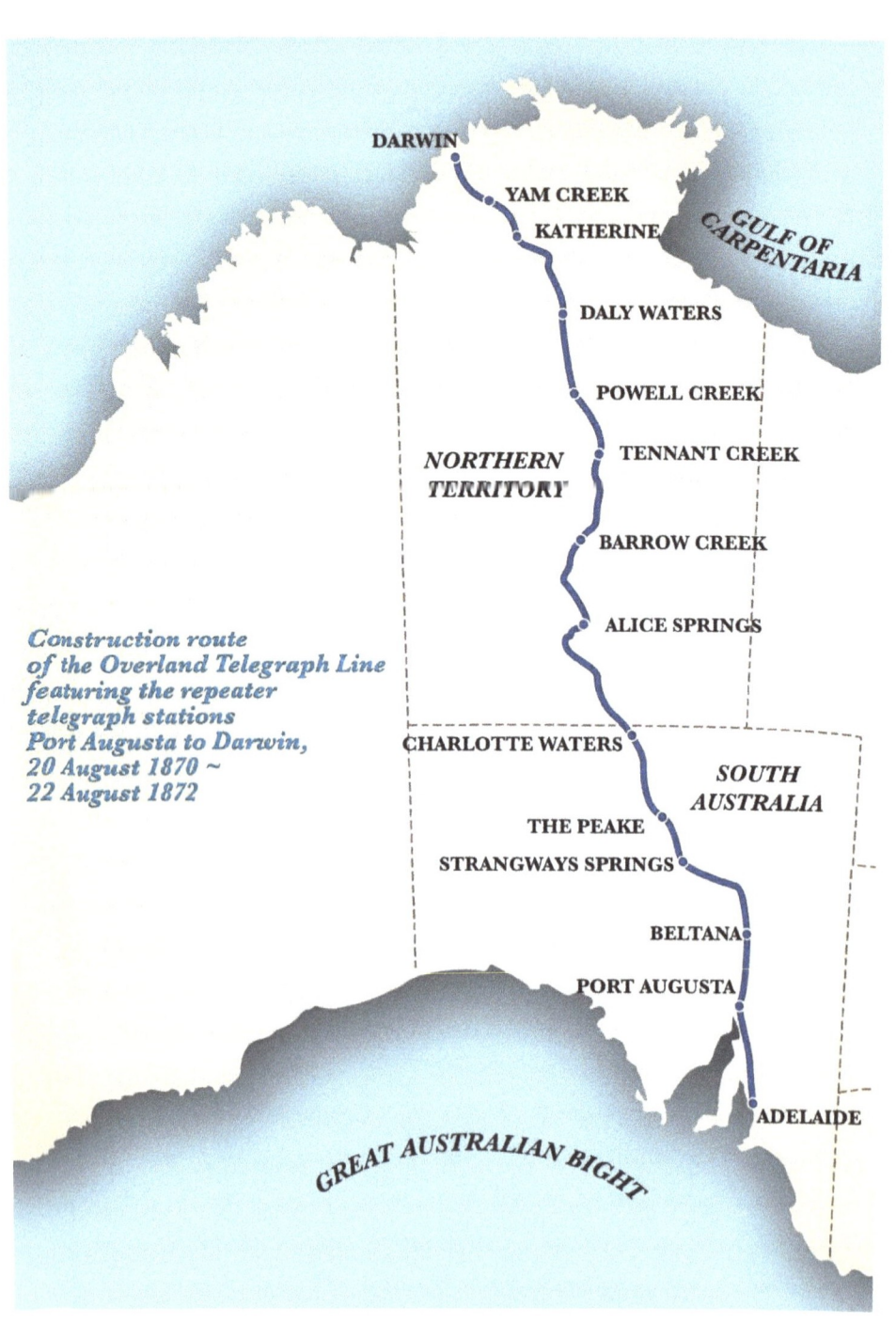

*Map of Overland Telegraph Line from Port Augusta to Darwin, NT.
Graphic created by Deborah Dawson, of Wongarbon, via Dubbo.*

did hurt somewhat, it stung, but it came good and never caused us to miss our work. Nevertheless it was so prolific in the colonial days it was said there was more scurvy on the Cooper Creek than there was on sailing ships. The Cooper of course is a major river, 1,300 kilometres long and sometimes known as the Barcoo since the Barcoo River flows into it. The Georgina, the Diamantina and the Cooper, when full, all constitute the Channel country and flow into Lake Eyre. They were what later attracted Sidney Kidman and others to the area.

At first the Aborigines had been afraid of the white men but with some familiarity they came closer and seemed friendly. However they resented the continued presence of the intruders and set fire to the three-metre-high grass in an attempt to burn them out. That failed so the Aborigines attacked and two men were speared. Bennet, the surveyor, had three spears in his chest but he broke off the shafts and managed to fire at and drive away his attackers. He then incurred the extra agony of being transported by horse to Darwin. When the doctor examined the surveyor he said if he removed the three spear heads that he would die within ten minutes. After writing two letters Bennet replied, 'I am ready doctor.' He died bravely, the first white man to die in Darwin, where he was buried. Some Aborigines in the Darwin area used spears that had up to seventeen barbs, possibly for fishing but more likely for hunting and fighting.

After that a regular 24-hour armed guard protected the camp, with rifleman Mills in charge of a watch. Some 145 years later the English researcher, Myra Fonceca, was in Perth where she read a mining memoir that casually mentioned, 'W. W. Mills came into the camp tonight. The best shot in the Territory and a great companion around the fire.' The work of surveying went on until the intended areas had been completed. The streets of Darwin were named after members of the expedition with Mills Street in the suburb of Millner. For an unknown reason no street was named after Goyder who returned to Adelaide, embarking on the *Gulnare* on the 28th September, 1869. With thirty-three men also going back to Adelaide, 101 remained in Darwin to carry out public works, undertake exploration and survey for the aforementioned possible Overland Telegraph Line.

Mills stayed behind and was in his element when on the 24th December he and three others returned in the evening, having shot more than thirty geese and several ducks for Christmas. In February 1870 all who had stayed on returned to Adelaide by sea. Many of those men were broken in health and some were unable to return to work for twelve months. It had been a successful but hard experience for all. A bonus was paid to the men, depending on their rank. Mills's immediate boss received £105, Mills himself £84 and the lowest amount paid was £3/16/7.

Having determined what the 'Centre' of Australia consisted of and put Darwin on the map, the South Australian Government now concentrated on the proposed Overland Telegraph Line. In July 1870 a group consisting of John Ross and four other men set off to find a route for the OTL. The South Australian Government recognised that the most difficult part of the line, that which passed through very inhospitable country was the Centre section, a 621-mile stretch of country from near Oodnadatta in the south to Tennant Creek in the north. As it happens, 621 miles equates to 999.4 km. The government decided that because of that difficulty it would appoint its own men from the Lands Office to construct that part of the line and that it would be divided into five sections, each approximately 200 km long and known as Sections A, B, C, D and E. Section C, of which Mills was a member, was to construct the line, specifically from 24 degrees south to 22.5 degrees south latitude, through the MacDonnell Ranges, the absolute centre of the proposed work. To complete the job by the contracted date of 31st December, 1871 and to avoid financial penalties the five sections would be operating at the same time. For the northern and southern areas the government signed up contractors to do the work.

The five surveyors in charge of the sections were R.R. Knuckey, G.R. McMinn, J. Beckwith, A.T. Woods and W. Harvey. All bar Beckwith had been with Goyder in Darwin, as had Mills who was appointed second-in-command of Section C, on a salary of £150 per year. The person in charge overall was Charles Todd and, like Goyder, he was an astute, thorough and practical man who achieved greatness by application of diligent and considered work. Todd was later firmly of the opinion that 'the successful carrying out of the Overland Telegraph Line was largely due to Mr. Goyder. The experience of the men he had trained being of great value.' In 1868 the Adelaide to Sydney telegraph line was

4
The Royal Flying Doctor Service and The Overland Telegraph Line

On the 5th October, 1870, Mr. Beckwith, in charge of Section C on the Overland Telegraph Line, was feeling unwell. Mills, second-in-command, shot a kangaroo for food to supplement the supplies of fresh sheep meat. Two weeks later, the group arrived at Thomas Elder's *Beltana Station*, a property he had acquired in 1862 from his brother-in-law, Robert Barr Smith. Elder, later Sir Thomas Elder, had a strong liking for and belief in camels for the opening up of Australia. In 1866, he had Samuel Stuckey import more than 120 camels and thirty-one cameleers. When not working the cameleers generally lived at Marree, Farina and Beltana. Elder's camel breeding proved successful and he provided camels for many of the exploration expeditions in Australia. *Beltana Station*, 540 km north of Adelaide, was popular as the assembly/starting point for the expeditions of Giles in 1872, Warburton 1873, Ross 1874, Lewis 1873/4, Mills 1882 and the scientific Elder Exploration Expedition of 1891.

The railway arrived at the nearby town of Beltana in 1881. In that year the town only had seventy residences but it could field a cricket team and support regular racehorse meetings. The population peaked at the turn of the century at 400 while its most famous resident arrived in 1911. This was John Flynn who immediately after serving for two years at Beltana's Presbyterian 'Smith of Dunesk' Mission, went on to found the Australian Inland Mission, dedicated to ensuring that 'hospital and nursing facilities are provided within a hundred miles of every spot in Australia where women and children reside'.

In 1928 John Flynn was at Cloncurry, north Queensland, where he founded the Royal Flying Doctor Service (RFDS) of Australia. Thanks to the Reverend John Flynn, his co-workers and people who financially have supported the RFDS ever since, Australia now has a not-for-profit comprehensive aeromedical organisation that provides emergency and primary health care to people in rural and remote areas. My home town has a RFDS base at the Dubbo Airport and there are similar arrangements across Australia. Some people say while the RFDS did commence in Cloncurry, John Flynn came up with the idea while he was based in Beltana. In any event he confirmed his intention after an incident in 1917 at Halls Creek in the Kimberley region of northern Western Australia.

You might know Halls Creek is 2,846 km north of Perth, along the Tanami Track and at the top end of the Canning Stock Route. It holds a prominent place in Australian rural life with its *Ruby Plains* being one of twelve cattle stations in the current S. Kidman group of properties, begun by the cattle king, Sidney Kidman. Whilst the aggregation is currently for sale, *Ruby Plains* was on the market in 2008 for $44 million. At auction the 9,674 square km property was passed in at $38 million. As the price of cattle has more than doubled, perhaps tripled, since then I imagine the asking price may be met or raised, or indeed the entire aggregation sold.

In 1917 a *Ruby Plains* stockman, Jimmy Darcy, suffered a ruptured bladder. It took 12 hours for his mates to transport him 48 km to Halls Creek where the only person with first aid training was the Postmaster, Mr. Tuckett. Knowing his ability was too limited to help Darcy, Mr. Tuckett tried to reach doctors at Wyndham and Derby but to no avail. He finally got through to a doctor, Dr. Holland, in Perth.

Using Morse code Dr. Holland directed the Postmaster through two operations. Mr. Tuckett's only sharp instrument was a penknife, so Jimmy Darcy was strapped down on the operating table, which was the post office counter, and rendered unconscious with a bottle of whisky. I gather he drank it rather than be hit by it. After the operation was completed Dr. Holland set off to see to the patient.

Travelling by way of a Model T Ford, a boat used to transport cattle, a horse-drawn carriage and on foot, Dr. Holland arrived in Halls Creek ten days later. Jimmy Darcy had died the previous day but not of the operation which had actually been successful. The cause of death was an undiagnosed case of malaria and a ruptured abscess in his appendix. It was that and similar cases of unrealistic hardship and suffering in remote areas that induced John Flynn to instigate what became the Royal Flying Doctor Service. Praise be.

There were countless outback injuries, most of which were never heard of in the public domain but one other has a story to it that I find hard to ignore for a young man's determination to prevail. A stockman suffered a serious upper arm injury which resulted in his arm having to be amputated. The arm was taken off at the socket of the shoulder. I am certainly not a butcher but I did learn on *Wingadee Station*, north of Coonamble, NSW, to kill and cut up sheep for meat. I like to think it stood me in good stead for the thirty-seven years I practised the art on our farm so I have to presume the bush surgeon did not cut the arm off with a saw but sliced delicately through the sinews and tissue that hold the arm into the shoulder socket. The pain must have been torturous for the patient but far, far worse came to him when the surgery was cauterised by applying a red-hot branding iron that seared the exposed shoulder. Appropriately cauterise comes from the Greek word *kauterion*, which translates as branding iron.

At *Beltana Station*, with Beckwith still unwell, Mills and the others encountered a problem. Most horses do not like camels and those of Section C were no exception. On the first night and after darkness fell, 150 horses, which included those of other sections, all hobbled and with a large bell on every third horse, were terrified by the smell and sound of the nearby *Beltana Station* camels. In their panic they broke loose and after being returned to the yards, six of Section A's horses were unaccounted for. After a bigger search three were found 50 miles away but after searching for more than 100 miles the others were not found.

Section C pressed on at a rate of 24 to 32 km per day, heading for the starting point for building their part of the Overland Telegraph Line, which would be up to and through the MacDonnell Ranges. On the last day of October they came to Strangways Springs, natural springs that bubble up from deep down in the ground. When Mills was there it was named Strangways Springs and situated on one of the great Australian cattle stations, by the name of *Strangways Station*. It was then close by *Anna Creek Station*, which in 1872 moved north to its present location, a little to the west of William Creek. At 23,677 square km *Anna Creek Station* is seven times larger than King Ranch, the largest cattle ranch in Texas. *Anna Creek Station* is also owned by the S. Kidman company whose current twelve rural properties total 101,000 square kilometres. *Anna Creek Station* has a carrying capacity of up to 16,000 head of cattle while the aforementioned *Ruby Plains* can run 24,900 cattle, depending on the seasons.

Section C moved on from Strangways Springs to Mount Margaret, which until the line was built, was the furthest point north for white settlement in South Australia. On 4th November, 1870, Charles Todd arrived from Adelaide. Finding Mr. Beckwith's health had not improved, Todd told Mills he now expected him to survey the line and attend to any exploration required to find timber for the poles for Section C.

Todd, later to be Sir Charles Todd, went on ahead to The Peake and arrived there on 10th November. Section C with all its equipment caught up on 21st November and it was then that Todd determined Beckwith was not fit to continue. He decided to replace Beckwith with Mills. Beckwith returned to Adelaide where unfortunately he died soon after. Todd conferred with the five section surveyors, Knuckey, McMinn, Woods, Harvey and Mills.

The OTL had to be completed by 31st December 1871 and if it wasn't financial penalties would be applied for every day it was late. Knowing it was impossible to build the line continuously in that time it was agreed that the line would be constructed by five teams or sections, each working their designated area simultaneously. Section C, being the third section, had responsibility for erecting its line through the absolute centre of Australia.

On 25th November, Todd wrote to Mills, saying, in part, 'I need not remind you how much in a work of such magnitude and difficulty as that before you, success depends on the example and tact of the officer immediately in charge of the men. I trust therefore you will do your utmost to complete the work successfully by yielding a ready and cordial compliance with the instructions of your superior officer, aiding him at all times to the best of your power and judgement' and 'to watch over the health and morals of the party, to regularly suppress all gambling and to endeavour as far as possible to promote all rational amusements.'

So it was that after just four years in the colony and a week after his 26th birthday, Mills took over the command of Section C. He led the section to what is now known as Charlotte Waters, a touch north of what became the South Australia/Northern Territory border. Charlotte Waters was founded on a tributary of the Finke River by two of the other surveyors/section leaders, Woods and Knuckey. I gather it was named after Lady Charlotte Bacon, the daughter of the rather comely Countess of Oxford and Countess Mortimer (two titles), the lovely Jane Elizabeth Harley, who numbered among her many lovers Lord Byron. Her son, Harley Bacon was one of the men who worked on the Overland Telegraph Line.

Putting that distraction at Charlotte Waters aside, Mills discovered that the terrain now changed from stony country to that which was sand. It stayed that way for the next 210 miles and he wrote 'Along the Finke the sandhills are such that they need to be travelled to be properly appreciated, continuing for miles in succession, many of them so steep a gradient that no horses in the world would hold a load coming down on any soil but sand.'

On 22nd January, 1871, Woods, the overall senior surveyor of the five sections, sent Mills ahead to look for a sufficient supply of water. On his return it was agreed that the route he recommended be accepted. Before that happened, Woods, McMinn and Mills rode out to a site three miles above the junction of the Hugh and Finke Rivers where it had been decided that the explorer John Ross and his men who were still looking for a way through the MacDonnell Ranges, would be met with food on their return. This was on 25th January and Ross and his men were not at the meeting place so late on the 26th Woods, McMinn and Mills turned back to their own camp. They had barely left when Alfred Giles, a member of Ross's team, heard a cooee. He answered it by firing two rifle shots and then Woods, McMinn, Mills and four others rode up with the supplies. After a sumptuous meal of damper, mutton, cheese and tea the Overland Telegraph Line men returned to their camps.

Alfred Giles was a member of John Ross's group and he said of the journey with John Ross, 'The flies were an awful pest, driving the horses nearly mad. Nearly everyone had bunged up eyes, the flies were a constant torment and nearly all the party were attacked by severe vomiting. We almost loathed the sight of food for everything was black with flies and the only escape was to remain in the mosquito net. We had no books, no papers or letters from relatives or friends since the previous November. The scorpions were an enormous size.'

Dingoes attacked the nearest mob of 2,000 sheep unless they were closely guarded. Mill's section however had already eaten forty of them. Quite a few men were suffering 'dislocation of limbs' and obstinate ulcers which was thought to be due to a lack of fresh fruit and a way had not yet been found through the MacDonnell Ranges wide enough for the working drays and wagons to be brought up with supplies for men and the line. There must have been a lot of timber in those days as a horse could be ridden through but nothing larger.

Woods was becoming frustrated by this delay and on 8th February he sent Mills with a small party to try to traverse the MacDonnell Ranges from the end of McMinn's Section B (Mills's Section C was responsible for erecting the line from thereon) into the Reynolds Range. Mills travelled up the Hugh River arriving in the MacDonnell Ranges on 18th February and then encountered heavy rain, which continued for five days and severely restricted his efforts. On 27th February he met up with McMinn who was also searching for a way through the Ranges. On 4th March McMinn returned to his Section B, leaving Mills to find the elusive way ahead.

On 7th March, Mills took one man and a young Aborigine and once more set off for the MacDonnell Ranges. They rode to Temple Bar which Mills named and is opposite Simpson's Gap on Roe Creek and about 20 kilometres west of what is now Alice Springs. Continuing on, to the east, Mills found an impressive array of waterholes and named them after the wife of his overall boss, Sir Charles Todd. On 11th March he wrote 'again arrived in the MacDonnell Ranges and was successful in finding a pass about thirty miles west of Stuart's Track with numerous waterholes and springs, the principal of which I had the honour of naming after Mrs. Todd.' Her name of course was Alice. Mills had found and named Alice Springs and when the town sprang up that was later its name. Temple Bar is these days known as Honeymoon Gap. The name was changed in 1942 after Bob and Vicki Darken honeymooned there. Must have been some honeymoon. Further along, seven kilometres west of Alice is the grave and memorial of the Reverend John Flynn, Flynn of the Inland, Flynn of the Royal Flying Doctor Service. Flynn, a great man, on the Aussie $20 note.

Mills rode on and also had the good fortune to find a way through the MacDonnell Ranges. The men continued on their way north. He also named Heavitree Gap, after his old school in Devon, England. It is the southern approach to Alice Springs and a sacred site for the Aborigine Arrernte tribe whose women avoided it until the construction of the eventual road and rail link. Now that Mills had found the way through the MacDonnell Ranges the work rate stepped up and from 22nd March to 26th June, Section C erected 75 miles of poles and had prepared poles for the next 27 miles. It had been expected this section would be short of timber but it had turned out surprisingly well as they were able to cut 150 poles from a clump of solid trees only 400 metres from the line. Camels brought up wire and stores.

There is a detailed, technical description of how the many men of all ranks combined to intricately construct the Overland Telegraph Line. I don't wish to overburden readers with an avalanche of information but those who are interested may wish to peruse the following by Peter Taylor from the book *An End to Silence*:

With good planning, as supplied and demanded by Sir Charles Todd, there was a distinct method as to how the Overland Telegraph Line was built. Each surveyor/overseer in charge of a section would establish the southern end of his section by latitude and then make a camp about 10 kilometres north as close to good timber as he could find. He marked out the first few kilometres of the line and men started preparing the poles. Leaving a man in charge he then took his second-in-command, in Mills's case this was Burt, and two or three men to survey the route ahead. After two days the second in command went back to supervise the work and direct it through the country they had just explored. The surveyor then continued north to establish his boundary with the surveyor of the next section. As he returned he roughly placed the route of the line by marking trees or putting in posts, marking them on his map.

The surveyor also searched out suitable timber and water and located camp sites to be used as the work progressed. The exact route having been determined it then had to be cleared to a width of 10 metres. This meant removing all the scrub and undergrowth as well as cutting down overhanging branches, so that there would be a perfectly clear space for five metres on either side of the line. The surveyor would have a small group of men clearing the route about 15 km ahead of the main working group. As it was cleared the surveyor would put in pegs to mark the approximate position of each pole, using large pegs where the line changed direction.

The poles themselves had to be about seven metres long, 25 centimetres in diameter at the base and 15 centimetres at the top. They needed to be perfectly sound, obviously. The bark was removed and the pole was charred over the bottom two metres. The top of each pole was bound with an iron band and a 12-centimetre hole bored vertically down from the centre of the top of the pole to take the insulator pin, which was then driven in and firmly fixed. If it was impossible to find timber long enough, two smaller poles were scarfed together and the join securely bolted and held by iron bands.

The poles were planted 80 metres apart, 12 to the km or 20 to the mile and as a consequence each twentieth pole was inscribed to mark another milestone had been passed. This meant they needed a good supply of suitable timber. It was better to cart good timber a considerable distance rather than use indifferent poles from poor timber closer to hand. A party of men would cut and prepare poles and take them up the route, dropping one at each peg whilst another team would be digging the holes. These were square with vertical sides 1.2 metres deep and had to be ranged accurately so they were all in a straight line. Rock had to be cut out by hand. With the insulator fixed, the pole could now be lifted into position and placed in the hole, a pair of poles being used as sheerlegs to support it until it was vertical. The ground was then well-rammed and the pole was self-supporting. Where the line changed direction the pole was strutted with an extra pole about five metres long.

Another team would then string the wire across the insulators on the tops of the poles and it would be strained so as to have a deflection of one metre over every 120 metres of length. As they came to the end of the coil of wire the next was joined to it by a Britannia knot, made by overlapping the ends of the wire and binding them tightly with a length of thinner wire which was then covered by solder. The surveyor had to inspect each joint before it was raised. Finally a length of wire would be stapled to every second pole as a lightning conductor. The top was seven centimetres above the insulator and bent clear of it, and on the opposite side of the line wire. The bottom was made in to a coil and buried one metre underground at the foot of the pole. Later, as the sections joined up, telegraph operators would move up behind the construction parties to test the line. With only basic tools it must have been cruel work, made even more so by high temperatures and the harshness of the country. Every operation demanded physical labour and in front of the men there was nothing but emptiness, day after day, pole after pole, until the low range in the distance was finally passed and another plain revealed.

I mentioned Alfred Giles who rode with the explorer John Ross's exploratory party, attached to the Overland Telegraph Line. Giles reported his wages from July, 1870, were £1 a week plus his food and kit which included three pairs of moleskin trousers, several shirts, three pairs of boots and two hats. In his book, *Exploring in the Seventies*, Giles recorded an occasion when Ross and his party had gone 36 hours without water in Central Australia and the grass was so dry in the scorching heat the horses were unable to eat it. Another time they went 72 hours without water but the air was cooler and the grass green and edible for horses. However, as we shall see, the camels were in their element.

A tiger for punishment, Alfred Giles crossed Australia seven times from south to north, one way or the other, mainly whilst on the Overland Telegraph Line and also when he later became a station manager in that part of the world. He discovered the Kintore Caves, 12 km west of Katherine in the Northern Territory and 330 km south of Darwin. The area is known for its extensive network of caves that contain rare fauna, beautiful stalagmites and stalactites and evidence of past human occupation. Giles once took the Premier of South Australia, Thomas Playford, into the caves to show him its treasures and unfortunately the Premier, a man of considerable bulk, became firmly wedged between two stalactites. He could not be removed until one stalactite was cut down. Mr. Playford was Minister for Defence in the Federal Government in 1905 and in the 1906 general election became the first serving Minister to lose his seat. His grandson, Sir Thomas Playford, rebalanced the ledger by becoming the longest serving Premier of South Australia.

As Mills pressed north he named the Everard Plains, not to be confused with the Everard Ranges named by Ernest Giles, which he rode out onto once he had cleared the MacDonnell Ranges; Forster's Creek, Burt Creek, after his second in command, Prowse's Gap, Allan's Waterhole, Bond Springs and Harry Creek, after his younger brother, Harry Mills, but like his former boss, Mr. Goyder, nothing for himself. On 13th July it became apparent the northern section of the line would not be completed anywhere near on time, 31st December, 1871. Accordingly, on 27th July Charles Todd sent an urgent message to Mills to complete his Section C work and then go north to assist Harvey with Section E and having done that to carry on to assist the northern area team.

While Mills and Section C were doing everything they could to comply with Todd's request, the Milner brothers, Ralph and John, with their stockmen, who as mentioned had left Port Augusta on 5th September the previous year, with sheep and goats to provide fresh meat along the way, reached Attack Creek on 30th August, 1871. One of the stockmen was Arthur Ashwin, who five years earlier at the age of sixteen had been working with drovers taking sheep through the Wimmera district of western Victoria. On their way they stopped at Lake Wallace which, at that time, was where the Victorian Cricket Club put together the first Aboriginal cricket team to tour England, in 1868. The men came from three neighbouring tribal areas and were of exceptional athletic ability. They trained and played at Lake Wallace before going to England where they played forty-seven matches against mid-level and higher-grade teams, winning fourteen matches, losing fourteen and drawing nineteen matches. The Aboriginal team was the first Australian overseas touring team in any sport. The team coach was the white man Tom Wills, whose father, Horatio Wills, was amongst nineteen whites speared to death by Aborigines in a retaliatory massacre at Springsure, central Queensland, in 1861.

Arthur Ashwin later worked on *Mundowdna Station*, at Marree, S.A. Aborigines, particularly those from the Lake Hope area, had become aggressive and resentful of white settlers taking up land, and from 1863 onwards were often spearing the sheep and cattle. In September, 1868, they attacked *Mundowdna Station* itself and burned it, while two of their men were killed. White men were also causing trouble and small police stations were established. Several of them were in the most isolated and dangerous of places. Their purpose was to catch white men who were stealing cattle and to protect settlers from Aborigines who were said to be sometimes cutting out the tongues of live cattle.

Some cattlemen understood they were utilising long-established native lands to feed and water their livestock and in return they tolerated the Aborigines occasionally spearing their cattle. However in various places and times the cattle-spearing was excessive albeit it may have been used to avenge a personal wrong committed by a white man. There were instances of Aborigines carrying the tuft of a cow tail on the human hair belt around their waist as an indication of their achievement and sometimes a man had seven such trophies. Others chose to carve a notch on their spear when they had killed a cow or a steer. Those who went far further and killed a white policeman carved the notch on their woomera, no doubt because there was little chance of retrieving the spear.

Spear points were originally made of bone, fine-grained stone or fire-hardened wood and attached to the haft by way of resin and tendon. With the arrival of the white man they gained the use of ceramic and glass, such as from the Overland Telegraph Line posts. Glass spear points were favoured by some because when they entered the body of a wounded animal they usually broke off and this caused haemorrhaging which in turn ensured a faster kill. I have heard that teeth were also used for spear points. At first this was hard to accept but two points have changed my mind. One is the initiation ceremony of *thaamba* whereby a young man had an incisor tooth removed. Surely those important and already sharp teeth were not simply thrown away. They would ensure a steady supply. The second consideration has to be that sound, healthy teeth can last for hundreds of years.

A great leap forward came with the arrival of iron in Australia. According to the extraordinary bushman, Ion Idriess, Aborigines initially gained their source from the settlers' worn-out, thrown away or stolen shovels. With the iron already worn and/or flattened they worked them into the shape of a long, broad spear head. How? With incentive they used stone, water and sand, persistence, sheer dint of unrelenting effort and many hands. Neither did they miss an opportunity to obtain more supplies. Farmers and stockmen built their wooden gates and hung them on hinges, especially around their homes and yards. At night the Aborigines would lift the gates off and remove the iron hinges. Others would follow a horseman through the bush until they had the opportunity to spear the horse, especially when they could see by the tracks that the horseshoes were well-worn. Such already worked iron was always highly sought as one accurately thrown iron spear could kill a bullock let alone a man. The owner of such a weapon could buy a girl from her father or trade it for other prizes.

As we know there is good and bad to be found on either side of the fence and I have quoted Arthur Ashwin, a highly regarded bushman and later, author, who did no more than call it as he saw it. Another bushman, Bill Hatfield, who was equally proficient in understanding and existing in the outback and in those demanding times which did not have the facilities of today, had gone into the outback to test himself and to make a go of this different way of life. He was a stockman on a large cattle station which also bred a significant number of horses and observed the following:

'The first handling of the colts was carried out by black boys, a thing that came as the biggest contradiction I had to swallow in all my Australian experience, these men of a race classed by ignorant observers in the first place as the lowest species of humanity on earth: lazy, useless, cowardly and incapable of organised effort. Instead of which I found them doing most of the stock work on all the big unfenced runs, where their bushcraft is unmatchable, doing all the hardest riding on all the roughest horses, under the direction of white overseers and head stockmen.'

Another stockman, employed on a Queensland cattle station recorded that the manager of a much larger station nearby, whom he regarded as an excellent manager, refused to employ any white men. He ran the entire station, most successfully, with Aborigines.

It might pay for us to recall the words of the archaeologist, Josephine Flood who determined that, 'If a time scale of human occupation of Australia were represented by one hour on a clock, Aboriginal society would occupy over fifty-nine and a half minutes, European society less than half a minute.'

5
Gold and Copper

Arthur Ashwin kept daily notes of each day's events and he recorded the following. Ralph Milner had ridden ahead to scout out the land and left his brother John in charge of their camp and the men. An Aborigine, described as a wild, tall, powerful fellow had come into the camp, and Ashwin as well as another man, Old Yorkey, were instantly distrustful of the man. In most such camps the Aborigines were kept at a distance and this was no exception, bar the easy-going manner of John Milner who shrugged off his men's constant warnings.

Arthur Ashwin had that day already seen large numbers of fresh Aborigine tracks nearby and couldn't help but notice a lot of smoke from signal fires to the west, north-west and south-west but without sighting anyone. He rode out to check on the grazing sheep and when he returned to the camp he found John Milner and Charlie's gin (Aboriginal woman), Fannie, with the wild man. The camp's dogs were unusually restless. Ashwin again warned Milner who replied the Aborigine was a fine specimen of a man and no danger. Being of a different opinion Ashwin had not taken his eyes off the unwelcome intruder, who had all his weapons with him and who just as keenly studied Ashwin's face and movements.

Ashwin wrote, 'I had tied my horse up to a scrubby bush. I left my rifle and revolver on the horse, as I had a double-barrelled duelling pistol on my belt and a large Pipe Brand butcher's knife for a sheath knife, just ground and like a razor. Fannie the gin said, 'Wild fellow no good. Piccaninny (Aboriginal baby) time him growl.' (My research says that in the language of the Powell's Creek Aborigines, and possibly other tribes, the word growl meant threat of war.)

Ashwin told Milner they needed to be around the sheep as they were moving away. Milner agreed and the moment Ashwin turned around to mount his horse, the Aborigine brought his club down on Milner's head and smashed his skull in. Fannie shouted to Ashwin and he turned back to see Milner's favourite kangaroo dog had a hold on the arm of the Aborigine who was now coming hard at Ashwin himself with a boomerang in his hand. Ashwin continued, *In a second I had the pistol out and cocked both hammers and fired straight into his belly or low in his chest. He was facing me and the dog on him. He had a boomerang in the air in the act of throwing it. When I fired it flew out of his hand and he fell, but got on his feet again and I fired at his back as he was running. He fell again but got up again. My horse bolted when I fired the first shot. I ran over to Milner's horse and took his revolver out of its holster and hooked his rifle down. I put the 200-yard sight on and aimed low at the man as he was again running, with the dog still on him, but the rifle would not go off.*

I then attended to the dying man. It was a heavy blow and smashed his skull in from the ear to the eye, both his eyes were out on his cheeks. We buried him under a large tree and fenced the grave in with heavy timber and pricked a sheet of tin with the date and name and age and cause of his death, and nailed it on the tree. Afterwards when the Government party came along there was a carpenter in the party who carved a large slab and put it at the head of his grave, which was full of spears. The Aborigines had been performing corroborees around it and throwing spears into it, and were too superstitious to take them out. They were showing their hatred of the white man.

Arthur Ashwin declared, 'Be kind to the wild native if you want trouble, he takes kindness for fear all over Australia.'

The men moved on and shortly afterwards came to an Aboriginal burial ground on land that is now *Newcastle Waters*, that Stuart named after the Duke of Newcastle and is today a well-known cattle station. It is 789 km north of Alice and 716 km south of Darwin. There were hundreds of bones and skulls and skeletons in different stages of decomposition. The Aborigines had made rough platforms in the limbs of the trees and put the bodies on them and then covered them up with sheets of paperbark. Ashwin picked up some of the skulls and found that a lot of them had been fractured and smashed in. He believed there had been a battle between two tribes a few years earlier. Arthur Ashwin may have come across so many skeletons because in some tribes the men were likely to have as many as four wives. In such a pitched battle when the tide had definitely turned against one group of combatants the losing tribe would often kill their own women to prevent them from falling into the wayward hands of the triumphant tribe.

I make no claims to knowing the intricate ways of Aboriginal deaths and burials but I have come across information concerning the Arrernte tribe that Mills often made contact with in his OTL surveying days. That tribe put deceased people on a platform of broken-off branches they placed in a tree well enough above ground level so as to provide security from animal attack. When the body had decomposed to the point that the flesh had gone, the men of the tribe would bring down the bones. If the deceased was female they would give the bones to the tribal women. A line of men, who were heavily painted with ochre of several colours on their chests and backs, and were otherwise completely naked, stood legs apart, over a recently dug trench, so that one leg was planted on either side of the trench and each man stood directly behind but close up to, the man who stood in front of him. When the women approached one of them gave an arm or other bone of the deceased to the men, who then broke the bone. The women, also naked, then got down on their hands and knees and crawled along the mortuary trench, between the wide-spread legs of the men of the tribe.

It was reported by the renowned anthropologist Herbert Basedow in 1925 that in northern Australia, particularly the Kimberley, the Aborigines used termite mounds to sometimes bury their dead and especially so if they had killed a stranger who intruded upon their land. If the latter happened they would break into a termite mound, which can be several metres high and weigh up to ten tonnes, and dig a hole in the ground, into which they would place the body of the victim. The termites, most conveniently for the locals, would soon repair the damage to the mound and conceal any evidence that would give an avenging party cause for concern. The mounds can vary in shape and colour let alone height and weight because they are constructed from the area's soil and the termites' saliva and excreta. As there are tens of thousand of termite mounds in Australia a search party, even if it suspected what had occurred, could never find the tomb. World-wide there are 2,000 types of termites and Australia has 350 species. Twenty of those are destructive, more than enough.

When a baby died in western Arnhem Land, its body would be placed in a termite mound so that the bones would quickly disintegrate, thus freeing its spirit to return to the same mother to be born again. Sometimes the mother would carry the bones around with her so that its spirit could return to the same mother and be reborn. Termite mounds in the north are thus treated with respect by Aborigines. In 1897, Roth stated that in Queensland's Boulia district, men who were convicted and sentenced to death by the tribal council for a serious offence were required to dig their own grave.

I find the matter of burying babies in termite mounds in the belief that the bones would disintegrate of significant interest because termites sometimes have an osteophagous or bone-eating diet. Such an appetite seems to have been a habit of the dinosaur-like archosaur to extract the salt and marrow while today's Bearded vulture definitely eats bones. Analysts have determined that fresh bones as consumed by the vulture contain 108 % as much energy as fresh meat and that dry bones retain 90% of the protein found in fresh bones. I have also heard that old graves in Peru have revealed skeletons in which the skulls have been substantially eaten away, apparently as the result of hungry termites. I have from time to time, I must admit over quite a few decades, observed cattle chewing on animal bones. This is said to indicate they are lacking phosphorous and/or calcium.

In the practice of inhumation, the method of burials, certain Aboriginal tribes used a form of tombstone to mark the burial places, of those regarded as having been of importance to the tribe. When such identities as celebrated warriors, powerful doctors or revered leaders were buried their grave was marked by taphoglyphs, arborglyphs or simply, glyphs i.e. carvings, incised into nearby trees around the grave as a memorial to the deceased. This was not an Australia-wide ceremony but one that appears to have been confined to inland NSW, not the coast. If you have a general geographical knowledge of NSW I can present a rough territorial outline.

These glyphs carvings were/are to be found within an area that runs from that good property, *Urawilkie* Station, 35 km north-east of Coonamble and almost bordering *Wingadee* Station, then due east to Gunnedah, south to Mudgee, further south to Mittagong and Exeter before fading out at Jindabyne at the foothills of the Snowy Mountains. From there they were to be found to the north-west at Lake Cargellico, north to Nyngan and north-east back to Coonamble. According to

Mr. Edmund Milne and another keen assessor, Mr. W. Jardine, the centre of the practice was along the Bogan and Macquarie rivers, particularly from Wellington to Warren and *especially around the site of the present town of Dubbo*. This indicates quite conclusively that it was important to the people of the Kamilaroi tribe of Gunnedah and the Wiradjuri of Dubbo and surrounding areas.

As a general rule one or more trees near the grave were heavily inscribed with details of the man interred. There seems to be only one recorded instance of a woman being awarded a glyph. Stone axes were initially used to carve the details of the deceased and his attributes into the trunk of the tree but from the arrival of the First Fleet there was a pronounced lift in the quantity of such carvings and that is attributed to the Aborigines gaining metal tools, particularly tomahawks, even though coastal tribes did not participate in such veneration.

Over time sapwood tended to cover many of the glyphs artwork while wind, fire and earth, man's clearing of land, insects, disease, chemicals, drought and fungal blight took out many trees. Fortunately numerous settlers and farmers took notes and recorded the names of participating men and places. The first white men to see one was the explorer John Oxley and his men in 1817, when they came upon the grave of a Wiradjuri man buried at Gobothery Hill, forty km west of Condobolin along the Lachlan River. The man had been buried inside a large mound and to the west and the north of the grave were two cypress trees, each seventeen metres away. The bark had been removed on the sides facing the tomb and curious figures carved thereon, the detail and depth of cut impressing the white men.

Edmund Milne, a railway superintendent and amateur ethnographer re-discovered them in 1913 and the NSW government decided to remove the trees to a Sydney museum. A ceremony was held onsite and attended by at least one Aborigine. It transpired that elderly lady was Wooroodumony, the great-granddaughter of the buried chief. Her mother had orally handed down the details to her. The chief drowned while attempting to cross the Lachlan River whilst it was in high flood in his bark canoe.

At Lake Cargellico, and also on the Lachlan, a glyph indicates the grave of a tribal head man who was killed in a fight between opposing forces from the Lachlan and the Murrumbidgee tribes. Another mark of respect lies along the Narromine-Dubbo road where a celebrated boomerang thrower of the Macquarie tribe (Wiradjuri) was killed in fierce battle against the Bogan River people, also Wiradjuri.

The tree carvings at this spot were inscribed in a series of semi-lunate cuts to represent boomerangs. Those cuts were made by Aborigines using ground-edge axes derived from basalt or greenstone that had their cutting edges ground and then highly polished. Quite a few have been found at burial sites.

In the Wallaby Ranges, south of Narromine, four trees are placed at the cardinal points, a high mark of respect to say the least when five tree carvings are the most ever found at the one grave. They surround the resting place of the medicine man of the Bogan River tribe, who died of a disease he contracted when attending professionally to the ill headman of the Macquarie River mob, who recovered. Of the four honouring trees, those standing to the north and the south were inscribed by the Macquarie men while those to the east and west were courtesy of his own Bogan River people.

At Coonamble's *Urawilkie* Station rests a man who had killed a fellow tribesman. The District Surveyor stated that the murderer was not only a generally troublesome man but also a thief. Amongst his trophies was the gin or woman he stole from a fellow tribesman. For that offence he was despatched without trial. Despite his disgrace he had friends in the tribe who incised grave trees for him. I have used the word gin as it was said in the 19th and 20th centuries. Aboriginal women were sometimes called that in a derogatory manner by those white men of the day who were ignorant of the fact that gin in classical Greek culture means woman and is therefore an honoured word. Another carelessly and sadly misrepresented word is boong, which is of the Malaysian language and means brother.

The well-known property, *Euromedah*, favourably situated by the Macquarie River between Narromine and Dubbo had five carvings of such note that they were assessed by J.T. Wilson as the best exhibits to be seen anywhere for hundreds of miles. Mr. A. D. Badgery's five glyphs at his Exeter property were also highly prized whilst the five carved trees three kilometres from the Dubbo railway station were similarly rated by W.M. Thomas. He reported four of the glyphs to be at the cardinal points and the fifth at the south-east of the grave. He added, *the glyph of one being — I believe — unique*. He estimated the tree carvings to be at least 150 years old, back then in the 19th century.

An interesting account concerns the burial place of Lowrie, famous headman of the Burrendong tribe near what would be Wellington. He went to Mudgee to pursue a love matter and returned safely to Burrendong. However he was tracked by the Mudgee men who speared him as he was fishing on the river. He was honoured by a glyph. Edmund Milne tells of three glyphs at a grave between Trangie and the Macquarie River. It marks the death and burial site of a man as a result of a duel between two warriors of the Macquarie tribe, who had fought over the possession of a woman.

Forty-eight km west of Gunnedah a carved tree indicates the grave of a headman or doctor from Guntawang. He may have been with a raiding party for according to a Forest Ranger he was killed in a fight between the Mudgee and Namoi tribes. He was a fair way from home for I have known *Guntawang* for a long time as a horse stud and quality farm on the Cudgegong River between Gulgong and Mudgee.

Henry Lawson's mother, Louisa, was one of twelve children born to a station-hand family on Guntawang. If you are fond of Henry's writing I suggest you would admire Louisa Lawson, for the women in her family believe she was the original for the hard-working, resourceful, kindly and long-suffering bush women in her son's stories. Louisa became prominent in writing and publishing whilst strong on womens' rights and social reform.

There are more but I shall conclude with *Dundullimal* the Aboriginal word for thunderstorm or hailstorm. Regarded as the oldest surviving slab hut house in Australia it was taken up in 1840 and with its surrounding land consisted of 6,500 hectares. It is situated on the southern edge of Dubbo and is within a lovely walk over a foot-bridge across the Macquarie River near our home. Only a road separates *Dundullimal* from the Western Plains open-range zoo, from where we sometimes hear the lions roaring in the still air of the pre-dawn. Captain R.W. Soane wrote of an extensive and old burial site with four glyphs at *Dundullimal* but today the trees cannot be satisfactorily identified.

From its inception *Newcastle Waters* has been prominent in the Australian livestock industry with its geographical position and large numbers of cattle. In 1886 G.R. Hedley was the first man to travel the length of the Murranji track from *Newcastle Waters* to Victoria River. The 245 km long track reduces the east–west travelling stock route via Katherine by some 630 km. However it is hard going. Much of the track is lined by bullwaddy and lancewood trees. Combined in thickets with the tough lancewood spikes capable of piercing leather, the trees formed a barrier that had repeatedly, for eleven sorties, forced explorer Stuart to turn back from his attempts to reach the Victoria River and the Top End of Australia. As if that hazard was not enough the track was all but devoid of water.

Remarkably but not too surprisingly, the Aborigines thereabouts knew how to obtain water when the white man could not. Termites often hollowed out certain trees and when the regular wet season came along the water built up in the trunk of the tree. Now those trees are hard to discern but when the Aborigines got it right they tapped into the bottom of the trunk and the water flowed out. When they had enough water they then plugged the hole to identify it and hold the balance for future needs. There was no shortage of drovers who were prepared to take their cattle along that shortcut but eleven of them, going by reports of the day, paid for their misjudgement with their lives. Many thirsty men died, on foot, in their attempts to reach the goldfields of the Kimberley by travelling that route, and history has recorded the names of barely but a few of them. More lonely, agonising deaths by thirst, of men who perished.

There was a man who had already forged his reputation, as most likely the greatest drover of them all and here he enhanced it. Drover Nat 'Old Bluey' Buchanan had earlier taken 20,000 cattle, successfully, from central Queensland to *Glencoe Station* in the Northern Territory, in 1880. He would go on to open up more land, for others, than perhaps anyone else on the continent. He was also known as *Far Away* Buchanan. While gold prospectors were taking their hopes and determination into the Kimberley region Nat Buchanan, in 1883, took the initial cattle there, 4,000 head in total.

Nat Buchanan became a legend in his lifetime for his droving feats, bush craft, sense of direction and his remarkable powers of observation. He was the first drover to cross the Barkly Tableland from east (Qld) to west (NT), the first, with 1,200 head of cattle, to the Top End of the NT, the first man on the Territory's longest river the Victoria River and the first on WA's Ord River with cattle. He established the Territory's famous Wave Hill Station which by 1907 carried an estimated 58,000 cattle.

In 1886, along with his son and Sam Croker, he took the first cattle along the Murranji track, from *Newcastle Waters* westward. He was fortunate that Aborigines twice took him to watering holes along the way but once more he did what no one else had then achieved. As government bores were later and gratefully drilled for permanent water the annual volume of cattle along the Murranji is said to have peaked at 140,000 head in the 1940s. The stock route continued to be used until 1967, when no doubt trucks overtook it.

In 1899 Nat and his wife Catherine retired to a small farm near Tamworth, NSW, where he died on 23 September,1901. Nathaniel Buchanan has an unequalled record of achievement in Australia's droving and pioneering history.

After the Northern Territory Government vetoed Kerry Packer's application to buy *Victoria River Downs*, once the largest station in Australia, in favour of cattleman Peter Sherwin, Packer and partners bought *Newcastle Waters* in 1983. They eventually sold it and other stations, I think eighteen of them, for a combined total of $425 million. Today *Newcastle Waters* consists of 1,033,100 hectares or 10,350 square km of well-balanced country that is home to some 60,000 head of Brahman cattle. Many of those are sold to Indonesia and Japan. Alfred Giles, who rode with John Ross on the OTL, was once the manager of *Newcastle Waters*. Back in the mid-1980s, Peter Sherwin owned *Victoria River Downs* and fifteen other stations, totalling some 70,000 square km, to run his herd of 270,000 cattle. Now 93, he has just bought a 2,600 sq. km Northern Territory cattle station. No retirement for that man.

Prior to the construction of the OTL, on 2nd March, 1860, the man considered to be one of Australia's best and greatest explorers, John McDouall Stuart, had departed from Chambers Pillar, 160 km south of Alice Springs, on the fourth of his six explorations. His goal was to find the centre of Australia and in so doing he found and named the MacDonnell Ranges, which have featured so prominently hereabouts. On the 23rd June he was at Kekwick Ponds, further north again and named by Stuart for William Kekwick his trusted second-in-command, when he was approached by several Aborigines.

According to his journal, he was impressed by the physical appearance of two of the men, for he wrote they were: *young, tall, powerful, well-made and good-looking and as fine specimens of the native as I have yet seen. One had a great many scars upon him and seemed to be a leading man. One was an old man and seemed to be the father of these two fine young men. He was very talkative but I could make nothing of him. I endeavoured by signs to get information from him as to where the next water is. After some time and having conferred with his two sons he turned around and surprised me by giving me one of the Masonic signs.*

(Stuart was a Freemason at the Lodge of Truth, North Adelaide. I was also a Freemason and I find this Aborigine experience extraordinary for Freemasonry is not a secret society but it is a society of secrets.) Stuart continued, 'I looked at him steadily; he repeated it and so did his two sons. I then returned it, which seemed to please them much, the old man patting me on the shoulder and stroking down my beard.'

Three days later Stuart and his men started off from Large Gum Creek. In the afternoon they were attacked by thirty Aborigines of the Warramunga tribe who charged them while throwing boomerangs at the white men. Stuart gave his men the order to fire but of casualties he mentions none. Ashwin however relates that Stuart's men used their revolvers and cutlasses. Retrieving their packhorses which had been frightened off by the noise of the affair, they rode away to safety. The site of the incident is now called Attack Creek. The Aborigines had discovered OTL insulators were useful for sharpening weapons and often smashed them or even climbed the poles to remove them in one piece. Days after John Milner was killed, Mills's party was two miles above Attack Creek when they were charged by boomerang-throwing Aborigines, who were also of good physique, determined and hostile. Despite his attributes with a rifle Mills was never known to shoot at Aborigine people.

On 25th November 1871, Mills left G.R. McMinn to finish off the remainder of Section C while he went ahead and helped Section E. That work was duly completed on 29th December. In a report he wrote on 12th December, Mills summarised the all but completed undertaking, at least all that he had been involved with, and followed up with a significantly longer report of the nature of the terrain and vegetation, a report which was said to be of inestimable value to landholders.

On 22nd August, 1872 the gap between the south and the north was joined in the Ashburton Ranges. Whilst the contract to build the OTL was not completed on time, the 31st December, 1871, any and all penalties became null and void when on the due date it was discovered that the British-owned overseas connecting cable was broken, and for a considerable time.

The construction of the Overland Telegraph Line is regarded as the country's greatest engineering feat in the 19th century and a good part of that assessment lies in the fact that it was over a distance of more than 3,000 km. Australia was connected to the world. The obituary of Sir Charles Todd states in part; 'What tongue however eloquent, what pen however facile, can do justice to the value of that thin streak of wire during the long period when on it alone was suspended the whole telegraphic communication between this continent and the wider world of Europe, Asia, Africa and America.'

Until there was competition the cost of sending a message, a cable, was one pound per word to London and one shilling per word within Australia. Receiving a telegram was a major event for it invariably concerned only big business, a marriage, birth or death.

Repeater stations were built along the line as after a certain distance the Morse code signal faded away. If it was weak when picked up at the next station it went on from there at its original strength. Port Augusta aside, such repeater stations were built at the following centres, with the distance from Adelaide attached in km. Beltana 540, Strangways Springs 877, The Peake 1,023, Charlotte Waters 1,294, Alice Springs 1,667, Barrow Creek 1,942, Tennant Creek 2,179, Powell Creek 2,361, Daly Waters 2,583, Katherine 2,850, Yam Creek 2,974 and Darwin 3,178. From Adelaide to London the line went via Darwin, Jakarta, Singapore, Penang, Madras, Bombay, Suez, Alexandria, Malta, Gibraltar, Falmouth, London; a total of 20,421 km.

Charles Todd acknowledged Mills who was paid a bonus of £50 for his work as 'Overseer and Surveyor' and another £100 bonus for completing the work of Section C on time. Todd later said, 'Dear Alice. Her name lives on, thanks to party leader William Mills, who named a pool of water in the heart of Australia, the Alice Spring.'

Mills returned to Adelaide after being away for nearly two years but gold was discovered south of Darwin and he went back there in 1873. In 1874 he was a surveyor in private practice at Yam Creek, where a syndicate of fifteen men from Kapunda, SA, arrived to prospect for gold. Shortly after he went into partnership with Mr. A Peachey in Darwin. From 1876 to 1878 Mills was a surveyor working out of offices in Jeffcott Street, North Adelaide. In 1879 he met Mary Jane Mullen, of Kapunda, 80 kilometres north of Adelaide. Her father John Mullen, born in Kells, County Meath, Ireland, emigrated to Australia, arriving in Sydney on 18th September, 1841, aged 20, on the 507-ton ship, *Canton*.

He went to work up on the Namoi, an agricultural district of the northern tablelands out to the north-west plains of NSW. It is believed he worked on the first station there. Today the area is renowned for the excellence of its cotton growing, amongst other rural pursuits. After two years he returned to Sydney and joined the army, enlisting in the 99th Lanarkshire Regiment of Foot, which had been raised in Glasgow in 1824. The 99th was sent to Mauritius and then Australia. John Mullen's Regimental number was 204.

In 1807 the Battle of Hingakaka in New Zealand was fought between two opposing Maori forces consisting of 16,000 warriors, in hand to hand combat. Then that format changed. From 1807 to 1845 the Musket Wars were fought in New Zealand between numerous tribes of the Maori. They had often been clashing but on gaining muskets from flax and timber merchants operating out of Sydney the inter-tribal killings intensified and there were up to 40,000 dead and wounded in that period plus another 30,000 Maoris who were taken into slavery, by their own race. As if that wasn't enough, there was more bloodshed to come.

In May, 1845, John Mullen was a member of two companies of the 99th Regiment that was sent to New Zealand where he fought in the First Maori War, which was caused by disputes over land purchases, five years after the Treaty of

Waitangi had been signed. The Treaty ceded all rights and powers of sovereignty to the Crown, as in Queen Victoria, while at the same time allowing continued Maori ownership of their lands. It was written in a bilingual manner, with the Maori text translated from the English. Although formally signed the issue of sovereignty came to be seen in another light by the Maori and consequently war between the two sides raged from 1845 to 1872.

The 99th Regiment participated in the Battle of Ohaeawai. Native villages and hillforts were known as a *pa* and mostly found north of Lake Taupo, in the North Island. The pa were usually located in defensive positions to protect fertile food and plantation areas. It was usual for the pa to be constructed on raised ground where the natural slope of the land could be terraced and defensive fortifications erected or built into the ground. These were considered adequate when fighting other Maori tribes with similar weapons but the British Army had far more formidable weaponry. The native people reinforced the Ohaeawai pa by placing bundles of protective flax over the exterior palisade which was composed of hard puriri tree trunks sunk 1.5 metres into the ground. The flax dissipated the velocity of the musket balls, making the defences effectively bulletproof and the strong timber and thick earth held firm against cannon fire which included solid cast-iron cannonballs that weighed up to 14.5 kilograms.

After days of unsuccessful bombardments by the British they were further surprised when the virtually unscathed Maori counter-attacked and captured a Union Jack flag. Taking it back to their pa the natives then hung it upside down, at half-mast and below the Maori flag, which was a Kakahu or Maori cloak. The insult so infuriated the British colonel he ordered a frontal assault that day on the pa. John Mullen survived but within seven minutes the British had lost thirty-three men dead and sixty-six wounded, one third of their force.

Encouraged by their success, the Maori built an even stronger pa, at Ruapekapeka. It was known as a gunfighter pa with two lines of palisades covering a firing trench with individual pits, while more defenders could use the second palisade to fire over the heads of the those at the palisade below. This pa included underground bunkers protected by earth over wooden beams, ditches, loop holes and the defensive earthen terraces. These were all needed as the British had superior, high quality percussion muskets, cannons, mortars, howitzers, rocket tubes and congreve rockets.

The congreve rocket weighed from 11 to 27 kilograms and could carry either an incendiary or an anti-personnel warhead and had been used by the Sultanate of Mysore in India against the British East India Company. The British further developed and used congreve rockets in the Napoleonic Wars and against the Americans in the War of 1812 at Fort McHenry during the Battle of Baltimore. The congreve rocket was known for its visually brilliant red glare and from that battle was incorporated into the national anthem of the United States of America, the Star-Spangled Banner. If you look at the first stanza of the anthem and read line five it states, 'And the rocket's glare, the bombs bursting in the air,' refers directly to congreve rockets as used in that fight at Fort McHenry.

On 10th January, 1846, the 99th Regiment was present at the assault on and capture of Ruapekapeka. The British suffered losses of twelve killed and twenty-nine wounded. John Mullen was badly wounded and repatriated to Sydney while 105 more men from the 99th arrived as reinforcements from Sydney and they also took part in ongoing fighting with the Maori. Mullen returned to Sydney and when he had recovered from his severe wounds, and according to his eventual obituary he was wounded several times, he moved to Brisbane and established the first saddlery in that city.

In 1860 the 99th Regiment was in China and in the force of 3,500 French and English soldiers who participated in the 'Sack of Peking' (Beijing) in retaliation for the extreme torture of two British Army officers whose bodies were afterwards unrecognisable, along with the deaths of twenty other ranks. The main city was left alone but to punish the Chinese Emperor, the Old Summer Palace was sacked. The Palace buildings and grounds covered 800 acres and it took all those soldiers three days to burn everything. Amongst the loot the 99th Regiment carried away was the Pekinese dog of the Chinese Empress. The Regiment presented the dog to Queen Victoria before being stationed in Hong Kong and later, after being inspected by the Duke of Edinburgh, this time in South Africa, fought in the Zulu Wars, with battle honours.

Before we leave New Zealand I would like to acknowledge a segment of its culture. The most time-honoured Maori practice was to have one's face tattooed as that is the sacred part of the body. Facial tattoos could represent the history of a man, his ancestors and his status as invariably tattoos were awarded only to men of stature. In the days before metal tools the tattoo practitioners used bones of sea birds, such as the wing bone of the albatross. The shin bone was highly prized for being small and sharp. The bone created the lines and patterns on the body not by piercing the skin but by carving a furrow into which the ink or pigmentation was deposited. The pigment was of charcoal mixed with oil from plants. The Maori later added gunpowder to the mix to create a blue tattoo on the skin.

They preserved the heads of their ancestors, storing them in ornate boxes and hiding them in caves, to be brought forth for sacred ceremonies. Preserved heads underwent the treatment known as mokomokai. First the brain and the eyes were removed after which all orifices, even the nostrils, were sealed with gum and flax fibre. The head was boiled or steamed in an oven and then smoked over an open fire, after which it was dried in the sun for several days before being treated with shark oil. Such was the quality of the tattooing and the mokomokai preservation it is claimed there are heads from 200 to 300 years ago that have the facial features as good today as they were all those centuries ago. Occasionally the heads of opposing tribe members were preserved and paraded around as war trophies. The exchange of mokomokai between tribes was an important component of peace agreements.

The naturalist Joseph Banks was able to obtain the head of a teenage boy by exchanging old white linen drawers, or underwear, for the trophy. When he returned to England and displayed the head wide-spread interest had certain people clamouring for the same. Collectors would place the heads on the mantle-piece, sometimes with a candle on top.

The demand for tattooed heads drove up the price until the peak was negotiated as being one musket per head. A musket was the most powerful tool a warrior could possess and they gained them from Australian traders. The colonials most sought-after trade goods from New Zealand then were flax, potatoes, timber, whale bone and the valuable whale oil. Thus began the blood-thirsty Musket Wars which consisted of 3,000 battles and raids as mentioned earlier. Some people were

5 Gold and Copper

*Top photo is a striking and clear-cut example of a tattooed Maori head.
Lower photo is of Major Horatio Robley, bottom right,
amongst some of his collection of thirty-eight heads.*

tattooed after death while slaves were tattooed and then killed and decapitated, in order to trade for muskets. Warriors raided enemy territory to steal the sacred heads of other tribes, in the race to have the most firepower and to dominate or eliminate other tribes.

The New Zealand government says there are some 600 heads in the hands of private and wealthy collectors, principally in Britain, Europe and America as well as in medical institutions and museums.

I am attaching photos of some such heads in the company of the British Army's Major Horatio Robley. Major Robley was a career soldier who served in India, Burma, New Zealand, Ceylon (Sri Lanka), South Africa, Mauritius and Zululand. Whilst in Burma for five years he learned the language and used the skills he inherited from his artist mother to sketch Buddhist temples. There he had an image of the Buddha tattooed in red on his right arm and he began a lifelong interest in tattooing.

Horatio Robley arrived in Auckland in 1864 for the New Zealand Wars, bought a Maori dictionary and books, and was at Pukehinahina, (Gate Pa). He drew sketches of that military action so vividly and accurately, of the scene of perhaps Britain's biggest defeat in NZ, including the tattoos of the wounded and the dead, that when published in England in the *Illustrated London News*, the public outrage at the deaths on both sides was instrumental in ending the Wars. It brought about the end of the tattooing and the decapitating of heads. Missionaries also saw to that although some converts to the growing Christian faith had their baptismal names tattooed on their arms.

Another reason for the disappearance of the moko or tattoo was that unless he was a highly regarded chief, any well tattooed man became a target to be killed and have his head sold to the traders. When the Maori social structure was so fractured by British conquest that it disappeared the rationale for the moko was dispensed with and could have stayed that way forever.

According to recent accounts from tattoo artists in NZ it was the priceless writings in Major Robley's two books, his detailed sketches and his many notes that brought about a revival, not of decapitation, but of Maori tattooing in New Zealand.

John Mullen, saddler, must have done well because in 1848 he was involved in outfitting the last expedition of the Prussian explorer Ludwig Leichhardt, which included five Europeans, fifteen horses, thirteen mules, forty bullocks, 270 goats, 180 sheep with carts and wagons and two Aboriginal guides; the experienced bushmen, Wommai and Flash Billy. From Moreton Bay they went to *Cogoon Station* on the Darling Downs and after leaving there, disappeared. They were never seen again and to this day, the matter is still of interest to more than a few people.

Mullen might have become infected with gold fever as in 1851 he was on the Turon River, NSW. That year was the start of the Gold Rush in Australia and Mullen must have been keen to get there because the Turon was where the first of the alluvial gold was to be found. From the Turon, 35 miles from Bathurst, Mullen went south to Braidwood, not far from where Canberra would one day arise. Braidwood was named after Dr. Thomas Braidwood Wilson and he owned a lot of land there. After he died it was bought by John Coghill. Braidwood was a small town with desirable surrounding land and after Mr. Coghill bought the good doctor's holding, he then owned all the land to the north, east and south of the town. Bank records of the alluvial gold escorted from Braidwood to Sydney between 1858 to 1874 show 32,757 ounces of gold were transferred. They don't state if any of it was written to the ownership of John Mullen but he was there in the early years. We do know that from there he went to the diggings at Ballarat, Victoria, and there he struck much gold. Initially riches were easily found as alluvial gold on or near the surface. A boy picked up a 435 gram nugget of gold thrown by a digger at a dog which was bothering him, while Jesse Lloyd saw another digger riding along Collins Street, Melbourne, on a horse shod with four gold horseshoes. Later the expensive and laborious quartz reefing and crushing would produce far, far more gold, massive amounts of it, from the depths.

The first Ballarat gold was ironically found at the local spot known as Poverty Point and it was ironic because unlike most gold fields the Ballarat lode was big and while the best may have gone a Ballarat prospector recently dug up a 5.5-kilogram gold nugget 60 centimetres below ground. At current bullion prices that would be worth more than A $410,000. The old-timers said Melbourne was built on Ballarat gold but not all that shone on Ballarat was golden.

From 1851 to 1860, hundreds of thousands of people came to Australia, principally from England and Wales, Scotland and China plus many more from Germany, America and Italy. The majority moved to Victoria and of those many sought the newly announced goldfields. To be a goldminer required a licence and to vote required a six-month residency along with the yearly mining licence that cost £8. That was a heavy fee and needed to be paid regardless. In 1854 there were already 25,000 gold miners at Ballarat. The government and the police treated the miners harshly, imposing severe conditions on them as if their tent city living conditions were not enough to contend with. The time came when the miners stood up for themselves as Governor Hotham authorised licence checks twice a week. The miners asked for the abolition of the licence fee and the right to vote.

The official response was to call for more police and the army; the 12th and 40th Regiments. The gold mining 'diggers' barricaded themselves in the Eureka Stockade which was overrun on 3rd December, 1854 and twenty-two 'diggers' and five soldiers died. It is often said that the goldminers' action was the only form of rebellion within Australia but it was no doubt required and just as many people believe it was the making of democracy in the new country, well before Federation came about. The right to vote was granted to all miners who possessed a miner's right now costing £1 and the despised Gold Commission was replaced.

With so many men from all walks of life competing for the golden prize there was bound to be trouble here and there. A likeable man, a good man, by the name of Gardner, joined up with a newcomer at Ballarat and they found considerable gold. The men were working their last gold-bearing hole and Gardner was standing in it, his head being level with the surface of the ground. His partner then drove a pick into the top of Gardner's head, killing him. Gardner slumped to the bottom and the murderer filled in the hole. When Gardner's body was eventually dug out, the pick was found embedded in his skull. Amongst the gold and valuable items the murderer took was Gardner's gold watch, a gift from his dear father. The inscribed watch was traced to a pawnbroker and so to the villain who was hanged.

In 1854 Chin Thum Lok, born in Canton, China, and later known as John

Alloo, opened the first Chinese restaurant in Australia, at Bakery Hill, Ballarat. He later opened a restaurant on the Eureka Lead, which was Ballarat's main gold seam and catered to the hordes of goldminers. At the time his establishment and its many successors were known as cookhouses or cookshops. Customers brought a saucepan to collect their take-away meals and as time went by they came with their bowls to eat at the cookhouse.

By 1890 one-third of all the cooks in Australia were Chinese. When the White Australia policy was introduced in 1901, partly as an attempt to prevent more Chinese people coming to Australia, their immigration ground to a halt. However such was the popularity of their meals that Chinese chefs were granted an exemption. I am advised that in Melbourne people continued the tradition of arriving with a saucepan up until the 1960s.

Also living in Ballarat was an Irish-born fruit and vegetable seller, one Henry O'Farrell. Henry had his problems, being an alcoholic and having spent time in a lunatic asylum. Whatever went through his mind it caused him to go up to Sydney where Prince Alfred, the Duke of Edinburgh, and second son of Queen Victoria was visiting the suburb of Clontarf. With security not being what it is today, O'Farrell was able to walk up behind the Prince and shoot him in the back. The bullet hit Prince Alfred a fraction to the right of the spine and rather remarkably he recovered, helped by the fortuitous presence of, and assistance from, six nurses recently arrived in Sydney who had been trained by Florence Nightingale.

As soon as Henry O'Farrell fired his gun he was tackled by a local coachbuilder, William Vial, who overpowered the gunman. The crowd all but lynched O'Farrell and it took strong action by the police to save him, temporarily. O'Farrell's barrister was Butler Cole Aspinall, well known at the time for having defended the leaders of the Eureka Stockade rebellion. He defensively referred to O'Farrell's recent release from a lunatic asylum but to no avail and the judge sentenced him to death by hanging. The verdict was quickly applied.

Following Prince Alfred's close call with death or maiming, the NSW Government erected a substantial memorial building to honour the Prince's recovery, with the general public mostly donating the funds. As one might imagine, it is known as Royal Prince Alfred Hospital or more commonly, RPA.

Situated on Missenden Road, in Sydney's suburb of Camperdown, it is today widely acknowledged as a premier tertiary referral hospital with an excellent reputation for healthcare innovation and research. For the record, RPA has a string of medical firsts in Australia including the first liver transplant, nuclear medicine department, major haemophilia centre, gynaecological oncology unit and other achievements. It conducted the first open heart surgery in NSW along with the first coronary angiography in the state. Such progress would have eventually occurred but a would-be murderer hastened this centre of lifesaving.

Arthur Ashwin also recounts that he rode past a country pub that had just been closed. The publican, in company with a horse dealer and a colt breaker had held up a bank manager making his way home to Ballarat. They shot and killed the banker, robbed him of his gold and callously rode on. However their horses' tracks corresponded in measurement in every way and so convincingly that after being tried for the crime, all three men were hanged. When he was eleven years of age Ashwin had watched with thousands of others as the ill-fated Burke and Wills expedition, seeking to cross Australia from south to north, paraded along Collins Street, Melbourne, prior to their departure. Burke's mount was a superb grey horse while Wills led the camels. Ashwin also saw them on their belated return. The bones of Burke and Wills were displayed in a glass coffin. He saw the funeral service and watched as the bones were buried.

John Mullen left the goldfields in 1856 and moved west, to Kapunda in South Australia. It was a big year for the man and he went on to live there for the last 34 years of his life. He established himself once again as a saddler and bought land on which he developed the East Kapunda Copper Mine. A newspaper article said: 'A fine block of ore from the East Kapunda Copper Mine is now on view at the shop of Mr. John Mullen, of Kapunda. The ore, the local paper understands, was broken from a newly-discovered lode, which has the appearance of being very rich, and promises well.'

That year John Mullen married Mary Kelly, also of Ireland. John and Mary were blessed with ten children, all of whom survived birth, but three did not live for three years, and in those days, 30 per cent of babies did not. Their second daughter, Mary Jane, married Mills in Christ Church, Kapunda, on 24th March,

1879. John Mullen also opened a saddlery business in nearby Terowie, became a Kapunda town councillor, a Captain in the local militia, was a prominent shot in the Rifle Club and was a sport enthusiast. He was of Irish Protestant faith and apparently even-minded about religion and all as well as sundry social matters and well-accepted by all manner of people in and around Kapunda. Mills was most likely fortunate to have such a fair-minded father-in-law.

Kapunda did not have the first copper mine in Australia but it can claim to being the first copper mining town. Kapunda developed many copper mines for the thirty years from 1842 when Francis Stacker Dutton and Charles Bagot discovered the first Kapunda copper on land they did not own. Keeping the find a secret they spent the next two years buying up the 80 acres of land at a cost of £1 per acre. At the same time they sent samples for testing to England. The results were astounding as the ore was 22.5 per cent pure copper, arguably the richest strike in the world. The mine was to be called the Great Kapunda Copper Mine. Initially the ore was transported by bullock-drawn wagons to Port Adelaide and then shipped to Swansea in Wales for smelting. Francis Stacker Dutton sold out for £16,000, which by equating that amount to the average weekly male wage in Australia today, 2016, I estimate that to be $48 million. Charles Bagot retained his 55 per cent shareholding.

Sir Sidney Kidman of Kapunda, South Australia. Exceptional stockman and the largest private landowner the world has ever known.

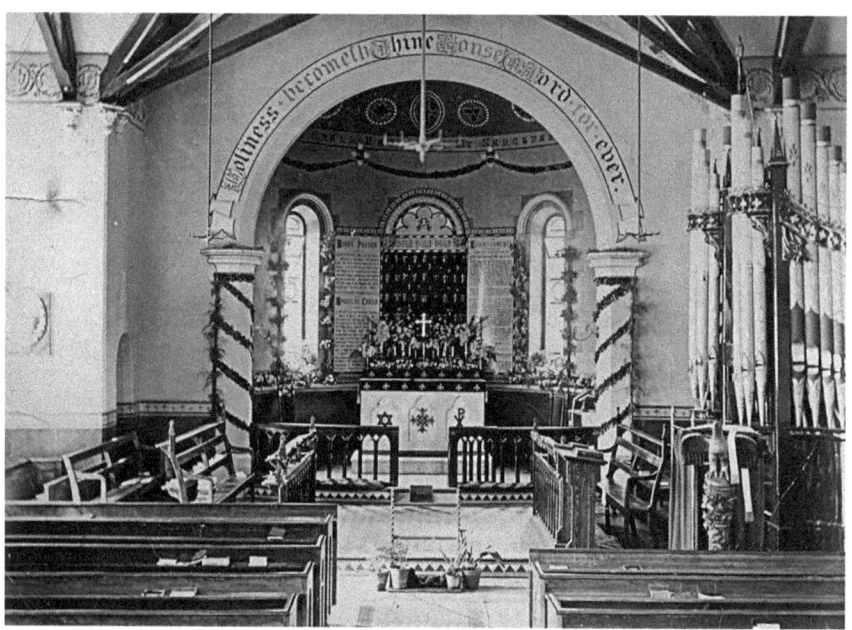

Christ Church, Kapunda, South Australia, where William Whitfield Mills married Mary Jane Mullen on 24 March, 1879.

6

Kapunda

In 2001 my wife, Janice, and I were travelling through South Australia and we stopped off in Kapunda. I idly wondered if some remnant of John Mullen's East Kapunda Copper Mine was in existence but after asking several townspeople all I received were blank looks, until it was suggested I ask Mr. Eli Hambour, a real estate agent. It was late in the day when I walked into his office and asked to see him. He had just left but I was able to make an appointment to see him the following morning at 10 o'clock. His secretary told me he always comes into the office right at that hour. I vaguely thought that's a bit late in the day but then again, that's his business.

At 9.50 the next morning I was quietly sitting in the waiting room and Mr. Hambour entered at precisely 10.00 a.m. and proceeded to his inner office. A few minutes later his secretary ushered me in and after introductions I sat down opposite him at his neat desk. I was struck by how well-dressed he was and his excellent manners, a gentleman to his bootstraps, one of the old school. Gaining those first impressions shielded me momentarily from suddenly realising the venerable gentleman must have quite a few years under his belt. Our talk revealed to me that he was ninety-five years of age and I thought he'd earned the right to come in at 10 o'clock. His mind was as sharp as a scalpel and he moved like a much younger man.

I asked if he recalled where John Mullen's copper mine was located. Straight away he told me, adding that when he was a boy, he and his mates used to hunt rabbits there and collect wild blackberries. I thanked him and shortly after took my leave. In recent years I wished I had talked with him for longer but too often I'm a slow learner. When I was writing this segment he came back into my mind and I phoned another real estate agent in Kapunda. I was lucky as the man had known him well and I asked how Mr. Hambour ended up. He said the elderly gentleman enjoyed running his business and worked every day until he was 101 years of age. He then moved to the coast and the following year he passed away at 102. So much for retirement.

I drove out of Kapunda for about 7 km, turned down a country dirt road and stopped near a small collection of rocks in an otherwise typical well-pastured and clean paddock. There was no one around but a few heavy drops of rain fell on the car windscreen and thunder rumbled overhead as the build-up of clouds darkened the sky. I thought that added character to the setting and that a little bit of rain would be as nothing compared to what those old timers went through. Besides, in a couple of days I had seen enough of Kapunda to realise I genuinely liked the place, it has a good feel to it. In addition, I felt there was something about Mr. Mullen, I would have liked him too.

I jumped the fence and as most of the paddock was open grazing land I moved across to the rocks. For some silly reason I looked around for rabbit holes and overgrown blackberry bushes from which the young Eli and his friends would have flushed out their quarry. I calculated that would have been about 1914 and guns then would have been even more exciting to those youngsters. I pulled my mind into gear and realised there was no sign of a mine entrance or apparent leftover workings from the 1870s when the copper began to fade out. I concentrated on the rocks and lo and behold there were some protruding from the ground that were grey with threads of faded green/pink running through them. Copper, what else could they be? The rain was heavy now but I barely noticed it. I was able to scratch and dig one piece out of the damp soil. It was the size of a football but of an attractive rectangular shape and it had that lovely raw copper shade flowing through it. And it was quite heavy. On the spur of the moment I decided to take it home. I was driving, not flying, so it would be easy.

I have since learned that when World War Two ended in 1945 Eli and a few mates established the Kapunda Harness Club. In his younger days Eli had been a 'powder monkey' so he blew up the stumps of the trees they needed to remove and the men built the racetrack, horse stalls, clubhouse and all the other facilities themselves. They did this on a section of the 50 acres of land that was donated to the Kapunda community by one of its most prominent citizens, Sir

Sidney Kidman, the Cattle Baron, as people liked to call him. Eli was the Club Secretary for thirty years and on the Committee for fifty years.

I never learned how John Mullen's copper mine eventuated but the Great Kapunda Copper Mine did well. After he cashed in his share, Francis Stacker Dutton went into South Australian politics and like several others in this account, he became Premier of South Australia, not once but twice. He was born in Germany, of an English father, educated in Switzerland and Germany and initially worked in Brazil, as a clerk. After his time in office as Premier he became Agent-General, similar to Ambassador, for South Australia and it is fortunate for South Australia that he was in that position for the British cable laying company was about to award the contract for the building of the Overland Telegraph Line to Queensland. Whilst Sir Charles Todd was the man who organised the physical construction of the line in South Australia it would not have been possible if Francis Stacker Dutton had not ensured South Australia gained the contract. The Queensland Government, which intended to have the OTL built in that state, made it very clear to the cable laying company it would rather not have any international communication at all if it meant co-operating in any form with South Australia.

Francis Stacker Dutton won the cable company over by promising to pay a default penalty of £70 per day if the line was not finished by 31st December, 1871, on condition their cable had been laid in place. As we saw earlier the OTL was completed late but the payment was not made because the cable at that time was broken and took a long time to be repaired. Francis Stacker Dutton did his state proud and he was always proud of South Australia.

In addition to copper, Kapunda also had several marble quarries and good agricultural land but what really kept the colony on its feet was the discovery of a massive deposit of copper at Burra Burra, now known as Burra, 80 km due north of Kapunda and like that town, east of the Clare Valley. The mine opened in 1848 and was called the Monster Mine. Unlike the other states or colonies, South Australia did not have any gold of note and copper was its salvation at so many levels. For fifteen years Burra produced 89 per cent of the colony's copper and 5 per cent of copper worldwide. Today South Australia produces more than 50 per cent of Australia's wine while the Olympic Dam mine site holds the world's largest deposit of uranium and the fourth highest of copper. Recently silver and gold have come in to production and if full development of the inherently expensive Olympic Dam project comes to fruition it will likely employ 23,000 people.

Now that he was a married man Mills found employment as a surveyor in the closer settlements of Kapunda and Adelaide. On 24th November, 1881, their first child was born, a daughter named Alice Thornton Mills. Thornton was a name that popped up every generation in the Mullen family and John Mullen's son was John Thornton Mullen. I can only surmise that Alice was named after Alice Todd, as a consequence of Sir Charles Todd's appreciation of Mills naming Alice Springs, as the name Alice does not show up in previous generations of the Mills and Mullen families. For better or worse Alice was destined, as a young woman, to be the central character of a love triangle that was nominated as the second greatest scandal in the history of South Australia. The affair and the case went on for many, many years, headlining newspapers and high society dinners while the associated legal matters reached all the way to the High Court of Australia.

The High Court was established in 1903 and until 1977 appointments were for life. Nowadays there is a mandatory retirement age of seventy. The Justices of the High Court who judged the case involving Alice Mills included the former first Prime Minister of Australia, Sir Edmund Barton, and the man I am assured was the greatest Governor-General the country has had the good fortune to be guided by, Sir Isaac Isaacs. Isaacs was of Jewish ancestry and like many other people who were drawn by the allure of a country that provided freedom and with no baggage from the past, his family left Poland, moved to England until they had saved enough money for the voyage to Australia, and then sailed to Melbourne, where he was born on 6th August, 1855. The family moved to Yackandandah which Janice and I found to be another rural area with a satisfying feel about it. I suppose today it would be regarded as a tree-change district, it is lovely. Isaac being blessed scholastically, the family moved to nearby Beechworth, yes, that is beautiful also, and was soon Dux of the Grammar School. At age fifteen he had passed not only his school exams but also the pupil-teacher exam and he began teaching at the school, at fifteen. Needless to say his life and career continued upwards.

I could but I can't readily relate the details of Alice Mills here because that involves people of great interest, of another family and I don't feel that I have the right to bring innocent parties out into the light of day, without their permission. I need to press on with her father as my example of a 19th century Australian. If that frustrates the reader I apologise for saying something and doing nothing about it, now. After the birth of his daughter, Alice, and with two of his numerous sisters-in-law raising her, Mills returned to the bush as the owner of a freight company, the Camel Carrying Company. The railway had now reached Farina in northern South Australia and Mills carried freight from there to The Peake and then on to Charlotte Waters in the Northern Territory.

Other telegraph lines were being built around the country and Messrs. J. and W. Bateman had purchased thirty camels from Thomas Elder of *Beltana Station* to use in the construction of a telegraph line north of Perth. Mills accepted the contract to deliver the camels and at *Beltana Station* he assembled his needs for the long ride with Charles Short as his offsider and five Afghan camel drivers. He could have taken the camels south to Port Augusta, across the Nullarbor Plain and up the coast to Northampton, the delivery point, 480 km north of Perth. Instead he opted to do it the hard way, my words not his, and go across the western half of Australia, from east to west, through desert country.

Mills had read John Forrest's journal of his trip in 1874 from Geraldton to The Peake, one of the repeater stations on the Overland Telegraph Line and from there down to Adelaide. He was aware that Forrest and his group of six men had been attacked three times by Aborigines on that exploration, once by one hundred armed men and on another occasion by fifty Aborigines.

In Central Australia, Ernest Giles had been attacked by more than 400 Aborigines but Mills was undeterred. He had a way, a persistence, about him. John Forrest, who would later become Premier, but of Western Australia, not South Australia, made the first crossing from west to east and at Weld Springs he was attacked by a large group of Aborigines and found it necessary to shoot some of them rather than be killed himself. Mills was going to attempt much the same trip but be the first from east to west and he and his men would be riding camels. Camels were the only way to go.

In the 15th century the Spanish brought camels to Tenerife, in the Canary Islands and in 1840 the Phillips brothers bought several of those to ship to Australia. Shortly afterwards they were loaded aboard the S.S. *Appoline*. The ship encountered a wild storm and only one camel, a male, survived and landed at Port Adelaide. The beast ended up in the hands of John Horrocks, a rather dashing Englishman of dignified height, good education allied with his swell manners and a desire to achieve.

On an exploration that had reached Lake Dutton, 100 kilometres north of Port Augusta, Horrocks was readying his rifle so as to shoot a rather rare bird in order to have it studied and recorded. His gun apparently held a ball in one barrel and slugs for the other. Whilst he was readying the rifle, as required for the job in hand, the camel turned suddenly towards him and being so close as to bump him, the rifle was fired. Most unfortunately the shot took off the middle finger of his right hand and then ploughed into John Horrocks's mouth where it shattered his top teeth. The pain must have been intense but after someone put a handkerchief over the remnant of that finger the man battled on. Mr. Horrocks, to all effects having been shot by his own camel, named Harry, and still the only one in Australia, soon ordered the offending beast to be shot, dead. Rather remarkably the bullet fired into its head had little effect on the bull camel and a second shooting was required. John Horrocks died some days later but there is a belief that it was the dirty handkerchief that was the cause of death as he developed gangrene in that finger.

Camels are not everyone's cup of tea and to some people are difficult to comprehend, plain stupid, certainly noisy, rather slow, somewhat unfriendly and when you need them to get a move on they can be frustrating, having a mind of their own. On the other hand when you are travelling through an environment of high, sustained heat with little, if any, grass and the water has run out, you cannot do better than to have a camel or two on hand. There are some 350 plants to be found in the Australian outback and I believe the camel can and will eat 325 of them. Having done so he sustains himself, not so much with a bellyful of water but with the fat that he has stored in his hump.

In a dust storm a camel keeps the fine grit out of its eyes by way of a protective eyelid and the durable round pads of its feet take it through sand country where vehicles become bogged. In the conditions found in Central Australia the camel is superior to the horse. Camels need to be loaded in a particular manner, one that accommodates the freight and suits the beast of burden and only knowledge and experience of that will prevail. The camel has to be loaded every morning and unloaded every night so it is not surprising that Mills and other explorers and pastoralists employed the Afghan cameleers, rather than Aborigines for travel. Mills departed Sir Thomas Elder's *Beltana Station* on 6th June, 1882.

On reaching Strangways Springs, which Mills knew from the construction of the Overland Telegraph Line, the party stopped to kill and cure meat for the journey ahead, leaving on 1st July. After two days riding the party arrived at *Anna Creek Station* where they were warmly welcomed by the owners, the Hogarth family, with whom Mills had dined in 1870, while surveying the OTL. He enjoyed the outback hospitality of the famous and largest cattle station in Australia and it was four days later before he moved on, no doubt savouring what might be the last vestiges of civilisation before the many arduous months ahead. On 11th July the party left the known track at the *Oogelima Trigonometrical Station* and headed west. The countryside varied wildly, swinging from saltbush, acacias and mulga trees to splendid pastoral land, undulating with light mulga and cotton bush but no water. After some days the soil deteriorated and light loam became pure sand while the mulga now grew like cacti, becoming so thick it was impenetrable. The salt and cotton bush were long gone.

Mills led the party into the Everard Ranges where he was confident of finding water. While Mills had named the Everard Plains, north of Alice, the explorer Ernest Giles found and named the Everard Ranges and it seems difficult to share Mills's optimism, for in Giles's book, *Australia Twice Traversed*, he wrote: 'Arriving at the first hills of the Everard, I found them all very peculiar, bare, red, granite mounds, being the most extraordinary ranges one could possibly imagine, if indeed anyone could imagine such a scene, everything and every place was parched, bare, and dry. We searched in many places for water without success.'

Mills's party entered a strip of boxwood and saw stony hills in the distance, fresh tracks of Aborigines and the remains of their fires. The Afghans came upon two Aborigines, and seeing them as prisoners of war, they captured them and put halters around their necks, insisting they stay that way until they led the party to water. The Afghans were disgusted when Mills gave the Aborigines some meat and bread and then set them free. In return, the Aborigines stayed with the party and two days later led them to a two-metre deep native well. Unfortunately the well was dry but just a few miles further on the Aborigines showed them a rock hole holding a little water. That night the Aborigines disappeared but the next day when the party had moved on and found a series of small rock holes, seven Aborigines came up and showed Mills a nearby white man's camp, which he believed had been Giles's.

Some of the Aborigines wore a fur string necklace and others a long bone nose ornament decorated with feathers, with other clothing, such as it was, consisting of a tassel-string pubic covering and a human hair waistbelt, usually made by a man's mother-in-law. In these areas food other than meat was scarce and the women would grind grass seeds. Small amounts of water were added to the seeds to eventually form a dark paste. This paste could then be eaten or made into a small cake and cooked in hot ashes. The sand content of those cakes contributed greatly to the worn state of Aborigine adult teeth.

As it was fourteen days since the party had last seen sufficient water, the camels were in dire need of a drink. Mills found water that ran in tiers down the side of a rock wall for several hundred feet, connecting one with the other by hard, smooth granite falls that culminated in rock holes. It seems Giles had not been so fortunate. The party remained at the rock holes for two days to refresh and supply their camels who had not drunk for the past fortnight. Setting off again, Mills made for springs that John Forrest, when he came from the opposite direction, had indicated were permanent. The party reached Ferdinand Creek but every known waterhole was bone dry. Relentlessly Mills pressed on and arrived at the Musgrave Ranges. Two more Aborigines appeared and tried to help Mills find water but without success. Mills decided to keep going west, to Beares Creek and in doing so met yet another group of Aborigines who led him to a small soakage, which he named Conundrum Soakage. The next morning the rain pelted down and it did so all day, easing off only after nightfall. In the last twenty-one days the camels had drunk water only once. Now, not only could they drink to their hearts' content but the party found a valley full of luxuriant salt cotton bush and acacias. The party stayed at Paradise Flat for thirty-five hours and scarcely knew the now energetic condition of their refreshed camels.

Mills now followed the route taken by Forrest and Gosse but in the next 80 km only once saw Gosse's dray tracks. When they arrived at Beares Creek they were within 240 km of the South Australia/Western Australia border, in the land of the Pitjantjatjara tribe, just a little below the South Australia border with what would one day become the Northern Territory. John Forrest would not only be WA premier but also the great great uncle of today's iron ore magnate Andrew Forrest.

They made their way to where William Gosse had camped on his exploration of Central Australia in 1873. Gosse named the Musgrave Ranges after the Governor of South Australia. Sometimes it strikes me that with its relatively small population, a lot of these explorers literally crossed each other's paths and were in various ways connected. Gosse certainly fits the bill on that count. He married Agnes Hay, a daughter of the pastoralist and politician, Alexander Hay. Hay took Gosse's sister as his second wife. In his marriage William Gosse had two sons and a daughter.

The first born was William Hay Gosse and in 1899 he enlisted for service in the Boer War as a Trooper. He joined the 2nd South Australian Mounted Rifles Contingent, which included Harry 'The Breaker' Morant, a name known to all students of Australian military history. William served in South Africa until 1901 and later signed on in the 17th Battalion in World War One. The 17th Battalion fought at Ypres in Belgium and Armentieres and then The Somme in France. This good soldier rose through the ranks to the position of Major and for his sustained gallantry was awarded the Military Cross in 1917. He was killed in action, leading his men against German forces on 5th April, 1918.

William's other son, George Gosse was a Lieutenant Commander in the Australian Navy in World War Two and for his heroism he was awarded the George Cross. At the 738-bed Hollywood Private Hospital in Nedlands, Perth, Western Australia, where a friend of mine was recently a resident, all the wards and units are named after Western Australians who were awarded either the Victoria Cross or the George Cross, such as the George Gosse Ward.

William Gosse, the explorer, moved on from the Musgrave Ranges to be the first white man to see and name Ayers Rock. As far as is known he did not climb the Rock but his second-in-command, Edwin Berry, is believed to have done so. It seems a little odd therefore that he did not mention what we now call The Olgas, the collection of extremely large rocks, as they should have been within his vision.

Mills found Gosse's Depot No. 18 and also some Aborigines who appeared to be friendly. They talked and laughed when Mills met them 200 yards from his camp and gave them bread. He was not so impressed when, in broad daylight, they stole into the camp unobserved and took off with three buckets, a gun and other items. Eight of them bailed up one of his Afghans and with loud yells surrounded the camp before being driven off.

Mills now realised that with the season being so dry his work was going to be cut out to make it across Western Australia to Northampton, as all the semi-permanent waterholes were dry and he would have to rely on rock holes and soakages that might have been replenished by any recent rains. He determined that he would get no more than 200 miles from where he believed there was a reasonable chance of coming across permanent water. To myself that still seems like a tall order, with a lot of risk in that assessment, as 200 miles would most likely take ten good days to travel.

The party continued on and came to the Deering Hills in the very corner of the north-west of South Australia. The men were thankful that the Aborigines in this part of the country had burnt much of the spinifex, for whilst this plant can be handled when quite young and fresh it is a pain in your trousers, or anywhere else it lodges, when old and dried out.

Spinifex grows, in fact it thrives, in the sand country of Central Australia, where the poorest and driest soils are to be found. It is a tough, spiky, plant, one that reminds me of tussocks by its physical shape. When fresh and growing it is green and edible for some animals but soon it becomes dry and coarse with its sharp edges immediately cutting those who venture too close. It then spreads out into a bush, the inner core of which hollows out as it dries. At least it can be handy for starting a fire, if handled carefully. It is what holds our numerous deserts together and ensures they do not become rolling sand dunes as found in the Sahara. The spinifex roots extend down for three metres and cover twenty-two per cent of the Australian continent. If you've encountered it, you've been out there. You don't forget it.

As always the ingenuity of man can create something out of seemingly nothing. The Central Australian Aborigines developed a method of extracting resin from the plant. They bash the base of the spinifex stem with a stick, on a clean surface. This results in a chaff, which is heated by means of a firestick. This process causes the contained resin to melt and they roll it into a ball. It then has the properties of an adhesive and is used to fix stone heads to spear shafts.

Mills was not to know, but later, mineral drilling disclosed that area to contain nickel and copper in one tenement while another held signs of vanadium and rare earth minerals.

From there they went on to the Tomkinson Ranges, so named by William Gosse for another politician, Samuel Tomkinson. Gosse's fellow explorer, Ernest Giles, used the Tomkinson as his base for pushing on to explore the Great Victoria Desert and the Gibson Desert. It was here that Mills found water but his camels drained it in one drink. However he was buoyed by the number of native and animal tracks and reasoned there must be ample water hereabouts. He turned to the south-west and in so doing crossed the border into Western Australia, into the Great Victoria Desert. For a short while the party passed through grass country but then it became sand, growing only thick mulga. That then deteriorated into sandhills and spinifex, lots of spinifex, with a scattering of quandongs and acacias. However it was the journey they needed to make to arrive at Skirmish Hill.

Neither Mills nor other explorers, Forrest and Gosse, who passed that way had much to say about Skirmish Hill at the time. I mention this now because they did not realise the historical significance they were in fact creating by their very presence but would not be evident until the dust of time had settled and permitted interested parties to follow in their footsteps. Their blazed tree would be the physical mecca to be pursued later in this narrative.

7
Smoke Signals

Skirmish Hill sits about 200 metres above the surrounding plains and due to the occasional rains a gully or two have been created over time. They don't descend in a straight line but wind their way downhill, their liquid freight creating a tree line that marks their passage from afar. One such is Moses Creek and in 1873 John Forrest, coming as he was from the west, circled Skirmish Hill to its eastern side and made camp 35 metres above that creek. To mark the spot, he blazed a grand eucalyptus tree. Due to the climate and lack of rainfall there are few such large trees in this part of the world. William Gosse had earlier camped there and he killed two bullocks, jerking the meat for future consumption. The bullock bones and the tracks of his dray remained visible for a number of years. Mills found the campsite and stopped. He blazed the same tree, with an axe, to first remove the bark and to then imprint his initials 'WWM' and the number 46, to indicate the site was his 46th camp on the trip.

For William Gosse Skirmish Hill had been his Depot No. 13 but now the well which had supplied him was dry. Mills decided to head north-west to Fort Mueller. As always, water was the burning issue and along the way, 160 km or so, all they found was a natural tank in a clump of granite rocks. They needed to use a billy can to tediously bring up just over 900 litres and as you can imagine thirty plus camels quickly made that disappear. Mills named the tank Short's Tank after his offsider. There were more bad tidings at Fort Mueller as they found the spring there to be dry. There is no mention of the actual construction of any buildings at Fort Mueller and I sense it was then more of a name than a substance. Ernest Giles had named it after his benefactor, the Victorian Government botanist Ferdinand Mueller. Born in Germany he was proficient in botany, geography and medicine. This highly intelligent man was decorated by Germany, Portugal, Denmark, Spain and France, and New Zealand and every Australian state bar Tasmania named places and flowers after the man. Whilst Mr. Mueller did not hold with Darwinism he was on friendly terms with Charles Darwin. His full title was Baron Sir Ferdinand Jacob Heinrich von Mueller, KCMG.

It has been well recorded that my great-great grandmother, Mary Kennedy, of *Wonnaminta Station* not only knew the indigenous names of plants but that she collected samples for Ferdinand Mueller. The rare *Grevillea Kennedyana* was formally described by Ferdinand Mueller in 1888 and the specific epithet (Kennedyana) honours 'Mrs. Mary Bozzom Kennedy, of Wonnaminta'. The 7,000 or so 1.5 metre tall plants grow on the Tibooburra stations of Olive Downs, Mt Wood, Yandama and Onepah.

In 1873 Ernest Giles had established a base for his second journey of exploration at Fort Mueller, in the company of William Tietkens, Alfred Gibson and Jimmy Andrews. On 20 April, 1874, Giles took Gibson with him to reconnoitre to the west of Fort Mueller, as the overall plan was to reach Perth. After making fair progress they were forced to turn back because of the lack of water. One horse died and the two men alternately walked and then rode the surviving horse back towards their main camp. At length Giles gave the horse to Gibson, telling him to go on ahead, to some kegs of water that had been earlier cached, no doubt for such an emergency. Gibson was to water the horse and then make for Fort McKellar. Ernest Giles stoically followed on foot.

It was 48 km to the kegs of water and Giles could not sleep because of his burning thirst. He continued following the tracks until the moon went down and the next day reached the kegs at noon. He could see that Gibson had watered the horse and gone on, leaving Giles 10 litres of water in one keg. He felt as though he could have drunk the lot but restrained himself. He found 11 thin sticks of smoked horse flesh and ate two of them, raw. He had to walk 100 km to the next water and it was a further 32 km beyond that to Fort McKellar where he could expect to find his colleague, William Tietkens.

The keg weighed 7 kilos and there was nine kilos for the water. With his revolver, ammunition and sundries, including fourteen matches, Giles carried a good 23 kilos, in an already weakened state and under a relentless hot sun.

He put the keg on his back. He later wrote, 'After I had thoroughly digested all points of my situation, I concluded that if I did not help myself, Providence wouldn't help me either.'

After two days Giles had eaten all the thin strips of horse flesh and, carrying the keg, averaged but eight km per day. Having covered 24 km he came upon the tracks of two horses they had earlier turned loose. Giles was naturally following his own earlier made tracks, running from east to west and as he had instructed Gibson to do. The two horses had cut those tracks and gone off on an east-south-east route and Giles could clearly see that Gibson had erroneously followed after them. As he trudged on he kept looking, keenly, for the footprints of Gibson to return, with the horse, to the original tracks. They never did.

On the night of the 29th April, Giles had drunk the last of the water and he still had 30 km to go. It was a moonlight night and somehow the man staggered on, reaching the expected water the next day. He drank his fill and as he set out for the final 32 km to the main camp, having already covered 100 km, he picked up a small dying wallaby, whose mother had thrown it from her pouch. 'It weighed about two ounces and was scarcely furnished with fur. The instant I saw it, like an eagle I pounced upon it and ate it raw, dying as it was, fur, skin and all. The delicious taste of that creature I shall never forget. I only wished I had its mother and father, to serve in the same way.'

Ernest Giles made it to Fort McKellar and after he had eaten and rested for a day, he and Tietkens rode out to search for Gibson. He was never found and in his memory Giles named the desolate area, the Gibson Desert. On Giles's fourth expedition he allowed two little girls to ride his camels, in Western Australia. One of those girls grew up to be the mother of Sir Ross and Sir Keith Smith, pioneer aviators. Ross Smith joined the 3rd Light Horse and landed at Gallipoli on 13th May, 1915, just eighteen days after the first ANZACs went ashore. The Australian Light Horse would go on to be known as the Flower of the Nation, and in similar fashion to the Imperial Camel Corps being founded in World War One by men drawn from the Anzacs and the British, the fledgling Australian Flying Corps, the forerunner of the Royal Australian Air Force, was established with men who had served in the Australian Light Horse. Two years later Ross

Smith was serving in the Australian Flying Corps where he won the Military Cross twice and the Distinguished Flying Cross three times. An air ace, he shot down eleven enemy planes, confirmed. He was also the pilot for T.E. Lawrence (of Arabia). In 1919 he and his brother Keith were the first men to fly from England to Australia. That fabulously unique Australian cricketer, Keith Ross Miller, was born that year, while the two men were actually halfway through their epic flight, and named after the two brothers. Apart from becoming Australian cricket's greatest all-rounder he was a pilot, flying Mosquito fighter-bombers over Germany in World War Two. He was also a phenomenal cricket player, extraordinary man and an individual to his bootstraps.

Mills's party rode on, this time moving north-west and after several days the Afghans found a trough-like cavity in a large flat granite rock. It was almost full to the surface and it held 9,000 litres of water and it was obvious why Forrest had camped there, for three cavern-like holes had been filled by a water course and supplied seemingly endless water. It was fortuitous as they were halfway between *Beltana Station* and their goal, Northampton.

Now they turned south-west, into the Barrow Range and here a change occurred. The party came upon a native well and the Aborigines there were so startled by the white men, Afghans and camels, all of which they had probably never seen before, that they ran away, leaving behind their long yam sticks, calabashes, gourds for carrying water, and a pile of mulga. The Aborigines extracted a form of sugar from the mulga. As they rode, Mills saw many native tracks and signal smokes every day but no living person. The Aborigines were now staying away from the party as it rode due west each day, into the setting sun and the Warburton Ranges, which Mills said was full of that 'diabolical mulga'. The Ranges were named after the explorer Peter Egerton-Warburton on his courageous journey from Adelaide to Alice Springs and across Western Australia via the Great Sandy Desert. He fell short of reaching the coast, being strapped to one of the two remaining camels (fifteen of the original seventeen camels had to be eaten) and he was conveyed to *De Grey Station* in a seriously bad way, suffering scurvy and loss of sight in one eye let alone dehydration and all that went with pitting oneself against such overpowering elements. Fortunately he recovered to live another seventeen years.

De Grey Station had been founded in 1869 and it consisted of three million acres, as it still does today. In addition to 6,000 head of cattle *De Grey* runs various numbers of sheep, camels and brood mares, plus stallions. In 1914 the station's 75,000 sheep provided wool for the British Expeditionary Force (BEF) on the Western Front in World War One. By the end of 1914, although they had stopped the German advance, the regular British Army had been all but eliminated by German forces. Thus the BEF was built up, to a standing army of two million men, but over the course of the war some 5.4 million men served in the BEF. Today Atlas Iron mines iron ore 10 km south of the station homestead.

After the Great Victoria Desert, the Great Sandy Desert is Australia's second largest desert. The next largest in area are the Tanami Desert, the Simpson Desert, the Gibson Desert, the Little Sandy Desert and the Strzelecki Desert. There are more, as based on rainfall, or lack of it, thirty-four per cent of Australia is rated as desert country.

Leaving the Warburton Ranges behind they came down into a valley and a glorious little spring that kindly produced 2,800 litres of life-saving water from what seemed to be a natural artesian spring. Mills named this Jane Spring, just possibly after his wife, Mary Jane. When they found the spring, the Aborigines' camp fires were still burning but again the people themselves were not to be seen. Mills marked 'WWM' 59 on a gum tree. After a day's rest they left Jane Spring on 23rd September, 1882.

Three days later they arrived at Blyth Watershed and followed a sandy creek until they came to an Aboriginal camp and a nice supply of water by digging. Mills decided to head for Alexandra Spring, which, if they reached it, would put them 350 miles from Fort Mueller. Two days later they came to a salt lake which looked so dry that Mills began to cross it. The crust broke and he jumped from his camel and led it to safety. They travelled around the lake and camped on the far side. Starting off the next morning before sunrise they were surprised to see large clouds of smoke, which were rapidly encircling them. They were able to go past the fire into lightly timbered sandhill country which did not burn.

7 Smoke Signals

Mills and Short had no doubt that by setting off before sunrise they had been too early for the Aborigines and had escaped the choice of rushing through the fire or into nearby quicksand, as the Aborigines had seemingly planned.

They moved on to Mt. Allott where John Forrest had found water but this year there was none. Forrest had spoken of springs up the gulley. Two men were placed on guard at the camp and the rest spread out to search for water. Mills soon found the springs but they were all dry save one. He scratched down as far as his arm would go and reached damp sand. He fired a shot from his rifle and all hands arrived and were soon digging with spades. However the digging ceased as low hanging thunderclouds rolled over, thunder roared and lightning flashed. The rain came down in the form of a waterspout, for just one minute, and a dry thunderstorm continued to rage for hours. Somehow they dug down to 4 metres and managed to get 27 litres per camel but it was not enough.

A decision had to be made. If sufficient water could not be found at once they would have to return to Jane Spring. At that moment a thin column of smoke rose up and the party set off in that direction.

Along the way they came upon a high brush fence, made by the Aborigines to trap wallabies and rats by lighting a circle of fire which was made smaller and smaller, thus driving the game into the fence where men armed with clubs, known as waddies, were waiting to kill the animals as they ran into the trap. Seeing the white men the Aborigines retreated but soon an enormous cloud of smoke rose up in the west. Mills guessed this was a decoy and that the water was to the east. Sighting a rocky cliff 2 km away the party made for it, following tracks to four rock holes at the base. The holes contained seven-tenths sand and three-tenths water. By shovelling, the men obtained 800 litres of water. Aborigines approached within 100 metres but would not come closer. The water situation was grim.

On the afternoon of Friday, 29 April, 1770, it had been smoke from Aboriginal fires that first told Captain James Cook that Australia was inhabited. It was smoke that sent the message to tribe after tribe along the east coast telling of the approach of a strange big canoe with white bird wings spread out to the winds. An Australian Aborigine carried three items; his spear, his boomerang and his firestick. Whenever circumstances required, he sent smoke rushing into the upper air as his token of warning or welcome, of invitation or defiance, of sorrow or rejoicing. Smoke called upon friends to join in the hunt for the flying kangaroo (shades of Qantas) or the racing emu, told of recently dried-up waterholes, invited others to lagoons of fish, told of the impending arrival of enemies and extended invitations to corroborees.

There were many Aboriginal languages and dialects for the great number of tribes and they were spread around such a large country. This made communication difficult when one tribe or group went walkabout and they came onto another's lands, for the local tribespeople could see from a great distance when someone was on the move through their territory. The Aborigines had not one but two ways to overcome this. The first one was by using smoke. They would light a fire and holding a green bough over it send up various signals. Using the ensuing smoke, two long puffs asked the approaching party, 'Who are you?' in the universal code of the land. If the reply was three dense clouds of smoke it told the landowners that, 'We are not of your tribe but we come on a friendly visit.' If no answer had been sent, the resident tribe would send up three puffs of smoke side by side, to pass the word along to their friends and neighbours that there are strangers in our territory and that with good intentions or not, they have failed to answer the first challenge. Four puffs would tell the tribe that a definite enemy is approaching. After that a line of smokes over the four puffs would indicate in which direction the intruders are travelling. If that was repeated it meant that the newcomers are in great numbers and the men who sent the first messages were now retreating before them. If the three puffs were repeated it said the strangers had given the friendly sign and would now be met. It was all rather short and basic but that was how they lived and it was sufficient.

Variations of such smoke were practised by way of colour or hue of the smoke, the size of the column raised, the more or less rapid change, when the change was made, even the time of day at which it was raised added more information as did the site of the signal. Long-distance signals required a larger, denser volume of smoke, more careful and elaborate manipulation and generally for a longer amount of time. Sometimes cut-off sections of smoke were employed, there

7 Smoke Signals

were side-puffs, parallels of smoke, adjacent fires and sometimes two in line. Different colours were created by the difference in the fuel used, such as spinifex, gum leaves, dry grass and dry wood. Animal skins were moved over the smoke to create the words.

A distress signal of pale thin smoke told of 'one feller sit down ill, send a man.' Another signal said, 'a blackfellow has discovered the presence of strangers.' Dry grass heaped up on a sandhill with a long train leading some distance for the lighting of the main body of grass meant 'Blackfellow dead'. A signal made of porcupine or dried out spinifex grass and myall bush, piled in small round heaps, translates as: 'Come here, we want to speak to you' while green spinifex was used to denote: 'Coming back' as there is no water to be found. A thin pale coil of spiral smoke derived from a circular grass fire with wood in the centre and with a train leading away spoke of a man's notification of the death of his lubra, his woman. A dark spiral smoke told all in sight, 'we are travelling and hunting.' Another coil said, 'All about, come quick, plenty kangaroo.'

An example of this good communication system was witnessed by Mills's former boss, Mr. Goyder, when he, Mills and others were at Port Darwin surveying in 1868–69. Mr. Goyder was told by one of his officers that war signals were being raised by the natives. He climbed an adjoining hill to watch and observed two spiral coils of light smoke being raised by the natives – Mr. Goyder's word but I shall use the same at times to keep to the mood and language of the day. Skins held by two natives were kept turning with a circular motion so as to cut the column of smoke at each revolution of the skin, and thus give a spiral motion and form to the smoke column as it rose, the fire being of dry wood. In the afternoon of that day there were but three blacks at the camp. At daylight the next morning between 600 and 700 painted and fully armed natives surrounded the camp. The natives had crossed Port Darwin in their canoes by moonlight during the night. The white men survived that time but sometimes, in later years, there were violent deaths and on both sides.

There were times when dark smoke-producing material was added to and laid in the centre of a clear fire of dry fuel. The resulting dark smoke was caught in the lower mouth of a bark tube, the upper mouth being held outside the

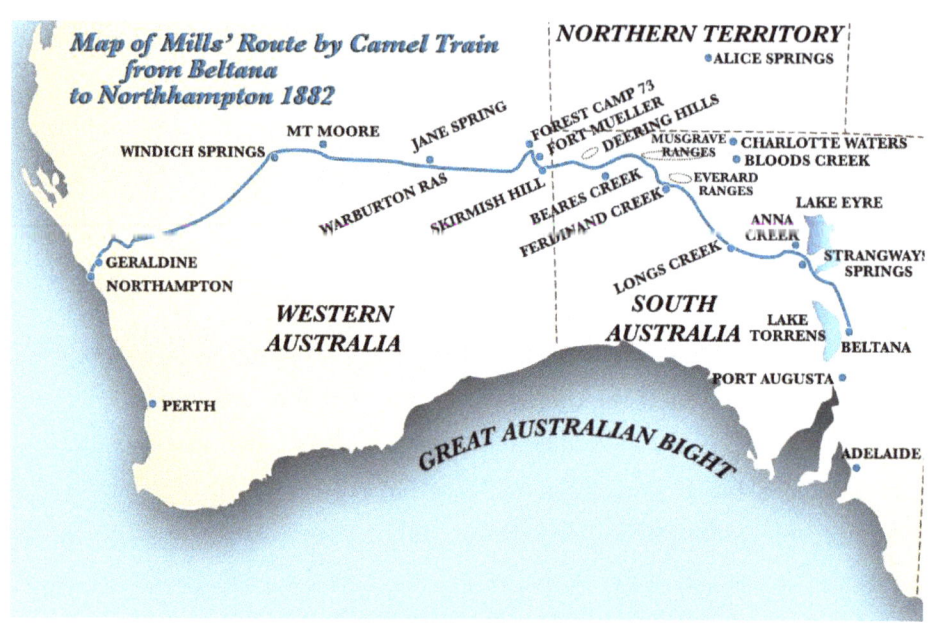

Map of W.W. Mills' journey 6th June – 25th November, 1882, by camel from Beltana Station, SA to Northampton, WA. Graphic created by Deborah Dawson, of Wongarbon, via Dubbo.

rising volume of pale smoke. The dark smoke was then made to rise outside of, but parallel with, the pale smoke so that there were parallel clouds of smoke of different colours, from the one fire.

John McDouall Stuart made his sixth, final and successful attempt, to cross Australia from south to north in 1861–62, the first expedition to do so. On their return journey news of their travel was sent by smoke to *Mount Margaret Station*. This information was relayed over 600 miles and accurately included the numbers of men and horses in the party and was known at *Mount Margaret Station* six weeks prior to their arrival. It proved that Aborigines could count beyond the generally perceived number of four or five. This was achieved by repeatedly opening and closing the fingers upon the palm of the hand. *Mount Margaret Station* is in 'the corner' of south-west Queensland, west of Quilpie. At one time its 1.5 million acres made it Queensland's and Australia's biggest sheep station, with double frontage to the Wilson River, the sort we played a hand of cards for when I was a young feller. The previous year Burke and Wills crossed the Cooper where the Wilson River runs into it.

The Aborigines could send messages much faster than the white man could convey his news by camel or horse and there are instances of Aborigines telling the boss on a cattle station of something that had happened hundreds of kilometres away long before he ever heard about it. One typical instance involved *Crown Point Station* which I have an interest in, not a financial interest but of its history and place in the Australian outback, today as well as back then. It is again a fast-growing cattle enterprise.

James Cowan was the owner of a milling business, a Member of the South Australian Parliament and the owner of *Crown Point Station*. He had been successful although perhaps he was aided by virtue of being an original investor in the Initial Public Offering in BHP, by way of his wife's brother-in-law. As noted elsewhere in this book the shares were offered at £9 each and a few years later were selling for £380. Mr. Cowan and his friend Mark Bullimore were one day in the north Adelaide suburb of Dry Creek and were crossing an often used railway line in their horse and buggy. For an unknown reason the horse stopped on the railway line as a train approached. The sudden onrush may have startled the horse even more for it did not move, either forward or backwards and the train killed all. News of the tragedy reached the Charlotte Waters telegraph station the following day. Natives there, learning the facts, sent smoke signals that evening to Mr. Cowan's *Crown Point Station*, 90 km away. The station blacks received the news but the manager and other whites did not believe it. Meanwhile the smoke signals travelled on, and early the next morning, were received at the Johannesburg Aboriginal Mission Station, 425 km north-west of *Crown Point Station*.

In a most practical manner, the natives often used code words in their smoke transmissions. The message about Mr. Cowan could be explained in seven smoke words, in this format. 1) Almerta boss – meaning headman, master or owner 2) Crown Point – each locality had a unique code signal 3) With comrade – an expression also in constant use 4) In wheelbarrow – every wheeled vehicle was termed a wheelbarrow in Central Australia 5) Nanto – horse 6) All swallowed up – all killed outright 7) Dichika – devil, i.e. railway engine. Reading the concise message the smoke said, 'Almerta boss belonging Crown Point with comrade in buggy with horse all killed railway engine.'

Crown Point Pastoral is not the most expensive rural property in Australia but when assessed on size, it now ranks as the fourth largest landholding in the country with more than five million hectares. It is interesting to realise the change in land ownership since the days of Australian cattle barons Kidman and Tyson. Nowadays the biggest foreign investor is the United Kingdom, which owns 10.2 million hectares of Australian land, closely followed by China with 9.2 million hectares, America with 2.7 million, the Bahamas with 2.2 million and Canada which now has taken up 2 million hectares.

The biggest single investor, with $3 billion in Australian agriculture, is Canada's Public Sector Pension Investment Board (PSP), which manages the superannuation of Canadian government workers including the military and the famous Canadian Mounted Police, the Mounties. In a sense we are working for them. Australia's Macquarie Agriculture controls $2.7 billion spread across 4.7 million hectares and in third place is the New York based Teachers Insurance and Annuity Association of America and College Retirement Equities Fund, which has $1.7 billion invested in our land and our water. When the Canadians bought Australia's fourth oldest and ASX listed company, Webster Limited it acquired not just 340,000 hectares of land but 153,000 megalitres of water. PSP paid $850 million for 12,000 hectares of almond plantations and included in that was 90,000 megalitres of high security water, valued at $490 million, more than 50 per cent of the purchase price. Sydney Harbour holds 500 gigalitres of water. China owns 732 gigalitres or 1.89 per cent of precious Australian water, which many of us would like to have returned to what remains of our waterways. Late news: Crown Point Pastoral has recently purchased Innamincka, Macumba, Ruby Plains and Mount Doreen stations to now have Australia›s largest landholding of 9.2 million hectares, so far.

The other method of communication was by sign language and again it was rather simple. Walking motions with the first two fingers and tilting one's head on the hand three times indicated that the destination is three days, or three sleeps, away. The sign word for kangaroo was the first two fingers held upright and together doing hops along the ground. Emu was all fingers brought together to make what would throw a shadow as a beak on the end of a long neck, the forearm. A turkey was the first two fingers together, held out stiff, with the little finger working together slowly up and down in conjunction with the thumb making the other wing. In many tribes if one man saw another 30 metres away he would not necessarily walk over to him or even call out but he would signal his message, by fingers and hand. To him it was quickly done and understood.

When hunting kangaroos the Aborigines needed to get as close as possible to give their spears a chance. They often stalked them carefully or while carrying a bush in front of themselves. They found that when an alert kangaroo raises its head, it is accustomed to seeing bushes around it but does not seem to consider the position of the bush if it has moved.

On another occasion and in another place, up in the Kimberley, a visitor asked a policeman what a nearby group of Aborigines were doing. He replied that they were his black trackers and with time on their hands they were making boomerangs. Those tribesmen were using pindam wood, a hard redwood, shaped from a natural knee in the timber. The Aborigines toughened it with fire and, he said, they smoothed it with a bit of glass. The officer produced two such boomerangs and gave an exhibition that had the boomerangs spinning and circling over the baobab trees before returning back to his feet.

The next three days took the Mills party though spinifex, wattle, mulga and quandongs, over more red sandhills and sandy flats, to dry creeks and empty rock holes. The five days after those saw them thread their way across salt lakes that briefly led on to grass flats lightly covered with mulga, then scrubby defiles, open spinifex and lightly timbered loam but none of the testing terrain nor the native tracks they came upon and followed, provided them with desperately needed water. A further three days uncovered rock holes and lagoons but they all were dry. The camels were now too thirsty to eat and were tottering along and staggering against the occasional tree. Mills expected them to drop but they held on. The age of Mills' camels is unknown but according to accounts from The Sudan and Egypt in World War One, camels are not fully grown before the age of six or seven years. They come into their prime at nine and can work on until they are twenty-five.

When close to Mt. Moore, they were on the move by 3.00 a.m., when it was cooler, and as the sun rose they saw native smoke no more than 1,100 metres away. Mills rode hard, pushing his poor, lumbering camel for all it was worth but the Aborigines had a head start and were gone by the time he reached their camp. They were soon sending up smoke after smoke to the east but he realised they were no more than decoy fires. So he turned west. This direction led him to Forrest Brook where he took a group of Aborigines by surprise, so much so that as they hurriedly rushed away they left behind their spears, shields and calabashes. They sent a man, painted in white, to ask for them back. Mills returned them.

On 24th October, having been virtually without water for fourteen days, and for the second time for fourteen days, the camels staggered into Windich Springs, where they found two magnificent sheets of water fed by natural artesian springs. From Jane Spring to Windich Springs the party had travelled 880 km and surely performed an epic feat of endurance. It is not surprising they stayed there for three days, the abundant water restoring men and camels alike to life.

Windich Springs is named after Tommy Windich, a native of the Kokar tribe who was born at Kellerberrin, Western Australia (WA) in 1840. His people taught him the traditional ways of bushcraft and the white man led him to understand the way of the horse. By all accounts Tommy was a hunter and tracker par excellence and an accomplished horseman. By his early twenties he was using those skills in the York district to help the police track down escaped convicts, missing horses and wanted Aborigines. One of the former was a man known as Moondyne Joe.

Moondyne Joe had been sentenced in England to ten years penal servitude for theft and was despatched to Western Australia where, after being pardoned, he continued his life of crime. The sentencing Judge, William Erle, seems to have been rather harsh on Joe as on that day similar crimes attracted lesser sentences but then again Joe had spoken up for himself quite firmly in court and that may have been a trait the judge did not want to encourage, at least not in his sessions. Judge Erle had a long and successful career but he did something special outside the court, on Gibbet Hill. A sailor had been murdered by three men who were caught and executed. Their upright bodies were then placed in iron cages that swung from a high post for all to see, rotting away. Sometimes convicted criminals were placed in those iron gibbets whilst still alive and they died horribly of thirst. It was meant to discourage further crime but it also upset many citizens. Owing to the fears of people living nearby, Judge Erle had such a gibbet removed from Gibbet Hill and replaced with a Celtic cross.

Moondyne Joe gained his name from the area in which he lived for a while in Western Australia. He pursued a life of crime and whilst he was gaoled many times, he gained a reputation for the similar number of times he escaped. He was good at that. For a long time a day's work for a convict was breaking five cartloads of stone. In 1865, Tommy Windich tracked him down and caught him and that helped Tommy's reputation. It was even more enhanced the following year when three Aborigines murdered a landholder. Tommy tracked them down and they resisted arrest, one of them spearing him in the arm. That episode saw Tommy employed by the explorer Charles Hunt, who explored east of York and with his Hunt's Track paved the route to what would become the Eastern Goldfields.

In 1869 Tommy joined up with John Forrest on his first exploration, which was to search for signs of the missing Leichhardt Expedition. The following year they surveyed the route along the coast of the Great Australian Bight, along South Australia and Western Australia. The big journey was in 1874 when John Forrest travelled up to the Murchison River and then turned east and became the first explorer to cross from west to east, from the Murchison to the Overland Telegraph Line running from Adelaide to Darwin. On reaching the OTL at The Peake he turned south and continued on to Adelaide.

In 1879 Tommy Windich was employed on the telegraph line being constructed from Adelaide to Perth. He caught cold that became pneumonia and died. John Forrest said:

Poor Tommy Windich died at Esperance Bay three weeks ago. This faithful and intelligent native has passed away, still in the field of exploration, as he has been for so many years. He was still quite a young man and has been intimately connected with every exploration in this colony for the last 10 or 12 years. He accompanied Mr. Hunt, Mr. Alexander Forrest and myself. Twice he crossed with me from Perth to Adelaide and took a very prominent part in those expeditions. He possessed great knowledge of the interior and I feel sure he was the most experienced and best bushman in the colony. He has died far away from his own home and from his friends, for his name is almost a household name in this colony. I will take steps to have the spot where he is buried fenced in and marked. To me, who has had him for my only companion on so many trying occasions, the tidings of Tommy's death is especially sad, and I feel that I have lost an old and well-tried companion and friend.

Those endearing words by the great explorer and first WA Premier are well-deserved and perhaps they inadvertently serve to emphasise the merit of resilient Mr. Mills in successfully and peacefully bringing his party through to its final destination, intact and without native guided assistance.

In 2002, the 'Year of the Outback', a friend and I were in a group of farmers from Gilgandra, Dubbo, Coonamble and Walgett along with a butcher from Sydney who went on a forty-day, 11,175 km, camping trip around the interior of Australia. We drove across much of that country Forrest and Mills rode and from Wiluna we set off to the north on the Canning Stock Route. It is a

1,900 km drive over 900 sand dunes with a prearranged fuel dump along the way. Unlike the explorers and the cattle drovers on the Canning we had ample water and other supplies but I am adamant that Windich Springs was the most attractive watering hole and it had the best water on the 1,900-kilometre track. I can quite understand the relief and satisfaction the Mills party must have felt on arriving there.

They weren't home, so to speak, but they were safe. Fully refreshed and in great spirits the party left Windich Springs on 27th October and struck the Murchison River on 2nd November. The Murchison rises in the Robinson Ranges, about 90 km north of Meekatharra, which is a little to the east of the centre of Western Australia. The river, the second longest in Western Australia, flows for 820 km until it reaches the coast at Kalbarri. On 10th November they were welcomed at *Mt Crawford Station* on the Murchison and Mills expressed his thankfulness at being finally released from the gnawing anxiety of such a dry ride. The camels, once more refreshed, the men rode on and arrived in Northampton on 25th November, 1882. The perils of the desert had been overcome and the end of the twenty-five-week journey saw the thirty Thomas Elder camels now delivered. They had travelled 2,650 km, a good 640 km more than had been anticipated and the last 800 were through extreme heat by day and night.

Mills paid tribute to the detailed and skilful exploration of William Gosse and the daring ride of John Forrest, without which he said he could possibly have been many weary months longer on the journey which was handicapped by the succession of droughts that had existed in the interior during the preceding years. John Forrest congratulated Mills on the successful completion of his stoic journey, one by which he proved his mettle and raised his standing amongst the few who ventured into the harsh interior as he had and the many who heard of it. Mills returned home to Adelaide and Kapunda.

Mills resumed his practice as a surveyor in South Australia and his second daughter Ethel May Mills was born on 1st May, 1885, in Kapunda. His father-in-law John Mullen had lost his beloved wife, Mary, and in 1888, Mills's wife, their second daughter Mary Jane, fell ill with phthisis. Today we call the illness tuberculosis and it is a shocking disease. The lists of births and deaths in

Kapunda in the second half of the 19th century show quite astonishing facts. Today too many young men die in car accidents but 140 years ago so many young men died of all manner of accidents; such as felling trees, mining, farming, drowning – particularly in flooded creeks, well-sinking and the wells falling in on them. There is a long list of varied accidents and horses were associated with many of them but overall and in the outback the biggest cause of premature death was listed as thirst.

Rarely was it the fault of the horse but in the early days it was the only form of transport and a high percentage of deaths was from people falling from their horse or being thrown from a horse-drawn vehicle. Perhaps it is not surprising to discover alcohol was all too often associated with horse travel, there then being no alcohol restrictions. When motor vehicles entered the more modern world drink-driving initially surprised the general population by continuing the carnage. By the same token the number of young women who died of phthisis would cause an outcry were that to happen today. There was no preventative vaccine and neither was there a cure. Tuberculosis is believed to still infect one third of the world population, with most deaths now occurring in developing countries.

In Mary Jane's time the disease was commonly known as consumption, due in part to the sustained loss of weight from chronic coughing that brought up blood tainted sputum along with fever and heavy sweating. It must have been an awful way to die, wasting away every day and still painfully struggling to emit from their lungs the ghastly disease that was destroying them in front of their family and friends. *Phthisis*; the word, derives from the Latin, *phthinein*, to waste away. Such a slow and agonising death is bad enough for one person but I was, and still am, saddened that so many young women succumbed to it.

Mills was left with his two young daughters, aged seven and three. As most families in those days had numerous children, it was the custom in such instances for maiden aunts to raise children. The daughter born after Mary Jane was Annie, just two years younger. She never married and the youngest daughter, Ada, married late in life. So Annie and Ada cared for Alice and Ethel while Mills moved to Broken Hill where he found employment as a surveyor for the next three years.

Camel-drawn wool wagon, Cloncurry, Queensland.

Overland Telegraph Line surveyors, W.W. Mills seated at right.

Aborigines find bicycle, Dalhousie Station, SA, 1896.

Camel train crossing Crown Point Station with Overland Telegraph Line faintly visible on the left-hand side, 1895. Courtesy of Victoria Museum, Melbourne.

Outback mail delivery by camel.

Shearers along with the most important team member, the cook, at Currawillinghi Station, on the border of Queensland and NSW, 1909. 540 km south-west of Brisbane, 40 km Goodooga, 5km Hebel. 90,000 sheep were shorn by hand (blades) on 60 stands in 1900. Note the broad collection of headwear, that 12 of the 16 men have moustaches, 6 are pipe-smokers as seen and the individual rugged and capable countenances of all.

Horse-drawn wool wagons.

Wedding of Dr. Hedley Ham and May Kennedy, author's maternal grandparents.

'Wonnaminta', Packsaddle, tennis court, 1880s.

'Wonnaminta' dining room, 1880s.

Wonnaminta Aborigines corroboree performed for the Kennedy family, 1888. In 1887 the Victorian Governor Sir Henry Locke, asked to see a corroboree but the Aboriginal Protection Board would not allow it. Instead he was given a painting by the Aboriginal artist, William Barak. See Chapter 22 photos.

Madge and eight-year old sister, May Kennedy, on the right, of 'Nundora' station, Packsaddle. May Kennedy would be the author's grandmother.

Mary Bozzom Kennedy, of 'Wonnaminta' station, author's maternal great-great grandmother and wife of Robert Henry Kennedy.

The Kennedy women of 'Wonnaminta' and surrounding family stations. Janie Kennedy, author's great-grandmother standing centre rear.

Dr. Hedley Ham, author's maternal grandfather.

Caroline Catapodi, 1791-1869. Daughter of convict Sarah Best, mother of Robert Henry Kennedy, and author's great-great-great-grandmother.

Caroline Catapodi, wife of John Kennedy. Ten of her children settled in the Western district of NSW.

Farmers travelling to Roseworthy Agricultural College, 1,600 hectares, 50 km north of Adelaide, 1908, for agriculture, horticulture and viticulture advancements.

Robert Henry Kennedy Jnr, of 'Nundora', adjoining 'Wonnaminta'. Author's great-grandfather.

'Wonnaminta' station buildings.

Aborigines at 'Castlesteads', Boorowa, NSW, family home of Francis Rawdon and Emma Hume, parents of Mary Bozzom Hume (Kennedy).

'Late Start', presented to the author's paternal grandfather, J. S. Stanford of 'Dangalong', Cooma, by the Australian Government's World War One official war artist George Washington Lambert.(American father, English mother, Australian citizen) See the artist's war work in Chapter 16.

'Wonnaminta' Picnic Races.

Gold was discovered at Gulgong in Central West NSW in 1870 and although it was all but gone by 1880 an estimated 23,000 people extracted a quoted 32 tons of mostly alluvial gold. The photo presents the Gulgong Argus Newspaper, General Machine and Printing Office constructed in the rustic 1870s style of the day. Gold was found locally at Red Hill (biggest find), Parramatta Reef, Home Rule, Canadian Lead, Salvation Hill, Brown Snake, Tallawang, Helvetia and Perseverance Paddock. Today Gulgong with 2,500 townspeople plus farmers is renowned for its agriculture, potters' clay, kaolin which is known as China clay and highly prized for its use in manufacturing paint, ceramics, high gloss paper and cement and also for having some of the state's oldest coal mines, especially of highly valued thermal coal—and what must be the narrowest main street of any town in Australia.

A de Havilland Dragon aeroplane of the Royal Flying Doctor Service at 'The Veldt' sheep and cattle station, Packsaddle, 1948.

8
Wonnaminta Station

Other people were also moving to Broken Hill, and amongst them were Robert Kennedy and Sidney Kidman. Whilst one of my ancestors, Andrew Hamilton Hume, has been mentioned, there is another branch of the family tree that flourished for some time in the early Australian pastoral scene. James Raworth Kennedy arrived in Sydney on the *Royal Sovereign* in 1795. After completing his education in England, his son, John Kennedy, followed him out, arriving in 1797. John, according to family romance, had seen a neighbour's daughter standing at her gate, at Appin, NSW, and announced that when she grew up, he intended to marry her. The child was Caroline and she had arrived in Sydney on the *Britannia* at the age of one, with her mother, who went by various names. At the time she was Sarah Best. Sarah had been married to John Roberts who was a partner in crime with Peter Catapodi, a forger who specialised in printing counterfeit bank notes. Sarah switched her attention to Catapodi and had his child, Caroline. Then she was arrested for stealing a bedspread from a lodging house and sentenced to seven years transportation to Australia. Under the bed were Peter Catapodi's homemade plates for counterfeiting. He escaped scot-free while his girlfriend, Sarah, was transported and his forger partner was hanged. Sarah's marital record reads: First marriage, John Roberts, forger, hanged; De Facto, Peter Catapodi, forger, escaped conviction; second marriage, Patrick Byrne, soldier, 102nd Regiment (they had five children with the eldest named Matilda) Australia; third marriage, William Sykes, pardoned convict. Sarah must have been pardoned by then as only the pardoned could marry.

So there is a second convict in the family. I gather James was not impressed by his son's mother-in-law's status. John and Caroline's son was Robert Henry Kennedy, his son was called Robert Henry Kennedy Junior or Bob for short and

Bob's daughter was May Kennedy, whose daughter was my mother. Therefore Robert Henry Kennedy was my great-great-grandfather. I should mention the first illustrious family convict. While Andrew Hume was the father of the explorer Hamilton Hume, another of his sons was Rawdon Hume. Rawdon Hume married Emma Mitchell and her mother was Elizabeth Huon, the daughter of Gabriel Marie Louis Huon De Kerrilleau and Louisa Le Sage. Gabriel fled from France after his property was confiscated and his life would have been worthless if he was captured by the forces of Robespierre during the time of 'The Terror'. My Latin teacher has a strong belief the authorities in England transported so many people to Australia to ensure that they were not around to follow in the footsteps of those across the Channel who participated in the French Revolution. They feared that the local revolutionaries might start chopping off privileged English heads.

Gabriel, or Louis as he preferred to be called, was a highly educated, industrious, well-mannered, honourable gentleman and to his Captain, John Macarthur, he stood out when he joined the ranks of the 102nd regiment of the NSW Corps as a private. So impressed was Macarthur that he employed Louis to tutor his children. John Macarthur, while apparently offside with so many people for his actions, was nevertheless responsible for the drastic improvement in quality of the Australian sheep flock and consequently the woolclip. As England was at war with Spain and short of wool, Macarthur's efforts in the wool industry were encouraged by the authorities in England, who ensured he received land grants in Australia. France and Spain at times cut the supply of wool to England.

Wool was important. It had financed Spain's expeditions of Christopher Columbus and the Conquistadores. In America's Massachusetts it was law for young people to learn to spin and weave. The eldest unmarried daughter had to do the spinning and from that is derived the word 'spinster'. Spain imposed the death penalty on anyone exporting sheep, until 1786. England's King George III made wool trading in the colonies an offence, punishable by cutting off a hand.

For some time there was a shortage of money in the colony of NSW and rum was used as a means of paying for goods or even wages. John Macarthur was among a group of officers in the NSW Corps who organised a buyers' cartel and they resold their goods for huge profits. At one time those Rum Corps cartel officers owned 77 per cent of all the sheep in Australia, 40 per cent of the goats, 32 per cent of the cattle and 59 per cent of the horses. John Macarthur died a wealthy man with an estate of some 13,700 hectares and much money, which passed on to his son, but he left nothing to speak of to his wife, Elizabeth. In those days a wife had no rights.

Louisa Le Sage was employed in London as a lady's maid. On 17th September, 1794, she was case Number 534 in the Old Bailey, where she was accused of stealing from her employer, Mrs Maria Brock of St. Georges, Hanover Square, a gunmetal watch, a petticoat, a key valued at one penny and two shawls, to the value of £2/17/7. She was identified by the pawnbroker to whom she had sold some of the goods but claimed the watch was a gift from the master of the house. The value of the theft was reduced to £1/19/0 and thus attracted the lighter sentence, being less than £2, of seven years transportation. The enchantingly named Louisa Le Sage was twenty-two years of age, spoke perfect French, little English and for her crime my great-great-great-great-great grandmother to be, was thrown in to Newgate Prison. Louisa was confined there until a ship, the *Indispensable* sailed in September, 1795. There were 133 female prisoners on board, two of whom died en route and the ship arrived in Sydney on 30th April, 1796.

Louis and Louisa met and married, the wedding being officiated by the Reverend Samuel Marsden, of the Church of England. In addition to doing the work of God the Reverend was busy on his own account. Macarthur's flocks were based on Spanish Merino sheep and Samuel Marsden favoured the strong-wool Suffolk breed and was successful, although Macarthur and his wife Elizabeth granted each of their daughters a dowry that, if the prospective husband agreed, would be paid in sheep. Marsden developed a keen interest in New Zealand, particularly the native people, and visited there seven times. He wrote of the Maori: 'A very superior people in point of mental capacity, requiring but the introduction of Commerce and the Arts, which, having a natural tendency, to inculcate industrious and moral habits, open a way for the introduction of the Gospel.'

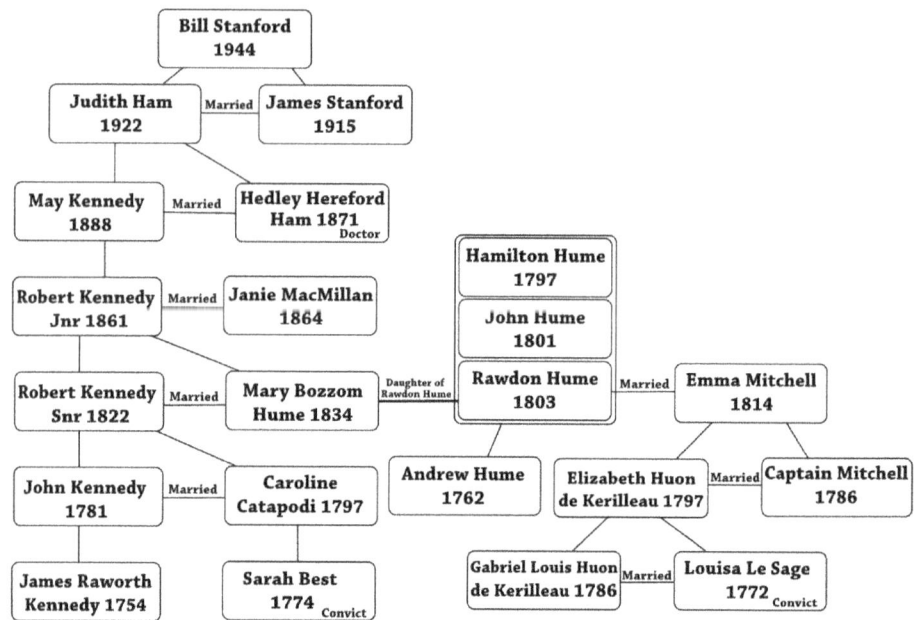

Family Tree.

Graphic created by Deborah Dawson, of Wongarbon, via Dubbo.

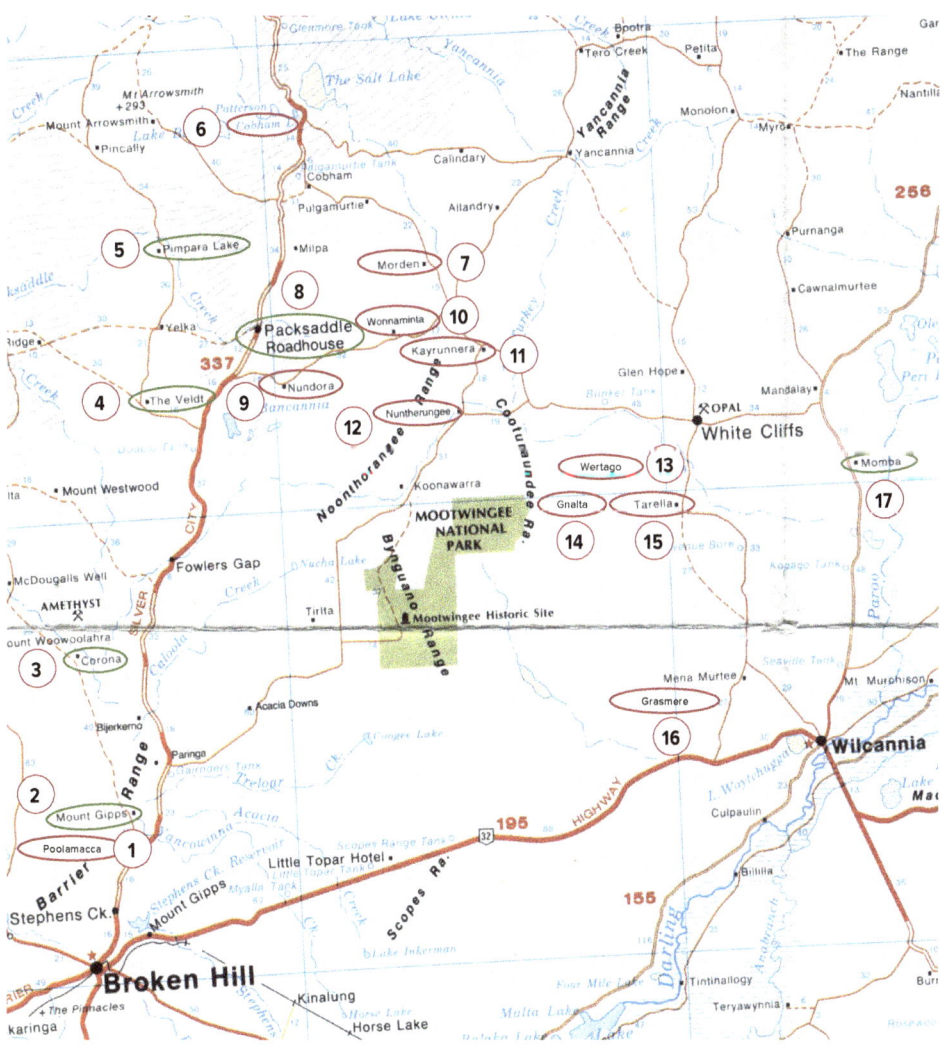

Map of area from Broken Hill north to Packsaddle, on the road to Milparinka and Tibooburra. Locations circled: 1 Poolamacca*, 2 Mt Gipps (BHP), 3 Corona, 4 The Veldt, 5 Pampara Lake, 6 Cobham Lake*, 7 Morden*, 8 Packsaddle, 9 Nundora*, 10 Wonnaminta*, 11 Kayrunnera*, 12 Nuntherungie*, 13 Wertago*, 14 Gnalta*, 15 Tarella*, 16 Grasmere*, 17 Momba. Asterisk-marked Kennedy family stations and others of note, Packsaddle area, Far West, NSW.

He was to be disappointed to later discover his missionaries at the Bay of Islands had bartered muskets and powder for hogs and potatoes. He thought a settlement there would be undesirable, 'as the Soldiers would be too much exposed to temptation from the Native Women.'

As that branch of the family tree is now crystal-clear I must now take you back to Robert Henry Kennedy, great-great grandfather and consequently my great-great grandmother, Mary Bozzom Hume. Another branch and a marriage that brought the Humes and the Kennedys together. History says that Mary had decided early in the piece that she would marry Robert. Equally it states that Andrew Paterson, who would be the father of Banjo, and Robert Kennedy had a horserace on the banks of the Yanco Creek to decide who would be the first to propose to Mary. Decades later one of Mary's granddaughters had the temerity to ask if that were true? Mary smiled over her half-spectacles and said, 'So I do believe, but what foolish, foolish gentlemen they were. I had made up my mind when I was nine years old, that I would marry Robert.' That union took place in 1858.

They first lived at *Wunnamurra*, on country Robert had taken up on the Billabong Creek, down Jerilderie way. They had a daughter, Emma, in 1859 and the second of their eleven children, Robert Henry, Junior, my great grandfather came along in 1861. Frank was born in 1862 and here follows an extract from Mary's diary.

Sept 27th 1862. A very fine flourishing Spring. A fine show for fruit, fine flowers, good peas and cabbage and everything thriving. Poor Doctor very low and ill. Children well. Hot weather promising. Some duck and hen eggs. Did not feel very flourishing myself. Annie's new room nearly finished. Wrote to Annie Hassall, Mother, E. Morgan and Annie James.

September 28th. Baby born half past six a.m.

September 29th Monday. Had visits from the Jerilderie family. Willie and Annie came. A later diary entry by Mary revealed that, *Robert back from Melbourne. Looks as though we will have to move. The banks are pushing us further out.*

In 1865 the family moved west to *Roto Station* at Hillston, NSW. I don't know the size of the holding in those years, but I phoned a stock and station agent who told me nowadays the station encompasses 56,000 hectares. Robert junior, my great-grandfather, remembered the arrival of the Duke of Edinburgh at the property. Like some other characters the Duke turns up every now and again in this little story. The seasons started well but when drought crept relentlessly onto the land, they left. In 1869 Robert leased *Collingwood*, at Gunning, NSW, once the home of Mary's parents, John and Elizabeth Hume, before John was murdered.

Some thirty years earlier the Humes had realised their close to the coast country, around Camden and Appin, incurred smut in the wheat and footrot in the sheep so they moved south, to the Yass Plains, to healthier, more open grazing and farming country around the likes of Goulburn and Gunning. Hamilton Hume had explored that area in 1824, with William Hovell, and believed it would be ideal for the production of Merino sheep, oats and wheat. Hamilton's bush knowledge had seen men ask him to find them suitable land for grazing, for farming, for timber, the climate and private reasons. He often obliged because he could but there were times when he needed to be paid for jobs that required many weeks of searching, investigation and consequent expenses. It was said that no explorer needs a compass if he can have Hamilton Hume in his party.

Speaking of compasses leads to a brief story. Hume was twenty-one years of age and on a government mission to determine the position of the gorges along the Shoalhaven River. A government officer had given Hamilton a compass for that purpose and the officer was later mortified when he realised Hamilton had given it to a wild blackfeller, as then called, but whose language he spoke. The senior fellow exploded about the matter but Hume calmly pointed out to the much older man that he had given the compass to the Aborigine who in return told him precisely where the gorges of the Shoalhaven River bend in through the mountains. 'The compass couldn't tell me that Sir, but that old native did'.

In 1873, while still at *Collingwood*, Gunning, Robert Kennedy had taken up 145,000 hectares of country west of the Darling River. He was forever moving west and you can't go much further west than there and still be in NSW. I imagine he had a feel for the big country. By 1878, Robert was itching to live out there but Mary cautioned him to wait until the youngest child was 'a safe age to be taken into the wilds'. So when Millie was eighteen months of age the family packed up.

It was then 1880 and writing in 1941 Bob recalled they travelled with a van drawn by six horses, two traps with four horses each and another three traps for lighter luggage. The men of course rode their horses. Mary wrote that she packed six rough foot-trunks with clothing to be refilled with soiled garments as they were used. They first stayed at *Cooma Cottage* with Mary's uncle, Hamilton Hume, and his wife, then for ten days at *Castlesteads*, Boorowa with Mary's parents, Rawdon and Emma Hume. After that, the fifteen people, including eleven children, pitched their camp each night along the track, the 1,137 km journey taking six weeks, setting up a new camp every night along the way, until they arrived at their destination, *Wonnaminta Station*, which in today's language is 220 km north-east of Broken Hill. Robert's two younger brothers, William and Edward, who had married the two Gayer sisters, took up neighbouring country on *Nuntherungie*, of 159,000 hectares. Soon Kennedy brothers and sons operated a quilt-like mass of surrounding properties. They would help each other and work together. They would prosper as one or all go under.

There is history to *Wonnaminta* before the arrival of the Kennedys. In 1859 William Wright had been searching for gold in the Barrier Ranges. In 1868, he held *Wonnaminta Station* and Alfred Howitt had *Wonnaminta South* but without any infrastructure on the holdings. Both men had been closely associated with the ill-fated Burke and Wills expedition of 1860–61, organised by the Royal Society of Victoria to cross Australia from Melbourne in the south, to the Gulf of Carpentaria in the north. Of the nineteen men led by Robert O'Hara Burke and William John Wills, seven died including the two leaders. Of the six officers in the party William Wright was third in charge after Burke and Wills. Knowing the area he guided the expedition from Menindee to Torowoto, which is a little south of the NSW/Queensland border but pedantically I have to say maps show he went on into Qld. He then established and was in charge of the Menindee Depot. Burke and Wills and two other men continued on to the northern coast, where they were stopped marginally short of their goal by mangrove swamps. On their return trip, Burke and Wills were reported missing, as is well known. The Royal Society of Victoria sent an expedition to find the men and appointed Alfred Howitt, one-time police magistrate, acting Secretary of Mines and Water supply, experienced bushman, drover and ardent naturalist, to be in charge. Mr. Howitt found the sole survivor, John King, who was living with Aborigines and who led Howitt to the bodies of Burke and Wills, which were buried. After arriving in Melbourne he was asked to go back and return with the remains of the two leaders, which he did. It seems extraordinary that the two men connected so closely to Burke and Wills owned *Wonnaminta*.

Whilst on the original trip north the Burke and Wills party camped, on Friday 8th February, 1861, at *Nuntherungie Station*, north-west of Wilcannia and soon to be owned by William and Edward 'Ned' Kennedy. Two days later, as they continued north, they camped at *Wonnaminta Creek*, obviously on *Wonnaminta Station*. From there they could see in the distance, the Koonenberry Mountain range. It is on *Wonnaminta* and William Wills referred to it as the *Wonnaminta* Mountain.

The Kennedy pioneers found mostly flat country, few watercourses and little or no permanent water supply, sparse timber but ample saltbush and bluebush but it is said that Robert had been developing the land for some years in preparation for this challenging move. The loneliness must have been testing for the women, the work was hard and the summers would assess anyone's mental and physical persistence. It was a way of life that spurred men and women to develop a fellowship that converted their initial simple shelters into work-inspired comfortable homes. They had no doctor, clergyman, chemist, general shopkeeper, dentist, post office or policeman. In fact, except for their immediate family of parents, sons, daughters and various in-laws who lived on nearby stations but mostly 50 or more kilometres apart, no immediate neighbours. The men constructed buildings from local materials of rammed earth, stone and timber as they commenced their sheep, cattle and horse breeding and selling ventures. Their women just as determinedly played their part. They kept house, bore children, taught them and made their clothes. Mary Kennedy not only educated her children but also Aboriginal children. Every morning she held a clinic and dispensed medicines and treatments such as Epsom salts, castor oil, Bates Salve and other medications. She nursed not just her family but everyone from her husband's manager to the newest jackaroo, the Aborigines and the station hands. They all swore by her and her word was law. Many a *Wonnaminta* shearer acknowledged he owed her his life.

Mary Kennedy continued writing her diary and extracts include:

Got Tom to hang the spiced meat to smoke (having killed a steer), also veal hams and made two mutton hams. I prepared an ibis for roasting and we had pigeon pie for dinner.

In late August she pickled cauliflowers, marked six new pairs of blankets, made new blinds for the bachelors' quarters under more difficulties with the sewing machine. She planted vegetables and flower cuttings. Cut out six chemises and seven cloth pinnies for Emma, finished the last of twenty-six sheets and made four meat bags and two sheets for Mary Carne. Wrote an order for flour, mustard, vinegar, candles and boots for the children. Heard with regret of the death of the second son of Archer Broughton to die of scarlet fever. She also catered to non-residents. Many an ill 'sundowner' was cared for and when cured sent on his way with a full tucker-bag. Late in November the dentist came to *Wonnaminta* and Mary had, *two teeth out and three stuffed, a very sore mouth in consequence, came to the conclusion that life on the blocks was hard.*

When the family became established they built the *Wonnaminta* homestead, in three sections, being the dining room block, the guestroom block and the large family living quarters. Mary Kennedy observed in her writings that they were 160 km from Wilcannia and the nearest non-family neighbour was 100 km away. As was her custom she had her usual signature coolroom built, partially underground and chilled by the breeze extracting warm air from a small louvered tower in the roof. Bob Kennedy, my great grandfather took up *Nundora Station*, where my grandmother was born, adjoining *Wonnaminta* on its south-western boundary. If you take the road north from Broken Hill to Milparinka and on to Tibooburra you will strike the small settlement of Packsaddle, about halfway along. To the east of that *is Nundora* and then *Wonnaminta*. To the west is *The Veldt* and above that is *Pampara Lake*. The latter two were not of the Kennedys' but all were and still are prominent sheep and cattle stations and the marked map shows the ones owned by the

Kennedy clan. I would like to tell you of *The Veldt* and although it means switching tracks again I shall do so now while we are in the area, before returning to the Kennedys.

I earlier mentioned the Australian $20 banknote. On one side is Mary Reibey, who came to Australia as a convict in 1792. After her trader/businessman husband died at a young age, she took over his operations and greatly expanded them, even though she was dealing with and against hardnosed business types from China, America and India. She became a trader, merchant and shipowner before expanding into buying prominent Sydney real estate. The Bank of NSW was founded in her house in Macquarie Place and she was renowned as a most successful businesswoman. She has been featured on the obverse side of the $20 banknote since 1994.

On the other side of that note is John Flynn, founder of the Royal Flying Doctor Service. His side of the banknote has recently been updated and whilst his face is unchanged the background is different. If you look at it you will see an aeroplane used by the RFDS, flying from right to left and in the original photograph, taken in 1948, the plane is flying no more than a few metres above three men, one of whom is holding a horse, and the wife and young daughter of the station owner. In the near background is *The Veldt* homestead. It is a well-positioned and timed black and white photograph, taken on a clear day with the vast open spaces of the Far West in the receding distance.

There is one significant difference between then and now. On the new banknote the plane has been deliberately reversed as in the original photo it is flying from left to right. Why would such a change of an historical fact be deliberately altered, and by such an august body as the Reserve Bank of Australia (RBA)? The position and direction of the plane was reversed in order to conceal hidden, microscopic security features within the banknote, so that villains cannot contaminate the system. It is interesting to know that after a recent publicity photo was taken, those present, went into nearby Packsaddle for lunch, where one of the attending officers from the RBA said that in his many years at the RBA, this day was his best ever, he was out there, in the real world.

The children grew up and began to marry; Bob, who drove a team of eight grey horses, bringing his wife on to *Nundora*, which was and still is next door to *Wonnaminta*, and Frank, his wife to the latter where he built a substantial homestead close by Robert and Mary. By all accounts, Frank Kennedy was an exceptional man in many regards. It was said of him that Frank, in the language of the day: *was a dominating figure, a good sheepman, as was natural being the son of his father, and the beau ideal of an all-round station man, as we viewed them in those days, a fearless rider and driver and a good athlete. As a four, six, even eight horse driver of the station coach his fame had reached throughout NSW and further. The writer has seen him handle an eight-horse team of spirited horses and knew of him turning them, with a full-size coach with undercarriage, in the main street of Wilcannia. An ordinary six-in-hand was child's play to him. He could also use a stockwhip as few men of the present day. To those who knew him he was a white man through and through and many an overseer and jackaroo in the back country had reason to bless his help and assistance.*

Some of the squatters of that era were inclined to be foppish, acting above their self-perceived standing in the world in relation to others by making a distinction between themselves and the working man. The Kennedys were not built that way. When Frank, for instance, was driving his eight well-matched greys in to Broken Hill, 215 km down the track, with all the splendour of the carriage, no swagman on the road was ever passed by without being invited to jump up and ride with him.

Edith married and matched her mother in having eleven children. Robert Kennedy bought more land, another 204,000 hectares along with 30,000 sheep for the price of £30,000. That brought their sheep numbers up to 105,000 head. That season was moderate but the following was a cracker and the men marked 50,000 lambs.

Wonnaminta in the 1880s was likened to a busy township, all built from scratch by those pioneering Kennedys. A photo from that time shows a line of buildings as would constitute a small town, being a coach-house, the blacksmith's shop, men's kitchen and hut, staff barracks, the main house and Frank and Amy Kennedy's homestead, with a lagoon of fresh water extending the length of them all. There was an annual one week gathering each year when all the squatting families for hundreds of miles around came to the *Wonnaminta* picnic races. More than 100 visitors would regularly come to celebrate a change from their everyday outback hardships. Each station brought their own tents and equipment. The tents were erected along the banks of the nearby creek and used by the men. All the ladies were accommodated in the station's two homesteads and other quarters and all hands somehow had their meals in the main homestead. Mary oversaw the many demands made by that generosity while Robert Kennedy's tact smoothed over any difficulties that arose. The picnic races, cricket matches, tennis with the court using fencing wire as the net, night concerts and dancing filled the week. The wholehearted enjoyment of those functions would astonish present generations.

A young Aborigine was one day chasing after horses when his mount stumbled down a rabbit hole. The boy's foot was caught in the stirrup iron and he was dragged some distance with his head bumping along on the ground. That didn't seem to bother him too much but Mrs. Kennedy, as usual, tended to him and consequently the young feller rode in the station races the next day. He went on to become a police tracker in Broken Hill.

The Kennedy men owned many properties while their sisters and daughters married into the Desailly, Brougham and Broughton families who also held country near Packsaddle and west of the Darling. The Broughams for instance owned Poolamacca Station, fifty km north of Broken Hill and bordering on Mt. Gipps Station, where the BHP lode was discovered. In the 1870s Sidney Kidman worked on Poolamacca as a stockman and boundary rider. Poolamacca owner John Brougham later erected a large building on the property as a sanctuary for the last remaining Aboriginal inhabitants, some fifty people, of the Barrier Ranges and adjacent areas.

Isolated white outback workers sometimes required assistance, such as the tank sinker who went on the drink and suffered the DTs, delirium tremens. He was seen chasing fairies through the nearby hills and ever since they have been named the Fairy Hills. There's a story behind every name. Such men were said to be difficult to catch and those that weren't mustered tended to die of exposure.

When country was first taken up there were boundaries to be determined by measurement. This was done by tying a rag around the spoke of the buggy or cart wheel and knowing the length and circumference. The number of revolutions of the wheel was given by counting the times the rag went around. This gave the distance required. The compass was used to go north, east, south or west.

One old Aborigine, who claimed to be from one of the wild tribes, told Keith Brougham (pronounced broom) the walkabout was a good sign to watch for at that time. A mob were looking for a new hunting ground and had camped at midday. While there, a pregnant woman had a baby. Next day they were off again, mother and child, and went straight to a waterhole, which the white people found by following their tracks.

In his reminiscences Keith wrote that on those stations west of the Darling, boys were brought up in the first place to ride bareback, then on a sheepskin saddle with a surcingle, which fastens around a horse's girth and after that, the saddle without stirrups. No doubt they could ride through all challenges.

Keith's father, Jack Brougham, was especially well thought of by the blackfellows, as called then. An old man with his own pronunciation of the English language and a sense of familiarity took to calling him Jacky Brougham. One day Jack told him to put a handle to his name and the old fellow replied, 'All right, Mr. Brougham Handle.'

Early one morning Keith and six men were walking down to the cattle yards when they saw a fox on flat country being chased by an eagle hawk. Every time the hawk came in low the fox threw himself on his back and with his four legs in the air disrupted the bird's flight and fought off the attack. The hawk lost its momentum and had to gain height and strike again. This went on until eventually the fox reached the safety of thick scrub which protected it from further attacks. Keith said it was curious to see how cunning the fox was.

Eagle hawks were so plentiful that the Pastoralists Protection Board wanted them destroyed and paid a bounty of two shillings and sixpence per head, literally. Like jackaroos in my day the station hands and others rarely rode out to work with money in their pockets. The men back then poisoned and used other means to reduce the eagle hawk population to a small one. They collected the heads and used their value to gamble, trade for goods or to pay off debts.

Across the border in South Australia the dingoes were numerous and killing so many sheep a bounty of five shillings was put on their head. In NSW there weren't near so many and consequently the bounty was four times as high, at £1 per dingo. A hunter working in South Australia realised the obvious difference and contacted a fellow scalper in NSW. They agreed to send all the S.A. scalps across to NSW and claim the bounty there. This worked a treat and the men were paid so much that the local authority completely ran out of money, twice, before they eventually realised what was going on.

The Broughams reciprocated the Kennedy hospitality and Robert Kennedy often stayed at Poolamacca. Another visitor, who stayed for several months, was Doug Mawson, who would later be famous as Sir Douglas Mawson of Antarctic fame. Before that he was known as a geologist and for his publication, 'Geological investigations in the Broken Hill area.' Mawson went to Antarctica with my boyhood hero, Ernest Shackleton, and another geologist, the dominant geological scientist Sir Tannant Edgeworth David. When I sailed aboard the barquentine, *Europa*, we came to South Georgia Island. I went ashore with four other crew members to Sir Ernest Shackleton's grave and we toasted the renowned inspirational leader of men, always referred to as 'The Boss', with a bottle of West Indies black rum, which one of my mates had brought along for just that occasion.

Douglas Mawson and Edgeworth David went on Shackleton's Antarctic expedition. On 16th January, 1909 Mawson, David, who was the leader at the time and Alistair Mackay, were the first men to reach the vicinity of the magnetic South Pole, man-hauling their sledges for 2,028 km. Shackleton's confidence in Mawson may be gauged from his instructions: should his own expedition to the South Pole not return in time, Mawson was to lead a search party. Edgeworth David said in public tribute; *Mawson was the real leader who was the soul of our expedition to the magnetic Pole. We really have in him an Australian Nansen, of infinite resource, splendid physique, astonishing indifference to frost.*

When I go on my early morning walks along the banks of the Macquarie

Inside country, bullock-drawn wool wagons on the road to Bathurst.

Outback country, camel train leaving Broken Hill on 400 km journey to Onepah Station, north of Tibooburra.

River in Dubbo I am sometimes accompanied by Sir Tannant Edgeworth David's great-granddaughter. To the Kennedys.

They started with wonderful years and were able to purchase a fabulous house in the renowned Adelaide Hills at Crafters. It was their home away from home in the summer when the temperature was often 46 degrees Celsius; it was *Wonnaminta House* and it had been magnificently built by master craftsmen for a member of the Hardy wine family with no apparent expense spared. It was so well built one could consider it to have been constructed recently. The house was built in 1867 from rock carved out of the side of Mount Lofty, and from where it was taken underground rooms and passages were created. From this house, the Adelaide Observatory received its rainfall records for the district. The Kennedys added on large rooms at the front of the house and two rows of servants' quarters behind it.

Just driving up a hill road, today, and as that road forks to left and right, having its immaculate gardens now immediately in front of you, draws your entranced eyes up to that glorious house on high. The Lady of quality homes. I was stunned by her magnificence. Behind the house are the excellent stables, for horses and coaches. The Kennedys didn't always ride the whole distance to Adelaide, as after taking the dusty track to Wilcannia, 160 km away, they boarded the boat downriver, depending on the season. When they went by road, there were always an extra thirty or so loose horses for the saddle and the coaches. The current owners graciously showed Janice and I through *Wonnaminta House*, a rare residence, exciting envy. They thrilled me by producing a photo of May Kennedy, my grandmother, as a young girl.

In 1889, the stock and station agency AML & F, Australian Mercantile Land & Finance, offered Robert Kennedy yet another property and 50,000 sheep for the price of its debts, those being £50,000. Hindsight is invariably an easy observation and Robert may well have hesitated but he played his cards and drew one more from the pack. Combined with the approach of both another drought and a rabbit plague it was the selection that brought them all undone. In 1892–1893 wool prices slumped at the same time that the Kennedys saw *Wonnaminta, Nundora, Poolamacca, Nuntherungie, Morden, Cobham Lake* and the surrounding properties eaten by rabbits and decimated by drought. They must have looked on in helpless horror as they were unable to prevent 80,000 of their lifeblood, their income-producing sheep, die. A separate report of the times states the Kennedys lost 92,000 sheep.

The remaining sheep were in too poor a condition to sell or be worth anything to anyone. All the family properties were in the same state. Compounding their woes was an interest rate of nine per cent on all the monies owed and that was while 25,000 sheep in the most recently acquired flock had also died. The losses could not be borne and AML & F moved in to reclaim the debt. The AML & F company was registered in 1863 and through the acquisition of foreclosed land in the 1890s, such as the Kennedy holdings, and failed land speculation and mortgages, overstocked properties and drought, found itself with a lot of unprofitable assets. The company managed to hold on and later unload them at good prices in better times but for a while it owned thirty-five stations in NSW with twenty-four of them in the Western Division, that being the large tracts of pastoral land west of the Darling River, i.e. *Wonnaminta*. AML & F would eventually be taken over by Elders in 1971.

In the Western Division, sheep numbers peaked from 1887 to 1891 at over 15 million. A seven-year drought followed and starving sheep and rabbits chewed the grass to bare soil and dust. Stock could not be moved from watering points and more than 10 million sheep died, due to starvation and thirst. On 8th January, 1900, the *Sydney Morning Herald* reported: *as if Nature herself fought against those who had wrestled the West from her ancient solitary reign, a series of perhaps the worst seasons ever experienced fell upon the pastoralists of the Western Division. So terrible has been the visitation of the last five years that millions of sheep have perished, without the possibility of soon breeding up again to past numbers and thousands of pounds worth of improvements in the shape of tanks, fences, homesteads and stock and plant for working the stations have absolutely vanished.*

On 13th December, 1894, the family departed from *Wonnaminta*. Most of the women and children moved on but whilst it was still in his son Bob's hands, Robert Kennedy first went next door to *Nundora*, just 40 km away. Only weeks later, in January, 1895, he passed away at Bob's home in Melbourne, naturally called *Nundora*, in the suburb of Minnamurra. It is not hard to believe he died of a broken heart. Mary's motto since she was seventeen had always been 'Whatever thy hand find then to do, do it with all your might' and she continued to do so. She settled in Melbourne, living on her small investment income, holding the family together and growing cabbages, tending folk with the 'epidemic', just as she had been the doctor at *Wonnaminta*, sending words of encouragement and newspaper articles of interest around the family, paying accounts and collecting botanical specimens.

On 23rd January, 1895 the *Western Grazier* newspaper wrote and I quote in part:

The late Mr. R.H. Kennedy, an appreciation; for indeed, his was a character that requires not many words from us, his epitaph requires neither fulsome flattery, nor gilded statement. When the plain unvarnished tale is told, when the pure fountain of truth is seen, his many acts of good entirely shall shine the brighter from their concealment in this life and shall increase a thousand-fold by the heart motive that prompted the hand to so freely give. In R.H. Kennedy then, the Church of England has lost a true and generous friend, Australia itself a bold and early pioneer, and the world at large a man whose attributes in collection cannot be expressed better than by affirming his to be that most noble of God-created beings, 'a Christian gentleman'.

The *Western Grazier* was established in 1880 and until 1940 it was published at Wilcannia. From then on it was printed and published in Broken Hill. Jason Smith Reid established the *Western Grazier* and later started up the *Silver Age* newspaper in Silverton, originally named *Umberumberka*, whose printing presses issued the first prospectus for BHP. The silver mining and railway town saw the formation of the Federated Engine Drivers Union, which would become one of Australia's powerful trade unions, the CFMEU. Some 57 million tons of BHP silver, lead and zinc ore plus 2.8 million passengers would be transported on the rail line up to 1970. At its peak Silverton maintained a gaol, newspaper, Masonic Lodge, stock exchange, hospital, several churches and a horseracing club. Today it has only about forty residents but many times that of visitors who travel long distances to soak up the still rather colourful surrounds and nostalgic atmosphere of long gone but genuine colonial days.

Robert's son, Bob, wrote a poem of the family's time at *Wonnaminta* from

1880 to 1894 and as it came from the heart I take the liberty, and your time, of reprinting it;

Fourteen Years

We left with happy faces, to make our home out west, with buggies, vans and horses in very great request. And we were very sanguine, and our hearts were all aglow, as we reached old Wonnaminta, just fourteen years ago.

A year it passed extremely quick, with very little rain, to keep our stock upon the run, to try it was in vain. A neighbour's place at Cobham Lake, we then were forced to go, and kept them all both safe and well, just thirteen years go.

Another year it passed along, and things were fairly good, the rain was fairly plentiful, for water and for food. We said to one another then, well this is not so slow, and hope was big within our hearts, just twelve long years ago.

Another year was ushered in, with times extremely dry, again were forced with flocks and herds our own country to fly. And Mother brought her maps right out and put her finger to, and said to Carrapundy at once you all must go. And truthful James was with us then, straight from Doughboy Hollow, and straightaway made his mind up then, our fortunes he would follow. He came out very well from this. Were our losses much? Well, no. Things looked fairly well for us, eleven years ago.

Ten, nine and eight were very good, and our spirits rose and rose, but then the little bunnie began to show his nose. They said 'You laugh at us just now, we very soon will show', and that is when they first began, just eight long years ago.

The best thing that can happen then, to me upon this earth, I met my dear old Janie, and am glad I knew her worth and time for me ran smoothly, on a very even flow, and she became my darling wife, just seven years ago.

And she and my two darlings, they make life very bright, and give one pluck and energy to go through this world's fight, and though we're down just now Janie, I'm sure bye and bye we'll win, and have many happy meetings with kith and kin.

Another year of dust and bog around the Lake, and very little water for our stock their thirst to slake. And our loss was very heavy, over thirty thousand oh! And that is just what happened, a short six years ago.

We pulled along and came out well, for we die very hard, and did not pull long faces as the sheep passed through the yard. For the year that we were in, looked very well and so, we thought we were right again, and that's five years ago.

But then the little bunnie, in earnest he began, and very soon the country, the whole he overran. He stripped it here, he stripped it there, and wherever he did go, he never left a vestige, and that's four years ago.

He followed on again next year, and had drought for a mate, and said they'd give us blazes, if we would only wait. We waited and we counted sheep, just eighty thousand short, and that is just three years ago, the time is getting short.

Three, two, one have passed away, and the old home now deserted, but let us try our luck again and be not disconcerted. For in spite of all the hardships that these few verses show, we still have many blessings to set our hearts aglow, as they were when we started, just Fourteen Years ago.

Those words are from my great grandfather, Robert (Bob) Kennedy Jnr, of *Nundora*.

The current owners of *Wonnaminta* told me there are graves all over the station and not in a cemetery but right along the creek, in clumps of trees, here and there and twenty close by the woolshed. There were so many deaths that men were paid to go out and dig enough graves. More remains turn up as the years go by. In addition to horse and other accidents, one cause of death was that many a swagman perished, they had died of thirst. A greater number of people died of typhoid, a bacterial disease usually spread by contaminated water or food, such as my wife and I recently encountered on a trip to India.

After the Kennedys had left the big country, a later manager-owner, Myrtle Rose White wrote:

In the old squatter's, R.H. Kennedy's day, Wonnaminta alone employed between eighty and ninety men. The almost denuded rooms that echoed to one's footsteps as if some invisible person followed, left a creepy feeling in one's bones. A large billiard room with a sitting room attached stood apart in what had once been a beautiful garden. The billiard table, cues and balls were still there just as if the last players had left in the middle of a game.

During my research I came across a photograph of a totemic ceremony conducted by resident Aborigines on Wonnaminta, Packsaddle, in July 1888.

Dust storm that struck Wonnaminta and Nundora (above with woolshed and shearers' quarters) on 6th November, 2018, Melbourne Cup day, former stations of the author's maternal great-great grandfather Robert Henry Kennedy and great-grandfather Robert Kennedy jr.

9
Cattle Theft

For too long the rabbits were literally everywhere on *Wonnaminta, Nuntherungie, Morden, Nundora* and the other stations. To reduce numbers and give the sheep a chance of survival, the tanks and billabongs were securely netted in and poison pens were constructed. The poison pen was made by netting off a triangle in which a small pool of water was poisoned. The outside of this enclosure was left raised from the ground, and the rabbits, circling the water, found the only access was there and crept under the wire to drink from the poisoned pool. It was taking a mean advantage but a very necessary measure if one is to breed sheep rather than rabbits. It was a common occurrence for 4,000 to 5,000 rabbits to be poisoned at just one pool in one night. Occasionally the number of fatalities was as high as 10,000 rabbits. That was one pool on one station and there were other stations. That, as much as drought, beat the Kennedys.

In 1892, when the first rabbits appeared on *Wonnaminta* and the other family stations there were said to be 62 million sheep and no rabbits in NSW. By 1924 sheep numbers were down to 32 million and there were now 500 million rabbits. It was somehow worse in 1932 when Broken Hill and Parkes were overrun by rabbits and the men were destroying 400,000 to 500,000 rabbits in a night by poisoning the water. Rabbits not only undermined the approaches to bridges by their burrowing but in the towns they ate all the gardens and undermined buildings and cricket pavilions. In places the rabbits caused irreparable damage that to this day can be seen in certain soil erosion areas.

On the other side of the coin it was the humble rabbit which kept many families in food for the hard times of not just the 1930s but also the previous decade. It wasn't the Roaring Twenties for all. Rabbits had another value prior to that. In 1905, entrepreneurs started offering to buy twenty-four rabbits for sixpence, for the lot. Sixpence must have been attractive or else the simple profusion of rabbits ensured it didn't take long to catch them. In no time, rabbit trappers were earning £3 a week, which I would suggest was three times the average wage at that time. Of course at 40 sixpences to the pound that meant a trapper had to catch 120 x 24 or 2,880 rabbits per week, for his £3.

A few years later prices went higher when rabbit fur was in demand for making felt hats, the hide into ladies' gloves and the carcases boiled down and converted into feed for chickens. Any residue soon re-emerged as garden manure. By 1910 the price of twenty-four rabbits had skyrocketed to seven shillings. In 1925 13 million pounds weight of rabbit skins were exported for the value of £3 million. In fact rabbits became more valuable than sheep. That same year wool was bringing 60 pence a pound and rabbit skins 101 pence a pound, there being (for today's young at heart) 240 pence to £1. A farmer who had sold both his wool and his rabbit skins in Sydney at the same time quickly left the local hotel and immediately hurried home. He explained he was going back to poison his sheep. On the Ivanhoe property, *Bellevue*, one night's bait setting well within a 2 km radius of the house tank resulted in 18,000 rabbits being picked up and taken away the next morning. One of Australia's most successful rabbit exporters, John McCraith, exported 130 million rabbits over his forty-five-year career.

At that time there was another market which, unfortunately, attracted a huge following. For thirty years, from 1888 onwards, an international trade centred on the clothing business in America, Canada and England, sought out Australian koala felt for hats, gloves and clothing. During that hard-to-believe time, some eight million koalas were shot and otherwise taken. Only when the open slaughter peaked with the killing of 600,000 koalas in Queensland in the one month, August of 1927, did public outrage bring a halt to the trade, although by then there were hardly any of those icons left alive. I didn't feel comfortable referring to this but over the years I have often vaguely wondered why I have never seen many koalas in the wild, except around Gunnedah, and it took a long time before I realised there are still only a fraction, some 88,000 koalas, of what there used to be and why. For reasons unknown to myself, the whole country was also said to be up in arms about the stately emu, whose feathers were only used to stuff cushions. The big bird carried a government reward and in 1888 at least 10,000 emus were killed in one district while 2,000 emu eggs were also destroyed in their nests.

Gunnedah is a prosperous rural town of 10,000 people situated on the banks of the Namoi River out on the magnificent soil of the famed Liverpool Plains, some 420 km north, north-west of Sydney. The early white settlers called the town The Woolshed before changing it to Gunnedah after the Aborigine tribe known as the Gunn-e-darr who lived there. Their greatest chief was an inspiring leader and formidable fighter, revered and known far and wide as Cumbo Gunerah or Red Kangaroo. After his death he was buried sitting up, befitting a Kamilaroi man of great importance. Today Gunnedah is home to Agquip, the largest agricultural field days event in Australia.

Most Australians know of Sir Sidney Kidman to some degree or other and as he now begins to take a role in this story I will take the liberty of referring to him also in shorter fashion. Whilst he was always known as SK in the outback and often as 'The Boss' I shall, with all due respect for the man, and only for the sake of my convenience and repetition, call him Kidman.

It was Kidman's strategy to have a series of connecting stations with, usually, sufficient water to enable him to move cattle from one to the other while always heading to the southern beef markets. As part of this strategy Kidman essentially acquired two chains of properties. One ran from the Barkly Tablelands which is mostly centred on the north-east of the Northern Territory, from about 100 km south of the Gulf of Carpentaria down to a line that runs from Tennant Creek, in the Territory, across to Camooweal and Urandangie in western Queensland. From there Kidman's properties went out across the Channel country and along the Birdsville Track down to the railway at Marree in South Australia. The second chain of properties started with *Ruby Plains* and *Sturt Creek*, not far from the Kimberley town of Halls Creek and the Tanami Track and extended across to the Northern Territory's *Victoria River Downs* and down to *Wilpena Station* in the Flinders Ranges of South Australia.

When the rains come the Channel country is superb, probably out on its own, in the manner that it quickly and efficiently fattens cattle courtesy of its three flooding rivers. In that region, Kidman held such renowned stations as *Innamincka, Annandale, Sandringham Downs, Bulloo Downs, Diamantina Lakes* and *Glengyle Station* amongst others. Kidman's Tree of Knowledge is a heritage-listed coolabah tree on *Glengyle Station* that is accepted as the restful setting where Kidman formulated and put into place his western Queensland strategy. It is regarded as the choice property of those selections as one third of it is a natural flood plain, carrying that wonderful feed, Mitchell grass, courtesy of the Georgina River. *Glengyle Station* is at the end of the world's longest mail run as it covers a distance of 2,000 km from Port Augusta and return. Nearby to Urandangie is *Tobermory Station* which was once owned by two brothers who married two sisters. The men then split the property into *Tobermory Station* and *Manners Station*, adjoining each other. I am told that at some stage the women swapped brothers and therefore they swapped cattle stations.

Back to Mr. Kidman. His managers, such as Con White, were required to inspect the travelling mobs as they passed through their respective country. The manager would decide which bullocks were too poor to sell well and which cows too heavy in calf to continue on. He and the men would cut them out and keep them on *Nundora, Morden, Wonnaminta* and other adjoining stations in that aggregation. When those stock were in stronger condition they would later join up with another mob, also heading to the markets. It was said a Kidman stockman was the worth of a Vestey's manager. Vestey's was a UK company which owned vast tracts of land in Australia and established themselves as dominant beef processors. They expanded their business by being the first to use refrigeration.

One day Con went out to *Cobham Lake Station*, 48 miles to the north and where Robert Kennedy had to send his stock soon after he arrived at *Wonnaminta* and ran into a dry season. He was awaiting the arrival of a mob of cattle from one of Kidman's most renowned stations, *Durham Downs* in Queensland, a property still in the Kidman portfolio, of some 9,000 square km and with a carrying capacity of 21,000 head of cattle. No doubt it was a big mob. The drovers were not yet in sight and Con climbed a sandhill so that he could look out over the direction from which they were coming.

He noticed a recent dust storm had uncovered some sawn timber and closer inspection revealed a railing around a grave. He cleared away the sand with his hands and found a curve of marble. Beyond that he discovered a headstone, which read, in part:

'To the memory of ---- who died in 1883 aged thirty-two years. Charity covereth a multitude of sins. She harmed herself but none other.' Her name had been erased by the land in which she died and yet it was when Robert Kennedy and his clan were thereabouts. Who was that rare woman in a land trod briefly by Burke and Wills and only when the rains prevailed, by Kennedy livestock? Who cared enough to provide a marble headstone in a land of travail?

By chance the head stockman then found an unburied skeleton, half a mile to the west of the boss's find. He had no idea of whether anyone else knew of it but he thought it unlikely as it was well off the beaten track. He had not reported it to the police, saying with the indifference of a bushman unconcerned with his own fate, 'What does it matter, anyway?'

Years later, a married couple were working on *Nundora* and the wife began flirting with the blacksmith. By all accounts she led him on, teased him and at the last moment resisted him. Due to his frustrations the blacksmith drank a bottle of whisky which not only inflamed his desire, but clouded his judgement. While the husband was lighting the early morning fire, the blacksmith picked up the kitchen poker and ironed him out. He then proceeded to the couple's bedroom, detached from the house, where the woman now definitely declined his advances. That brought the poker again into play and as he gave her a touch-up with it she began to scream. As station men came running the blacksmith went the other way and off into the distance. He managed to make his way to a boundary rider's hut on *Wonnaminta*. When he defied arrest he was shot dead, the walls of the old hut retaining the numerous bullet holes.

On the north-west side of the aggregation there is a place known as Hard Hill Gate and there are four graves spread out over two miles, in an area long known to only a few of those early pioneer pastoralists and drovers. One contains the remains of Old Jack Stoker, who died in 1885, when the Kennedys were in their prime and perhaps he worked for them. Who knows now? A man and his half-caste wife went that way with a horse team. When the woman blamed him for not finding some of their missing horses she became upset and shot him dead. The third grave does not have a known story but the fourth does. It harbours Tim Wilks, the jockey. He claimed many a horse had been ridden by him as a 'dead finish'. Now he lies at the foot of what the bushmen call a dead finish tree.

Back in time a mob of about one thousand head of cattle, whose I do not know, were being moved from *Boolka Lake*, which had dried up. They had a two-day walk without water to *Wydga Well* and from there it was another two dry days to reach *Cobham Lake Station*. The lake was found to be dry save for a hole in the neck of it and where a spring or soak normally sustained it. The cattle were held on this minuscule hole for three days while men rode out to inspect the route ahead in the hope of finding water along the way. The lake did not suffice so the mob pushed on, now making for *Wonnaminta Waterhole*. When the cattle were still 24 km short of reaching that water they broke away and stampeded ahead.

Straight for the water, the scent of which maddened them, they went, first at an amble, then a slow trot, which quickened to a breakneck gallop. Mile after mile the thirst crazed cattle thundered on. The horsemen tried everything in their experienced repertoire to restrain, let alone bring them under control but they may as well have tried to stop a dust storm. When they came to the water there was no regard for one's bovine brethren. The cattle to the fore were trampled underfoot and then covered over by the never ending on-rushing hordes behind them. The slaughter continued until the waterhole was saturated with the dead and the dying.

On the mail road north to Tibooburra, just short of the Queensland border, there were a few pubs, each separated by 40 km to 50 km and convenient for travellers to stop overnight. They were also utilised by station hands, miners, shearers, salesmen, one and all. Sometimes, after shearers had cut out a big woolshed they would come in with their cheque and leave it behind the bar, instructing the proprietor to take the costs of their accommodation, meals and alcohol out of it, for as long as the cheque's proceeds lasted. Some of those blokes were known to be generous and to share their hard-earned with whoever was about.

9 Cattle Theft

At the nearby Bancannia pub, which the map shows to have been on *Nundora*, an old feller who had been out in the bush for three full years turned up with a particularly healthy cheque. When he handed it over the bar he announced he was going to stay there and drink it out. He invited everyone to help him along and many men did so, to the best of their ability. An unexpected problem

Jockey Tim Wilks was one of the most colourful personalities to grace Broken Hill and other Outback tracks. An accomplished horseman he rode countless winners in NSW, Qld and SA. In his day he was the idol of the large race-going public. In 1925 he rode the winner of the Strezlecki Stakes and then took out the following race, the Innamincka Cup on Nile Fruit (above). He died in 1936 of an accident while droving at Palgamurtee, south of Milparinka, on the Broken Hill to Tibooburra road.

In 1871 four men and three youngsters drove a mob of cattle from John Conrick's Nappa Merrie Station, 40 km north-east of Innamincka, 1,200 km to the markets in Adelaide. To celebrate their success they then bought new clothes and had their photo taken—with John Conrick standing.

The Innamincka Hotel beer bottle heap—said to have been one hundred metres in length, of similar width and two metres high.

An initial stage of the initiation ceremony that accompanied circumcision of Ngalia boys from the Vaughan Springs region in the Northern Territory.

Among traditional tribes the Kadaitcha man had the authority to take revenge and/or to kill offenders who transgressed tribal ways.

Except for a gunyah, an Aboriginal shelter of bark and branches, being available on days of extreme heat, the remote outpost of Innamincka had no provision for prisoners. Offenders were chained to the prisoner's post as shown by a police tracker.

Abdul (Waid) Wade was an outback entrepreneur/businessman from Afghanistan who prospered in Australia, the land he loved but whose authorities used the White Australia policy to break his heart, as you will read in Chapter 26. In the above photo his camel-drawn wagons cross the Cooper at Innamincka to deliver supplies to outlying stations.

arose due to the fact that not having had a drink for three years he was out of condition and about halfway through his marathon he up and died, at the bar. His unfortunate passing was not enough to deter his new-found friends from continuing on with his generosity and they proceeded to drink the cheque dry. He was propped up on one end of the bar counter, nodding with each shout until, when rigor mortis set in, his head no longer responded to the manipulating hand behind it.

There was another bloke who enjoyed a drink and after having a fair few he bought two bottles to take home. He left the pub a bit wobbly, mounted his horse and set off. A rabbit, surprise, surprise, ran across his path, his horse shied and he was thrown to the ground. He landed heavily, breaking the two bottles that were shoved inside his shirt. He was knocked unconscious and someone sent a message through to his station manager. The boss turned up and wasn't too concerned about his employee having damaged his head as much as he was about the man's stomach. The bottles, having broken, had cut open the man's stomach for a width of 13 centimetres and some of his intestines were hanging out. The manager did what he could for the fellow. He took a darning needle from his saddle bag and a few long hairs from the tail of the horse that had thrown the man and after pushing the intestines hopefully back in place, he sewed the folds of the patient's stomach back together. A fortnight later the stitches were removed and it appeared as though the manager had re-inserted the intestines the right way up. They functioned remarkably well, in fact his mates reckoned they were better than they were before the accident.

I referred earlier to the Reverend John Flynn starting the Royal Flying Doctor Service due to the hardship incurred by the *Ruby Plains* stockman, Jimmy Darcy, when he suffered a ruptured bowel. One Sunday, my wife, Janice, and I went to an Open Day at the Dubbo Royal Flying Doctor Service (RFDS) and I was struck by the dental service that is provided in addition to the well-known RFDS medical care. The next morning I had an appointment with my dentist and I asked her what dental facilities would have been available to outback people in the second half of the 19th century. She said, 'None, and there still isn't. It's third world out there. Last week a man walked into the Brewarrina Hospital and said he had a tooth problem. They examined him and found he had an abscess on a tooth. He had treated it himself, by pouring battery acid on it. Ruined his gums as well.'

The Kennedys had gone but Mills had arrived, not at *Wonnaminta* but at its nearest town, Broken Hill, in the Barrier Ranges, where he worked for three years as a surveyor. Between *Wonnaminta* and Broken Hill was, and still is, *Mt Gipps Station*. Kidman, born 9th May, 1857, was the fifth of six sons and after his father died his mother took up with and married a much younger man, one who turned out to be less than desirable. When he was twelve years of age, Kidman was working in his home town of Adelaide at Dean and Laughton's slaughter yard, handling stock brought in by drovers. Arthur Ashwin had also worked there before going to *Mundowdna Station*, which Kidman would one day own. Kidman earned five shillings a week and handed most of it to his mother, as did his brothers, who despaired of her second marriage. The only good thing that fellow did was leave her.

At age thirteen, Kidman left also, to follow in the footsteps of his brothers, particularly Sackville Kidman who was two years older and named after his grandmother's employers' titled name, in England. Kidman had saved £2/10/0 and he bought himself a horse and headed north, to Kapunda. He briefly worked there before being employed by German Charlie, who ran a grog shanty. As his alcohol was often doctored with nicotine in the brandy, sometimes turpentine, and flat beer was frothed up with a bar of soap shaken in the keg, Charlie kept a weather eye on his more susceptible drinkers and maintained a freshly dug grave for those patrons who expired. A one-legged traveller left without paying and German Charlie later met up with him on the Menindee common where he chopped the man's wooden leg in half with an axe. He escaped conviction by producing his licence to cut wood on Crown land, so it was said. From there Kidman progressed to being an offsider to Harry Raines, looking after livestock for eight shillings a week and always listening to and learning from everyone.

After one year and now aged fourteen, he packed up his swag and walked to *Mt Gipps Station*, forty km north of Broken Hill. There is some doubt as to what happened to his horse so I won't enter into conjecture. Neither do I know how far he walked, but when Broken Hill started up mining it is a well-known fact that men walked the 515 km from Adelaide to be there, usually pushing a homemade wheelbarrow with their lifelong possessions, swag and tucker on it, in order to strike it rich or at least to find work. *Mt Gipps Station* was then 407,000 hectares in size and his luck was in. Kidman landed a job as a station hand. Now he was earning 10 shillings a week on the biggest property in *The Barrier*.

He joined three of his brothers there, with Fred earning £1 a week for general work, George on the same money as a boundary rider, and Sack (Sackville) on 15 shillings a week as a water drawer. In a sense Kidman at that age was a boy among men, there being forty men employed on the station but he was always observing his surrounds. The overseer sacked him when he asked for a pay rise and he moved to Cobar and entered the butchering business, where he learned to accurately know the live and the cut-up weight of beef. He did well and progressed to transporting rations and goods to re-sell profitably at Tibooburra before going into partnership with a knowledgeable horse dealer.

He started dealing in cattle and horses, always buying to resell. As with all beginners he took a loss here and there. In time he reasoned that if he could bring cattle down from those new stations being opened up in Queensland to the southern markets, it could be a profitable exercise but how reliable were those three rivers, the Cooper, the Georgina and the Diamantina to help him along the way? Then, like everyone else, he heard of the exploits of Harry Redford and his two accomplices, George Dewdney and William Rooke. The three men stole the best part of 1,000 head of cattle from *Bowen Downs Station*, 60 km north-west of Aramac and so close to the centre of Queensland. The property was blessed by being covered with Mitchell grass, which stretched across its plains for 200 km and enabled the station to run 60,000 cattle. They wanted their 1,000 back.

Redford's plan was to take the cattle south to Adelaide and that meant crossing some of the harsh country that had brought Burke and Wills undone. It was one hell of a gamble but the three men succeeded and they didn't even have to reach Adelaide. Against the odds they worked their way south until they came to *Blanchewater Station*, 128 km north-east of Lyndhurst, which in turn is just below Marree, at the southern end of the Oodnadatta Track. At *Blanchewater*

Station the three men sold all their stolen cattle for £5,000, an absolute fortune. They were able to travel a little faster after that and made it to Adelaide, while behind them the pursuing *Bowen Downs* station hands were still marvelling at the skill of the cattle duffers (rustlers) to move the cattle so far south and in such good time. The three men were eventually arrested but when Harry Redford appeared in court the jury was so impressed by what he had achieved and in appreciation of his skill, they found him not guilty. The judge said, 'I thank God, gentlemen, that the verdict is yours and not mine'. A few years later *Blanchewater Station* was owned by Thomas Elder, of *Beltana Station*.

There was an unusual outback code that seemed to say cattle stealing or duffing was outside mere low-down theft. A man could participate in cattle duffing without losing his standing among men who would run a pickpocket out of the country. In the north-west of Queensland cattle stealing was only surpassed as an industry by copper mining. Cloncurry had fifty-three cattle stealing cases listed for one sitting of the court and there was not one conviction. Things were so bad that eventually the criminal court was closed and the sessions removed to Townsville, where it was hoped there might be twelve good men and true, without a cattle thief or sympathiser among them. There was a feeling around the north-west that cattle stealing was no crime. If people had such large herds that they couldn't keep them branded, it then presented opportunity for anyone smart enough to put his own brand on them. Unbranded cattle running wild in unfenced country could not be classed as private property.

That sentiment did not only prevail among the landless class or the small landholder taking up country with the aim of stocking it from the herds of the surrounding large stations. Retailers and businessmen did not feel they had anything in common with the large operators who were so wealthy that they would purchase their goods wholesale in the south at better rates than the local retailers could obtain. They could replenish their cattle stations without spending one penny in the district.

Invariably, whenever a cattle stealing case arose the jury would retire and at least one man therein would bluntly state: 'My verdict is Not Guilty, and you can wake me when you agree to that. I didn't see the man take the cattle and I won't convict on circumstantial evidence.' That reasoning was played out many times and it was a face-saver if someone dared to openly accuse the proclaimer of bias. Additionally the cattleduffer/ thief would arm himself not just with a good rifle that he carried at the ready across his saddle but also a dingo scalper's licence. A scalper's licence afforded such men carte blanche, the French term for blank paper but in the English-speaking world it granted complete freedom to do whatever one wanted to do, to ride over anyone's land and a perfect alibi if they were challenged. One had to be careful when confronting a man who carried his rifle at the ready.

The cattle duffers were hard men as exemplified by one who was out on bail due to a cattle stealing charge. In the street he saw the stock inspector who was appearing as the chief witness against him. He not only attacked the stock inspector and brutally broke his jaw but escaped the grievous bodily harm charge although his victim was in hospital for several weeks. Another man rode into the police paddock where seventeen head of stolen cattle were being held as evidence against him. He shot the cattle, cut their brands out and burnt the pieces of hide. Yet another cattleduffer, by the name of Matthews, got into a hotel brawl with three policemen. He knocked them all to the ground. He leapt onto his horse at the rail outside and galloped away, yelling, 'You'll *ride* if you want me, you bastards......' They say a night without half a dozen fights in Cloncurry was quiet. The police went about with almost permanent black eyes, until eventually the prices of both copper and cattle dropped.

The *Western Grazier* newspaper, at Wilcannia on the Darling, gives further insight to the happenings of those days. The rural paper reported as many items then as the major capital cities do today. To select any date I happened to choose 9th September,1882, by which time Robert Kennedy and clan had been at nearby *Wonnaminta Station* for two years.

Just the first page recounts that: *an Albury grazier has bought a place in Queensland and the task of moving his 20,000 sheep, his horses and all his stores up north will take six months. A man died of 'congestion of the brain, accelerated by alcohol' and yesterday's race meeting at Randwick was well attended although Twilight fell (the horse I presume) and two jockeys were injured. The NSW Premier Sir Henry Parkes was seriously ill and St Mary's Cathedral in Sydney was opened today. Dysentery is rife amongst the British Army troops in Egypt where they still managed to repulse an attack by Bedouin Arabs. Yesterday 9,000 bales of Australian wool were sold in London and 5,000 bales in Antwerp, Holland. In Melbourne bullocks sold from £17 to £20 per head while calves sold at extreme rates of £4/7/6. The Crown Lands Office had 17 applications for land purchases, the majority of which were for 640 acres or one square mile.*

Four shearers and woolrollers had gone on strike at a western woolshed and gone to another shed for work where they were arrested under the Masters and Servants Act.

Author's note re. the Masters and Servants Act. By the 14th century wages paid to workers in England were tightly controlled by the ruling classes and the employers. Then chaos and indeed disaster struck from 1346 to its peak in 1353 when the Black Death, also known as the Plague covered not only England but much of the world. Some 75-200 million people died in the largest fatal pandemic ever recorded in human history. Records show that friends who lunched together were often dead within mere days. A prince would die as readily as a pauper, there was no protection from the plague. Such was the scarcity of able-bodied men that survivors of any classification became wealthy in the shortest time for there were so few to bury the dead let alone sustain other facets of what had been normal life, such as transport, food supply etc. Those alive charged and received vast sums of money for their services. In Paris fifty per cent of the population died and Florence and Sienna fared worse. Ships arriving in Venice were commanded to sit off-shore at anchor before unloading for quaranta giorni, which translates as forty days and thus we have the English word, quarantine. Some people did likewise.

In 1351 the Statutes of Labourers were introduced to enforce service at rates of hiring that existed prior to the plague and to ensure that if a man left his service, his job, before the time agreed upon, it was not that he could be punished but that he would be punished, by imprisonment. This draconian legislation was introduced after the plague surged like a tsunami through England and it was updated in 1747, 1766 and 1823. In Australia all states passed similar laws, such as NSW in 1823 and Tasmania with its infamous Van Diemen's Land Act of 1854.

Absence from service without leave would see offenders suffer solitary confinement for thirty days or three months with hard labour. In Tasmania the authorities believed that solitary confinement was actually beneficial as it would protect convicted workers from indiscriminate association with vicious characters in prisons. In addition wages due to the employee would be forfeited. The Masters and Servants Act was not repealed in Australia until 1986 courtesy of the Industrial Relations Act.

They were each fined £2 plus court costs of £2/2/6 or in default seven days in gaol. Local stores were offering tea for sale at 18 pence per pound, sugar at 4.5 pence per pound and rice at 3.5 pence per pound. Full-size shirts with lined backs were 1/11 while men's good boots and best moleskin trousers were both 7/11 per pair. A Wilcannia station owner wanted a tank sinker for 12 months work. A book ruled and printed to contain a daily analysis of the shearing – for rams, ewes, wethers and hoggets – with leaves sufficient to last 14 years in a shed of thirty men or seven years for sixty men, could be made to order at the Hay office of the Western Grazier, for £1. Raven Wade, having completed extensive improvements at the Murrumbidgee Hotel, near Hay, invites his numerous friends and patrons to call in. At the same time any person found trespassing, damaging fences or cutting timber on Uardry property will be prosecuted according to law.

I have to assume that the *Uardry* property is today's *Uardry Station* as it also is 40 kilometres east of Hay and as mentioned herein was bought a few years back by Tom Brinkworth. He walked his purchase of 18,000 head of cattle from Queensland to the 35,000-hectare *Uardry Station* with its 32- kilometre frontage to the Murrumbidgee River. *Uardry* is an Aboriginal word for yellow box tree. Everyone who grew up in Australia knowing and using the old pounds, shillings and pence currency until 1966 would have handled the shilling coin which from 1938 until 1966 carried a sheep's head. That unique Merino ram was *Uardry 0.1*, Sydney Grand Champion 1932, but otherwise known to the trade as Hallmark.

10
Sidney Kidman & the Broken Hill

Kidman was also impressed by Redford's escapade but he saw a lot more in it than others did. To him it indicated he should pursue his plan of breeding or buying cattle on those well-grassed plains of the north, bring them steadily south by way of well-connected and watered stations for fattening and then have holding and delivery properties to take them to the southern and eastern markets. Three things happened in the meantime.

On a trip back to Kapunda he met Miss Isabel Wright and he soon realised she was, hopefully, to be Mrs. Kidman. Second, he was surprisingly bequeathed £400 by his mother's father, back in England. Third, something special occurred on *Mt Gipps Station*. While Robert Kennedy and his sons and brothers were now established on *Wonnaminta*, *Nundora*, and *Nuntherungie* mere miles to the north of *Mt Gipps Station*, something happened at the latter that would make the resultant mining company the largest the world has ever seen.

The man known in Australia as Charles Rasp, boundary rider, was born on 7th October, 1846 in Stuttgart, Germany and his given names were Hieronymous Salvator Lopez von Pereira. He was of Portuguese descent, a highly intelligent man as evidenced by his qualifications in economics and as an edible-oil technologist who spoke five languages. It seems his lungs were not suited to the cold of German winters and he departed for warmer climes, thus arriving in Australia in 1869.

Charles Rasp was earning a pound a week for his duties on *Mt Gipps* and during his time riding the station boundary and mustering sheep to take to the long, stone built, shearing sheds, he often rode by a 45-metre-high ridge of a broken hill that extended for 3.2 km. He was not a geologist but he studied books on minerals and metals and believed the black oxide contained tin. Rasp was a popular employee on *Mt Gipps*, liked by all for his manner and good nature and being so knowledgeable was known as 'the walking encyclopaedia'. He was close to David James, who was a tank (dam) sinker and fencer on *Mt Gipps* and James's employee, James Poole.

The three men decided to stake a claim on part of the broken hill and they did so on 3rd September, 1883. The date was deliberate. On 3rd September, 1758, armed men had made an assassination attempt on King Joseph of Portugal while he was travelling in his coach. The king was shot but he survived and the retribution saw several families of the nobility, who had opposed the king and his rule, executed en masse. Rasp's grandfather, a member of the aristocracy, was forced to flee for his life and to change his illustrious identity. If it were not for the flow-on effect of those shots, Rasp would not have found the riches he did, precisely 125 years later, to the very day. He was also conscious of 3rd September, 1870, the day that Napoleon III had been taken prisoner by Bismarck's army during the Franco-Prussian War, an event he saw as a propitious and favourable omen. Sooner or later, someone else would have had the BHP honour but that's how history unfolds.

Rasp, James and Poole gathered at their chosen spot and James, perhaps because he was the tank sinker and fencer, more accustomed than Rasp to using his hands, staked out the claim. There could have been another reason but 16 hectares were pegged out on the broken hill and then the men registered their claim. Having done that they told George McCulloch, the station manager. McCulloch was annoyed the men had done so on station land but ownership of land in Australia did not and does not necessarily extend to what lies beneath the surface. He then suggested they stake a claim on a much larger section of the broken hill and having brought in three more station employees that is what happened. Their extra claims covered virtually all of the 3.2 km length of the black broken hill, the hog's back, as it was called.

The men formed The Syndicate of Seven and it consisted of: Charles Rasp, boundary rider; George McCulloch, station manager; Philip Charley, jackaroo; David James, contract tank sinker and fencer; James Poole, David James's employee; George Urquhart, sheep overseer and George Lind, station bookkeeper. In those days it would have been unusual for a jackaroo to be entering into a financial arrangement and ownership with a manager but in many ways those men lived on the same level and life was hard for all in such remote areas.

Each man contributed £1 a week to the syndicate and owned one-seventh. Their money paid for the title and legal expenses plus the cost of digging the first shaft. In another twist of fate, that first shaft was dug on the one spot of the entire claim that was worthless.

In accordance with that disappointment the shares began to change hands. Before I get to that I might ask you to consider the seven syndicate members, above, and hazard a guess as to which of them would go on to have a faint connection, by marriage, to Mills and our story.

Charles Rasp bought out the disappointed sheep overseer, George Urquhart, for £10. Mr. Rasp married but died childless in 1907, leaving his widow an estate of £480,000, a sum no doubt far greater than that bequeathed by Mr. Urquhart, who passed away in 1915 at nearby Silverton and was the only one of the seven buried in Broken Hill. George Lind, the bookkeeper, sold out to the manager, George McCulloch, for little if any profit and moved to Victoria. McCulloch, then wanting to capitalise on that purchase, offered a one-fourteenth share to a casual station bookkeeper, Alfred Cox, for £200. Cox made a counter offer of £120 and neither man was prepared to budge. Cox then challenged McCulloch to a card game of euchre, to decide if the sale price would be £120 or £200. They were not to know but that one hand of euchre was most likely for the highest stake of all time. McCulloch lost and Cox the bookkeeper left with a fabulous share. It is claimed that six years later McCulloch's lost share would have returned him £250,000 or more.

Philip Charley, the jackaroo, sold half of his share for £100 but fortunately for him he retained the other half and consequently became a very wealthy man. As a youth he had moved to Broken Hill where the hot, dry climate was seen as beneficial to his health, his lungs in particular, aggravated as they were by moister, colder climes, similar to those which adversely affected Charles Rasp. With his remaining half share and the massive income that was soon derived from it, he purchased a large landholding at Richmond, a little to the west of

Sydney and on those rich plains before they rise up to the Blue Mountains. This area has long been known as the breadbasket of Sydney although every day more and more of that valuable and irreplaceable soil disappears under the developers' machinery and concrete.

The former jackaroo was still only twenty-six years of age when he bought that significant property in 1889. The following year BHP, which had begun production in 1885, returned a profit in excess of £1,000,000 as it also did in 1891. Yet it was just getting started. The property Charley bought was called Belmont Park and had long been established and loved by previous owners. The widow of the most recent owner had tragically died after her dress caught fire.

The word jackaroo is derived from the Aboriginal word, *tchackooro*, which describes the noisy jay bird that goes around in flocks of a dozen or so, incessantly chattering, and as a result it was the early Aboriginal name for white men. *Tchackooro* is a wonderful word as it is one of those intriguing utterances in that the sound of the word is similar to the noise it describes; it is in fact onomatopoetic.

Philip Charley demolished all the buildings that came with his purchase and spared no expense over three years in constructing a 25-room grand, multistorey, mansion. He then set about breeding top quality livestock, cattle and horses, and followed that up by devoting himself to various Agricultural Associations for the benefit of many other interested people. After the fortuitous move to Broken Hill for health reasons, he lived another sixty years. He and his wife raised eight children and they bought the first Rolls-Royce in Australia. The estate was sold in 1952 and the magnificent home and buildings of Philip Charley and his family today belong to the St John Church of God organisation which operates it as an 88-bedroom private mental health hospital. It all stems from that section of a broken hill, an awkward-looking otherwise nondescript outcrop of Mt. Gipps station...

James Poole, David James's employee, sold half of his share to Kidman, who knew all seven men, especially as he had previously worked on *Mt Gipps Station* and afterwards supplied them and others in *The Barrier* with beef from his butchering operations. Kidman said: *About this time Broken Hill was moving along. After the drought I went to Cobham Lake Station, where Robert Kennedy had moved his livestock to when he encountered drought conditions as soon as he moved on to Wonnaminta in 1880, and I bought 900 cows and bullocks, all they could muster out of 10,000, at £3 a head. I travelled the cattle via Broken Hill and sold them at the Burra. On the way I met Jim Poole, who was with David James, sinking a tank at the Nine-Mile, which is a few miles from where Broken Hill now is. I gave Jim Poole 10 of the culls for a one-fourteenth share in the Broken Hill and also left 10 bullocks to be broken in. The culls were worth about £60.* Kidman always claimed he was offered the share for £60 and he paid for them with the culls, not, as his detractors would later say, with the working bullocks, which were far more valuable.

James Poole kept his remaining half share until he later sold it for £4,500. He then took up farming in Western Australia before, like several others in this story, moving to Kapunda for the rest of his life. It was and still is a great little town in South Australia. David James kept all of his one-seventh share. He sold his working bullock team and moved to Kapunda where he married and lived in the town while building up a team of thoroughbred racehorses. In 1884, he entered one of his horses in the Australian Cup, in Melbourne. It was then the premier staying race in the country, at two and a quarter miles, being longer than the Melbourne Cup and only two years younger, the inaugural race being run in 1863. With most owners' preference being for a quick return on their money and consequently a dearth of genuine Australian bred stayers, the race has been steadily eroded in distance and, perhaps, quality. Many of today's so-called stayers run barely half that distance or 2,000 metres. The name of David James's great stayer was Broken Hill. He won the 1884 Australian Cup.

He had other horses in the stable and the following year he trotted out a lovely brown three-year-old filly sired by that good stallion, Trenton. Lightly raced due to sore feet, Trenton won the Melbourne Stakes and from thirteen starts had eight wins, three seconds and one third. He may have been better in defeat as he was placed third in the 1885 Melbourne Cup and second in the 1886 Melbourne Cup, losing by a neck to Arsenal who carried 13 kilograms less weight. Trenton was fortunate to even exist as his sire was the English bred stallion, Musket. The fifth Earl of Glasgow originally owned Musket and unfortunately the earl had a rather bad temper with a disposition for being rid of horses that displeased him on the training track. He had slowcoaches shot on the spot. He once had six horses executed in one morning and when unable to flush out any foxes for the day's hunt he was quite likely to designate one of his beaters or huntsmen as the quarry, to be pursued relentlessly across the undulating countryside.

When Musket was a two-year-old and displaying only little promise, the Earl of Glasgow, despite the protestations of his trainer, intended to have Musket put down. Something happened and the earl died instead. Musket left England and thankfully sired not only Trenton but the great Carbine, winner of the 1890 Melbourne Cup while carrying the steadier of 66 kilograms and winning in race record time. To this day, many racing aficionados rate Carbine the greatest stayer to grace the Australian turf. David James's three-year-old filly, Auraria, sired by Musket's son Trenton, won the South Australian Derby and Mr. James then had his heart set on winning the Victorian Derby, which, as it dates back to 1855, is Australia's oldest horserace. Auraria did not win but was placed in the Derby and that plus the fact that Mr. James was a small bettor saw her price for the 1895 Melbourne Cup blow out to odds of 33 to 1. She won the race, one of only three fillies ever to do so. Auraria proved her win was no fluke by also winning the Flemington Stakes, the VRC Oaks and many more races, including a dead-heat for first in the C.B. Fisher plate with the great Wallace, son of the mighty Carbine. Mr. James was proclaimed by the press to be the King of Kapunda, where he had established his racing stable, *Coalbrook Vale*.

1888 marked a period of great prosperity in Victoria and that year the Melbourne Cup with prize money of £4,888 was the richest race in the world. As Melbourne in particular flourished so did horse racing. When Carbine won the Cup in 1890 the prize money was a staggering £13,230 and in Tarcoola's 1893 victory it was similar at £13,124 but when Patron greeted the judge in 1894 it had dropped dramatically to £5,000. After his racing career Patron moved to Germany and sired cavalry horses. When Auraria won the following year the prize money was at its lowest ebb, just £3,667. I doubt that unduly concerned David James for he raced his horses for the love of doing so and did not need the prize money as others might. But why did the financial reward plummet?

The discovery of goldfields in Australia, especially in Victoria, saw a surge in the population. Victoria grew to have a larger population than NSW with Melbourne outgrowing Sydney. Most gold was to be found in Victoria's Ballarat and Bendigo and as people prospered so the demand for housing escalated. In Victoria the peak of the population growth and residential housing and house prices was in 1888. It was observed that the price of building land was 1,000 times higher than the valuation sixty years previously. Oversupply reduced the price of property which eventually went into freefall. The following year property prices began to fall in Melbourne with a flow-on effect. Then living standards fell and perhaps worst of all there was not only a banking sector crisis but disasters in the non-bank financial sector, with Melbourne suffering the most.

The Australian depressions of the 1890s and the 1930s were similar in that the initial fall in real output on both occasions was 10 per cent. However the depression of the 1890s was substantially deeper and more prolonged than the depression of the 1930s, with real GDP continuing to fall the following year by 7 per cent. It was not until 1899 that the level of real GDP surpassed the peak of eight years earlier while in the 1930s depression, growth resumed in 1932 and by 1934 had surpassed the previous peak of 1930. Real GDP fell by 20 per cent over the 1890s as against 10 per cent over the 1930s and the degree of openness of the Australian economy was similar over both time periods.

Making matters worse was the lack of actual productivity from 1861 to 1891. For those thirty years GDP grew on average at about one per cent as compared to 3 per cent per annum for the thirty years following World War Two. Whilst that is so, it is fair to say that from 1875 to 1891 building activity as a percentage of GDP averaged about 14 per cent, making that time period the most extravagant of all building booms in Australia's history. Around 1890/91 private investment expenditure, building activity and bank credit all halved as a percentage of GDP. In 1887 there were twenty-six banks operating in Australia but due to the severe economic depression only six survived by 1893. The Federal Bank of Australia ran out of money and closed. Then the City of Melbourne Bank went into liquidation. The Commercial Bank of Australia, one of the country's largest, suspended operations.

People who had put their savings into building societies, as well as those who had borrowed heavily to fund their own speculative investments, found themselves in dire straits. Businessmen, pastoralists, farmers and land speculators were not able to pay their overdrafts and thousands of small and large investors were ruined. So I can assume it was not surprising that the prize money allocated to the Melbourne Cup spiralled downwards.

David James lived in Kapunda and when his wife died, he married for the second time. On this occasion his wife was Ada Mullen, the sister of Mills's wife, Mary Jane and youngest daughter of John and Mary Mullen. With her sister Annie, Ada had raised Mills's daughters, Alice and Ethel, and now, late in life, she finally was happily married. David James entered the South Australian Parliament in 1902 and lived until 1926. According to the Cambridge English Dictionary definition, the marriage of Ada Mullen to David James made Mills, via his wife Mary Mullen, his brother in-law, with David James quite possibly one of the wealthiest men in Australia. Not that it affected Mills.

After Kidman had sold his cattle at the Burra and bought that one-fourteenth share in the Broken Hill mine he went down to Kapunda to see Isabel Wright, again. On his return trip to Broken Hill he travelled in a Cobb and Co. coach. Kapunda is 434 km from Broken Hill and whilst Kidman was good in the saddle he was travelling to Kapunda quite a few times, although not staying long as he had work to do. He did not write letters to Isabel, he was a good talker instead. No doubt to save time he found the coach convenient. On this particular trip he fell into conversation with a fellow traveller whose line of work was as a commission agent. Kidman had a share in three mines and told the man he was prepared to sell his one-fourteenth share of the Broken Hill mine for £150.

The man, named Harris, agreed to do what he could and they parted company in Broken Hill. Soon after that the young jackaroo Philip Charley picked up some rich silver chloride from a dumped pile near the original shaft. It was assayed and found to contain 600 ounces of silver to the ton. Silver was then worth four shillings per ounce. Another report stated there were 35,000 ounces to the hectare.

It was an absolute bonanza however anyone looked at it. Kidman had instructed Harris to sell for £150, which was now a pittance and he desperately tried to cancel the proposed sale of his share. There was no communication as there is today and if Kidman was not normally disposed to letter writing he certainly was now. He wrote to Harris and despatched the letter. It crossed in the mail with a letter from Harris that detailed the successful sale he had made on Kidman's behalf and for which a cheque was attached. The sale was watertight and try as he did to make it null and void he was unable to. To add insult to frustration the cheque to Kidman was for only £100. Harris had kept £50, not for nothing did he describe himself as a commission agent.

Kidman said, 'How hard I tried to get that share back. But I could not. After that little romance I went away into Queensland again to buy cattle out on the Mulligan at *Sandringham Station*. I went into partnership with my brother Sackville and remained so until his death.' For the rest of his life Kidman maintained an interest in the affairs of BHP. In 2011 the capitalisation of BHP was $241 billion. If David James had held his stock and taken up all further issues his one-seventh shareholding would have reached $34 billion and Kidman's ten cull cattle payment for a one-fourteenth shareholding would have turned in to $17 billion, by 2011.

The Syndicate of Seven had been reduced in numbers and the men decided to form a new syndicate, of fourteen. Charles Rasp and George McCulloch held three-fourteenths shares and David James two-fourteenths, thus retaining his one-seventh holding. Some members now had one-fourteenth shareholdings. With new members and new money, the initial development work could be carried on. One of the new members was James Dalglish, the District Surveyor for my home town of Dubbo where he lived and worked from 1872 until 1883, the year David James pegged out the Broken Hill site. Such was the exemplary nature of all his work it is reputed that he was never in error and his remarkable talent and finished product was highlighted by the government as the standard that all other officers of his profession should seek to attain.

One of his uncles was Sir Robert Torrens whose likewise diligent application to his endeavours was instrumental in introducing an efficient system of land title, Torrens title. In the early days of settlement in South Australia tens of thousands of land grants were dispersed and such was the quick and wayward nature of that largesse, the vast majority of them ended up worthless, in accord with the old Latin quotation *Nemo dat quod non habet* or *No one gives what he does not have*. Sir Robert instituted a replacement for the accepted method of recording land transfers that hitherto were conducted by way of a paper trail. He was successful in having his relatively straightforward system of land ownership validated by being recorded onto a register and guaranteed by the state government. Torrens title is now used extensively in many countries. He built a substantial home, *Torrens Park* in the upmarket Adelaide suburb of Mitcham and today that constitutes the well-known Scotch College School which occupies 20 hectares. The annual Sir Robert Torrens Award honours the man by being awarded to the person whose contribution in the South Australian real estate field most raises the reputation of the industry.

In 1885, the fourteen men issued 16,000 shares in their business, now to be known as the Broken Hill Proprietary Company Limited (BHP). Whilst 14,000 shares were spread amongst the men according to their percentage and numerical holding, only 2,000 shares were available to the public. Five hundred shares were distributed to each of Sydney, Melbourne, Adelaide and nearby Silverton. As Silverton had been appropriately named after the local silver strike in 1875 there were many people who knew the characteristics and workings of silver bearing country and they readily took up the shares, even though they were issued at the high price of £9 each. Sydney and Melbourne residents were much more hesitant to act.

The NSW Government had earlier prevented South Australia from extending its railway line across the border but after the NSW Minister for Mines inferred a line could be built by private enterprise that is what occurred and progress was quickly made. Over the succeeding years the prices of lead, silver and zinc varied for a variety of reasons but then World War One boosted demand when Britain bought the entire zinc output until 1930.

From the first 48 tons of ore sent from Broken Hill to the smelter came an unbelievable 35,600 ounces of silver. However it wasn't always that easy and as time went by the miners required specific knowledge of processing the ore and extracting the zinc, lead and silver by magnetic separation, distillation and electrolytic means. Before any of those methods came into play the miners had to reach the ore. Many years ago Janice and I went out to Broken Hill and then on to Silverton. We were shown some of the original homes that the Silverton miners lived in. They were built of local rock and stone and consisted of one room of three rock walls with the fourth side open to the elements. It was just big enough for a man to lie down and the roof consisted of two or perhaps three sheets of iron with rocks placed on it to hold it down. A dog in a hollowed-out tree trunk for its kennel lives better.

We were stunned to discover how narrow were the early tunnels, dug out by men using hand tools. Many of the miners succumbed to lung problems from constantly breathing in the regular swirling dust of the area which was given its name *The Barrier* by the explorer Charles Sturt after he found his way was blocked by what he initially named *The Barrier Ranges*. When the miners went underground the lack of ventilation caused them to incur more severe breathing problems via forms of silicosis. When they returned to their Silverton rock houses after a long day inhaling those deadly particles, they found they could not sleep lying down as their lungs were so contaminated they coughed all night. The only way they could eventually gain some relief was to sit against the interior wall of their dwelling with their back upright and hope that tiredness would induce sleep. Many of them came from Cornwall where they had been tin miners. The tunnels are as narrow as a man's body but cut to the same height and whilst they lacked little in the way of intestinal fortitude those men were short of stature. The brave miners had another issue to deal with and hopefully overcome, the perennial problem of water. For some time their water supply, for which they paid one shilling per bucket, a monstrous price, was brought in from the Mingary tank, a journey of 73 km. Remote Mingary only existed because it was noticed that just a little rain thereabouts sent vast volumes of water down its creek which was then dammed. It was good clean water but when it reached and mixed with Silverton's refuse it became dirty or contaminated water and the population suffered from typhoid as happened in 1884. That year half of Silverton's population went down with the typhoid and although there was a local doctor the busiest man in the town was 'Bob the Finisher', the undertaker.

Mary Gilmore, famed author, journalist and patriot and later to be Dame Mary Gilmore, arrived in Silverton in 1887 and was an assistant at the Silverton Public School until December, 1889. She then moved to Sydney's Neutral Bay and began a close relationship with Australia's greatest writer of short stories and more, a young Henry Lawson, one that extended from 1890 to 1895. Henry was two years younger than Mary and while he died at age fifty-five, she lived for ninety-seven years. The Australian ten-dollar paper banknote features Henry Lawson and intriguingly the more recent polymer ten-dollar banknote has Banjo Patterson on the obverse side, joined by Mary Gilmore on the reverse.

The Broken Hill Library has a fabulous, dark, but intriguing photo, taken in 1885, of ten men working on the top of that broken hill. They are digging out an air shaft and above them, suspended from a tripod, is a sail to deflect wind in to the shaft. They later dug tunnels from the other side of the broken hill into the hill itself, in order to ensure air reached the men in the working shafts. As in much of rural Australia the area suffered greatly from a lack of water, let alone safe water, and it was 1952 before a consistent supply via a pipeline from Menindee was in place.

To reveal a brief but first-hand picture of life at Broken Hill I shall quote relevant extracts by Mr. Edmund Harral who was engaged by *Pictorial Australian* newspaper for an assignment to Broken Hill. He afterwards wrote of what he found out there, on 2nd February, 1888:

At last I have an opportunity of narrating the varied experiences of my trip to the Broken Hill Silver Mines. The occasion of our visit was the completion and opening of traffic of the railway from Adelaide to the mining district. This now world-famous silver field is in New South Wales several miles over the border, but being so much easier of access from our capital than Sydney, it is really looked upon as a South Australian undertaking and principally worked with South Australian money. It is only two years since operations were commenced here and now 60,000 ounces of silver are turned out per week. Dividends amounting to £225,000 have already been paid.

Around this mine have sprung up many others. Some may prove good but many profitless. No doubt, however the mining fever is so great here now that shares in everything are rising tremendously. Investors and brokers are making fabulous sums of money, some even £10,000 pounds per week. The reaction will come sooner or later but those who have their money in the two or three original mines have not much cause for fear, as their prospects are brilliant, to buy at present prices is absurd.

One street in Adelaide is a scene of great excitement every day, hundreds of people representing all classes of the community buying and selling shares. The remainder of the day I spent in sketching and never shall I forget the trying ordeal through which we had to pass. Imagine a place completely burnt up, not a green leaf or blade of grass, not a particle of shelter, and the heat of the sun about 170 degrees (F). Add to this dust such as I have never experienced. Must tell you the ground was so terribly hot that all the time I had to keep picking my feet up, for it felt like standing on hot coals. The township itself would present a novel appearance to an English eye but it is without exception the vilest place I ever saw. The habitations are principally wood or iron and a good number reside under canvas. I should dread spending a night in Broken Hill for the rough element strongly predominates and was told as the night wore on, it was pandemonium. They make plenty of money, the miners, and spend it on living. Since writing about those shares they have risen from £320 to £380.

Precisely four days earlier, on 30th January, 1888, the *Sydney Morning Herald* reported the following numbers of livestock held on various stations in the Wilcannia district; *Morden* 117 horses, 44 cattle and 85,000 sheep; *Wonnaminta* 250 horses, 15 cattle and 66,568 sheep; *Nuntherungie* eighty horses, 40 cattle and 7,500 sheep, *Nundora* 100 horses, 600 cattle and 70,615 sheep, *Momba* and *Mt Murchison* 425 horses, 200 cattle and 387,834 sheep. Going due north from *Mt Gipps Station*, the next stations are *Poolmacca*, owned by Robert Kennedy's sister Caroline and her husband John Brougham, *Corona*, later owned by Kidman and then *Nundora*, Robert Kennedy junior, and *Wonnaminta*, Robert Kennedy senior, placing the Kennedy family incredibly close to that massive BHP wealth. Caroline and John were to lose four young children from diphtheria in one tragic week.

After years of not making an offer, Kidman finally rounded up the love of his life and made his bid for Bel (Isabel). They were married in 1884 in the Congregational Church in Kapunda. Bel was a good-looking young woman, certainly well-educated and indeed respected in Kapunda and highly regarded in her teaching profession and her church. In those days men invariably established themselves financially before committing to support a woman in matrimony and Kidman was now well and truly in that league. As with most marriages there was something that seems to have taken him by surprise. He did not have a house. He was twenty-eight years of age and had lived less than half his life in a house. As he said, 'I never knew what it was to be in a house until I married. I was more used to sleeping black fellow style with a fire at my head and feet and one on each side of me.'

An Aborigine naturally proclaimed the blackfellow's fire is the best. It is very small, permitting him to lie close to it all night and to enjoy an even temperature. He added, 'White pfeller big fool. Him make um big fire, can't get close. By'n' bye fire go down an' white man catch um cold. No sense 'bout that.'

As a house was a priority for Bel he gave her the best one possible. *Bald Hill*, Kapunda, was their first home. It was a Victorian bluestone, a large family home but not a grand mansion. Photos show a well-constructed attractive, brick house with a turreted entrance area and sweeping views from its high ground. It would have set the man back a few pounds. In their fifteen years at *Bald Hill*, Bel produced four daughters while four of Kidman's brothers threw nineteen sons, plus a fair share of daughters. Finally Bel had a son but sadly the boy died at sixteen months. Bel was thirty-eight when she did produce Walter Sidney Palethorpe Kidman and rarely was a baby boy more carefully cared for. When interviewed in 1935 and queried on his cattle trading, Kidman was asked: 'What was the greatest deal you ever made?' He didn't hesitate to answer, his eyes aglow, 'My wife. She's been my mate for fifty years.'

11
Cobb and Co. and first car Adelaide to Darwin

From July, 1853, beginning with the short run from Melbourne to Port Melbourne, to the running of the last coach from Yeulba to Surat in Queensland in 1924, Cobb and Co. was the premier transport service in Australia. The company was established by four Americans who were well versed in that mode of travel in their homeland. Freeman Cobb is the best known but his companions, John Murray Peck, James Swanton and John Lambour were essential to the overall success of the company.

In January, 1852, fifty-seven ships had arrived in Melbourne and 500 crewmen, three men in every five, deserted and fled for the goldfields. Ships carried from 65 to 265 passengers and many came from California, chasing the new and much bigger Australian goldfields. When a large quantity of gold was reported as being found on the headwaters of the Amazon in Peru, three-quarters of the Americans in Melbourne headed off there. The only beneficiaries of that large scale and hurried movement were the shipowners, in what was known as the Peruvian Swindle. By 1853 immigrants had arrived not only with feverish hope but also scarlet fever and aggressive measles, not previously present.

When the first of them landed, Melbourne was a solid brick town. The south bank of the Yarra River was soon covered by so many tents it was known as Canvas Town as additional accommodation was not available for itinerant butchers, bootmakers, shopkeepers, barbers, prostitutes and sailmakers. Some newcomers slept in the street on a plank where more than one mother bore her child. There was no railway, telegraph system, gas, waterworks or sawmills. People could only buy water from a monopoly company which filled barrels at exorbitant prices from the Yarra River into which the sewage drained. Water had to be boiled. Men cooked their meals, such as they were, on a shovel. The roads were dirt tracks and in the middle of winter, wagons sank axle deep into the mud. Respectable women were hard to find. The best paid jobs were for bootmakers, coach and carriage makers, painters, wheelwrights, trimmers and saddlers. They commanded double wages or more.

London-born Charles Brown Fisher had arrived in Adelaide on the good ship HMS *Buffalo* and by 1851 he had just begun buying all the cattle he could when, fortuitously for him, the Victorian gold rush began. Mr. Fisher quickly moved all his cattle to Victoria as the price of a fat bullock rose quite remarkably from £2.50 to between £15 and £17 pounds. He later bought the prized *Bundaleer Station*, in South Australia, and for some time was the largest pastoralist in Australia. Renowned for buying the best livestock of whatever category he went into, his great love in cattle were Shorthorns, a sentiment my wife, Janice, and I fully shared for thirty-seven years on our Dubbo farm. Interestingly, Kidman's preferred cattle were Herefords for droving long distances and Shorthorns for short distances.

Coaches provided a quick way of arriving on the goldfields but it was expensive. That didn't stop the coaches invariably travelling with a full load of passengers, freight and mail. People were charged a staggering £10 from Geelong to Ballarat for the 87 km. The fare for the 150-km trip from Melbourne to Bendigo was £7, the price of four weeks wages for most. But the bookings were full as police were scarce and bushrangers plentiful. Although bushrangers might attempt a hold-up of a coach, it had drivers who could fight back and were armed accordingly. Not only did they have to be good drivers but they were required to be sober. There were passengers seeking gold who would stand up for themselves, especially in numbers while those who could not afford protection had no option but to travel on foot. They were far more likely to be robbed and even if they evaded the villains of the road they had to acknowledge that by being a latecomer to the gold fields, the easy pickings could be gone. At Ballarat the numbers went up to 47,000 miners.

From 1850 to 1860, the colony's numbers grew from 76,000 to over 500,000. Men paid heavily to be aboard a good coach and there were none better than the Concord. American Concord coaches were imported by Cobb and Co. It was much the same with the horses as Cobb and Co. initially brought in American horses, thoroughbred trotters. Unlike the heavy framed English coaches with steel springs, the American variety were of a lighter, rounder build, of hickory and ash, that rested on leather straps made from the hide of the American bison; sad to say in a way, as, Shorthorns aside, that is my favourite land animal. This created a smoother ride for the passengers as did the wider axles which were placed well outside the body of the coach so as to prevent it tipping over at speed on the corners. Cobb and Co. had another innovation, of staging posts, on average every 20 km, so fresh horses were always ready to go and could maintain a fast non-stop pace.

The American drivers were superb at their craft and initially were superior to their Australian counterparts, due to their stagecoach handling experience. However, the Australians were also good with horses and as they were employed and as they plied their trade they learned to be on a par with the Americans. Each driver could select his preferred horses and expect them to be ready and waiting for him at the next stop and, knowing that he could then go all out, he gave many passengers the ride of their lives. Accordingly the better, efficient and more reliable drivers, known Australia-wide as whips, became household names with their ability to control either six or eight horses in a team, using only four reins; perhaps they were the forerunners of today's sports stars.

Possibly for showmanship and publicity, Cobb ensured that over short distances his drivers did have horses of the same colour, as in a team of bays, blacks, chestnuts, greys, roans or even white horses. Over the major and longer distances the drivers had access to the best of stayers for their stamina and endurance, of any colour. He paid his whips £8 a week and later it escalated to £14 per week, plus they were 'found', i.e. with their meals and accommodation provided, such was the value of mail and passengers. Using a 12-foot thong on a whip, ex Wells Fargo stagecoach drivers could cut a cigarette from a man's mouth without touching his nose.

An English gentleman once shared a red Cobb and Co. coach with an American gold prospector in Australia. He afterwards wrote of the experience: *He was a coarse, hideous, dirty-looking man, without an attempt or even neatness* in his dress: yet he wore in his ears a pair of earrings about the size and shape of a wedding ring. He wore a pair of pistols in his belt and the words 'put a bullet through his brain' were continually in his mouth.

The biggest hazard for drivers and passengers was not bushrangers but bushfires. Fire can travel as fast as a galloping horse and I know that. I have seen a bushfire in the Blue Mountains outrun a fire truck that was racing alongside it on a dirt track, endeavouring to get ahead of the fire. In the 1850s little land was cleared and eucalypts, which no European had seen until the end of the 18th century, burn their oil fiercely, particularly in summer. The horses would become unmanageable amongst the blazing trees.

Bushrangers were still a problem and part of their vernacular arose from the first horned cattle to arrive in the colony, as brought onto the *Guardian* when Andrew Hume helped load them aboard in Cape Town. Those large-boned and heavy African beasts were harder to handle than the conventional British breeds, especially when it came to milking them. It wasn't enough to drive the cow into the bail and tie her nearside rear leg back to a post. They invariably had to be cajoled, even talked into such submission. So as to render the cattle pliable forever and a day to the exercise the man or woman doing the milking would command the cow to 'bail up'. In similar fashion bullock drivers when yoking up their teams would call out to the animals to 'bail up'. As with certain words of today the expression caught on right around the country, and before long, bushrangers were demanding that their intended victims in a stagecoach, (walking or riding along the roads, operating their store or other business), needed to 'bail up' in the sense of stand to order or surrender.

Another bushranger quirk was to rob their target and then tell the people not to move for half an hour, while the nefarious made their escape. The victims must remain where they were and not raise the alarm. It seems nearly everyone obeyed that directive but those who did decline to comply were tied to a tree and left there. Problems arose when the villains tied men to a tree well away from the road or building. In some instances they were not found in time and died of starvation and thirst.

Surprisingly Freeman Cobb sold out after just three years but for a reported £16,000, a fabulous sum of money at that time. Australian interests bought in and the business continued to flourish. By the beginning of the 1870s, Cobb and Co.'s 6,000 horses were covering up to 448,000 km every week through New South Wales, Victoria and Queensland. Such transport developed and opened up vast regions of Australia and no one noticed this more than Kidman.

Kidman and his brother Sack ran their stock-dealing operation at Silverton, which, while it is still 25 km north-west of Broken Hill, has seen its population decrease from a once thriving 3,000 residents to today's fifty. As it is so close to Broken Hill, when the mines started operations there and people moved to the much bigger town they often took their Silverton house with them. Most things were simpler in those days. Kidman was the man out in the bush, securing suitable sheep and cattle for Sack and his men to process and sell as meat to the mining community. All the while Kidman was buying working horses to sell in Adelaide and noticing what Cobb and Co. was doing. He thought there was room for him.

Kidman went into partnership with a man who had been one of Cobb and Co.'s best drivers, Jimmy Nicholas of Wagga Wagga. The two men built up a strong network of mail delivery runs. They did business in all states bar Victoria and were strong in New South Wales and in Western Australia, where Kidman's brother partnered Nicholas. They became big enough to stay on the road against Cobb and Co. and were its strongest opposition. Whilst there are different opinions of Kidman, Nicholas said: *Regards Sid Kidman, I don't think Australia has seen many men as smart as he was. We were young fellows together and great pals. He was one of the nicest men you could ever meet. He was a great horseman and would ride or drive anything and was probably Australia's best judge of a bullock. He could hop off the top rail of any yard onto any bullock, ride him around, slip off him onto the top rail well before the bullock knew what had happened. He would buy and sell anything from a penknife to a station and one deal did not disturb him a bit more than another. He is one of Australia's supermen. I never saw him drink, swear or lose his temper. He could box, if necessary, as well as the best of them and was not a bad poker player but five bob rises were his limit. I think that he with those few different characteristics in his favour, and I think with my considerable knowledge, we should have been able to run a successful coaching enterprise.*

Nicholas and Kidman did just that, along with 1,400 horses, 40 coaches and 150 men. They rose through the ranks to be second only to Cobb and Co. Gold was found in the Pilbara of Western Australia (WA) and that was followed up by that colony's Murchison River in 1891 and Coolgardie the following year. Coaches were needed for goldfields such as Kalgoorlie, Coolgardie, Norseman, Lawlers, Menzies and Laverton to mention but a few.

Nicholas and Kidman bought out Cobb and Co. Limited in Western Australia and whilst their expenses were high owing to the lack of water in WA they prospered. Across all their transport, meat selling, cattle, sheep and horse trading, the Kidmans used Elder Smith as their banker and for their stock and station agency business, except in WA where they utilised the services of the Emmanuel brothers and John Forrest, explorer and WA Premier. Kidman bought the first of his cattle stations, *Owen Springs*, near Alice Springs, in 1886, and from then on required the services of the much larger Bank of NSW.

On the eastern goldfields of WA, the Nicholas and Kidman, Menzies–Kalgoorlie coach which could carry twenty passengers every day and twice a month it also carried from one-half of a ton of gold to one and a half tons of gold. The daughter of Jimmy Nicholas, Hope Margaret Nicholas, married Lang Hancock, the Western Australian iron ore magnate. Their daughter is Gina Rinehart, currently Australia's wealthiest person who has just bought the Kidman cattle empire. I imagine Kidman would be surprised but pleased to know how his legacy will continue on.

Kidman often travelled from Broken Hill on his stock buying and dealing runs and he liked to ride his coaches but rarely as a passenger. He would sit upfront and would usually take the reins in short bursts. Back in Kapunda, Kidman had bought a building in the main street, which just happens to be called Main Street. A large building, he divided it into two sections and rented one half to Mills's father-in-law, John Mullen, and his saddlery business, and the other half to the Bank of New South Wales. It is still named the Kidman Building.

Next door, on the corner of Main and Franklin Streets, is the North Kapunda Hotel. At the rear of the hotel was where Kidman held his regular horse sales.

The North Kapunda Hotel was opened on 7th November, 1849, and is still going strong. From its verandah the Riot Act was read in Australia for the first time. The Act was introduced in 1715 due to civil disturbance and riots in England during 1714 and 1715. It stated that any group of more than twelve people who were engaging in unlawful or riotous behaviour could be ordered to disperse. If they failed to disperse within one hour, any one of the group who remained gathered was guilty of a felony punishable by death. A point of effective law was that the precise words of the Act had to be proclaimed aloud. The Riot Act still exists but in Australia it was significantly amended in 2007.

Kapunda is derived from two Aboriginal words, *cappie* and *oonda* and translates as a spring. The Great Kapunda copper mine was the first successful metal mine in Australia and together with the copper mine at nearby Burra, saved the infant colony cum state of South Australia from an economic crisis in the 1840s. The Great Kapunda copper mine became operational on 8th January, 1843, and went on to produce 14,000 tons of copper. Most of the ore was high-grade but to process the low-grade ore required dissolution in hydrochloric acid. The miners were very adept at using the ore body itself to do this. They manufactured sulphuric acid by burning pyrites, one of the mine's gangue minerals. Gangues are simply valueless material such as sand, rock or other in the ore deposit. In this case the gangues were the pyrites, a shiny yellow mineral that is a compound of iron and sulphur. The miners then blended the resultant sulphuric acid with common salt to produce hydrochloric acid.

At its peak, in 1861, the Great Kapunda Copper Mine employed 338 men and boys. The first company housing in Australia was provided for the mine's employees and miners, on the average wage for copper miners of £1/10/0 a week. They paid 10 shillings a week for their family housing. Those are interesting figures as they seem proportionate to housing costs/wages today of about 30 per cent. Hawke's Foundry in Kapunda was founded in 1857 and by the 1890s had sixty men producing mining equipment for Broken Hill. The Foundry closed in 1984, after 127 years of manufacturing work.

The Aborigines shown herein who permitted the anthropologists Baldwin Spencer and Francis Gillen to take their photographs gave their approval and cooperation. In the book, 'The Photographs of Baldwin Spencer', the Preface clearly states that: *there are no images of the Aboriginal secret rituals, religious objects or sacred ceremonies. The images presented here were selected in consultation with some of the descendants of the people Spencer photographed. Although activities of a secret nature were omitted at their request, a stunning imagery depicting Aboriginal secular life and culture is reproduced for all to appreciate and enjoy.*

Dancing entrance of another tribe as they ask for permission to enter the land of the Arrernte people 09/05/1901.

Women throwing fire at Illpongwurra, Engwura.

Running man, Alice Springs, 1896.

Alice Springs corroboree, 1901.

Four dancers in the Tjitingalla corroboree, wearing white cockatoo feathers, April, 1901.

Arrernte women dancers, Alice Springs, 1901.

*Man releasing woman from the ban of silence,
Warumungu, Tennant Creek, 1901*

Emu man at corroboree of the Arrernte, Alice Springs, 1896.

Arrernte men, Alice Springs, April, 1901.

Returning avenging party.

Initiation process, known as thaamba, the knocking out of a tooth.

Arrernte Erkita corroboree.

Arrernte men preparing for a corroboree.

Men gathering at Alice Springs, 1901.

Arrernte rain ceremony.

The above photographs are courtesy of the Victoria Museum, Melbourne.

The oldest Australian Rules Football club in South Australia still playing under its original name is the Kapunda Football Club, which was created in 1866. If one happens to be a lawn bowler you might like to know that the first game of lawn bowls in South Australia was played at Andrew Thomson's private green in Kapunda in 1876.

The railway reached Kapunda in 1860 and to give an idea of the times, that resulted in not one but two hotels being instantly constructed, one at each of the two gates leading into and out of the railway station. In the latter half of the 19th century the railway opened up much of rural Australia.

There was a marble quarry in Kapunda and many quarries from which came the stone that endowed the town with its substantial stone houses, most of which were enhanced by wrought iron or lace work. It truly was and still is a lovely town. I find it quite remarkable that it resides in a pristine part of South Australia, retains its glorious rural characteristics and has not been overrun by an avalanche of new residents while being no more than 80 kilometres from the beautiful capital city of Adelaide.

The North Kapunda Hotel has a reputation for being Australia's most haunted hotel. There is much talk of prostitutes, suicides and murders being associated with the hotel but I take that as hearsay as I have heard little to confirm those matters. However there is support from too many people for the following to be easily dismissed.

A great number of people have encountered two young girls, both named and one aged fifteen, who haunt the upstairs former accommodation areas. More have been frightened by the appearance of an aggressive looking man in black clothing and wearing a wide-brimmed hat. A former maid has several times been sighted as an apparition by the front desk and an indigenous man who was murdered in a revenge killing because he broke a hotel window also haunts the establishment. Another man died when he was crushed to death by a bale of hay in the hotel courtyard and he still makes his presence known while the heavy doors of the gaming room are well known for opening by themselves. The person of most interest to myself is Matthew Henry Smyth Blood who when alive was known by one and all as Dr. Blood. He was said to perform strange experiments on people.

I tended to take that with a grain of salt until I discovered he certainly existed. The foundation stone of the Anglican Christ Church of Kapunda, which I entered to check on the marriage of Mills and his wife, Mary Jane Mullen, was laid in April, 1856, by Dr. M.H.S. Blood. Not only that but the Corporation of the Town of Kapunda was proclaimed in 1865 and Dr. Blood was no less than the first mayor of Kapunda. He also haunts the North Kapunda Hotel. Tours are conducted of the premises by those who are interested if not fascinated by these spiritual beings.

Apart from the Kapunda residents, John Mullen, Sidney Kidman, William Mills, James Poole and David James there is another of particular interest, leastways to myself. His name was John Hill and he was the Bosun on HMS *Buffalo*, a ship built at the Sulkea shipyard in Calcutta, India, in 1813. She was bought by the Lords Commissioners of the Admiralty and initially used by the Royal Navy before being utilised as a store ship. In 1833, she was fitted out as a convict ship before being recommissioned in 1835. In December 1836 HMS *Buffalo* arrived in Adelaide, not with convicts but 176 colonists, including Captain John Hindmarsh who was about to become the first Governor of South Australia on Proclamation Day, when the province would be granted its own government, on 28 December, 1836. The Proclamation was drafted aboard HMS *Buffalo* and read out while the flag of South Australia was raised, for the first time, anywhere, on board HMS *Buffalo*. The man who raised the flag was John Hill, the ship's Bosun but otherwise another resident of Kapunda.

That year HMS *Buffalo* sailed through Investigator Straits as Aboriginal smoke was first raised on Yorke Peninsula and then in quick succession at Cape Jervis, Peeralilla, O'Halloran Hill, Mount Lofty, Barossa and northwards to the bounds of one's vision. The Aborigines' smoke signals were letting others know what was coming their way.

In 1837 the ship sailed to Quebec, Canada, with 300 British soldiers, reinforcements for the British military dealing with the Rebellions in Lower and Upper Canada. In 1839 HMS *Buffalo* departed Quebec with eighty-two American patriots, men who had tried to liberate Upper Canada from British rule. They had been taken prisoner along with fifty-eight French convicts who had also participated in the Canada Rebellion. During the voyage the Americans and the French conspired to murder the ship's crew but they were overcome. The Americans were taken to Van Diemen's Land, of which it was said, 'Alas, there is no road from Van Diemen's Land to heaven, while a thousand lead downward to the regions of eternal death.' The Americans seem to have avoided the dreaded Port Arthur penal colony, where the main method of rehabilitation was to lock up prisoners in mind-destroying isolation. Instead they were placed at Battery Point, Hobart, which was named for the great array of guns along the shore. The Hollywood film star, Errol Flynn, renowned for his action-packed swashbuckling roles, drinking and womanising would be born at Battery Point. I sometimes recall his personal observation, 'My problem has been in reconciling my gross habits with my nett income.' It is perhaps of some interest that his only film role in Australia was *In the wake of the Bounty*.

Errol Flynn's mother came from seafaring stock and one of her ancestors was Midshipman Ned Young, who sailed with Captain Bligh on the *Bounty*. Ned was the only sailor on the ship to sleep through the mutiny, in real life, not the film. When he woke he had to decide to join the mutineers or stay loyal to Captain Bligh. As Ned was Fletcher Christian's chief aide he sided with Christian and the other mutineers. In doing so he obtained Captain Bligh's sword, which may account for the fact that a painting of the mutiny portrays a mutineer throwing another sword to Captain Bligh as he stands, without weapons, in the longboat.

Mutiny need never have taken place on the *Bounty* if not for a collusion of circumstances. British naval ships carried a detachment of Royal Marines whose duties were two-fold. They ensured the security of the ships' officers and the maintenance of discipline in the crew and in battle they engaged the enemy.

On 14 February, 1779, Captain James Cook went ashore in Hawaii, accompanied by four Marines. He was attacked by natives and cruelly bludgeoned to death on a beach, while the Marines escaped. Captain Cook had earlier seen the qualities in William Bligh and honoured the young man by appointing him as his sailing master. Bligh witnessed his mentor's death and the horrific event may well have reinforced his strong attitude about discipline.

Bligh has been criticised for his pettiness, his weakness of finding fault in others and not being backward in letting them know. This was in an era when a man's honour was more important than his life but there was far more to him on the positive side. Five versions of the film *Mutiny on the Bounty* have been produced and four of them portray Bligh in a negative light, as a cruel man. Yet there are those who believe he became embroiled in the mutiny because he was too soft. In those days one of the most dreaded punishments a soldier in the British Army could suffer was to be transferred to the British Navy, where sailors were known to be lashed as many as 1,000 times, a limit imposed by King George 111. According to Scott Claver's *Under the Lash* individual captains designed their own instruments of torture to keep control of their crews. Men were press-ganged into the Navy and the nautical paymasters were misers. Nearly 10,000 Americans were pressed into the British Navy, contributing to the War of 1812.

In his seventeen months in command of the *Bounty*, Captain Bligh ordered eleven floggings for a total of 229 lashes while Captain Cook, albeit with a bigger crew, ordered one or two floggings per week.

In 1789, William Bligh was selected to take *HMS Bounty* to Tahiti to procure as much bread-fruit as could be taken on board and prepare it to go on to the West Indies to be grown as food for black slaves on sugar plantations. Such was the high priority awarded to the bread-fruit, Bligh was not given room for Marines, let alone other Naval officers to assist him in controlling the crew, half of whom later mutinied and returned to the good life in Tahiti.

To arrive at Tahiti Captain Bligh opted to go via South America's notorious Cape Horn after which he would be able to sail comfortably across the more placid Pacific Ocean. Sailing down the east coast of South America he came to Isla de los Estados, which in English we call Staten Island. The island is 29 km from the eastern extremity of Argentina's Tierra del Fuego. The *Bounty* passed between the two and entered the Le Maire Strait which put it on a direct course to Cape Horn, another 220 km to the south south-west.

According to the logbook of the *Bounty* the ship and the crew variously encountered heavy snow squalls, hail which was sharp and severe, freezing rain, fresh gales and sleet and rain with a very high confused sea, fresh gales with frequent squalls of hail and sleet, the sea broke over much of us, much lightning all around the compass, the sea from the frequent shifting of the wind is very irregular and breaking, etc, etc. On top of that the seas were reported of height and swell as never seen before, by any sailor.

I have sailed exactly the same course and can attest to the conditions for nothing on earth, or of the sea, has at times so terrified me as similar conditions in those waters. We sailed in the same manner by hauling on ropes and being without winches or other aids but our barquentine is a 500-tonne boat while the *Bounty* was but of 215 tonnes. Captain Bligh ensured his men were kept well fed and every day served boiled wheat with sugar and butter, soup and sauerkraut and other such sustenance. He wrote that *Laying to as before and a most heavy storm of wind, hail and snow. Obliged to be lashed with a rope to get my observations, and is the only way I can perform them*. On each watch he had two men who somehow maintained fires below deck to ensure not only warmth but that every man had dry clothing to hand. In addition Bligh ordered his *cabin to be appropriated at nights to the use of those poor fellows who had wet berths by which means it not only gave more room between decks but rendered those happy who had not dry beds to sleep in*. For twenty-nine days the tenacious and leaking *Bounty*, which had to be pumped out every hour, battled ferocious elements that have to be experienced to be believed but finally it was accepted that there was no way round Cape Horn. Sailors' Creed: Below 50 degrees south there is no law, below 60 degrees south there is no God. Captain Bligh then declared, *the wind not so violent I bore away for the Cape of Good Hope*. The sailors cheered but there was never a hint of mutiny. It was because of Tahiti with the good life, the short-sighted pleasures of life, that some men later mutinied, but not while they were being tested for their very existence.

William Bligh was a blend of characteristics, like all of us. He was a man of immense courage, one of the finest navigators in maritime history and a talented cartographer. His strong sense of duty was enhanced by his relentless energy and devotion to his career. His attributes as a seaman could have no higher endorsement than the responsibility bestowed upon him by Captain James Cook.

Appointed Governor of NSW in 1806 Bligh was harried by the powerful Rum Corps but admired by the settlers of the colony, whom he cared for. Tombstones in the Ebenezer and Richmond cemeteries of western Sydney reveal many boys born around 1807 to 1811 received the given names of William Bligh, as did William Bligh Turnbull, 08/06/1809, of Windsor. Young William would be the ancestor of Malcolm Bligh Turnbull, Prime Minister of Australia.

Ned Young eventually sailed to Pitcairn Island, where he died of asthma in 1790. Errol Flynn said the sword was kept in the family and handed down through the generations until it came to his mother. As a boy he played with the sword. He also recalled, 'A beach, Sandy Bay, was not far away and I was often there, swimming at the age of three. The beach was of hard, brown sand, the water was freezing cold. Mother was a good swimmer and she took me there often. I have never been out of ocean water for very long since.' Whilst some people dispute the following , Flynn also said, 'My father ultimately gave this souvenir to the Naval and Military Club at Hobart where it still hangs on the wall. I could have choked him for giving it away.' Nonetheless, the American prisoners were just in time to participate in building the second Prince of Wales Battery, built in 1840, and more of the wharf and associated buildings. Thirty years of convict labour were required to complete that work. While the guns were there for defensive measures they were also a deterrent to any convicts who might attempt to escape by stealing a ship, as thirteen of them once did. They sailed past the guns unnoticed but how much further they proceeded I do not know. Meanwhile the French, no doubt French-Canadians, were put to hard labour, helping to build Sydney's Parramatta Road by breaking stone and dragging it to the work site. In addition they cut woodblocks for paving Sydney streets. One French-Canadian later set himself up as a blacksmith at Irish Town, today known as Bass Hill, out on the Liverpool Road.

Some of the convicts died, married free or settler women in Australia or stayed in the colony after they were all eventually pardoned. Most of course returned to their homeland but it is interesting to learn that the first Americans to be prisoners in another country found that dubious honour in Australia. I had sometimes wondered how the Sydney suburb of Canada Bay derived its name but now I know, along with the small bays of Exile Bay and France Bay. If the British at the time had not been at war with the Americans it is vaguely possible they could have named HMS *Buffalo* as HMS *Bison*, as there are no buffalo in America. Those wonderful animals are bison. My wayward imagination suggests that in that case John Hill, of Kapunda, would have been the Bosun on the *Bison*. Yet another one-time resident of Kapunda was Richard Knuckey who went to school in Kapunda before joining Mills as another surveyor on the Overland Telegraph Line.

On the 18th March, 1879, a testimonial dinner was held at Host Hooper's Prince of Wales Hotel by the citizens of Kapunda to honour John Mullen. It has been stated more than once that he was respected in his community for the assistance he had always given others. Whilst we saw that he served in the Maori Wars it was noted that when the Crimean War broke out he joined the militia in Adelaide in 1854, specifically the No. 1 Artillery battery and was the second man enrolled. In a reply speech he said of his volunteering, 'namely, the protection of our land, for I hold it to be in such cases one of the noblest instincts in a man's nature to be a true patriot to the land of his birth, next to that the land of his adoption and above all that to the Sovereign of your native land.'

In appreciation and as a token of respect from the community, John Mullen was presented with a new Martini-Henry rifle. The first such rifle was produced in 1871 but it had cartridge ejection problems after too much use. This was rectified by three succeeding models over the next eight years so that when John Mullen received his gift it was an excellent rifle, as proven less than two months earlier, when the weapon was instrumental in 139 British soldiers holding off between 3,000 and 4,000 Zulu warriors at the battle of Rorke's Drift in South Africa. Over the ten hours of engagement they killed many hundreds of the attacking Zulus, and eleven of the British soldiers received the Victoria Cross. At that time the Victoria Cross was not awarded posthumously.

John Mullen did well in his saddlery and harness making enterprise and opened branches in Terowie and Yarcowie. Considering Kidman's coach business and his horse requirements it seems assured Kidman would have conducted considerable business with his tenant Mullen.

Inevitably, John Mullen passed away, on 19th June, 1890, and according to the *Kapunda Herald*, 'his employee for the last twenty-five years, Mr. Duncan Barron, has entered into the well-established Kapunda business of saddlery, harness, collar, coach trimming, etc, of the late Mr. John Mullen. It will be carried on under the same name and style and the workmanship and expedition which characterised the business of the late Mr. Mullen will be adhered to.' An historian sent me an index of Kapunda businesses for the year 1927 and it states that, 'J. Mullen, Saddler' was still trading.

Years later another saddler came to Kapunda, one by the name of Reg Williams, who had left school at age thirteen to go and live in the Australian bush, the land he truly loved. Legions of people would know him as R.M. Williams, whose company name and personal reputation live on. Back in his early days he needed money for his son's medical costs and he asked Kidman would he buy his products, saying, 'Some day a better pack-saddle will be made using a higher fork in the steel, a deeper side and rigged with double girths, instead of carrying breast plates and breeching. And the bags will have gussets for items that have to be carried upright.' Kidman answered, 'I will give you an opportunity.'

Kidman's first purchase from R.M. was a pack-saddle for which the cattleman paid £5. R.M. was on his way. He said, 'Kidman gave me a start making pack-saddles and that started me off.' Saddle bags cost ten shillings or half a pound. Regular saddles and other leather goods came to the fore as R.M. established his business on land his father owned in Percy Street, Adelaide.

Today the saddles are outsourced to be made by Marsh Carney in Scone, in the Hunter Valley of NSW, but the saddlebags are still produced in Adelaide, as are those wonderful R.M. Williams boots. R.M. made each boot from one piece of leather, with a single seam at the back of the boot. That system still applies. Today those boots continue to be hand crafted, passing through eighty sets of hands. Customers can have their boots made of leather from a variety of sources, such as Australian cowhide, ostrich, expensive but luxurious crocodile, bass and more to produce suede, water-resistant, patterned, heavyweight, chrome-tanned, dressed, oiled or other durable types. President Bill Clinton wore R.M.s at his inauguration. Hugh Jackman once owned 5 per cent of the company and nowadays iron ore magnate Andrew Forrest owns 100 per cent of the Australian icon company.

Are they expensive at many hundreds of dollars for regular dress boots? Yes and no. I bought a pair of tan dress boots in 1998 and they have aged better than I. In 2003 my daughter gave me a pair of black dress boots as a birthday present. With regular maintenance both pairs will probably outlive me. R.M. and fellow investors later took a chance and bought a run-down gold mine near Tennant Creek. The gamble paid off when they struck good gold. R.M. said, 'I used to stagger down the street to the bank with these bags of gold, a shotgun on each side, and thinking I was pretty important.'

He was once asked to keep his eyes open and buy ten coloured horses for Adelaide buyers and ten likely buckjumpers for the Marrabel Rodeo. He filled the order and trucked the horses to Kapunda. From there they were walked north to Marrabel, which is 43 km by road but across country 23 km.

One of the horses was destined to be famous as Curio, regarded by many as Australia's greatest buckjumper. You wouldn't have thought that likely when you first looked at the fourteen hands high roan mare bred from a draught horse stallion out of a small grey brumby mare.

Many rodeo riders attempted to make their name by getting on top of the mare, and staying there. Her favourite technique was the 'hat-trick'. To effect that manoeuvre she would drop her shoulder, twist around so severely that her rear end would be looking at the front of her turning head and then 'suck back'. This resulted in the rider being sent flying through the air within 2.1 seconds. It was eight years before she met her match when Alan Woods stayed with her for ten seconds. If you look at the photograph of her, with him way above her, it is surprising that he was able to regain the saddle. Curio did not retire for another eleven years and by then the crowds numbered up to 16,000 spectators.

Another man who did business in Kapunda was James Shaw. Like Mills's father-in-law he fought in the Maori Wars in New Zealand and was a member of the Kapunda Rifle Club. He is better known for his success as a builder, for amongst his many achievements are the Governor's residence and the substantial Hindmarsh School in Adelaide. He was invited by the NSW Government to attend the Centennial Banquet in Sydney on 26th January, 1888. His buildings were so admired that his tender for constructing Parliament House in Adelaide was not only accepted but on completion it was regarded as the most beautiful building in the southern hemisphere, replete with Kapunda marble. He became the Mayor of

Adelaide and over time people said he was the most popular mayor ever.

As were many people of the day, he was drawn to the Western Australian goldfields and with masses of others, he settled in Coolgardie, where he was soon managing director of the Londonderry gold mine and then the first Mayor of Coolgardie, amongst many honours. Mr. Shaw was a good man with not just business know-how but appreciation for his fellows.

I more or less stumbled upon Mr. Shaw, and a few days later, I came across an old photo of a car in Alice Springs. Why might that be of interest, I hope you ask? Well because there are two men sitting in the front seat of a British manufactured Talbot motor car and because Alice Springs is invariably of interest, as is Kapunda. In 1907, Mr. Harry Hampden Dutton, of Kapunda, of course, and Mr. Murray Aunger set off to be the first people to drive from Adelaide to Darwin. They had a 1907, 3.7 litre, 15 horsepower edition Talbot car which they named *Angelina* and it was fully prepared for the trip ahead. On 25 November, 1907, they left Adelaide from King William Street as the clock tolled 12 noon. *The Observer* reported that, 'Mr. Dutton took the seat at the steering pillar—'.

By Christmas they were near Barrow Creek and on their way to Tennant Creek when in the wet season they became so bogged that a pinion in the back axle broke. The spare had earlier been used and the men had to abandon the car. They covered it as best they could against the wet weather and apparently started walking back to Oodnadatta. Fortunately for them in the summer heat and humidity, a camel train supposedly came along and took them to Oodnadatta where they boarded a more conventional train back to Adelaide.

Determined to succeed, Mr. Dutton, who I believe was the grandson of Francis Stacker Dutton, the man we saw earlier who part owned the Great Kapunda copper mine and became the Premier of South Australia, bought himself a 1908 Talbot car to pursue his goal. Harry had attended Magdalen College, Oxford, and rowed in the bow against Cambridge. He was wealthy, being the twenty-eight-year old heir to a pastoral fortune and owned amongst other assets, *Anlaby Station*, which is one of the historic stations of South Australia.

Harry Dutton's great uncle, Frederick Dutton, brother to Francis Stacker

Dutton, took up the original 160,000 acres of *Anlaby Station*, which is just 19 kilometres from Kapunda and a mere 100 kilometres from Adelaide. It must have been so easy then. The place measured, in the old vernacular, 25 miles by 10 miles and so you have 250 square miles or 160,000 acres which in today's metric is 63,000 hectares. All you needed was the right someone to support your land application, old chap, in 1841. Good land of course, if not the very best still available. Land began as leasehold but one could transfer that to freehold, keeping only the very best, when later the government resumed such land for closer settlement, to wheat farmers and later to ex-servicemen. *Anlaby Station* consisted of a manor house for the family and cottages for the head gardener, the coachman and the kennel master. The grounds held a deer park while peacocks paraded in the many acres of formal gardens. The property was known for its good livestock and famous for its elaborate garden parties. There were enough talented staff to maintain both cricket and football teams.

In 1908, there were no more than 500 cars in South Australia and that may be why the number plate on the new Talbot was 474. The Model T Ford had not yet reached Australia. Murray Aunger had helped establish the Adelaide business of Lewis Motor Works, which supplied Talbot cars to mostly wealthy people, in the late 1890s, and he built the first car in South Australia, in 1900. Murray Aunger was regarded as a genius at anything mechanical. A keen cyclist, he held the South Australian one mile and the Australian 50 mile records.

Harry Dutton's 1908 Talbot had a lower axle ratio and its power was increased from 15 to 19 horse-power, giving it a recommended cruising speed of 70 kilometres per hour, which would be impossible to attain on this overland trip. Talbot cars were good but expensive. A factory refurbished chassis cost £450 and a car body £350, at a time when the average annual wage in Australia was £158.

Still and all it was an audacious attempt to drive to Darwin. In that era motorists faced horse-loving reactionaries, regressive law makers, overzealous police and the luddites of the day. The latter not only opposed new technology or industrialisation but in the early 19th century there had been workers, in England at any rate, who actively destroyed machinery.

English cars had no oil seals. That sounds too simple today but that's the way they were and so they blew out or dripped more oil than they actually used. They also consumed vast amounts of water. However the Talbot was equipped with a water pump which made it more suited to Australian conditions than most cars. In those days cars needed regular greasing, such as at the recommended rate of every 900 kilometres. The four-cylinder Talbot had a three-speed gearbox which fortunately included reverse gear. The footbrake worked off the transmission and the handbrake activated a contracting band on the rear wheels but there were no front brakes.

The Talbot weighed 1,280 kilograms but added to that were the two men, provisions for a week, kerosene lamp lights, a shovel, a mattock, an axe, block and tackle along with the survival kit, a set of spare tyres, vulcanising matters for making repairs, assorted spare parts, clothing and other necessities, modifications to carry the 385 litres of fuel and a rifle rack up high behind the heads of the two men who sat in the front seat without the windscreen. The Talbot then weighed two tonnes plus. Extra supplies of petrol and oil were sent ahead to Oodnadatta, Alice Springs, Katherine (then known as Catherine Creek) and Pine Creek. I don't know but I imagine camel trains were used to deliver those necessities for bush motoring.

The more immediate problem was not having a regular road, for a distance of 3,400 kilometres although the men reported no initial problems on the way to Hawker, in the heart of the Flinders Ranges. From there they often followed the Overland Telegraph Line and the horse track that ran beside it. When the men reached the sanctity of Alice Springs they told the *Melbourne Table Talk* magazine that the notorious Depot Sandhills, which ran for 40 kilometres between Horseshoe Bend and Alice Well, just a little to the north of Charlotte Waters and along the Finke River, 'are too much for any car without assistance.'

Assistance was certainly lacking as were roads, bridges, service stations and maps. What they did have were giant sand dunes, swollen creeks, dusty tracks, gigantic termite mounds, boulders, protruding mulga stumps, ant hills twice their height, long grass and bushfires. They used their water bottles as pillows and early on, at Burra, experienced so cold a winter night that their pillows froze. Dutton and Aunger were progressing carefully at Daly Waters, which is

400 km north of Tennant Creek and close to 600 km south of Darwin, when they were confronted by a raging bushfire and as they later recounted, 'We'd been going very slowly but that day was the fastest time we'd made as we were racing against the flames.'

When skirting Lake Eyre and going over sand prior to crossing waterways, the two men placed corduroys or mats on which to drive. That type of mat can be made of thin saplings about two metres long and lashed together for a length of four metres. They can then be rolled up and used again and again, however they may need to be kept moist to be flexible. Bamboo, if available, makes for excellent sand mats. The car was fitted with Michelin steel-studded, non-skidding tyres but on the heavier, higher sand dunes the men had to call on nearby stations for the use of their teams of mules to pull *Angelina* up and over the dunes. Stations bred mules to meet the demand from South Africa.

When they arrived at one of their unattended fuel dumps they discovered that the daytime temperature of 45 Celsius had caused the fuel and oil tins, left out in the open air, to generate so much pressure that the seams of the tins had sprung and much fuel was lost. At times they had to use the Spanish windlass to extricate themselves from being bogged. The bed of the Goyder River was loose, heavy sand which they found difficult to go through. When the car had to cross the 360-metre wide Finke River a telegraph line repairman told them it would never happen. They judiciously selected the most likely spot and raced the Talbot down the sloping river bank and hit the water at 32 kilometres per hour. Remarkably it never dropped below twenty as they ploughed on through the water to climb up the far bank. Dutton and Aunger rated that episode the best part of the trip.

At night they somehow slept in the car but when circumstances, such as being bogged, made that impossible, they slept on the ground. When it rained on them those nights were the worst part of the trip. The overall greatest discomfort came courtesy of the flies. The men had to tuck trousers into socks, tighten belts and on several occasions go without their meals, such was the saturation of the flies. During the day when in timbered or tropical country beetles and spiders dropped on them as they drove without a windscreen or roof. Along the way the two men witnessed a corroboree at Barrow Creek, ten Aboriginal women in mourning who had completely covered themselves with white pipe clay at Tennant Creek, a long, long camel train at the dry Bloods Creek and the mailman with five fully loaded camels delivering the mail at Horseshoe Bend and onto other outback stations. In Alice Springs they were joined by the Alice Springs telegraph station officer, Ern Allchurch who was a Justice of the Peace/magistrate. He was known for making commonsense decisions in surroundings and circumstance far removed from capital cities where the law was more likely to be played out by the book. He was almost unique on account of the understanding and the compassion he had for the Aboriginal way of life. He travelled with Dutton and Aunger to where they had left the 1907 Talbot the previous year and Murray Aunger set to work on it. The car's tyres were partly deflated and the vehicle was exposed to the tropic sun for seven months while it had also been swamped by 450 millimetres of rain but within a few hours Mr. Aunger had the first Talbot running.

They arrived in Darwin on 20th August, 1908. The journey had taken fifty-one days of which forty-one were taken up by driving and ten days given over to some form of recovery from their physical efforts of keeping the Talbot and themselves in working order. The car suffered only a few punctures and broken leaf springs and did the trip on the one set of tyres. Quite remarkable, I would suggest. Both men had lost considerable weight. In some quarters, their feat has been lauded as the motoring equivalent of the epic Burke and Wills venture, to open up the way north.

Back home the car was used as a farm vehicle for years and was driven into Kapunda each day on a mail run. In 1959, Harry's sons drove it once more from Adelaide to Darwin and in 2008 it accompanied a centenary drive back to Darwin. It arrived there on the 20th August, 2008, one hundred years to the day after its first coming of age. These days the Talbot is in the National Motor Museum, Australia's largest with over 400 great cars, at Birdwood in the Adelaide Hills of SA. The town of Birdwood was formerly called Blumberg, a German name, and like many such others in World War One, Blumberg was Anglicised and became known as Birdwood, after the famous Australian general who commanded the ANZAC soldiers. The old girl is still driveable, by the lucky few. By 1913, a few cars around the world had reached speeds of 100 miles (160 kilometres) per hour but till then no car had covered 100 miles in an hour. The first to do so, was a Talbot.

When T.E. Lawrence of Arabia was exhorting Arab forces to fight the Ottoman Empire and its German allies in desert warfare his favourite vehicle, if not weapon, was the Rolls-Royce armoured car. Lawrence had nine of the armoured cars with their Silver Ghost chassis and engines. He then heard about the qualities of the Talbot and ordered six of them to join his desert forces. Lawrence had the body strengthened and the rear of each Talbot was a tray, like a utility and it held a ten-pound gun, more like a cannon. At the front, protruding over the bonnet and operated from the front seat was a Vickers machine gun. The ten pounders were normally off-loaded and fired from ground level but it was found that due to the strengthening the gun could be fired from the tray. The ten pounder's lack of a recoil system then caused the Talbot chassis to visibly bend but every time it was fired it sprang back into place, perfectly. Lawrence enjoyed his mobile artillery. In World War One Talbot sold large numbers of their tough vehicles to Russia, to fight Germany in 1915 and Austria-Hungary in 1916. Instead of paying England for the military Talbots, the Russians sent much needed grain crops. This scheme continued until the Russian Revolution began in October, 1917.

By chance, I suppose, Harry Dutton bought *Corona Station*, in 1910. It was stocked with 60,000 sheep, 280 cattle and 190 horses. That property is situated 74 km north of Broken Hill and in its northern reaches is what is today known as the *Fowler's Gap Research Station*. A similar distance further north is *Wonnaminta Station*, my great-great grandfather, Robert Kennedy's place. Kidman had bought *Wonnaminta* and seven years after buying *Corona Station*, Harry Dutton, of Kapunda, sold it to Sidney Kidman, of Kapunda. Kidman said *Corona Station* was his best property in NSW, perhaps in part due to being well-watered by two good creeks.

12

Aboriginal Maps and Outback Water

There was an even more remarkable coincidence. On the same day, 20th August, 1908, that Talbot 474 arrived in Darwin and became for all time the first car to cross Australia and at the same hour, one of the most powerful navies in the world was sailing into Sydney Harbour, for the first time. Sydney had a population of 600,000 people and well over 250,000 of them turned out to welcome the sixteen battleships of the American Atlantic Fleet. Some reports of the day quoted many more people than that number but I will stay with the conservative figure. It was a monumental moment in the city's life and the largest gathering in the new country. Seven years earlier Federation of the nation had not stirred and galvanised the citizens to anything like the extent that these foreigners did.

They were foreign only in a word accompanied by an accent. Britain had a squadron of ships in Sydney that was meant to provide security for Australia should it be attacked but with the exception of *HMS Powerful* the very ordinary class of ships clearly failed to give reassurance about the perceived threat of Japan, which in 1905 had totally destroyed the entire Russian fleet and proven itself a world power, a power on the prowl. Australia paid England £200,000 annually for this so-called protection and, from the Prime Minister down, the people felt it was money wasted. Now, three years later the American visit excited and possibly overwhelmed the locals, who gave the visitors such a welcome in Sydney, Melbourne and Albany that more than a few of them stayed behind. The American Navy was on a fourteen-month, 75,000 km circumnavigation of the world and of all the ports it called into it was said that none of them exceeded the warmth of welcome that was so willingly given in Australia.

The American warships were painted white, to represent peace, and thus were known around the world as the White Fleet. The American Navy had arrived and observers had to accept that American warships could proceed through one ocean as much as they would another. Nonetheless the vast majority of Australians endorsed the American way in line with the then official Anglo-Saxon White Australia policy.

Prime Minister Deakin had gone against established British protocol by directly asking America's President Theodore Roosevelt for the visit and that action upset the British Admiralty and the Foreign Office. For his part President Roosevelt had organised the worldwide naval tour to show that America had arrived as a new force, the more so by bringing the American Atlantic Fleet into the Pacific, especially in the face of Japan. He didn't hesitate to support the Australian request and the resultant government and strong public interest went a long way to creating the establishment of the Australian Navy, which was celebrated by its entry into Sydney Harbour for the first time in 1913. In 2013, our navy celebrated its centenary with a re-enactment and at the time I was fortunate to be sailing on the three-masted Dutch barquentine *Europa*, which itself was then 102 years old. We were invited to join the celebrations and sailed from Hobart and through the Sydney Heads along with ships from around the world, precisely 100 years after the Australian Navy did so for the first time.

Before we return to the main story there was another car of interest. In 1909, the cattle king, Kidman, had been in England where he bought a new Thornycroft car. However by the time it arrived and was registered for use in Australia it was August, 1910. Whilst Kidman gave it his all he did quite a bit of damage to the car on what passed for roads in those day. He was used to riding horses or travelling by coach, both of which allowed him time to look around at the countryside and at the livestock. He discovered it took far more concentration to keep the vehicle going in a straight line and the following year he gave it to his daughter, as a wedding present. Neither was she short of a quid, travelling as she did, to England to buy her trousseau. She married a New Zealander.

In 1913, Kidman departed Kapunda for Adelaide and from there took the train to Melbourne and then another to Sydney, where he headed off to the Homebush livestock saleyards. Homebush was then the major selling centre in NSW and when I sold a few livestock there in the 1960s it still was but not for much longer. By then its odours were permeating the new and surrounding Sydney suburbs and it was closed down. That move enabled the rural saleyards to rise to prominence and it made good sense getting out of Sydney. It suited buyers and sellers, transport companies, speculators and dealers, owners, auctioneers, abattoirs and stock and station agents to operate across the state where since World War Two there had been a wool boom, increasing livestock numbers and a growing economy. There was an exception in 1960 when the Australian Treasurer, Harold Holt, declared that interest on borrowing would not be tax deductible and, as I recall, there was a credit squeeze the following year.

At Homebush, Kidman had 300 head of cattle for sale and he surprised one and all by instructing the auctioneers to accept the first bid offered on those cattle. The buyers were no doubt impressed, at least the ones who quickly realised what he was doing. He cheekily told them it meant he would pay less commission. He didn't repeat his instructions during the rest of the fortnight he spent in Sydney and during that time he privately sold 12,000 cattle in the Sydney and Brisbane markets. At the same time his many stations across the country were also selling his cattle into the Adelaide, Melbourne and Sydney markets. It was said that from one Kidman station alone came 6,000 bullocks.

Kidman and others of that time would no doubt be taken aback if they could have seen the Homebush site eighty-seven years later when it showcased the quite brilliant Sydney 2000 Olympic Games.

He then bought a new car in Sydney, a Ford, and set off to inspect thirteen of his cattle runs and another twenty stations, nine of which he was already interested in, owned by other men. He inspected them to see the lie of the land and how many cattle they could reasonably carry, with an eye to future acquisition. I often heard it said that Kidman would ride discreetly or perhaps blatantly, his horse across prospective properties and having determined the carrying capacity, make an offer to buy. It usually transpired that his estimations of what the current owner had or had estimated the place would run, were much closer to the mark than the owner's figures. Consequently, Kidman was often making money on the buying transaction before the ink was dry.

He and his men drove over the Blue Mountains to Bathurst, Orange, Wellington and on to Dubbo. He wasn't selling cattle then in Dubbo but in 1896 he had sold 300 horses in our town and achieved an exceptional average price of £28/10/0. I say that because in 1896 the average weekly wage in Australia was £1.27 pounds. If you divide the former by the latter you will realise that it took more than twenty-two weeks to earn the price of a good horse. Compare that to today if you will.

In 1896, Australia followed New Zealand in being one of the first countries to set a national minimum wage. Today Australia has one of the highest minimum wages in the world.

In 1894, three men owned *Bulloo Downs*, the famed cattle station centred on the mighty Bulloo River south-west of Thargomindah, in the south-west of Queensland. That year the men had 43,000 cattle on the 9,842 square kilometre property. Later the usual drought set in and in 1903 they were down to running just 3,000 cattle. That was when Kidman stepped up and bought the place for a modest £20,000. The man made an art form of buying when others would not, or could not.

Shortly after, Kidman walked some 1,000 store bullocks i.e. male castrated cattle that are not fat, not in prime condition, down to Dubbo where they sold for a few pennies less than £10 each. This was a record price for store bullocks and he sent another 800 store bullocks which averaged £8/10/0 after all that travelling. In 1906 the average weekly wage across the country was £1/6/4 and if we look at just the lower priced bullocks that means it took 6.44 weeks to earn the £8/10/0. If you multiply today's average weekly wage by 6.44 you release that beef then was an amazing price. If men like Kidman had good prices and the weather running with them, they were making a fortune. It is little wonder that so many other men were out there stealing cattle.

Kidman inspected many properties in Queensland and then turned south into NSW where amongst others he visited *Wonnaminta Station*. He would later buy that and *Nundorah Station*. He noted that it, 'was wonderful country before the rabbits came but they seem to have left the district now. They came in millions, got into the sandhills and the people could never get them out.' After reaching Broken Hill he returned home to Kapunda. He said the Ford had stood up to the 5,000-kilometre trip in splendid condition.

Perhaps you should know the reality of the working day for others. In a Parliamentary Board of Inquiry during 1893–1895, sworn testimony submitted by factory inspectors showed, for example, that two shirtmakers worked for twelve to thirteen hours a day in order to earn between them ten shillings, or $2.43, a week. A family of father, mother and two sons made knickers and collectively earned seven shillings and six pence or $1.82 a day, while a tailor who made tweed trousers, worked thirteen to fourteen hours per day and sometimes on Sundays in order to earn 12 shillings, or $2.92, a week. Life was grim for the masses and social security benefits non-existent. We shall now return, belatedly, to Mr. Mills.

Annie and Ada Mullen continued to raise Mills's two daughters in Kapunda and in 1891 he made his way to Western Australia. About that time Sir Thomas Elder was financing the scientific Elder Exploration Expedition. The expedition operated under the guidance of the Royal Geographic Society, Adelaide. The party, under the leadership of David Lindsay, was probably the best equipped and organised expedition in to the remote areas of Australia, consisting as it did of six scientific officers, four assistants and five cameleers. The forty-four camels came from Sir Thomas Elder's *Beltana Station*. The objective was to fill in on the map the unexplored areas of Australia that had not been traversed by Ernest Giles in 1872, William Gosse in 1873, John Forrest in 1873 and W.W. Mills in 1882, while they crossed Western Australia. The party left Hergott Springs, today known as Marree, on 2nd May, 1891.

Despite looking for new areas, the party camped at Skirmish Hill on 20th July, 1891 and saw the tree marked by Gosse, Forrest and Mills. They reported the temperature that night dropped to 19 degrees Fahrenheit or 13 degrees below freezing, the coldest night on their journey. They continued on their way and on 31st December, 1891, disharmony unfortunately bubbled to the surface for the final time and the scientific officers resigned. David Lindsay continued on to Geraldton, which is on the coast about 420 km, by camel, north of Perth, with the remainder of the party and from there he was directed to return to

Adelaide. The expedition was abandoned and Sir Thomas Elder was a most disappointed patron.

An interesting article came my way, from the *Geraldton Telegraph* of 16th March, 1894. It seems that Mills was a regular contributor to the newspaper as evidenced by his column, entitled 'Out East', of that date. He was writing of his gold exploration journeys in the winter of 1893, when he had set out on a prospecting trip commencing from the Star of the East goldmine, a little south of Meekatharra. He remarks to the paper's editor that a journalist had referred to Mills as a member of the Elder Exploration Expedition and corrects that assumption by saying: 'This was a mistake doubtless caused by the fact of my having ridden as a freelance with the expedition for a few hundred miles, out east, after their arrival at Southern Cross.'

Whilst there appears to be no mention of Mills being on the expedition officially it makes sense that he says he was there for the last few hundred miles because he certainly knew the Murchison area, having ridden through there in 1882 and most likely again since his arrival in WA in 1891. Additionally, if the scientists were at odds with David Lindsay he may well have welcomed Mills's impartial company and regional advice for what would be the last section of the journey. It is several hundred miles from Southern Cross to Geraldton. As confirmation of Mills's presence, the expedition's surveyor and the man who would take over from David Lindsay, Mr. L. A. Wells, was quoted in the *Express* newspaper, saying in Southern Cross he met Mills, who told him where water had or had not been found.

It was not unusual for bush-hardened and capable men such as Mills to be employed by syndicates of gold-seeking men to do their exploration for them. Not only would there be payments from their employers but the WA Government offered a reward of £5,000 to anyone finding payable gold that produced 10,000 ounces within two years of the discovery. The gold was required to pass through a customs point so that the government could take a payment that was levied as a gold tax.

The goldfields of WA were instrumental in Australia becoming a country, formed from its colonies. In 1898 a referendum was held in the colonies so that people could vote on the constitution. Queensland and Western Australia did not participate and in New South Wales it was not approved. A bone of contention was where the national capital would be built. A second referendum based on an amended constitution and promoted by pro and against parties took place in 1899. Western Australia was still holding out but two things swung the vote to the pro-Federation group. The miners on the goldfields, who accounted for a third of the colony's population and who for the most part came from other colonies, were so much in favour that they threatened to leave the colony, to secede from WA, and form their own state of Auralia. In addition WA was assured that after Federation the Federal Government would construct a transcontinental railway track.

Even so WA's vote was only 69.4 per cent in favour as compared to the six-colony average of 75.5 per cent. It has to be said that many people chose not to vote and apparently some sectors of the population were excluded from voting, such as; the indigenous, most women, the poor and those of Chinese or Indian descent. I am curious to know what defined the poor in those days of no social security benefits, let alone the other restrictions. The Commonwealth of Australia Constitution Act 1900 was passed on 5th July and proclaimed by Queen Victoria on 17th September. Federation came into being on 1st January, 1901. Australia, an independent, democratic nation.

Gold was found in Halls Creek, 1885; Southern Cross, 1887; Cue, 1891; Coolgardie, 1892 and Kalgoorlie, 1893. In 1891 there were 49,782 people living in WA and four years later there were 100,515. Another six years after that and the number was 184,124. Gold, gold, gold. It was Charles Hall who, in 1885, found the first successful gold rush in WA at the area and the town that is now named after him, Halls Creek. For the record Halls Creek is close to 2,900 km north of Perth and some 1,300 km south-west of Darwin. A big country.

The Geraldton newspaper of 16th March, 1894, published a two-page report from Mills of a gold prospecting expedition he made in company with Ned Heffernan, Charles Hall and Julius Anderson, all three being prominent gold prospectors, in May of 1893. In March, 1892, Mills found a waterhole which four men could span around. When they passed that way in May, 1893, he found it had enlarged, due to a good season, so that fifty men could enjoy a comfortable swim in it. There were areas and times that were not so bounteous. On one occasion Mills and the other three exhausted their supplies of food and water. It was decided that two would ride back to replenish their stocks while the other two remained out in that harsh season prospecting. I don't know which men carried on but I suspect Mills did as he was an acknowledged marksman. I do know that when the men returned with supplies the other two were reduced to eating what they shot, crow. Men boiled their crow meat and where possible ate it with nardoo, which was an aquatic fern resembling a four-leaf clover. I don't know that there was such a plant in those arid parts of WA. Burke and Wills were said to eat nardoo as a bread, knowing that the Aborigines grind the seeds and convert them into a paste to make bread. As their food supplies dried up Burke and Wills are believed to have existed on such bread for a short time. However they seemed to have been unaware that the Aborigines first soaked the paste in running water, for up to five days, in order to leach out the enzyme thiaminase, which depletes the human body of vitamin B. Life was hard for the early settlers and to be reduced to living off crow meat seems as good an example as any.

A Mills entry reads in part: *We then travelled north-easterly, one day's stage bringing us to a sandstone cliff range and the second day to another auriferous belt, the intervening country undulating with alternate belts of open spinifex and mulga thicket running diagonally to our course. We prospected this belt northerly to Latitude 27 degrees and getting colours, one being over 1 dwt. but found nothing payable. We then struck westerly for Lake Wells, making for the high bluff range on its western shores that loomed up boldly against the sky long ere we reached it. Here we found splendid prospecting country, and although we only obtained colours I left the locality with regret and quite believe there will be a rush there yet.* See Lawlers, Barrick Gold, below…*

Another article says: *News has come into town of a new find on the Murchison. It appears that a surveyor named Mills who had been prospecting lately with Heffernan and party, 300 miles east of Cue, and formerly with Lindsay, recently returned to Cue, in quest of some stray camels. While in Cue he disposed of some coarse gold and* stated that Heffernan and party were on gold but that the find was not sufficiently developed to warrant a report to the Warden or a rush. The general impression at Cue is that the party are on good gold.

The prospector and pastoralist Arthur Ashwin kept detailed diaries and he wrote: *On the bank of the creek I came on a hole sunk six feet deep and Ned Heffernan's initials and Mills. Mills and Heffernan came out from Cue before Paddy Lawler had found the Donegal. I heard all about their trip, they stopped on the way back and found a reef two miles north-east of the Great Eastern and they lost their camels there and Mills and a black boy tracked the camels right back to Cue, 230 miles, a long walk. I knew Mills, he had been a surveyor. I met him when he camped with us one night at a soak about sixty miles north of the MacDonnell Ranges on the Overland Telegraph to Port Darwin. I was with Ralph Milner in 1871. Mills was a good walker and a good shot with a rifle.*

Another newspaper said, *Lately Mr. Mills came into Cue and many are saying this party has struck something good in the far interior and several parties have started out to cut his track and follow it to where his companions are busy raking in the shekels.* Taking Arthur Ashwin at his word, and his writings are worthy of that, his remarks pose the distinct possibility that Heffernan and Mills not only found gold but that it was in the area that the following year was claimed by Paddy Lawler and became known as Lawlers. (*This would one day be owned and operated by Barrick Gold, currently the largest gold mining company in the world. How tantalisingly close to those riches were Ned Heffernan and William Whitfield Mills?)

On the Victorian and New South Wales goldfields ample supplies of water meant extracting gold from the ground was hard work but relatively straightforward. The other colonies had less available water and the dry to desert areas of WA had no water with which to separate gold from other matter. Water became a commodity in its own right and therefore expensive. It was more valuable in combating disease and dehydration than in mining and so the Royal Gold Commissioners set a reward for the best water saving technique.

To overcome that drawback Stephen Lorden and John Banfield invented the dry blower. Essentially, the dry blower sifted through soil for alluvial gold rather than the usual method of panning for gold with water. Mounted on a wheelbarrow-like stand, the dry blower box used a manually operated blast of air to separate the dry earth from valuable pieces of gold. Placed just above hand-operated bellows, a riffle board caught the gold. Set on a framework above the riffle board was a classifier screen-feeding hopper. The hopper box directed classified fines onto the riffle section. The dry blowers were made in Fremantle, weighed 45 kilograms and were designed to be carried on a horse or camel. While camels carried huge amounts of mining materials and supplies to the goldfields, and really they were invaluable in that sense, horses also played a part. In 1895 there were estimated to be more than 600 teams and about 4,000 horses on the road between Southern Cross and Coolgardie, a distance of 366 km, the latter town being the centre of the goldfields.

When the horses arrived at a roadside condenser their owners sometimes had to pay £1 for a single drink of water per horse. To appreciate that cost after converting one Australian pound to two Australian dollars today, the two dollars is multiplied by the increase in the real purchasing indicator since 1893 (to the most recent update) and that just happens to be 100 times. So that drink of water was costing the horse owner $200 and if you do the calculations by way of the labour value of the commodity and/or the income value, the resultant figure is 4.23 or 7.87 times higher. The lower figure of $200 tells the story by itself. As was often the way, people who provided services, such as water, food, mining equipment, transport, alcohol, basic accommodation, female company, boots, clothing, you name it; they were most often the real winners out of a gold rush.

An independent miner wrote, 'two men who were camped near me died of thirst and two others went mad, one shot himself.' Mine employees were paid a gallon of water per day as part of their wages but in such dry land the act of obtaining the water was the very problem. Necessity being the mother of invention a few father figures soon had condensers of various shapes and sizes out on the goldfields. What water that was available was too brackish to drink as it came from underground bores, the quality of which may have been suitable for animals but it was not fit for human consumption; or from salt lakes, claypans and underground mines where such seepage was known to cause goldmines to become water mines. A wood fired furnace would be constructed to boil the collected water. As it was heated, the water changed form to gas and the steam rose through a pipe at the back of the boiler. As it travelled away from the fire and the heat, it cooled and changed back into a liquid. The resultant water was potable but not palatable, usually just good enough to drink. One prospector described it as: 'resembling boiled water with a dash of galvanised iron and several unrecognisable substances including smoke'. As late as 1912, the manager of the Beltana Pastoral Company told a nineteen-year-old looking for work he could start as a boundary rider on *Cordillo Downs*, but also told him that often the thick drinking water did not splash.

In 1896 the Premier of WA, John Forrest, authorised a water pipeline to be built to carry 23,000 kilolitres or 5,100,000 gallons of water per day from a dam on the Helena River near Perth to the goldfields but it was not completed until 1903. The 760-millimetre diameter steel pipe was 560 km in length, the longest freshwater pipeline in the world. The water had to be conveyed up a 400-metre gradient and required eight relay stations to ensure it finally arrived in Kalgoorlie after eleven days. Each of the pipeline's 60,000 sections, most of which were laid by hand, weighed one tonne. That engineering feat is still required today and yet the man who oversaw its design and construction was heavily criticised by those who thought it could not be done or the gold would run out and the pipeline would be a white elephant.

That Irish-born engineer-in-chief of Western Australia was Charles Yelverton O'Connor and he had already gained fame by constructing Fremantle Harbour. I gather he may have had health problems as well as undue criticism, but in any event a letter was much later found in a vault at the State Records Office. It was written by Mr. O'Connor and says in part, 'I feel that my brain is suffering and I am in great fear of what effect all this worry may have on me – I have lost control of my thoughts.'

Tragically, on 10th March, 1902, before the pipeline's completion, Mr. O'Connor rode his horse into the water at a beach near Robb's Jetty, south of Fremantle, W.A., and shot himself, dead, at 4.40 a.m. There are several monuments to honour Mr. O'Connor. The beach where he died is now named

C.Y. O'Connor Beach and thirty metres out into the sea is a bronze statue of him on an unsaddled horse. A steel pylon that is sunk six metres into the seabed keeps horse and rider in place at the sea level. Also, in his memory is the Federal electorate of O'Connor, which encompasses the southern wheatbelt and most of the goldfields of Western Australia.

'The explorer is necessarily insatiable for water, no quantity can satisfy him, for he requires it always and in every place,' so wrote that extraordinarily resilient explorer Ernest Giles. 'Doing a thirst,' quickly came into the expressions of Western Australia's goldfields and yet when smoke signals were seen in the far distance denoting Aborigines in yet another desert, the stunned white man would wonder, 'How can this be?'

As with their smoke signals, the Aborigines had an expertise derived of practical knowledge, experience and adaptability to their environment, handed from generation to generation. I have been to Ethiopia where I flew over the one tribe that still insists on staying in their remote desert village, dependent on one animal alone to completely sustain them in all aspects of their existence, for food, clothing, housing materials, milk, transport and food. The authorities find it impossible to entice them into the civilisation that their countrymen and women adhere to, as long as they still have their saviour camels. So to some degree I can understand Australian Aborigines, in the past, living in areas that no one else could survive in, living off the land.

They knew where to find water and what made that possible was understanding the attributes of certain trees. The principal water trees are the mallee, needle-bush, the desert kurrajong, the casuarina or desert oak, acacia, mulga and probably the bloodwood. The mallee is a good example to work with as its roots extend out from the trunk of the tree for distances from 12 to 24 metres. An attraction of the mallee roots is that they lie just a few inches below the surface. Sometimes they can be noticed by a rise or bulge in the soil or a crack as fine as a human hair, on the surface.

If the ground is hard the Aborigine prises the root up with his wooden shovel and if it is loose he positions his spear-point under the root and loosens it up and out. Using both hands he then pulls the root up all the way to its point. He breaks the root into sections, about the length of one's arm and stands them upright against the tree trunk so that the water flows out and down into a wooden coolamon or a kangaroo-skin bag. Roots about the size of a man's wrist are generally best as the water then flows freely. One long and well-stretched mallee root can usually satisfy the thirst of two or three men. An end of the root can be covered or sealed with clay for travelling with the water.

The red mallee produces even more and arguably better although if the water is left standing for a few hours it turns cloudy and there are not all that many red mallees to be found. I did come across one clump of the red mallee with its striking appearance while setting out on the Canning Stock Route in Western Australia and that was a sight to behold. The desert oak holds water in its roots and in its stem. The water from that tree is quite cool and there are 8 to 10 roots, enough for that many men, but exposure to the air for a few hours is enough to turn that water a pale brown. When we were later heading for Skirmish Hill, we would find any number of lovely desert oak trees between the Docker River and the Great Victoria Desert.

The other clue to find water is to be aware of the bird life. Possibly the most reliable bird for indicating where water is to be found is the diamond bird, also known as the zebra finch. They drink often. The popular pigeon, crested, wire-winged or topknot, would rank second and the ever-noisy white cockatoo, which I personally have always found most reliable when it comes to sourcing water, is generally placed third in the find-water stakes. I say that because our Dubbo farm was 20 kilometres as the crow flies from the Macquarie River where the cockatoos like to congregate. It didn't happen often enough but whenever the white cockatoos flew out to the creek below our farmhouse and went ballistic with their frenzied screeching we knew rain was coming, every time, for thirty-seven years.

In its journal dated 82:17-25, 1999, the Royal Society of Western Australia published a most informative article written by Ian Bayly, of the Department of Biological Sciences, Monash University, in which he describes how the indigenous people managed for water in the desert regions of Australia, not only as above (via trees), birds and animals, but by maps.

He states that the last of the small groups of Aborigines living a strictly traditional life in the desert, probably disappeared in the late 1970s, in the Gibson Desert. Up until then such people relied on oral instruction and stylised mapping regarding the type and location of water supplies. The sequences and locations of water sources were memorised by the Aborigines and the adults would instruct the children as groups passed along a chain of waterholes.

When I have told some of my friends who travel by 4WD through the outback that the Aborigines used maps to aid their travels they have been understandably but politely disbelieving and asked what proof is there of that. Well it so happens that Mr. Bayly has the following to report, as is disclosed in the Journal of the Royal Society of Western Australia.

Thomson (1962), in a narrative of the Bindibu Expedition of 1957, described how he spent several weeks with Aborigines in what is probably the most formidable of all the Australian deserts – the Great Sandy Desert, Western Australia. Just before departing these people he was given a very generous gift; a tutorial about their desert waters and a priceless map to assist their location. It is worthwhile reproducing Thomson's account of this episode.

Just before we left, the old men recited to me the names of more than fifty water-wells, rock-holes and claypans – including those that I have described in this narrative; this in an area that the early explorers believed to be almost waterless, and where all but a few were, in 1957, still unknown to the white man. And on the eve of our going, Tjappanongo produced spearthrowers, on the back of which were designs deeply incised, more or less geometric in form. Sometimes with a stick or with his finger, he would point to each well or rock-hole in turn and recite its name, waiting for me to repeat it after him. Each time the group of old men listened intently and grunted in approval – 'Eh' – or repeated the name again and listened once more. This process continued with the name of each water until they were satisfied with my pronunciation, when they would pass on to the next.

I realised that here was the most important discovery of the expedition – that what Tjappanongo and the old men had shown me was really a map, highly conventionalised, like the works on a message or letter stick of the Aborigines, of the waters of the vast terrain over which the Bindibu hunted.

Tindale (1974) reproduced a comparable map of water resources prepared by Katabulka of the Ngaatjatjarra tribe in the Warburton Ranges of Western Australia. This again used spirals to show the location of pools and soakage-wells. The importance of native water maps and associated names in the establishment of the Canning Stock Route was discussed.

I believe it is worthwhile to give a little space to another form of finding lifesaving water. Bayly refers to Carnegie who related how his friend, *was perishing from thirst, and at the last gasp, he came to a claypan which, to his despair, was quite dry and baked hard by the sun. He gave up all hope; not so his black-boy, who, after examining the surface of the hard clay, started to dig vigorously, shouting, 'No more tumble down, plenty water here!'*

Struggling to the side of his boy, he found that he had unearthed a large frog blown out with water, with which they relieved their thirst. Subsequent digging disclosed more frogs, from all of which so great a supply of water was squeezed that not only he and his boy but the horses also were saved from a terrible death.

Once deprived of its bodily supply of water the frog soon dies but it was often saved from that form of demise by another, when the Aborigine then ate the frog, whole. The man would sometimes exclaim, 'Bullya Marra,' which translates as Good! Good!

Although laughed off at the time by most of Carnegie's companions, the essentials of the story were, as Carnegie himself realised, factually based. Those wonderful photographers of well over a century ago, Baldwin Spencer and Frank Gillen, provided a good account of the behaviour and ecology of the water-holding frog (*Cyclorana platycephala*), which has the ability to take up a large amount of water stored in the bladder before burrowing beneath the surface of a claypan where he, or she, may aestivate for more than a year. Aestivation is a state of animal dormancy, similar to hibernation but taking place in summer rather than winter.

Baldwin Spencer was an Oxford graduate, zoologist, photographer and anthropologist while his companion Frank Gillen was an autodidact, i.e. he was self-taught, in photography and anthropology. They both were utterly fascinated by the Australian Aborigines. They described how their native guide had the uncanny ability to appreciate the significance of some indistinct marks on the surface and how they cut into the rock-hard clay with a hatchet to recover one of those frogs at a depth of about 30 centimetres. It was a common practice for Aborigines to squeeze the body water out of the frog and drink it, 'and the Australian native will win through where unattended white men would perish of thirst.' Aborigines could also detect hidden chambers of aestivating frogs by tapping on the hard surface with the butt of a spear or after a long drought by stamping on the ground, and listening for the faint croaking of the frogs.

Thirst was a widespread problem in the colonial days and in blistering heat it was not unknown for stagecoach horses to drop dead in the traces and for the driver to sometimes having to walk to the nearest station for a replacement, contend with removal of the body and deal with passengers. Probably the worst disaster on outback coaching occurred on the Northern Territory's *Powell's Creek* to *Anthony's Lagoon* mail run when the driver, passengers and horses all died on a dry section of the run, for want of water. *Anthony's Lagoon* is 440 kilometres from Tennant Creek, the nearest town for shops and doctors. Today stores are delivered to the 934,900-hectare *Anthony's Lagoon Station* once a fortnight via a road train from the much larger city of Mt Isa, Queensland, 700 km away.

On the lighter side, a stagecoach was bogged in a creek courtesy of unexpected and recent rain at Packsaddle, a little to the west of *Wonnaminta*. Two station hands came upon the coach with the driver and passengers deep in the water endeavouring to move the horses forward. One passenger, a Chinese man heading for a border station, was up on the driver's seat with reins in hand, making a worthwhile contribution while shouting his helpful instructions. 'Pullee gley 'orse round more better. Hit 'em the black cow – my wor, lazy blute. Gee up, horsee.'

In addition to frogs, the Aborigines' diet included snakes. If the snake carried venom it was important to kill it without breaking the skin. It therefore needed to be pinned to the ground, as done with a well-shaped implement before its neck was snapped. A good fire was required so that the chef could drag the snake to and fro through the burning embers until such time as the snake's scales had dissipated. Then, in similar fashion to pricking sausages on the barbecue to prevent them blowing up and bursting, a sharp blade was inserted along the body of the snake, to relieve that pressure. The snake was then cooked on the fire's resultant coals with its body coiled and the tail of the snake in its mouth. When the cooking was complete the snake's body was completely opened up so that the Aborigines could drink the juices therein before eating the meat.

They also ate witchetty grubs, cooked or uncooked, according to taste. I might say I have eaten Australian witchetty grubs, uncooked and found them quite agreeable. Of course I took the head off first. That experience came in quite handy when I was staying in an eco camp in the Orinoco jungle of Venezuela. Four Warao Indians came along in their canoe, as the only form of travel is on the river, with four freshly killed iguanas, for their dinner that night. They signalled for our canoe to stop and offered me, not the iguanas but the local witchetty grubs. Knowing what to expect I took one, bit its head off and promptly ate the body, which pleased the men. In Puerto Rico I saw several middle-class people with pet iguanas. They walk them on a lead just as we walk a dog.

In those remote areas of the Australian outback it could not be reasonably expected that all the children of pioneers, settlers and itinerant workers could be educated beyond the lore of the bush. A well-intentioned minister of the cloth came upon two barefoot outback kids on his rounds at a distance far beyond his norm, children who through no fault of their own had no understanding of academic or ecclesiastical matters. When he asked of them, 'Haven't you heard of Jesus Christ?' the elder one replied, 'Na-ow, but if he's been boundary ridin' round 'ere me Dad'd know him.'

The photographs below are courtesy of Dr. Philip Jones, Senior Curator of Anthropology with the South Australia Museum, as published in his outstanding historical and photographic book, 'The Images of Australia.'

The Birdsville mail coach crossing sandhills near the Cooper River on its fortnight long 500 km journey from Marree, South Australia, to Birdsville, Queensland.

The first plane to land on the Birdsville Track was a Sopwith Camel, in April, 1921. Among the onlookers was Bridget, the camel.

Two Wangkanguru boys playing with toy spears at Mungeranie, 1920.

Yawarraka tribesmen at Mungeranie demonstrating the dueling method when using the heavy two-handed non-throwing Murrawirri boomerang, 1912.

Wangkanguru women at a Mungeranie ceremony, east of Lake Eyre, 1920.

This 1930s hunting party incorporates European hunting dogs and a rifle.

Arrernte women and girls at Alice Springs, 1896.

Arrernte men decorated and armed for an avenging expedition, 1896.

Tjitingalla ceremony at Alice Springs, 1895.

Family life with man adzing his spear, two wives grinding seed and children playing, near Alice Springs telegraph station, June, 1897.

White men traveling through the spinifex and desert oak country of the Musgrave Ranges, on the SA/NT border, are accompanied by local Pitjantjatjara tribesmen.

A Ngadatjara girl holds a dingo pup, in the Warburton Ranges of Western Australia. Dingoes were kept as pets and occasionally used for hunting but mainly as food.

Pitjantjatjara women collecting water in wooden bowls at the Cabi Yura rock hole.

Aboriginal red ochre and pipeclay rock paintings at Uluru (Ayers Rock), showing emus, kangaroo tracks, ancestral figures, Europeans and a rare image of a white man shooting a horned bullock.

13

Waltzing Matilda

As in Victoria and New South Wales, where the Australian gold rush started, the largest contingent of foreigners were the Chinese. In 1850 Melbourne had a population of about 25,000. In 1855 there was an influx of 11,493 Chinese to that city and Australia-wide there were 38,337 arrivals from China, of whom only eleven were women. Dr. Thomas Wood remarked, I *have seen the Chinese and marvel. Is there anything this race cannot do? They have filled their own country; spread over Malaya and the East Indies; established themselves in Europe, Africa and America; flooded the South Seas. Distance is no more to them than discomfort, privation, time and death. They know nothing, or give no hint that they know anything, about the eight-hour day, a standard of living or birth control. If the most prolific race is to govern the world some day, as is quite possible, is there any reason why China, centuries hence, finding Australia still a vacuum, should not fill it?* Prescient words from 1932?

The Chinese then made up three per cent of the Australian population and today six per cent of Australians have Chinese heritage and this figure is rapidly growing. In Sydney the figure is eleven per cent. Billy Sing was born in Clermont, Queensland, in 1886, of a Chinese father and an English mother. Billy was one of approximately 200 Chinese-Australians who managed to enlist in the Australian Army in World War One, as did a similar number in World War Two.

Many more men of Chinese heritage would have joined up but at that time men needed to be, generally, of European/Great Britain descent to enlist in the Australian Army. Billy Sing joined the 5th Light Horse Regiment in October, 1914, and was sent to Gallipoli, where he excelled as a sniper. On 23rd October, 1915, the ANZAC commander, General Birdwood, complimented Trooper Sing on his 201 kills of Turkish soldiers. Major Midgely, who later told Lord Kitchener of Billy Sing, said he estimated Billy's tally at close to 300 kills. A sniper invariably had the services of a spotter and for a long time Billy Sing's spotter at Gallipoli was a man called Ion Idriess, who was a well-known Australian author. The spotter's job was to observe the surrounding countryside and seek out targets for the sniper. Kills were only confirmed when seen by the spotter. Ion Idriess wrote for *The Bulletin* and published more than fifty books, two having more than forty reprintings. He was wounded at Gallipoli, and Beersheba, Palestine, and continued writing until the age of seventy-nine. Billy Sing killed 'Abdul the Terrible', the Turks' leading sniper, when he endeavoured to get Billy at Chatham's Post, Gallipoli.

Billy Sing received the Distinguished Conduct Medal and articles about him were published in England and America. He transferred to an infantry battalion and was sent to the Western Front, where he was wounded many times. He led a counter-sniper operation in Polygon Wood and was awarded the Belgian Croix de Guerre and recommended for the Military Medal. He never did receive the latter. In November 1918, an army medical report noted that in the past two years he had been badly gassed and had gunshot wounds in the left shoulder, his back, and left leg. He died a lonely man in a Brisbane boarding house in 1943, leaving behind a mining claim worth £20 plus five shillings cash in his room. His employer still owed him £6. It was many years afterwards before a few people got around to honouring a man who served his country, Australia, to the utmost of his body and mind.

Frank Fisher, born in Clermont, Queensland, was one of at least 1,000 Aborigines who served in the Australian Army in World War One. He signed up in August, 1917, when he was a labourer. As Frank was married with three children he allocated three-fifths of his Army pay, which was the same for all men, to his wife and children, consented to being inoculated against smallpox and enteric fever and disembarked in Egypt with the 11th Light Horse Regiment in January, 1918. The regiment had recently participated in the charge at Beersheba and in battles at Gaza and Sheria. During Frank's service, the regiment fought Turkish and German forces in Palestine. The regiment initially consisted of 25 officers and 497 other ranks. By war's end 95 men had been killed and 521 wounded, resulting in over 100 per cent casualties. After Armistice Day, 11

November, 1918, Frank stayed on as the regiment was required to put down riots in Egypt until July, 1919, when he returned safely to Australia.

On a perfect evening in Sydney on 25th September, 2000, my family and I were amongst a crowd of 112,254 avid spectators who were enthralled by the spectacular array of athletic prowess from the world's best competitors. The night culminated in a young Aboriginal woman powering home in the straight to convincingly win her event, the women's Olympic Games 400 metres track gold medal final. Her name is Cathy Freeman, great-granddaughter of Frank Fisher.

When Australian soldiers who had served in Egypt during World War One returned home, they put wire netting on the sand areas as it then enabled them to drive cars and trucks where they would otherwise have been bogged, a lesson they learned from the Egyptians.

The usual water shortages in Australia were exacerbated by the drought that severely struck the eastern half of the country from 1895 and extended to 1903 and in some places for longer. Due to the hardship it caused to farmers, pastoralists, miners and so many associated industries it was called various names but overall it was known as the Federation Drought. Those who study such challenges state that it was in effect three El Ninos following hard on each other, i.e. from 1895 to 1898, 1899 to 1900 and 1901 to 1903. If some of us think recent events have reached too far beyond the normal they may be thankful they weren't around in 1897–1898 when the extremes of heatwaves, dust storms and bushfires lit up Tasmania, Victoria, South Australia, New South Wales and Queensland, and in those trying times there were not the defences and protective arrangements that we have today. In addition, Victoria was reeling financially due to a bout of depression, agricultural land was beset by plagues of rabbits and the ploughing of land had undermined the capacity of nature's systems to resist drought. It also gave credence to the expression that drought follows the plough. The subsequent decline in water in quantity and quality, combined with poor sanitation procedures, brought about new highs in disease and death, specifically typhoid, influenza, enteric fever and diphtheria. In 1896, western New South Wales had temperatures of 52 degrees centigrade and in Bourke, 160 people died of the heat and disease. 1897–98 was hotter. Sydney was covered by smoke from Victorian bushfires, let alone its own.

The land of the pastoralists was laid bare by the rabbit and stripped of vegetation while their weakened sheep succumbed to wild dogs. Stock values fell to virtually nothing as those who might have an interest in buying had no feed to take advantage of depressed prices. To quote a South Australian pastoralist: 'While I am writing this the dust is blowing in clouds; no lambing for the last three years and a bad prospect for one this year; high rents and wild dogs galore; three parts of this country blown further east. It will take three good seasons for the country to be of the same value as it was before the drought set in.' Henry Lawson wrote *The Drover's Wife* at that time of increasing unemployment and hardship. More and more men turned to the swag as they tramped from homestead to homestead, with the expectation that if they could not find work they would at least be offered a meal and somewhere to sleep for the night. According to the author Don Garden, there was then a widespread fear in rural Australia that to refuse a swagman could result in a carelessly thrown match. Perhaps it was no coincidence that *Waltzing Matilda* was written in 1895.

There was a system in place in some parts of the country that served to alleviate rural hardship, although more so where the landholdings were smaller and closer together. In that way the men on foot could walk from one place to another in a single day. It went by the name of the traveller's huts. Each station had such a hut. Generally swagmen carried their swag from station to station and sought work while it was the sundowner who was not so desirous of seeking paid labour but the free life. The huts provided overnight security from the elements for both and the station served up breakfast and supper, for up to ten men. The more generous station owners provided a cook and an offsider to cater for travellers only. The more largesse the stations handed out the more they were utilised. One was known to have sustained and replenished one hundred men in a single day and the traveller tended to stay at such properties for longer. They would mostly assist in times of local bushfires.

When swagmen walked from station to station they began to identify and name the track from one place to another by the amount of food they received or the amount of effort they were expected to put into singing for their supper. For instance there were flour tracks, garden tracks, wood tracks and the White

Man's track. The flour track designation indicated that a swagman could expect to receive a pound of flour and if he was fortunate, a piece of meat. The garden track required him to dig up a patch of land, in the shape of a square that was already pegged off and precise as to its area before he could be fed. If the station manager had a predilection for firewood the wood track meant the station would have two stakes about a metre high and a metre apart. The visitor would need to cut wood to a certain length to the height of the top of the stakes. If you were favoured by the White Man's track you were assured of a good reception and treated with excellent food and secure shelter.

There were sundowners who made an art form of living off the goodwill of others for a year, or much longer, as there still are in today's society, and there were those who felt they were owed more. That type was not beyond taking the pound of flour and down the track burning not only the grass but a wooden fence of those who had fed them. They also indulged in taking the odd jumbuck or sheep from the station and from whence came *Waltzing Matilda*. Unlike their brother swagmen, sundowners arrived at sundown, too late to work for their meal and accommodation.

Dagworth Station, near Winton in central west Queensland, was established from nothing by the two men who took up that country in 1876. When I say near to Winton, it is about 130 km to the north-west of the town, in the direction of Cloncurry, and along the appropriately named Matilda Way. The two newcomers built and lived in a grass hut until they had the place up and running. In 1891 the great shearer's strike began across Australia and although settled it broke out again in 1894. By then *Dagworth Station* was owned by the MacPherson family and came into Australian history during the widespread protests by shearers over the amount of their wages. This resulted in the woolshed of the 100,000 hectare *Dagworth Station* being burnt to the ground by sixteen disgruntled shearers and in the process 143 lambs which had been penned up in the shed were burnt to death. A man was shot dead the following day, while seven nearby woolsheds were also destroyed by fire.

The strike of 1891, over the proposed reduction in wages paid by the sheep owners to their shearers, was spread right across Australia and resulted in action at Robert Kennedy's *Wonnaminta Station*. Five non-union shearers, uncomfortably known as scabs, turned up for work and were attacked by one hundred union shearers who had gathered at *Wonnaminta*. Two of them were beaten up and the other three were locked in a cave created out of an old mining shaft in the Koonaberri Mountain Range on the northern part of *Wonnaminta*. They survived only by the fortuitous arrival of the police who rescued them and then locked the union leaders in a gaol at Milparinka for six months.

Prior to taking over *Dagworth Station* the MacPhersons had lived at *Peechalba Station*, Wangaratta, and in 1865 the entire family was held up by the bushranger Mad Dan Morgan. Also known as Mad Dog, he was probably the worst of all Australia's villains, the rural ones at least, with a vile temper and a propensity for murder. Dan Morgan committed robbery under arms on many occasions, holding up stagecoaches and bailing up the magistrate in Wagga Wagga. Morgan was once sentenced by Judge Redmond Barry, a man of the law who came to Australia from England and steadily worked his way up the ladder, due to his good endeavours. His mother's maiden name was perhaps appropriate for his new country. She was known as Phoebe Drought. Along the way he was the judge in the Eureka Stockade treason trial, where all thirteen miners were acquitted. He was in the chair when the fifteen convicts who murdered an Inspector General were on trial. Seven of those men were found guilty and sentenced to death by hanging. The hangings occurred within a three-day period. When Judge Barry sentenced Ned Kelly in similar fashion he said to the condemned man, 'May God have mercy on your soul.' The transcript shows Ned Kelly boldly replied, 'I will go a little further than that and say I will see you there when I go.' Twelve days after Kelly's hanging Judge Redmond Barry died.

If you look at my limited family tree you will see that Dr. Hedley Ham married my mother's mother, May Kennedy, a daughter of Robert Kennedy Jnr. When Hedley Ham was but a boy he was able to attend the hanging of the bushranger Ned Kelly, at Old Melbourne Gaol. There was an official party of some twenty medical personnel, the sheriff, the governor, magistrates and representatives of the press in attendance on that day. Whilst he was certainly not one of them, he was numbered amongst the favoured few of the general public who were given admission passes. He was too young to receive such an invitation on his own merit and it came courteous of his father, David Ham.

Five minutes before the execution hour of 10.00 a.m. on 11th November, 1880, the official party appeared in the courtyard of the gaol and was followed by the chosen spectators to the main building, where the gallows were situated. The officials proceeded up and onto the upper platform near the hangman's drop. Everyone else was gathered in the long corridor below with the reporters at the front. I don't know if my grandfather and great grandfather were close up behind the press or further back but they were amongst the people who witnessed the executioner step forward and place the noose of his rope from the strong overhead beam, around the neck of the condemned man.

David Ham had earlier arrived in Ballarat as a nineteen-year old migrant from Cornwall, England. He tried his hand at a butcher's shop, at storekeeping, saw-milling and real estate before finding significant gold at Ballarat. Over the next thirty years he was a promoter or investor in at least 175 gold mining companies. One of those was the fabulously wealthy Madame Berry GMCo mine which went on to pay out nearly one million pounds in royalties and dividends, The lease over that goldmine extended for just half a kilometre and produced more than twelve tonnes of gold. He was also credited with finding the famous Ballarat deep fields. Elsewhere at Ballarat, his friend, Edward Morey, and six lucky sailors made a claim on twenty-four square feet or two square metres. That smidgen of land produced over one tonne of gold. David Ham extended his activities to being a share broker and a member of the Melbourne and Ballarat Stock Exchanges. He was also a Member of the Legislative Council for eighteen years.

Before we leave grandfather Hedley Ham I would like to mention he not only became renowned for his work in the field of dentistry in Australia but he travelled to England and gained his Licentiate of Dental Surgery at the Royal College of Surgeons. Dr. Ham would walk from his nearby lodgings to the Royal College via the pathways of Hyde Park. On those mornings he fell into the habit of every day greeting a regal lady who passed by in her phaeton, an open carriage popular in the late 19th century.

He would tip his top hat to her, bow his head and wish her good morning. I do not know what words Queen Victoria of England uttered, if any, in reply but he said every day he would receive a nod and a smile as she came to recognise him. She was consistent in acknowledging my then young, gentlemanly grandfather. I imagine that few people of the time could have said they had seen the visages of two such disparate people as bushranger Ned Kelly and Queen Victoria.

Queen Victoria reigned for 63 years and 7 months. Dr. Karen Jones, Senior Lecturer at the University of Kent co-wrote the book, *A Cultural History of Firearms in the Age of Empire*, which states that the Second Boer War of 1899-1902, in South Africa, was the 226th of 230 wars that Britain engaged in during the reign of Queen Victoria, a lady who until the day she married slept in the same room as her mother. Victoria's then unusual white wedding dress set that ongoing colour fashion for the brides who came after her. Now back to Dr. Hedley Ham.

He went on to Paris and Rome for further study before working in Bucharest for three years, where he was the dental surgeon to Pauline Elisabeth Ottili Luise of Wied, (1843–1916), perhaps better known as Queen Elisabeth of Romania. Subsequently Dr. Ham went to America where he obtained the degree of Dental Surgery at the University of Pennsylvania. He returned to Melbourne and for the balance of his long career operated from his rooms in Collins Street, next to the Independent Church. A renowned gardener, he grew outstanding hydrangeas, was a fifty year member of both of Melbourne's horseracing clubs, played golf off scratch, was President of the Sandhurst Golf Club, founded the Bendigo Golf Club and was one of the earliest members of the Melbourne Golf Club.

He was photographed at the latter with one of his closest friends, Arthur Mailey, one of Australian cricket's greatest leg spin bowlers. In twenty-one Test matches Arthur Mailey took ninety-nine wickets. Cricket aficionados will know this but in the second innings of the Fourth Test of the 1920–21 Ashes series against England, in Melbourne, he took nine wickets, (of the possible ten) for 121 runs. Nigh on a century later that performance is still the Test record for an Australian bowler. In a First-Class match in England, playing against the Gloucestershire team, Arthur Mailey took all the wickets, ten for sixty-six.

Also a dear friend of Hedley Ham was another Arthur, the rather unique

(Sir) Arthur Streeton, whose paintings were influenced by the Heidelberg school of impressionism, featuring distinctly Australian attributes of space, distance, heat and light. Today some of his work hangs in galleries around the world and several have sold for millions of dollars, not that one sees money when admiring them but subtle characteristics that reach out to the Antipodean heart. Arthur Streeton would write to Hedley Ham and complete his letters with off the cuff light-hearted drawings, a lovely and friendly touch.

Back to that Australian personification, the bushranger. The judge sent Morgan to Pentridge Gaol for twelve years, the first two of which he spent in chains. Released after six years he resumed his murderous ways, killing civilians and policemen. After he killed Sergeant Smyth the government declared Morgan to be an outlaw, which meant anyone could shoot and kill him on sight.

Morgan held the entire family hostage at gunpoint, in the *Peechalba Station* dining room. When the nursemaid was required to attend the fifteen-month-old baby Christina MacPherson, the woman took that opportunity to escape. Once away she warned others of what was happening. When Dan Morgan walked out of the homestead the next morning a station hand shot and killed the man who was probably Australia's most bloodthirsty bushranger.

In 1895, after the shearer's strike was settling down the baby girl, Christina MacPherson, was a grown woman and visiting the family property, *Dagworth Station*, when a guest, Banjo Paterson, he of the steel blue eyes, arrived. He wanted to know more about the strike. You will recall that Banjo's father Andrew Paterson, was Robert Kennedy's rival for the hand of Mary Bozzom Hume.

One day Christina's brother took Banjo Paterson on a horse riding tour of the property. They came upon a waterhole or billabong where they found the fresh skin of a sheep that had just been killed. That was all that the swagman had left behind as he had obviously taken the sheep meat with him. Banjo also learned that the man who had been killed, Frenchy Hoffmeister, the day after the station's woolshed had been burnt down, was one of the ringleaders of those who had denied their employers a year's income. He committed suicide, apparently from remorse, the next day, by shooting himself.

Christina MacPherson wrote all these details and more in a letter she never posted. It was not until 1991 that the letter came to light, revealing her part in providing the music of what would be an iconic Australian song, the unofficial national anthem to many. In her letter she also threw more light on the doings of the swagmen when they walked from place to place. She said, 'There are always numbers of men travelling about the country, some riding and some on foot and they are usually given rations at the various stations that they come to, but in Queensland the distances are so great that they help themselves without asking.'

Banjo took all the above into account, the taking of the jumbuck, the sheep, the suicide of the ringleader by gunshot and altered it to death by intentional drowning in the billabong and the walking or waltzing of the swagmen as they carried their matildas or swags.

One day at *Dagworth Station* Christina was playing a tune she had picked up at the Warrnambool races. She played it on her zither or autoharp. Banjo Paterson heard it and asked her to play it again, and again, as he wrote first one verse and then another, all based on what he had learned above. The joint result of course was *Waltzing Matilda*. In 1891, Henry Lawson wrote another of his wonderful poems, *Freedom on the Wallaby*.

I mentioned Cloncurry, to the north-west of Winton. If Alice Springs was the centrefold of colonial Australia I could not place Cloncurry on page three, that would be reserved for the attractions of Albany, Kapunda, Yackandandah, Beechworth and more. The back pages would be for where the action was, the hard action as seen at Broken Hill, Derby, Coober Pedy, Marble Bar and Cloncurry.

For a year or so, Derby was my home town in the Kimberley and had toned down from earlier days. The famous boab tree which housed Aboriginal prisoners outside the town still exists but in my day if a white man transgressed, up to a certain limit, the police would simply drive him out of town for 15 to 20 km, and leave him by the side of the road to reconsider himself as he walked back to town in the usual stifling heat while they drove back to Derby.

It was Broome that was then the problem child. If the reader does not mind I shall digress, as briefly as I can, and that's not easy for me. These days Broome is a highly popular and decidedly different environment for people from all walks of life and many countries to visit. It attracts travellers who come with their own transport and accommodation and also those who happily bestow their hard-earned on the relaxation and other benefits of resort living, at least in the Australian winter.

I make no bones about the way it was in my day for it was a wonderful experience. I merely wish to tell it as it was so others may know, if they are interested. I had several good friends on the island where I was employed out in the Indian Ocean and after I had been there long enough to have paid my dues a good mate and I decided to take some time off and go down to Broome for a look around. He was a German by the name of Alf and had been a soldier in the German Army before deciding he wanted to have a much bigger look, on the other side of the world. Like myself he had been flown to the island by the mining company. So Alf flew to the mainland and then from Derby to Perth. He had left his VW car at the Perth Airport and I don't know what the cost for ten months parking would be today but it was negligible, if anything at all back then, in 1971. While Alf drove from Perth to Broome I flew from the island to Derby and took a bus 220 km south to Broome. With Teutonic timing Alf met me in Broome as I stepped off the bus.

The Roebuck Bay Hotel was the only hotel in Broome and we went there to see it at first-hand and then drove out of town to see what we could of the surrounding cattle stations and anything else of interest, such as the famed Cable Beach. The tide ebbs and flows a long, long way in that region of 11-metre tides and at low tide people reverse their vehicles as far out as the receding water permits. They unhitch, drive their vehicle back up on the beach and when the tide comes in it floats their boat and they are away. Every so often someone gets stuck or doesn't move their vehicle out in time and they go underwater, to some degree or other, wondering how on earth did that happen?

When mother-of-pearl was initially found at Broome, the local Aborigine women and girls were forced to dive for them, until Britain abolished slavery in 1883. When diving suits became available, the white bosses used Pacific Islander and Japanese divers to do the dangerous diving. I imagine they were paid for their endeavours but I doubt it was enough reward as 919 Japanese divers paid with their lives, in Broome. Today Broome produces cultured Australian South Sea Pearls and I am told they are the most desired pearls in the world, bar the rare natural version, which is found only once in many, many thousands of oysters.

At the southern end of Cable Beach, so named on account of the underwater telegraph cable that runs from there to Indonesia, are the 130 million-year-old tracks of nine species of dinosaurs but I imagine everyone more or less knows of local interests like those. You would hardly believe it but twenty or more years ago some blokes stole a few of those dinosaur footprints. They cut them out of the rock. Fortunately they were later retrieved. There are more mundane matters such as Alf and I propping up the bar of the Roebuck Bay Hotel during some of those long daylight hours, to unwind. We talked with locals and travellers, had a few bets with the SP or starting price bookmaker on the Perth horseraces, listening on the radio over a distance of 2,200 km, depending how one travels. On more than one occasion I received a tap on the shoulder and turned my head to look straight into the close visage of a full-blood Aboriginal girl. Her coal-black face and attractive large eyes were invariably studded with weeping sores to which the ever-present flies had attached themselves like limpet mines. She didn't have to speak English to tell me she was offering herself to me, and to Alf.

The region then consisted of men who were engaged in the search for oil and gas, who work on cattle stations, of road gangers and miners like us. There were few members of the fairer sex and once when a beauty contest was promoted on our island there were only two ladies, who worked in the office, who entered. One smart alec nominated his dump truck and it won the contest. No, not really, it came second.

We did not encounter any trouble during the day but by the end of the week some men were steamed up, and not just on account of the weather which turns to prickly heat late in the year as cyclones and monsoon rains build up. Tensions rise and tempers flare, fights erupt from truck to chair. Fridays were when the hot water bubbled over and the lid came off the restraints. It was usual on a Friday night for the king black man of the week, to fight the king white man, of that time period, to decide who was the overall man of the week.

Alf and I were not there for that entertainment let alone participation and as it was always in the wind we left the pub as darkness fell and drove along the beach. We camped there, above the high tide mark and undisturbed we slept well for six nights. It didn't bother another good friend of mine. Don was a former Aussie Rules player, for St Kilda in Melbourne. Well over two metres tall and with beef to match he played first grade for many years. The knuckles at the back of his hands were enlarged and rough as I had never seen before, no doubt from many years of striking. I had no doubt he could have held his own on Fridays.

Don took a regular room in the Roebuck Bay Hotel and one night, not a Friday night on this occasion, he was asleep when he was woken by the sounds of a great ruckus in the corridor outside his room. He wasn't perturbed by it until two men burst through his door. They didn't open it but they came through it, taking it completely off the hinges. They fought their way around his room, throwing non-stop punches and then reeled back into the corridor and continued fighting each other to a standstill some distance and time further on.

Meanwhile Kidman was busy. Since buying his first stations, *Cowarie Station*, a little to the north-east of Lake Eyre and *Owen Springs*, near Alice Springs, in 1886, the latter costing only £1,500, Kidman had built up his holding to seventeen cattle stations. *Owen Springs* came with its 4,000 horses and the price may have been so low as there was not a single fence on the place. The portfolio soon came to include other Alice Springs properties such as *Hamilton Downs*, the aforementioned *Crown Point, Stirling* and *Bond Springs* and his aim was to build up a line of secure north to south cattle stations. The Federation Drought however made no exception for Kidman. At first it stopped him buying up more land and as it progressively took a stronger grip on the country it began to shake out those stations he did have. The figures are difficult to collate, not just now but at the time because Kidman was not of the mindset to be telling others of his woes. A conservative estimate of his losses, by the author, sniper-spotter, Ion Idriess, was that Kidman would have lost 2,000 head of cattle from each station, on average. Other analysts and critics claim his losses would have been twice that, with some estimations at 70,000 head of cattle lost.

To his undying credit he kept all his cattle stations except *Owen Springs*, selling it for a good profit and then having its huge herds of horses to sell. Due to the drought his first 500 horses for sale were in poor condition and not worth the £1/10/0 cost of freight to sell in the saleyards. He offered them to his men in lieu of wages but they declined so he paid them as normal. Twelve months later, in a good season, they were strong and fat. He sold them for prices between £24 and £38 a head. The others were sold in following sales and if the 4,000 averaged £25 to £30 each, the gross total for Kidman and his brother Sack must have been heading for £100,000, if not £120,000. Amongst the seventeen stations he had acquired was the mighty *Victoria River Downs*, (VRD), in the far north-west of the Northern Territory. This station was far better watered and grassed than most properties and while Kidman had 69,350 head of cattle on it in 1907, in later years *VRD* would run 120,000 head of cattle. Due to receiving the northern monsoon rains *VRD* had plenty of feed, and cattle were fattened and sold from there. That and his relentless dealing in sheep, cattle and horses kept Kidman going, while many people were of the opinion the drought would break the man. He may well have been on his knees at times and he certainly suffered the loss of tens of thousands of head of cattle but as Jimmy Nicholas said, 'Kidman was a smart man.'

He also had an excellent relationship with his bankers, the Bank of New South Wales. I don't suggest by any means he was too big to fail but he had the ability and the nerve to keep the bank onside, even though he was often stringing out the settlement of his latest station acquisition for several years and paying the bank when it suited him. The bankers may have grumbled but they reasoned Kidman always did pay. Having said that I should balance the scales and say that I have a friend whose grandfather, a cattleman from *The Barrier* region of western New South Wales, was employed by Kidman as a buyer/drover to go up into Queensland and put together a suitable mob of cattle at the right price and bring them down south to be sold. He was gone three years on the job and he said, when he returned, Kidman did not pay him.

Another opinion of Kidman comes from the author/sniper-spotter Ion Idriess. He said that several of his informants encountered Kidman and spoke well of his treatment of Aboriginal workers. According to one, Kidman believed that Aborigines brought good luck. Which brings to mind the Australian Aborigines' use of their rather unique weapon the boomerang. I am indebted to Dr. Philip Jones, Curator of Anthropology at the Museum of South Australia, for just a few of his observations, below.

Most hunting or throwing boomerangs were thrown to hit their targets, not to return. Boomerangs can travel for 150 metres but thrown at a range up to 100 metres, the different forms of medium-weight throwing boomerangs used across Australia were all capable of inflicting death or serious injury. This was particularly so if they were sharpened and spinning fast at contact. Ricocheted off the ground towards an enemy, the swerving flight of these boomerangs was almost impossible to avoid. The hooked boomerangs of northern Central Australia were potentially lethal. The hook would catch on a parrying shield or club, causing the boomerang to swing around and strike the defender.

Boomerangs were thrown in every possible way to damage the enemy, sometimes directly at them, striking the ground first as mentioned, to skim horizontally along the ground or high in the air but in every instance the boomerang is held with its points towards the object. It has been known to rip up an individual as does a knife. When thrown the unequal air speed of the two rotating arms – the leading arm is followed by a trailing arm – causes the boomerang to veer to one side and thus it begins to turn in an arc towards the thrower. The boomerang rotates up to 10 times per second.

A significant number of boomerangs were never thrown and across eastern Central Australia that includes the long, heavy boomerang known as the Murrawirri. It measured up to two metres in length and was 7.5 to 10 cms in width. It was carried in the belt at the back of the body with the end sticking up over the owner's head. They were formidable fighting weapons and were used in hand-to-hand combat after the smaller boomerangs and clubs had been thrown. Combatants exchanged blows and blocked each other's moves. The men would grasp the Murrawirri with both hands, each hand grip about 30 cms apart and use it as a sword. The Aborigine, Mundowdna Jack, presumably from Mundowdna Station or nearby, said he fought two men armed with boomerangs and throwing sticks. He split the skull of one man and struck the other through the wall of the chest. Both died at once. He was untouched. He was strong and the Murrawirri was the big man's favourite weapon.

Alice Springs, Northen Territory.

13 Waltzing Matilda

Late Acknowledgement.

It is now six years (2023) since I wrote the bulk of the book, arranged the photographs and created the cover, with Arrai-iga of the Arrernte tribe standing in front of a strongly shaded Alice Springs waterhole, thanks to Luke Harris' artistic talent. The other night while doing research I discovered the great-great granddaughter of Arrai-iga. I tracked the lady, whom I shall refer to for now as T, down and asked her his name to confirm his identity and when she told me she didn't know my disappointment was almost audible. I only know because the anthropologists, Spencer and Gillen, recorded his name. She said she is sixty and he died before she was born, adding that once he was gone no-one was allowed to speak his name, a traditional custom. It was understood by all that when a person died it was not by natural causes as white people might say but because of tribal belief in sorcery.

His granddaughter, i.e. her grandmother, knew him and long ago handed down his history to T, her sisters and their mother. She told me he was known as Emu Feather, due to his ability to cover the tracks of man and beast. He was a hunter, as were many men, for his family, the tribe in general and for the seven dogs and dingoes he owned. He always carried three or four spears and they were made of mulga or ironwood. Without hesitation T said those hardwoods contained toxins and if an enemy was not killed outright or if the spear was not removed quickly the victim would die of septicaemia, of blood poisoning. I imagine such spears would invariably be dirty and infectious.

I asked T if she knew when or where her great-great grandfather died and she does not know, but when I asked where did he live we hit the jackpot. If you have been to Alice and to the nearby Telegraph Station you will hopefully recall that after leaving those lovingly restored buildings you can walk down a well-grassed slope, passing by and admiring the monument to William Whitfield Mills, as you go to the western bank of the Alice Springs waterhole that Mills found and named on 11 March, 1871.

On the eastern side of the water, as seen on the previous page, large boulders form the base of a hill that rises up to a plateau enhanced with several trees that barely intrude on the 360-degree view of the surrounding countryside. That was the home of Arrai-iga, as befitting he who was also the tribal medicine man. In that honoured capacity he assisted and invariably accompanied the Kadaitcha man, following behind him when he set out to kill a man who had been condemned to death. To do so each of the two men carried a shield and a spear while wearing a girdle around his waist, made from the hair cut from a warrior after his death, to grant the wearer all of the war-like virtues of the dead man.

If you go to the front cover of Skirmish Hill you might look at Arrai-iga , specifically above his left shoulder and up to the top of that hill, close to the trees. That is precisely where Arrai-iga, medicine man, hunter, certainly an Elder and possibly a one-time chief of the tribe, lived. In addition a sentry always patrolled that area looking out for intruders from other tribes intent on attacking the men, stealing the women or desirous of the ever-valuable water. T added that Arrai-iga was the first of the tribe to see white men, at the waterhole. As Mills was there on that day it is likely they acknowledged each other and possibly raised a hand to signify peace for as we know due to his six-month camel ride from Beltana Station to Northampton, and elsewhere, Mills was so inclined. I find it extraordinary and pleasing that after four generations have passed the cover photo is now found to contain such Central Australian history. T said she is thrilled to hear from me, to share her and my knowledge and to see in the book the wonderful photos of 'my people'.

I earlier mentioned the role of the anthropologists Baldwin Spencer and Francis Gillen, who took the original photograph that I have amended. Professor Marcia Langton, AO, anthropologist, Boyer Lecturer, geographer and since 2000, Foundation Chair of Australian Indigenous Studies at the University of Melbourne and historian of the Yiman/Bidjara nation said: *The Arrernte tribes of Central Australia are fortunate in that there are such detailed records of life in their societies when everywhere else in Australia, Aboriginal society was falling to colonialism, to the gun, and records were simply not produced. There were no Gillens or Spencers.*

14

The Boer War

As just noted Banjo Patterson wrote Waltzing Matilda in 1895, between the first and second Boer Wars. The second Boer War raged from 1899 until 1902 and amongst others David Jonathon Ham was deeply involved. He was the son of David Ham Snr, whom I have already briefly mentioned. A gold mining entrepreneur he was also a businessman, politician and philanthropist. In addition to supporting charities he donated the two carved Sicilian-marble lions placed at the entrance to the superb one hundred acre Ballarat Botanical Gardens, still resplendent today. When he died the newspapers reported the whole of Ballarat, including the children, turned out for the funeral. He had made clear his wish that Handel's *Dead March* not be played at the funeral but rather the poem of Alfred, Lord Tennyson *Crossing the Bar* be read to mark his transition from life to death. *And let there be no moaning of the bar when I put out to sea....*

The Prime Minister, the Hon. Alfred Deakin, who had written part of the Australian Constitution telephoned Mrs. Ham from his holiday home at Point Lonsdale to express his utmost heartfelt sympathy. Prime Minister Deakin also sent a telegram of condolence to Mrs. Ham and the family.

David Ham built a grand residence for his wife in 1857 and I mention it because the Ballarat house can be seen in all its magnificence today. The family sons who grew up in that house included my grandfather Dr. Hedley Ham of Melbourne, Mr. Fred Ham, barrister of Ballarat, Mr. W. S. Ham, sharebroker of the Melbourne Stock Exchange, Dr. Nathaniel Burnett Ham, (he tackled the problems of bubonic plague for which he received worldwide recognition, food adulteration, sanitation and infectious diseases and was the first Commissioner of the Queensland Health Department), Mr.

William Ham, stock and station agent of Brisbane and David Jonathon Ham, farmer and soldier. There were three daughters but the little I know says that one married the Queensland Attorney-General while gracious Ethel Ham married wealthy Mr. Arthur Baillieu of Melbourne. Ethel and Arthur did have a daughter, Sunday Baillieu. Her friends came to include Dame Nellie Melba and Arthur Streeton. After a privileged and sheltered upbringing she left the establishment and after the setbacks of an unfortunate illness and an abandoned marriage Sunday and her second husband, John Reed, used Sunday's trust fund to purchase a fifteen-acre former dairy farm, *Heide*, on the Yarra River at Heidelberg, in 1934.

They became patrons of the arts, supporting many artists and today it is the Heide Museum of Modern Art. It is another story but she had a close if not intense relationship with the artist Sidney Nolan. Sunday lived in a menage a trois with Nolan and her husband and when Sidney Nolan finally realised he could not have her entirely to himself he departed in emotionally charged circumstances in 1947. He left his Ned Kelly paintings at *Heide*, with Sunday. He had once told her to take what she wanted but he later demanded their return. She handed back 284 of his paintings but she refused to give up the remaining 25 Ned Kellys. It was only in 1977 that Sunday gave those paintings to the National Gallery of Australia, to settle the dispute. Sunday was the aunt of the 2010 Premier of Victoria, Ted Baillieu. Nicole Kidman's father Anthony Kidman stated that Nicole named her daughter Sunday after Sunday Baillieu/Reed. Sunday and John Reed financed the Communist Party of Australia and John helped fund CPA candidates in Federal elections. My mother would never mention her by name but she always admired and spoke highly of Sunday's younger brother, Everard. Sunday and my mother were cousins and Sunday and I are first cousins once removed.

David Jonathon Ham left school at age fifteen and for the next three years he was to be found in the Wimmera district of Victoria, experiencing dryland farming. At age eighteen he returned to Ballarat and attended Grenville College for two years, where he was the college champion in rowing, swimming and running. Grenville College no longer exists but the school produced an Australian Prime Minister. Sir Robert Menzies was P.M. from 1939 to 1941 and later oversaw the post-war economic development from 1949 until 1966.

After leaving Grenville College David Ham went to outback Queensland where he was engaged in droving cattle and sheep and managing rural properties. From there he moved to NSW and bought country just as a major shearers' strike began. Moral persuasion being a waste of time he offered to fight the best union man in the strikers' camp over a few rounds, presumably to decide the strike issue locally. When no one was prepared to take him on he promised to shoot the first man who molested any of his working men. That need did not arise so he put up £50 for a race meeting among the men. He was handy on a horse himself and when compelled to undergo a journey of 100 miles he did so without taking a break other than to change horses. He could ride across country with only a compass to guide him and when he rode a distance of 140 miles he stopped for only a ninety minute spell. When he had improved his NSW property by clearing and fencing the land he sold it and returned to Western Port Bay, at Hastings, Victoria.

He bred both sheep and cattle on his new 1,300 acre property *Warrenda* and his brother William and he bred horses together. He married Margaret Weston and he and William joined the Hastings Football Club, that being Australian Rules for foreigners like myself who are of the Rugby Union persuasion.

The team contained several farmers but it was the fishermen of Hastings who supplied many of the fit and healthy young men of the initial football team. Throughout the 1880s Hastings had about sixty hardy adventurers who would sail out on a Sunday night, after the Sabbath, and not return until the following Thursday with their catches. Their backgrounds, combined with their occupation's hardy lifestyle, meant that Hastings footballers would quickly gain a reputation for rugged determination. In the 1860s the father of John and William Jones had come from Nassau in the Bahamas to fish at Hastings and together with two more of their brothers the Jones Brothers were known as tough and outspoken fishermen of renown. George, aged 20, and Daniel Sheehey, 18, were in the first Hastings team of 1889. They were the sons of a wild Irishman, Daniel Snr, who had run away from home at the age of fifteen to avoid being sent into the priesthood by his devout Catholic parents. He arrived in Australia as a cabin boy in 1852, jumped ship and became one of the first fishermen in Hastings, where he married a Welsh girl and became an Anglican. William Lamble was another valuable member of that first Hastings team. He was tall and wiry, a blacksmith like his father, and a tough and determined young man. He continued to shoe horses until he was 82 years young.

David Ham played in the Hastings team for several years and was then elected Club President for six years, from 1894 to 1899. Like his father he committed himself to community work, was president of nine differing societies, twice Shire President and a Councillor for ten years.

As earlier mentioned there was fear around Australia that Russia would invade the country and being prior to Federation it was up to the states to do something to protect themselves. Hastings elected to form a battery of heavy guns for that purpose. They acquired no less than four forty-pound Armstrong guns. That might not sound so much but they are big artillery guns, each weighing two tonnes. A battery was formed and David Ham was requested to be in charge but he initially deferred to another.

When the guns were limbered up with their gun carriage and wheels and all that was required the total weight came to nearly four tonnes per gun. The Armstrong guns were housed in sheds but required to be mobile as to fire from the most advantageous position, often up a hill, when an enemy sailed in. Unless the ground was particularly firm heavy horses could not manage the job. The horses were inclined to jump obstacles they encountered, breaking shafts and harness in the process. In India the British Army had used elephants but that was not possible in the Hastings area. David Ham, who then held the rank of Lieutenant, suggested they use bullocks. Although they could only proceed with the guns at two miles per hour the bullocks tended to plough through at a steady rate and that was sufficient. The group acquired the name of the Beef Battery. No less than forty men joined up, excited to be working not just with the big guns but also being taught by professional bullockies who lived in the region, to learn the art of being a bullock driver themselves. Cricket and football teams had to compete strongly for their own numbers.

An annual camp was conducted during Easter at Langwarrin and in previous years the Hastings men had attended but trained and drilled on smaller guns. In 1899 Lieutenant Ham had passed his Captain's exams with flying colours and he now proposed bringing their big guns to the gathering, drawn by the bullocks. The Defence Department denied the request but on Captain Ham's insistence they granted permission, most reluctantly. Their arrival in the camp created a tremendous stir and the Beef Battery was re-named the Ham and Beef Battery. I am indebted to Lance Hodgins for information about Hastings and its people.

Everyone wants land and the British settlers in South Africa claimed they were being harshly treated by the Boers, the Dutch word for farmers, and the Boers resented both the Anglicization of South Africa and Britain's anti-slavery policies. There were other reasons of course but after the Dutch established themselves in the Transvaal and the Orange Free State and the British gained control of the Cape Colony, minor fighting broke out in 1880-1881. I imagine the possibility of gold and diamonds had something to do with the differences of opinions. In October of 1899 full-scale war erupted and 15,000 Australians set off to aid England, along with other colonials from New Zealand and Canada. The pacifist Mohandas *Mahatma* Gandhi served in the Boer War as a stretcher-bearer with the Indian Ambulance Corps at the Battle of Spion Kop, for which he was decorated.

There was no Australian Army prior to Federation so men joined up on behalf of their state, in contingents known as Bushmen. According to the Official Records of *Australian Military Contingents to the War in South Africa* that I received courtesy of Lieutenant-Colonel P.L. Murray of the Department of Defence all the men who joined up had to be bushmen who were hardy riders, straight shots and accustomed to finding their way about in difficult country. They were selected by a committee and passed a strict test in riding and shooting as well as a medical examination and preferably were unmarried. Of the Victorian Contingent 230 were farmers. The men were fully clothed, supplied with weapons and horsed, although many men brought their own horses with them, some more than one horse. Privates were paid two shillings and three pence per day. Ten Australian nurses, all single, accompanied the troops.

Captain Ham was commander of the 3rd Contingent, Victorian Bushmen. There were then five and later eight, Victorian Contingents. They sailed from Melbourne on 10th March, 1900, on the transport ship, *Euryulus*, and after calling in to Cape Town, continued on up the east coast of Africa where they went ashore at the major port city of Beira, Mozambique. The men proceeded westwards to Marandella in Rhodesia, (Zimbabwe) and on to Bulawayo. From there they continued on to Mafeking where the seven-month Siege of Mafeking had been broken on 17th May. Captain Ham records being there but does not say if it was with or before the arrival of the relief force or after it. Either way it must have been a close thing. The commander of the besieged British garrison at Mafeking was Colonel Robert Baden-Powell who would go on to create and lead the world-wide Boy Scouts movement and later the Girl Guides.

Having beaten off the 7,000 Boers the goal was to trek east from Mafeking and take the Boer capital, Pretoria. The 3rd Contingent Victorian Bushmen was involved in several engagements along the way and eventually came to a supply camp at Elands River, a way point on the route between Rustenberg and Zeerust, in the Transvaal. Food, livestock and ammunition were stored there for British and Colonial forces, not by the river itself but one km away from where the ground sloped down to the river, with two exceptions. There was one small ridge and a hill, Cossack Post Hill. Around the camp and across the river the ground was decidedly higher. Such a position could be seen as a trap. On this occasion the troops at Elands River were from the NSW

Skirmish Hill

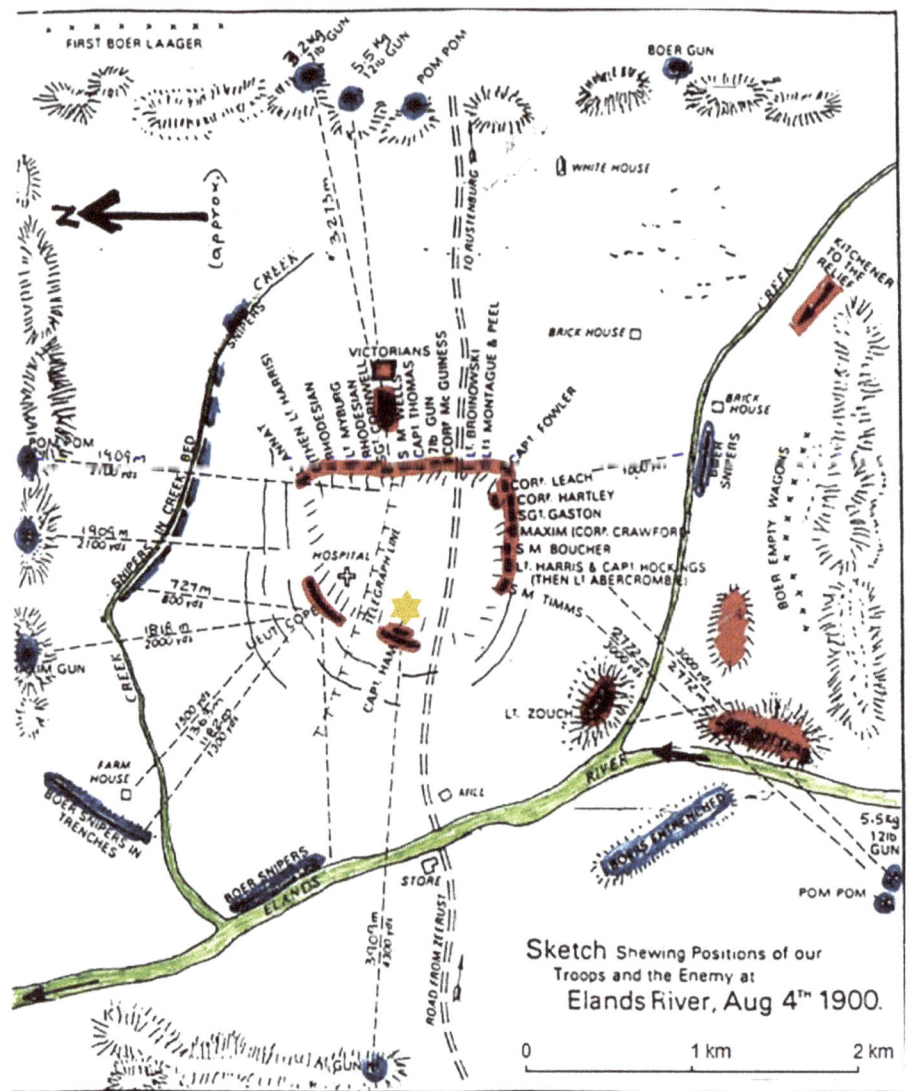

BATTLE OF ELAND'S RIVER

PLAN DRAWN FROM SKETCHES BY CORPORAL KELMAN AND TROOPER
DONKIN, OF MAJOR TUNBRIDGE'S FORCES; FURTHER EMBELLISHED BY
CAPT COPE AND CHAPLAIN GREEN, ALL OF WHOM WERE PRESENT
ADDITIONAL INFORMATION ALSO ADDED

Redrawn in 1978 by JF

Bushmen, Queensland Bushmen, Victorian Bushmen and Rhodesia, numbering close to 500 men in total.

The map of the Battle of Elands River was drawn from sketches by Corporal Kelman and Trooper Donkin. It was further embellished by Capt. Hope and Chaplain Green, all of whom were present. The circular double trench of Capt. Ham is highlighted by a yellow star near the centre of the map. The following are extracts I have taken from the twelve-page letter written by Captain Ham to his wife Margaret the day after the Battle of Elands River. The letter passed to my mother and she handed it down to me for he was my great-uncle. The letter's faded and yellowed words are sometimes illegible but fortunately my mother made a copy to go with the original letter which I still have.

Elands River Camp 17 Aug. 1900.

Dear Meg,
Little did we think that on the 4th just as that old grey light of dawn broke upon us that 2,800 Boers with nine artillery guns would be hurling hails of shells and bullets around us. In the darkness of the previous night a commando of the above strength under General Koos de la Rey, gained possession of the surrounding hills, which overlook our little garrison. There was no faltering. I rushed for the nearest cover and my men followed in a tremendous hail of bullets. Ten minutes later Corporal Norton and Trooper Bird were lying on my right hand and Corporal Smith close by. A shell struck Bird's leg, completely severing it, hurling it with great force against me and the shell passed through the side of Norton, yanking his arm off and continuing on took the woodwork off Smith's rifle and passed on, splintering the rocks and covering us with dirt. I gave a look at the poor fellows and Norton begged me to shoot him. I ordered two men to carry him to the ambulance wagon which had been erected a few days earlier as a temporary hospital.

As there was a good deal of confusion I ordered all the Victorians to follow me and we took up a position that I had slightly banked up the day previous. None of us anticipated an attack from the Boers and it was with difficulty I could get the men to even put up this small a shelter and it was more to keep them engaged that I did so. This small cover went over to just behind our horse-lines, and behind 700 oxen that were tied up the night previous. Through the hail of lead we took up our place there lying behind only six inches of cover while we heard the whistle of the bullets, just like a hive of bees swarming. The shells screeched and broke in fragments above our bodies. Soon the enemy found the dense mass of cattle close to us and two guns and a pom-pom played and the oxen went down twenty to thirty at a time. There was panic amongst the oxen, they broke loose and for half an hour threatened to trample us to death in their wild stampede. We had to leave our shelter and cut them loose and still the shells burst amongst them. Trooper Fortune showed the utmost coolness and sharpening his knife walked amongst the maddened bullocks and cut them loose.

I sent a blackfellow to complete the cutting loose and gave him my knife and he had only cut two loose when a twelve-pound shell took both his legs off and burst all over us. Here, we had to stop, there was no getting away from it. Soon we were out of the ammunition we had on our belts and Fortune and Hillier went to the tent and brought us two boxes, a case of biscuits and some water. Both of these men exhibited the greatest coolness and I watched them go and come expecting every moment to see them scattered to pieces.

After all the cattle were cut loose the enemy began to attack our horse lines with two pom-poms and a seven-pounder. Every time the gunners appeared we poured in well-directed volleys and silenced them for more than half an hour. Our sole gun, a seven pounder, could not answer all the enemy's guns and finally choked and was a target for their guns. At nine o'clock we had only sixteen horses left and the NSW Bushmen had about forty out of one hundred and seventy. This fire continued until six o'clock at night. I got a couple of scrapes from the shells, one burst three feet from me and cut my face, another took a piece out of my hand. I often wondered how I would feel under such fire, well all through the day I never felt the least anxiety for myself, and I felt I would come out perfectly safe.

On the other side I heard the groans of dying and wounded men. Some were cursing, some praying and still the carnage went on, particularly in our horse lines. I saw a shell strike the end horse on my lines and go through twelve horses, it did not burst and was picked up later. The agonies of the horses I shall never forget and the scene of horses swinging their legs, some with them off altogether, some crawling about on their stumps, or with their entrails dragging on the ground, can only be seen to be realised. I never want to see such carnage again, it was a sad sight.

Night came and under its cover until nearly daylight we worked to entrench ourselves with bayonets and I had not to ask my men twice to dig for their lives. During the night we buried our dead but had no time for funeral ceremonies. It was like sending me from Zeerust with that big convoy of fifty-three wagons and only twenty-nine men that I wrote to you about. I went, arrived here safely but it was a miracle and we were only attacked by de la Rey because he was short of supplies after being driven back by Lord Kitchener. We had been in a hot sun all day and had no water, the enemy held all points of the river around us, but we had to get water or surrender, so we decided to fight for it and after a fight in the night our horses got water and we brought back enough to last each of us for a day, each of us proportioned a quart (one litre of water): we lost two men and several horses in this fight for water and had to do this regularly after fighting all day. One man not far me from me got a bullet in his arm, it passed out through the top of his shoulder and into his jaw and he spat it out of his mouth, uttering the exclamation, 'Oh Christ'.

Our second day at daylight opened up with hot fire from rifle and gun of the enemy and up to ten o'clock in the day 600 shells were counted. We were however protected by timber from smashed wagons for head cover and used this protection to make ourselves more secure and by night time we were like a lot of rabbits in a burrow. We had the usual fight at night for water and lost two more men and whilst seeking the water we poured in volleys along the river banks and kept down the fire of the enemy.

Despite the darkness the Boer artillery continued until one o'clock in the morning, using a pom-pom rapid-fire gun that could do a lot of damage.

This was too much for the Australians and Lieutenant Annat, a young Queenslander, took twenty-five Bushmen into the night to raid the gun. Half an hour later they crept up on it, killed the crew and wrecked the gun. In retaliation the Boers opened up again with their shells. I was just going to headquarters to report the day's proceedings when a fifteen-pounder shell struck Lieutenant Annat in the stomach and scattered blood and fragments over me. Poor fellow, he groaned once or twice and died immediately. He was one of the best Queensland officers and was at the Relief of Mafeking, a very cheery and plucky fellow.

When I returned to my dug-out I found that a poor blackfellow had dragged himself in there and laid on my rugs and he was dead, having bled to death, saturating everything. That night we had only three horses left and two of them were mine. The next day at twelve o'clock there only two, the cobby bay horse I had brought from Victoria and Major Viall's horse that we were taking on. That evening there were none left, Old Kruger, as I called him being the last to go down. I have a piece of the shell that killed him along with my Boer rifle which was shattered by a bullet. I am going to get it back to Victoria as a memento.

Major-General Carrington attempted to break through and relieve us but the Boers drove him off and on the third day General de la Rey asked us to surrender, saying he had taken two other posts and repulsed Carrington and congratulated us on our defences under fire. His messenger, under a white flag, said that if we refused he would put a ninety-four pounder on us the next day and that the best men he had met were the Colonials. Colonel Hore sent back the message that our position was held by troops of Her Majesty and that we refused to surrender. The English Colonel added that even if he wanted to surrender, which he didn't, he was in command of Australians who would cut his throat if he did so. He concluded by saying that I don't expect your artillery will change the minds of these men.

Colonel Baden-Powell also made an attempt to relieve the Elands River camp but did not succeed.

I never slept at night for three nights as I was afraid of an attack and had *the weakest spot to defend and visited our sentries four or five times every night and slept in our trench during the day. I knew we could not silence their guns and were now perfectly safe from an attack during the day. The dust is frightful and we had the option of washing our faces with our quart of water or drinking it and it is needless to say it went inside instead of outside. We were unshaved, dirt begrimed and powder-smoked beggars at the end of the second week. To make things worse in the hot weather the dead beasts were putrefying and no relief came for the stench from the dead horses, bullocks and mules day after day, night after night. Yet in all this time our men were in good heart and there would have been no surrender until the last bullet had been fired and the bayonet had found a resting place in the heart of the foe. All our fellows behaved splendidly and Major Tunbridge of the Queenslanders did a lot of good work.*

On the morning of the 16th, yesterday, forward scouts from Western Australia came into the camp at two o'clock and informed us that Lord Kitchener would relieve us at eight o'clock in the morning. During the night we had seen three rockets go up in the air and it was the signal for the Boers to leave. General Kitchener rode in with 25,000 soldiers and never had I seen so many soldiers. They took well into the next day to all come to our five-acre camp in to which the Boers had fired more than 7,000 shells. This was more than the Boers fired at the seven-month Siege of Mafeking.

The first troops to come in were Rimington's Guides, a British Light Horse unit led by Major Mike Rimington. These men always lead the way. They wear leopard skin hat bands on their slouch hats and are known for their night marches and stealth-like movements. Every man in the unit is an English-speaking South African, obliged to also speak Afrikaans--- daughter language of Dutch, 90 to 95 per cent so----and at least one indigenous language. They are armed with a carbine and a pistol.

Author's note. Others that the Australians and Rhodesians cheered on their arrival were the Scots Greys, a cavalry regiment formed in 1681. In 1693 the entire regiment appeared in London with every man riding a grey horse.

The Household Cavalry arrived, consisting of the two most senior regiments of the British Army, the Lifeguards and the Blues and the Royals. They date from 1660 and are the Queen's personal bodyguard. Next were the Grenadiers, an infantry regiment from the Indian Army and one of India's most decorated regiments, active since 1778 with twenty-three battalions. And on they came.

Lieutenant Gartside and I were the first officers introduced to General Kitchener who told us he had only heard two days ago that the Elands River garrison was still holding out and he and that his men had marched or ridden 54 miles in those two days. He said it must have been the hottest shell fire with the exception of what Cronje got from England when he surrendered, since the war began. I got great praise for my original trench. Lord Kitchener said it was a splendid affair; it was a circular double trench and I could command it better than one long one: the front men were protected from the fire of those behind by the covered bomb proof shelter. I used the bullock bows for the purpose and it was lucky they were there for there is no wood here. I have no time to give you a description of Kitchener. The Union Jack flag is still flying in the centre of our camp. I have been promised it as another memento, and needless to say, I shall prize it very much although it has been riddled with shot and shell. I am writing this under a wagon at desperate speed. I have a lot to do yet.

We had a military funeral today over the poor fellows that were killed. We placed a memorial cross over Corporal Norton's grave and the effects of Lieutenant Annat were sold by public auction and realised £100 which will be sent to his widow. I don't expect we shall ever see such shelling again as all the officers who have seen our position say there could not have been hotter fire. At any rate I am satisfied with my first experience of grim warfare. I met Botha junior's wife. She was crying bitterly. She and all her children were dressed in black. She said that her husband had been killed at Elands River by us. She asked me where we come from and I told her we are Australians. She said you have come a long way to fight the Dutchmen. *I told her we are going to fight until all the Dutchmen are killed or give in.*

Trooper Bird survived the battle and his leg that had been taken off by an artillery shell was buried before being just as quickly dug up when the soldier remembered he had £4 in the trouser pocket. In the Garden of Remembrance at Elands River three of the six memorials are dedicated to the men from Australia. The aggressive Boer general, Jan Smuts, said of Elands River, *Never in the course of this war did a besieged force endure worse sufferings but they stood their ground with magnificent courage. All honour to those heroes who in the hour of trial rose notably to the occasion.* Another Boer wrote, *For the first time in the war we were fighting men who used our own (guerrilla warfare) tactics against us. They were Australian volunteers and although small in number we could not take their position. They were the only troops who could scout into our lines at night and kill our sentries. Our men admitted the Australians were more formidable and far more dangerous than any British troops.*

The 3rd Victorian Bushmen were then attached to Lord Methuen's force and marched back to Mafeking. All their horses had been killed as were all but a handful of the total of 1,539 horses, oxen and mules. They were on foot for the 230 km journey but were re-equipped on arrival and then sent out to Kimberley and Blomfontein, fighting the Boer at Silbrants' Kraal, Wagon Drift and other places, culminating in the last pitched battle of its kind at Rhenoster Kop on the 29th November, 1900. Captain Ham's companion at Elands River, Lieutenant Gartside was badly wounded. It was here for the first time Bushmen from all the Australian states fought together but not for the first time with the New Zealanders. The latter had fought with British forces who to them were of unknown quantities but they soon learned they could trust the Australians with whom they were often associated. The legend of the ANZAC grew out of Gallipoli and the Western Front but the bond was melded in South Africa.

Arthur Conan Doyle, who had retired from his successful medical practice eight years earlier, as it allowed him to devote himself to write his Sherlock Holmes series, volunteered his medical services. He served as a medical orderly at the Langman's Field Hospital in Blomfontein. He wrote, *And so fortune yielded, as fortune will when brave men set their teeth. When the ballard-makers of Australia seek for a subject let them turn to Elands River, for there was no finer resistance in the war.*

David Jonathon Ham returned to Hastings, Australia. The Ballarat Star interviewed Captain Ham and noted that *in addition to scars on his hands and the back of his head from shells he had been shot in the fleshy part of the leg by a Mauser bullet.* Captain Ham stated that the British *are not now fighting the Boer so much as renegades from other countries, soldiers of fortune in the worst form, in the shape of men who have got into trouble in their own country and had to leave. Out of every twenty prisoners captured, he states, fully twelve will be found to be the scum of other nations.* Captain Ham was promoted to Major and awarded the Queen's Medal with four clasps.

Lord Kitchener was the man who signed the contentious death warrants for the execution by firing squad of the Australian soldiers in South Africa, Lieutenants Harry 'The Breaker' Morant and Peter Handcock, for killing twelve Boer prisoners of war. The two men were defended by Major James Thomas, who had been educated at The Kings School, Parramatta, and graduated in law at Sydney University. He was a solicitor in Tenterfield, NSW, where he owned the Tenterfield Star newspaper, which has been in continuous operation since 1871. He volunteered for the Boer War, served with the NSW contingent and fought at the battle of Elands River alongside Captain Ham and the Victorians. Major Thomas was directed to defend Morant and Handcock and allocated the briefest of time to prepare their defence, despite the fact that he was up against six legal prosecutors. Thomas, by all accounts a thoroughly honest and decent man, was aghast at the hurried and prejudiced trial. Lord Kitchener departed for distant lands so as not to be present to hear Major Thomas lodge his legal objections to him in person. The one sure thing to arise out of the process, and due to Major Thomas, was that henceforth the Australian Government, which was denied knowledge of the trial and its outcome for many months, in its turn denied the British military the right to execute members of the Australian forces under British Command, as would be the case in World War One. Sadly, as a consequence of the executions which took place eighteen hours after sentencing, James Thomas became and died a broken man.

Kitchener's face was on millions of posters in Britain that showed Field Marshall Lord Kitchener looking straight ahead, pointing his finger forward and with the words WANTS YOU below him, exhorting volunteers to join the British Armed Forces in World War One.

During that time he was the Secretary of State for War and in 1916 attempted to sail from Scotland to Archangel in order to negotiate with Czar Nicholas II of Russia. He stopped off in Scapa Flow in the Orkney Islands and changed ships, departing on the armoured cruiser *HMS Hampshire*. The warship had barely gone three km when it hit a mine recently launched by a German submarine and quickly sank. All but twelve of the 749 men aboard died, amongst them Field Marshall Lord Kitchener. That incident is of particular interest to me for I sailed in the three masted barquentine, *Europa*, from Ireland to Norway and Sweden and after leaving Scapa Flow, we sailed over the location where *HMS Hampshire* and Britain's favourite soldier of World War One are said to have gone down.

Documentary film-maker and author Nick Bleszysnski and military and civilian lawyer and author James Unkles believe Kitchener sacrificed the Australian soldiers who had obeyed his orders to take no prisoners in order to appease Germany as it was rumoured that country may be about to enter the Boer War. If so it seems ironic that Lord Kitchener later died due to a German submarine.

Major David Ham,
Commander of the 3rd Contingent,
Victorian Bushmen,
Boer War, South Africa, 1900-1901.

From the left, Lieutenant Peter Handcock and
Lieutenant Harry 'Breaker' Morant

Major James Thomas of Tenterfield, NSW at the grave of Lieutenant Harry 'Breaker' Morant, Pretoria, South Africa

15

James 'Hungry' Tyson

More knowledgeable people than I have written of Kidman and I bow to their efforts but as I was involved with cattle, in a small way, for forty-one years altogether and as he was a Kapunda man, as were Mullen and Mills and later in life so were David James and James Poole, I am interested in who he was and what he achieved. I make no claim to writing about him but merely wish to add what I feel is relevant to this story because Kidman's lifetime, like that of Mills, Mullen and others, covers so much of Australia's development.

Just before Kidman sold *Owen Springs* he took 350 horses from there to Kapunda and sold them, in 1900, at what would be the first of his regular horse sales in the town for the next thirty-six years. The Kidman Kapunda horse sales were not only the biggest in Australia but in the southern hemisphere, growing as they did to accommodate up to 3,000 Kidman station horses annually, with the sales continuing for as long as fourteen days. They would have been good business for John Mullen's successor, as they were for Kapunda in general. The town benefited from the throngs of buyers and onlookers, who were charged admission prices.

Horses were sold in big numbers as remounts to India, for the Indian Army, and as polo ponies to Kashmir. Farmers from Victoria and South Australia, and so they say, Germany, came to buy horses for their wagons, drays and buggies. Women purchased ponies and hacks. The final day of the sales became Ladies Day. Horses were bought and sent to Western Australia and Queensland. And at that time Adelaide city tram companies bought their horses at Kapunda. The sales ceased after 1936 because of mechanisation and the passing of Mr. Kidman in 1935.

Despite the deaths of two of their young children, Kidman and Bel now had three daughters and one son and Kidman felt it was time to give them, and Bel in particular, a bigger home. Alexander Greenshields was born in Lanarkshire, Scotland, in 1843. He emigrated to Australia in 1861 and settled in Kapunda where he established a thriving drapery business, one that was said to be the largest in the state outside Adelaide. That success enabled him to build an architect designed home, *Lanark House*, for his family. The house was completed in 1879 at a cost that exceeded £4,000 and the *Kapunda Herald* said: 'a pound was not withheld by Mr. Greenshields where it would add to the beauty or accommodation and the residence was regarded by those acquainted with its interior as one of the most convenient and comfortable homes in the northern districts.'

With the drought still raging in 1902 and most of his cattle enterprise struggling to stay afloat, with people eager to say Kidman was about to be brought undone, the man bought *Lanark House*, paying more than £8,000 for the privilege. In addition to the grand gardens there was more than enough attached land for Kidman to place a lot of his horses, while the size and fittings of the house alleviated him from buying property in Main Street to have a substantial office. He did change the name of the house to *Eringa*, most likely after *Eringa Station* that he owned, in the north of South Australia.

Kidman never had any hesitation to employing the best of men for his enterprises; be they station managers or drovers. When conditions improved for a while, one of those drovers, Joe Gleeson, brought 1,200 bullocks down to Marree, South Australia, from where they were taken to Adelaide and sold for a most welcome £15,000.

Kidman sent his best drovers to buy cattle from the Barkly Tablelands in Queensland and take them across the north to coastal markets. He made profits and began buying more stations. He bought *Lake Albert Station*, in 1903, for £85,000 and within six months had sold it off in blocks so that he cleared a profit of £25,000. Then he was criticised for buying stock, let alone property, at low prices and taking advantage of the vendors but he was paying for what he bought and he was buying when others could not or would not.

By the end of 1904 he had 129,680 square km of territory. That was good but disaster struck the same year. He was home for Christmas when the house,

Eringa, caught fire and despite everyone's best efforts the house was burnt down. He regretted losing a piece of wood from the famous Dig Tree near where the explorer Burke had died. Kidman went back to sleeping under the stars with his men while he sent the family to Adelaide. The house was underinsured but Kidman had it rebuilt. His daughters aroused comment when they were seen at the beach indulging in, heaven forbid, mixed bathing. How the world evolves.

In 1907 Kidman owned or had an interest in twenty-nine stations for 152,000 square km of country and said:

People think I have been making a lot of money. They make a mistake. My desire has been to build up a big herd of cattle. My ambition is not to be rich but to hold the largest herd of cattle in Australia, if not in the world, and the same with the horses. Droughts might come along again as they have before and give things a hit back but with the present prospects, I think I will attain my ambition.

On 25th March, 1909, Kidman was in England on a family holiday but still finding time to make deals, as was his wont. Kidman, holding a six-sixteenth share, announced he and his partners had sold *Victoria River Downs*, (VRD) of 32,300 square km, plus the smaller *Carlton Hill* of 4,000 square km. Kidman and his partners had paid £27,500 for *VRD* less than ten years earlier and now they sold it alone to an English company for a staggering £180,000.

In July, 1913, Kidman inspected his eastern cattle stations which now included what had been Robert and Bob Kennedy's properties, *Wonnaminta*, where he stayed, and *Nundora*. In the following years he was extremely generous in contributing to the World War One effort, not only to the Australian Government and military but he started the Belgian Fund in Australia. It raised over £700,000 by voluntary subscription to assist Belgian farmers after German troops had devastated their country. The German aggression during World War One affected the Victorian Football club, St. Kilda, based in Melbourne. Their colours were red, white and black which were the same as Germany's. St Kilda therefore changed their club colours to red, yellow and black, the same as Belgium's national colours. When asked how many of his men enlisted, Kidman said: 'every mother's son of them, with the exception of two whom I retained because they were absolutely necessary to me as managers.' He said he would keep their jobs for his men who went to the war and a life pension for any man injured.

By the time he died, on 1st September, 1935, aged seventy-eight, he was knighted and owned sixty-eight stations over an area greater than 260,000 square km. If you add in those he controlled or had an interest in, the total came to about 150 stations over 414,000 square km, 40 million hectares or some 102 million acres. Kidman, Dame Nellie Melba and Don Bradman, were then the best known and most popular people in Australia. Rather than sell their magnificent Kapunda house, *Eringa*, Kidman and Bel donated it, in 1921 when they moved to Adelaide, to the South Australian Department of Education to be used as a school. My wife, Janice, and I have visited it and it was a thoughtful, exceedingly generous gift to future generations.

There was another great Australian cattleman and he, James Tyson, has always had his admirers, including Kidman who met him here and there. In similar fashion to, but starting before Kidman, Tyson built up a chain of cattle stations but in better country, closer-in, as they say, in the eastern states. Like his parents he had an interesting start in life.

As of much interest to me is James Tyson's mother and the twists and turns that life takes. It was the *Indispensable* that brought Louisa Le Sage from London's Newgate prison to Sydney in 1795 and the former French ship, which had been captured by the English in 1793, made a second convict voyage to Sydney in 1809. For most of the time in between, the ship was a whaler.

One of the convicts in 1809 was Isabella Coulson, accused of stealing twenty-three yards of gingham valued at ten pence and a leather purse valued at two pence. The leather purse contained three shillings and six pence and Isabella was sentenced to seven years transportation. The ship carried sixty-two female convicts and Isabella, who was said to be a most attractive woman, was fortunate that her husband and firstborn son were somehow able to travel, for free, on the ship. They had to leave their three-year-old daughter behind and sadly they never saw her again. As a convict, Isabella was assigned on landing in Sydney to her husband until the completion of her sentence. Isabella appears to have been remarkably fortunate when compared to other convicts.

Nonetheless the family had a hard start overall in their new homeland, as did most arrivals. They were granted 43 hectares of land at Appin, near Campbelltown and some 70 km from Sydney, where the Humes and many others had made their mark and their homes in the colony. With Isabella assigned to her husband the couple had to clear the land of timber and then build a slab hut with a dirt floor and a bark roof. Their only tools were an axe, a hoe, a mattock, and a spade. Part of the chimney on which the children sharpened their slate pencils survives to this day. When James, now also known as Jimmy, was nine years of age his overworked father died and Isabella, already shunned for being a convict, married one. Jimmy always loved his mother but he left the family home at age seventeen, with his sum wealth, that being a half-crown or two shillings and sixpence, one-eighth of a pound.

For two and a half years he worked as a farm labourer, earning £30 a year. Of that £75 total he had saved £60 and given an indication of his attitude to the value of labour and money. From there Jimmy took a job as overseer at a place on the Ovens River in Victoria and after that he was employed by Henry O'Brien, of *Douro*, at Yass. He was now working with cattle, was a crack shot and could live off the land. His rations included wheat that he ground between two stones to make flour for his damper, which he washed down with water. He acquired the nickname of Daylight Jimmy for his practice of rising at dawn and settling down to sleep at dusk, thus not having to burn the oil in his lamp.

Having proved himself at *Douro*, Henry O'Brien sent Jimmy to manage another property he had, *Groongal Station*, on the lower Murrumbidgee. Henry must have been impressed by Tyson for *Groongal Station* was no ordinary place that he took up in 1839. O'Brien was always a man of action and by 1849 he had built it up to 23,350 hectares. Not content with that he purchased *Benerembah Station* in 1847 and whilst it was 15,000 hectares at the time, it was 36,000 hectares when sold at public auction for £340,000 in 1924. The auctioneer proclaimed '*Benerembah* is not a station, it is a principality.' As with everything on the property the appointments for man and beast were simply superb although the new 40-stand woolshed was not rated as magnificent as its predecessor, that having been burned to the ground five years earlier by an argumentative soul who turned to arson for his revenge. I don't carry much knowledge of the superbly watered Riverina country but I have heard that *Groongal* and neighbouring *Benerembah* occupy prime areas of the MIA, the Murrumbidgee Irrigation Area. The current family owners of *Benerembah* have held the property since 1924.

After some time at *Groongal* Jimmy teamed up with younger brother William and they bought cattle for resale. Drought soon sent them droving in an effort to keep their cattle alive. As fences were then non-existent they took up what was known as slow grazing, in other words moving their cattle as slowly as possible through other men's landholdings and fattening on the growing grass of others. They came upon Bendigo where gold had been discovered and sold their cattle at good prices. Tyson then took that operation further. Leaving William and two other brothers to handle the sales to the goldminers, he rode out along the tracks leading to Bendigo and, offering good money, he bought up the cattle herds that other drovers were bringing to the goldfields. After months of droving most of them were happy to quickly and easily sell out for the ready cash. Tyson then adopted his steady method of slow droving and over the final weeks or more put so much weight on the animals that he made greater profits than those who had sold to him. The brothers did this for four years and then sold the business. James Tyson walked away with £20,000.

He rarely visited a city and when he did he travelled second-class but only because there was no third-class. He stayed at the cheapest hotels to save money and in the bush he would swim across a river rather than pay the toll of one shilling. At those times he would carry his matches and his cheque book under his hat or in his mouth. Having done precisely that one morning he rode on and in the afternoon used that chequebook to buy a property for £30,000.

Years later he was sitting around a camp fire when a man asked him, 'And how Sir, did you make your money?', before proceeding to strike a match and light his pipe. 'Well,' said Tyson, calmly and courteously, 'There's one thing I didn't do. I'll tell you that. I never used a match when a firestick would do. Money, muscle and brains were made for use, not abuse. Money, poured down a man's throat or wasted in useless luxuries might just as well be thrown in the sea.' Tyson reasoned he had things to do with his money than spend it as other people thought he should. He tended therefore to avoid people and it is said he never saw the inside of a pub, a church or a theatre. As with Kidman it was not the money that drove him but the creating of his land and overcoming the elements to achieve his actual goal. In similar fashion to Kidman, James Tyson never drank, smoked or swore.

Tyson began buying land. It was always good land and often he was ahead of his time and unlike Kidman, not hesitating to spend money on roads, modern fencing and water supplies, thus boosting his stock numbers and enhancing the value of his country. He repeated his system throughout Victoria, then in NSW and into Queensland. He led the way in accessing the artesian bores at Boulia and Cunnamulla and he had the first hydraulic wool press on Queensland's famed Darling Downs.

On *Tinnenburra*, Cunnamulla, he spent money drilling nine artesian bores. Producing a bottle of water from the ninth bore alone he displayed its softwater qualities, telling the enquiring *Brisbane Courier* that the bore was yielding between 14 million and 18 million litres per day. He initially ran cattle on that country but the rise in wool prices saw him decide to run a few sheep. He built a woolshed that cost £7,000, which would be at least $6,000,000 today. The more important figures are in the construction of the shed which was reputed to have between 100 and 120 shearing stands and was built upon 1,000 cypress pine logs. On *Tinnenburra* it is said James Tyson ran 250,000 sheep, 50,000 cattle and 2,250 horses, while other properties carried 100,000 or so sheep plus cattle and horses.

Tyson liked the Aborigine people and put land aside for them, decreeing that no wagons enter their land and that their culture was not to be interfered with. He described them as a gentle people and said if you treat them right, they treat you right. In a sense he was gentle himself, despite his imposing 1.94-metre height. He was always shy but in a rare moment he told a friend of the time he was in new country with a mob of cattle. As night came on, he was unsure of the lay of the land when he saw a light in the distance. It drew him to a house and when he knocked at the door he said it was opened by, 'the finest woman I ever laid eyes on.'

The woman was tall, clear-eyed and rosy of cheek and with her inherent kindness and concern she insisted he come in and sit by the fire while she prepared him a meal. Tyson seems to have been bowled over by the charming young woman moving around the cosy room on his behalf and despite the intense impression she made on him he was too tame, in this one regard, to say anything of that nature to her. Over time he would ask after her until the day came when he was told she had married. That was as close as James Tyson came to a liaison with a woman.

He settled down on *Felton Station*, on the best country of Queensland's Darling Downs. There he ran 70,000 sheep, 1,000 head of cattle and seventy horses but other places he owned put those stock figures in the shade. Mr. Tyson was no absentee landlord. He was always calling in on his many properties and usually unannounced often travelling by the name of Smith or Shiels. Shunning the nearest hotels let alone his station manager's homestead he would camp out as it suited him, often along a nearby creek. Wherever he was he insisted his tea was brewed in a modest billy can, tea as it should be. James Tyson had excellent men, the best of the best, in the livestock and station management industry, working for him to the extent that Tyson cattle were shifted by Tyson drovers riding Tyson horses from Tyson breeding properties to Tyson fattening country.

When James Tyson passed away in 1898 Kidman made sure he enticed some of Tyson's men to work for him. They included the intriguingly named Pierce 'Barbed Wire' Edwards and his brother Albert 'Tie Wire' Edwards. Kidman said of Tyson: *I worked with Jimmy in the 1870s and travelled with him during the big 1891 strike. In spite of numerous legends of his meanness, I always found him a good man to deal with. His pay wasn't big but he used to say if he paid a man too much he would get rich too quickly and leave him. A man had to be a topnotcher to stay on Jimmy's payroll.* Tyson was another self-made man who succeeded as Kidman did. Neither did they accept waste, in any form.

When he passed away at *Felton Station* in 1898 Jimmy Tyson owned 2.1 million good hectares and his estate was valued at £2,500,000. He was Australia's first millionaire, a long way down the track from when he was once earning 12 shillings a week. His obituary was carried in the newspapers of Australia and in the *New York Times* and the *London Times*.

I hope the reader has realised that Henry O'Brien who employed the young Jimmy Tyson was the same Henry, 'Black Harry,' O'Brien who was a good friend to Andrew, Hamilton and Rawdon Hume and who tracked down the murdering bushrangers who killed John Hume. Bear with me a moment, if you will, while I refer back to the arrival of convicts to support my interest in Isabella Tyson.

From 1788 to 1868 there were 162,000 convicts transported to Australia in 825 ships. Of those 65,000 were consigned to Van Diemen's Land; Tasmania. If you've been to Port Arthur you would know the penal settlement was to break people not to rehabilitate them. Discipline was what the convicts were to expect when their ship reached Australia and to sustain themselves there was one item they craved above all, tobacco. Its addiction was such and its availability so restricted, that there were those that desired it above food, sex and it is said, even freedom. Possession of tobacco was punished by flogging, repeatedly for those who were so addicted they could not help themselves.

The voyage of the Second Fleet was under the control of private contractors who were paid per convict. It was the worst of all the transportation voyages. The ships included in 1790 were the *Surprize* on which thirty-six convicts died at sea out of 254, the *Neptune* which lost 158 convicts out of 499 and the *Scarborough*. When the *Scarborough* sailed in the First Fleet, under navy control, no one died but in the Second Fleet, seventy-three of her convicts died out of 253. A soldier who witnessed starving and unexercised prisoners on the *Surprize* said they lay chilled to the bone on soaked bedding, covered to one degree or another with salt, vomit and excrement while succumbing to scurvy and boils.

When the ships reached Sydney an Anglican chaplain found that 269 of the *Neptune's* surviving 341 convicts were incapacitated. Of the original 499 only seventy-two convicts were in reasonable health. The numbers for the other two ships were only marginally better with the chaplain estimating one man had 10,000 lice covering his body. Ships' captains had deliberately served short rations to their convict charges at sea then sold the conserved food to the starving colonists in Sydney at exorbitant prices. The Third Fleet had less deaths at nine per cent or one third of those of the Second Fleet. It is not meant to make light of convict sufferings but on one of my voyages on *Europa*, from Brazil to Chile, the First Mate wore a T-shirt saying, 'The floggings will cease when morale improves.'

On the *Britannia*, which brought Robert Kennedy's mother, Caroline Catapodi, to Sydney in 1798, one unfortunate convict received 800 lashes over two days, the second session with pieces of fresh horse skin braided to the cat-o'-nine-tails. He took several days to die and six other convicts were also lashed to death. About that time medical staff could not be spared to accompany the ships due to the Napoleonic wars. After 1815 when they were available conditions improved but they were still ghastly. Perhaps, in a way, the war was fortunate for some convicts, in that instead of being transported they were required to work in the docks. Even so, such was the flow of convicts that by 1800 there were only twenty-three free settlers in Sydney and, so I believe, convict ships were identified at sea by the red and white pennants they flew. There are countless other gruesome and disgraceful facets of the transporting of England's convicts to a foreign land, an exercise by the way which was never repeated anywhere else, but perhaps they are for others to recite. I have veered off the track and gone back several decades because the circumstances struck me that, as a convict, Isabella Coulson was incredibly fortunate and good luck to her, and her hardworking son James 'Hungry' Tyson.

Back to Mills who was still in Western Australia engaged in surveying but for the most part he was out in the bush prospecting for gold. While life was hard for many there must have been days when it was simply thrilling to consider that having come from the relatively closed confines of life in England, where you generally moved no more than 20 km from your birthplace in a lifetime, a man could ride off into the vast, wide-open lands of Australia, with or without his mates, experiencing a freedom hitherto unknown to him and with diligent application to his endeavours and the luck that most of us need now and again, especially when it surfaces unexpectedly, prove and satisfy himself.

In his later life Mills was prospecting around Norseman and Coolgardie. In his last years he set up a camp with a few mates, including Mr. Knuckey, who had been one of his fellow surveyors on the Overland Telegraph Line. He lived until 18th August, 1916, three months short of his 72nd birthday and considering the times that was a good life span. From what I can ascertain from a life table of people born from 1850 and onwards, only 10 per cent of people lived longer and Mills was an 1844 drop.

All the same he died in hard circumstances. A policeman from Coolgardie was nearby and confirmed the death which was then recorded in the *Kalgoorlie Miner* newspaper. In his report the policeman stated that Mills left personal property of £1/3/0. I found that amount confirmed by the Curator of Intestate Estates as issued for the Supreme Court of Western Australia, in the probate jurisdiction. The document is stamped 'Not Exceeding Two Pounds' so I imagine quite a few people passed on with less than £2 to their name. Fair enough, as they say, you can't take it with you. For all we know Mills may have had a premature farewell wake with his old mates.

16

Islamic attack and Railways.

I thought that was the end of the story but in 2015, I was having a talk with a man in my home town of Dubbo whom I knew well enough to say hello to here and there. Then he joined our Latin class and we found we had a few things in common. So one day we met in the early morning sunshine for a cup of tea and a talk. He was telling me he has done a fair bit of 4 Wheel Driving (4WD) in the Simpson Desert and other parts of Central Australia over the past ten years when up came the name, Skirmish Hill. Now for the life of me I can't be sure if he, and Roger is his name, or I, said the magic words, but that's what happened. I had an interest in the name because I knew Gosse, Forrest and Mills had blazed that tree and Roger knew a lot of colonial Australian history and specifically that those men had been to Skirmish Hill and that tree and it seemed to be well off most people's radar. I asked if he would be interested in going out there to find it and he replied he would. Things went from there.

I think I mentioned somewhere I was on that camping trip around the interior of Australia in 2002. We stopped for a couple of days in Alice Springs and whilst there, I met a lovely American lady who is a journalist in Alice. She is still there and we keep in touch so I phoned her and asked if she could recommend a local who knows the Skirmish Hill area and who could also help us obtain the necessary permits. She put me in touch with a retired surveyor and whilst he was interested he said there is one man, and one only, who has the knowledge but more importantly the connections to get us there. Skirmish Hill is on Aboriginal land and permits to visit such places are not only required but can be difficult to obtain.

I was passed along the line until I spoke with David Hewitt on the phone. By now several people had spoken highly of the man. He is an Alice Springs resident who, with his wife Margaret, has lived and worked amongst Aboriginal communities on and off for the past forty years. An electrician and builder by trade, he also assists Aboriginal people who have suffered kidney failure by providing dialysis treatment. He is widely known and trusted amongst the Aboriginal people and after I outlined the plan Roger and I had for making our way to Skirmish Hill, he said he knew about the tree and roughly where it is but that he had never been there. He said that he would like to find it and agreed to assist us in acquiring the permits and if that could be done he would guide us out there. Going by the maps and written reports of some of the explorers, Roger and I reasoned that we could find it ourselves but without having a man of David's stature along, we would most likely be rejected by those in authority.

Roger and I decided we would head off to Skirmish Hill the following winter as while it would be cold in the Great Victoria Desert of Western Australia at that time of the year it would be much safer and more sensible than attempting to go out there at any other time, let alone the summer. The explorer, Charles Sturt, in company with my great-great-great grandfather, Francis Rawdon Hume's brother, Hamilton Hume, journeyed along the Macquarie River through Dubbo country blasted by drought and searing heat. Dubbo did not exist then, in 1828, and the party continued on to the Bogan River before coming upon a much bigger river, one that Sturt named the Darling. He wrote, in part, that 'the blasts of heat were so terrific that I wondered the very grass did not take fire.'

And, *At noon I took a thermometer, graded to 127 degrees, out of my box, and observed that the mercury was up to 125 degrees. Thinking that it had been unduly influenced, I put it in the fork of a tree close to me and sheltered from the wind and the sun. I went to examine it about an hour afterwards, when I found the mercury had risen to the top of the instrument and had burst the bulb, a circumstance that I believe no traveller has ever had to record. I cannot find language to convey an idea of the intense and oppressive nature of the heat that prevailed.*

If our vehicle, which in this case would be Roger's 4WD Land Cruiser were to break down, or should we become lost, we wouldn't want to be out there in heat like that or even hotter. That reminds me of a friend of mine who is a Dubbo builder. He took on an apprentice, who came from the coast. When he arrived in Dubbo for his first day on the job the young man rather apprehensively said he had heard the temperature that day would be 40 degrees in the shade. My mate then said to him, 'That's alright son, we won't be in the shade.'

We needed that timeframe, not so much to prepare for the trip but to gain the approval we required. It was not just a matter of phoning someone or lodging an application. The tribal elders for the Skirmish Hill area live in the Great Victoria Desert community at Blackstone, WA, and David told us he would approach them personally.

Blackstone is 800 km west-south-west of Alice Springs and Warburton, which is named after the explorer Peter Warburton is a community 200 km further west. Another 550 km further on is the town of Laverton, known as British Flag in the gold rush days but changed in honour of Dr. Laverton, a highly regarded and dedicated medical practitioner who rode a bicycle wherever he went. The town, on the western edge of the Great Victoria Desert, was famous for gold and nickel and regarded for many a day as the wildest town in the west.

Laverton's Windarra mine was where Poseidon struck nickel in 1969. Due to speculation and its old companion, greed, the price of Poseidon shares raced up from $1.80 to $280, before just as quickly falling back to earth. I recall a friend who had invested in the company when it was on the way up and when it fell so fast he could not get out in time. He pasted his Poseidon share certificates on the wall alongside his toilet; I guess as a painful reminder.

If you keep going south-west for another 1,000 km from Laverton you will arrive in Perth. To the immediate north of Blackstone is the Gibson Desert and beyond that the Great Sandy Desert, while to the south is the Great Victoria Desert and in that is Skirmish Hill. Roger calculated it would be a 3,000 km drive from Dubbo to Skirmish Hill but as it transpired he was a good eight km short.

David had to wait until he was heading out to the Blackstone area on the 800 km drive to do maintenance work on Aboriginal houses that would give him the opportunity to talk to the elders about our proposed trip and when he arrived in Blackstone not all three of the men were there, two having gone walkabout. The man he did speak with about the trip was okay with it but he wouldn't commit himself until the other two did. Roger and I were concerned by the name, Skirmish Hill, because of the clash between Gosse and local natives in

1873 and not surprisingly the Aborigines can be touchy about such things. We discovered, fortunately, they refer to it as Kata Ala, the name before the white man rode onto the scene.

It was a few months before David was able to meet up with all three men and discuss the matter. They not only gave their approval for him, and Roger and me, to accompany David, they admitted even though it is on their tribal lands, they had never been there. They asked if they could come with us. That was a pleasant surprise but now we had to obtain permits from the Aboriginal Land Council that meets once a month in Alice Springs. We missed the next meeting by the skin of our teeth and the following month they did not have a meeting. Even when they did meet, our application was considered for quite some time before it was approved, thankfully. From go to whoa it took us ten months to gain that approval and David emailed copies to Roger and me. In the fine print I noticed it said that, 'this permit can only be revoked by the Minister for Aboriginal Affairs' and I now felt confident of our chances.

There is a particular reason I say that and I have been undecided for some time now as to whether or not I should mention it, but in keeping with calling it as it is, I shall. Before we set off on that camping trip around the interior of Australia in 2002 I had discussed that tree at Skirmish Hill with the leader of our group. He, Lloyd, felt that if we had permission to visit Skirmish Hill we would and that we could, indeed we should, set aside some time to find a tree with that historical significance. In those days I didn't know anyone in Alice but there was a man on the Dubbo City Council who might be able to help me, with his connections.

He, Warren Mundine, is an Aborigine and a man of interest who soon became Deputy Mayor of Dubbo. He later went on to become the President of the Australian Labor Party. He left the ALP in 2012 and in 2019 joined the Liberal Party. To cut a long story short he obtained a permit for us to those tribal lands and said before we did that we must call in to see the elders at the Wingellina Aboriginal community, not the ones at Blackstone, and let them know we were there and wished to continue on to the tree. Come the day and Lloyd and I drove into Wingellina at the appointed hour; we had been asked not to drive in before 9.30 a.m. so as not to disturb anyone, at that late hour of the day. To be fair, it seems that at least in days gone by, it was the accepted way of life that Aborigines did not get up until daylight had established itself, unless there were extenuating circumstance, which we were not. We of course had been up and about at 5.30 a.m.

Well we found the tribal elders and had a friendly but difficult talk with them for some twenty minutes, as they spoke little English. They were okay with us continuing on for the next 90 km or so to Skirmish Hill and Lloyd and I were just about to take our leave when a white man suddenly appeared in our midst and said, 'Who the hell are you? What are you doing here?' He wasn't exactly interested in shaking hands or exchanging the compliments of the day but yelled at us to get out. It seemed that he was the manager of the food store in particular and the community in general and he didn't want any outsiders nosing around and determining how he financially runs the place.

Now he probably bluffed us but we did not want to antagonise anyone on their Aboriginal land so we left to keep the peace but I have to say he acted just like a little Hitler. He tossed our permits aside and would not even let us explain our presence. A right so and so. When I later related that sorry episode to David he said straight away what we should have done was report the matter to the Aboriginal Central Land Council in Alice Springs and that would have been the end of him but that's easier said than done from an isolated area as we were in and without mobile phone connection. Anyway these new permits were going to see us reach our goal, Skirmish Hill.

Sunday, 3rd July, 2016. At 5.00 a.m. I was waiting on the footpath outside our house in Dubbo. It was a black night in the depths of winter but within two minutes the headlights of the already packed Land Cruiser curved around the corner and on straightening up exposed me standing motionless under the front tree. Roger stopped alongside me and I put my swag and daypack in the remaining but neat space in the back of the vehicle. I jumped into the front passenger seat and we were away. This was to be a boys' own trip and our wives said they didn't mind if we left them to sleep in their warm, dry, beds for a couple of winter weeks.

We headed north up Macquarie Street and turned left over the Macquarie

River. For the next few hours we held her steady on a westerly course with a bit of variety here and there. Dubbo sits at latitude 32.25 degrees and our first goal, Broken Hill, is 31.95 degrees. Not much difference there but there's a gap of 758 km in between them. We passed through long established and renowned rural towns such as Narromine, Trangie and Nyngan before refuelling at Cobar.

The first two hours passed in darkness and normally that entails the risk of meeting a few kangaroos at close quarters but that year, after a dry summer, it seems like it hadn't stopped raining. As a result, the crops looked excellent and there is stock feed in every paddock. With daylight came the hundreds of emus and the thousands of wild goats but they generally know enough to steer clear of man and his machines. There wasn't a solitary kangaroo in sight. There must have been so much grass around they didn't need to come in to the roadside table-drains where a bit of run-off moisture creates a little feed for them most of the time.

Roger and I shared the driving and cruised along a good road, doing it comfortably. The sky was clear, we had ample visibility and soon, good conversation. We stopped by the road for morning tea and later, lunch, and demolished our homemade sandwiches and thermos of tea and at 2.30 p.m. we came to Broken Hill. We drove around that rather unique town and soaked it up. In its heyday the main street of Broken Hill had more hotels than any other city in Australia. I know there were once twenty-six hotels in that street. I imagine if it hadn't been for the mining in and around the district it would however have struggled. Broken Hill is 1,147 km from Sydney and 515 km from Adelaide and fortunately it has a magnetism all of its own. It is not just distance that sets it apart. The city has an aura, a difference. If you haven't done so I hope you will come to experience it. Despite saying and believing that we didn't stay there that night as we have both been there before and as we were looking for an interesting alternative we moved on. On the outskirts of Broken Hill is a solar plant that is producing enough electricity to power the requirements of 17,000 houses while the one we passed at Nyngan supplies renewable electricity for 33,000 homes. We had a look around the Broken Hill solar system and were impressed by its modern-day infrastructure.

With the unfortunate rise of Islamic fundamentalism these days it is of interest to note that Broken Hill incurred a related incident on New Year's Day, 1915. On 11th November, 1914, after signing a treaty with Germany, the Sultan of the Turkish Ottoman Empire announced a holy war against Great Britain and her allies, obviously including Australia, describing them as the 'mortal enemies of Islam'. At the time there were few disaffected Muslims around the world who took up the call, except for some in Egypt and two in Broken Hill.

As recounted by Nicholas Shakespeare, there were two particular cameleers living in the North Broken Hill camel camp. They were Pathans, people of the Pashtun speaking region between Afghanistan and Pakistan. That is the area of the rugged Khyber Pass, which Janice and I travelled many years ago, on our honeymoon, and where we received the distinct warning that if we strayed off the road we would have our throats cut, as had just happened days earlier to three Frenchmen. They had engaged in a drug deal with local Pathans that went horribly wrong.

One of those Broken Hill men, Mullah Abdullah, was a community butcher and in the eyes of some he transgressed in two ways. He slaughtered his livestock in the halal manner, according to his religion, but worst of all he was not in the union and in Broken Hill that was just not on. The man who resented Mullah Abdullah far more than anyone else was a newly appointed but unqualified sanitary inspector. The man had twice failed to pass the required inspection certificate test. He picked on his fellow whites for their uncleanliness but he drove the Pathan to despair, fining him in the court system until he had no money left.

The second former cameleer, Badsha Mahomed Gul, was distraught because he had been laid off from his smelter work with the outbreak of war and contracts with German smelters being cancelled. Lead produced at Broken Hill was being used in Germany to make bullets, to be used against the ANZACs. The Muslim men decided to act against the wrongs perpetrated by Australians, on them.

On that New Year's Day the Broken Hill Independent Order of Oddfellows organised a picnic at nearby Silverton for their families and friends. A train from Broken Hill, consisting of forty open ore trucks was cleaned and fitted out with tables and seats and 1,200 people, all dressed up for a happy and relaxing day out, climbed aboard. In the meantime, Abdullah and Gul were taking up their ambush position on an embankment three km from town and just 30 metres from where the carefree families would pass by them. They were armed with knives, a Martini-Henry rifle and a Snider-Enfield rifle.

As the train load of innocent passengers, happily sitting up or standing in the open ore trucks drew abreast of the two gunmen, they opened fire. At such close range it is surprising they only killed four people and wounded six. A seventeen-year-old girl had the back of her head blown away and a bone fragment from there struck another girl with such force that it wounded her.

Until that happened, the passengers were not aware what was taking place but when it became obvious soldiers, police and irate citizens attacked the two men. After firing at the Pathans for some time they then charged their rock covered position and found Abdullah was dead but Gul, despite having been shot sixteen times, was somehow still alive. A reporter afterwards said the militia was 'desperate in its determination to leave no work for the hangman'. Both attackers had left written statements, Mullah Abdullah revealing 'but owing to my grudge against the sanitary inspector it was my intention to kill him first.' He missed. Badsha Mahomed Gul left a letter that said he was dying for his faith and that he was a subject of the Ottoman Sultan and that: 'I must kill you and give my life for my faith, Allahu Akbar.'

After 50 km we arrived at Cockburn, which the locals call Coburn. As we drove in we saw low down in the long grass a marker post that defines the border of New South Wales (NSW) and South Australia (SA). The town is in SA but as close as you could be to NSW without having a foot in that state. In those days Australian states had railway gauge lines of different widths and Cockburn was established to facilitate the changeover of trains and crews. Aided by the boom in mining, seven trains serviced Peterborough, Cockburn and Broken Hill. Cockburn's population jumped to 2,000 and in 1892, 83,194 passengers passed through the town. Today there are thirteen residents and some of those work away.

We pulled up outside the sole remaining 128-year old pub and walked past the motorbikes of a couple of blokes having a beer in the late afternoon sunshine that was already tinged by the quickly cooling air that presaged a cold night to come. The lady publican welcomed us warmly which was also nice on account of the quickly dropping temperature and before long she had used her own fair hands to cook us a hot meal. There was a fire inside the bar. The ceiling in the old hotel must be five metres high, which is good in the summer heat. She also owned an old building up the street and rented its single rooms out so we each took one of those for the night. There is room for a single bed but not much more. An early model air conditioner hangs over one's head and acts like it is a World War Two bomber warming up on the tarmac. I had the choice of trying to sleep through that racket or freezing all night. I soon worked out the best way to cope was to take it in turns with noise and cold.

In the morning I was refreshed by a hot shower in the amenities block and then Roger and I served up our travelling breakfast, which that morning was porridge on account of the chill but normally it was Weet-Bix. We stepped out into the fresh air, waiting for the sun to say hello and when it was light had a look around the old place. When the railway started up Kidman used Cockburn as a trucking centre as from here he could send his cattle that had come down from the north straight on to Adelaide by rail. In the latter days he also owned a number of stations in *The Barrier* region, in addition to *Wonnaminta* and *Nundora*. In 1908 the industrial activist, trade unionist and socialist Tom Mann had been barred from public speaking in NSW where he was also a union organiser for the Broken Hill Combined Unions Committee. That meant he could not address the workers of BHP in the bitter dispute that raged between the entities, especially over proposed pay cuts. So 3,000 BHP workers took the train to Cockburn and Tom Mann addressed them in the town of 2,000.

There were 1,000 square metre blocks of land for sale in Cockburn at prices ranging from $500 to $2,000, in 2016 annual land rates were $49.50. Water is delivered by tankers from Peterborough in SA or from Broken Hill with a fixed charge of $700 per year with a household allowance of 150 litres free per day per household. Above 150 litres water costs $13.98 per kilolitre. By comparison, in Dubbo we pay no fixed charge and $1.91 per kilolitre.

We drove the 233 km to Peterborough and stopped for a walk around the old town. It was mid-morning and while the people were pleasant and helpful, life seemed to move ever so slowly, perhaps influenced by the staid old buildings that have not been renovated or replaced since way back when. The tourist information office was in a 1916 railway carriage and we arrived one hundred years later. It is as though the carriage has been hand-crafted and no doubt it was, a century ago. The interior was lovely, the woodwork reflecting the style of the day and that includes the first-class sleeper compartments with toilets and showers. While one seems to enter a time warp, the delightful young lady tourist officer, born and bred in Peterborough, and there to enlighten the traveller, is of this era and helping to maintain today's population of 6,723.

Peterborough was another town with many German migrants. It was initially called Petersburg, until World War One altered people's opinion on numerous matters.

It takes some imagination to realise that a century or more ago Australia was serviced to such a large degree, first by the humble camel and then by a wonderful network of railway lines. With its natural resources and a far higher percentage of the population living in the bush, overall good weather and flat surfaces, the railway was the natural way. Well before the end of the 19th century Peterborough was linked to Adelaide, Port Pirie, Ororoo and Broken Hill. Ore from Broken Hill was transported by rail to the smelters at Port Pirie and by 1898 there were seventy trains per day engaged in that business and that wasn't the peak. That came over the following fifteen years and from 1911 to 1914 the Broken Hill to Port Pirie line was the busiest single railway line in the world. In 1923 there were 102 trains recorded as moving through Peterborough during a 24-hour period. Remarkable.

It wasn't only BHP that brought about the great surge in rail travel. It added to the development. From Sydney the railway went south to Goulburn, west to Wallerawang and north to Murrurundi. There the progress stopped, short of Bathurst to the west, for example, which upset people living there and further west. Then the NSW State Government had a brainwave. In 1872 it began selling off Crown land and during the next ten years it disposed of 25 million acres, five times as much as Victoria could do in the same time period. NSW debts disappeared, salaries went up and taxes went down. Caution went out the window and the government dispersed money with gay abandon, with one of its major projects being the politically popular decision to create the widest possible network of railways. From the 1850s to the 1950s government railways were Australia's biggest employers.

The NSW Government was then led by its longest serving Premier, Sir Henry Parkes, and the career Colonial Administrator, Sir Hercules Robinson, who served as the fifth Governor of Hong Kong, the fourteenth Governor of NSW, first Governor of Fiji, eighth Governor of New Zealand and Governor of South Africa's Cape Colony. By 1920 one-third of the world's 1,200,000 km of railway lines were in America which had twenty times Australia's population but only ten times the Australian railway length. With state governments pouring money into rail and refusing to exist in the dark ages of pre-rail transport, Australia then had a greater rail coverage per head of population than any other country. Would that it were still so, especially outside the capital cities, for those who live in and visit the bush.

As I have available space I shall pass on a little humour from those days, one each from man, woman and child.

Man to his drinking mates, 'My shout and it's me block and tackle.'

'What do you mean Jacko?' asks one.

'Me sixth. When I've had five double whiskies I do me block but when I've had six I'll tackle anything.'

Middle-aged woman surrounded by a troop of children is asked by a census taker if he can ask her some questions. 'Good-O, ask away,' she says.

'What's your name, ma'am?'

'Anthea Walton,' she replies.

'Married?' he enquires.

'No, I'm an old maid.'

'Whose are the children?' the census taker asks.

'Mine,' the woman replies.

'But I thought you said you're an old maid.'

'So I am; but I'm not a fussy one.'

Little girl excitedly runs home from Sunday school, gushing, 'Oh! Mummy. You'd *never* guess what we learned today?'

'What dear?'

'The O'possum's Creed.'

And for good measure you might like to know that at that time Australia had a collective welter of bookies and a glut of bishops. Daylight saving commenced on 1st January, 1917, and the reason back then was not to play golf after work but to conserve energy supplies for World War One. The Chinese who came to Australia to work the goldfields introduced opium to their new home and it was the principal ingredient in many medicines such as Siegels Operating Pills, Dr. Morse's Indian Root Pills and Pink Pills for Pale People. The 1912 Pure Foods Act put an end to those practices but by then opium and cocaine dens were in the major cities aplenty. Early amputations were done without anaesthetics and the patient either took alcohol, opium or a blow to the head. Infections caused a major loss of life.

The Australian stockman did not use the lasso, the bowie knife or the hand gun as did the American cowboy but he was pretty good with his constant rifle, certainly with the stockwhip and, many say, supreme at riding buckjump horses. There was another exceptional skill he developed during down time in a mustering camp or elsewhere as circumstances permitted. He would practise throwing a tomahawk at a small circular mark, about 76 mm in diameter, on a tree. The aim was to bury the blade in it from a distance of 10 metres, while on his galloping horse. A more dangerous exercise was for two men to stand a metre or two apart and engage in a tomahawk duel, each catching the other's weapon, or not, by the handle as it revolved rapidly towards him.

On occasions, some stockmen were of a mind to dress for the moment, as it took their fancy, but they must have been among the few men with a damn good income. The most favoured outfit for going out on the town consisted of snow-white, tight-fitting moleskin trousers, coloured shirt, black coat, a gaudily coloured silk neckerchief, cabbage tree or wide-brimmed felt hat, Cossack boots and long-necked spurs, those being inseparable from his stockman's heels. The spurs jingled him to dinner and kept time to his pirouetting around the dance floor. When he removed his boots at night the spurs invariably stayed strapped to them and if he was camping out he often slept with them still attached.

By 1910, the closer-in and settled districts had farms producing record wheat and other crops thanks to progress such as the famous McKay harvester, developed in the 1880s, and the constant introduction of better wheat varieties along with superphosphate, steam machines, tractors, chemicals and fertilisers. In 1915, the government bought wheat direct from farmers to stop it ending up in German hands. That action brought about the introduction of the long-established Wheat Board, which is now gone and today we have a myriad of grain traders, big and small, in a free market.

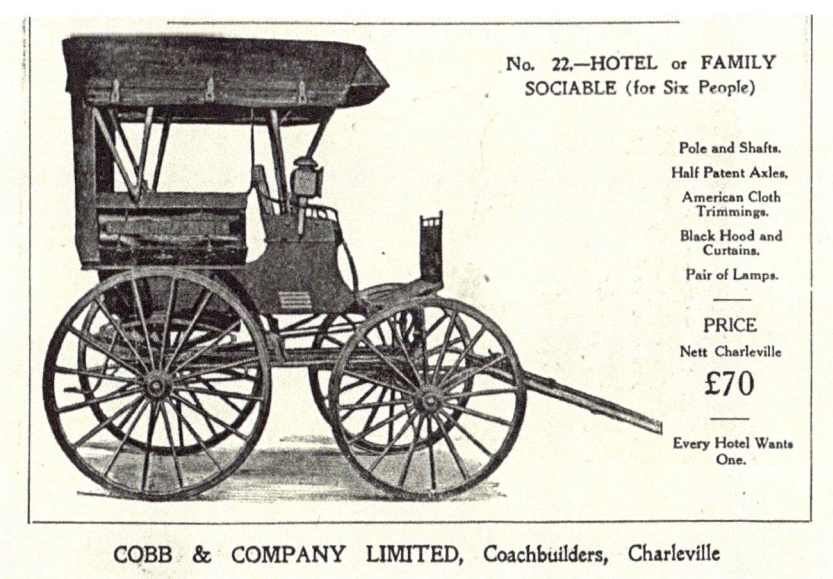

Cobb and Co built coaches at Bathurst, Hay and Goulburn but when coastal timber was used it tended to crack in the outback. So factories were built in the heat of Bourke and Charleville where the locally used timber cured perfectly and lasted longer. Coaches built for Victoria and NSW were usually painted red and yellow while Queensland was to be seen in white. After servicing Australia for 70 years, first trains, then cars and trucks and finally planes brought Cobb and Co undone, in 1923. On 2 November, 1922, Qantas, although based in Winton, made its first regular mail and passenger service, from Charleville to Cloncurry.

Ancient mesa scree slopes with duricrust of silcrete at Theldarpa Station, west of Milparinke. Photo by Ruth Sandow, Pimpara Lake, Packsaddle.

Central Australian police.

The 34 kilogram 'Golden Eagle' nugget, found at Widgiemooltha and photographed in Kalgoorlie, WA.

Station hands on Cardawan station, WA.

Harry Dutton on right, of Kapunda, with mechanic and co-driver, Murray Aunger, in Harry's 1908 Talbot motor car, Angelina, as they set off to be the first to drive from Adelaide to Darwin.

A rifle was deemed necessary.

As were station-bred mules to pull Angelina over the sandhills.

With no roads in existence there were numerous obstacles to overcome, such as being bogged in dry country.

Bogged in water.

A good section of the track.

Two Talbots, the first cars to travel from Adelaide to Darwin.

A Talbot vehicle with a Vickers machine gun on the front and a 10-pound gun in the covered rear.

A World War One gathering of T.E. Lawrence's military Talbot and Rolls-Royce vehicles.

The man in white robes and on a white horse, ninth from the left is Lawrence of Arabia, with his Arab bodyguard.

A force of T.E. Lawrence's six Talbot vehicles and nine Rolls-Royce armoured cars.

Men of the Fourth Contingent, Queensland Imperial Bushmen, days after returning from the Boer War on 17th August, 1901. The photo features an Aboriginal soldier on the far right, courtesy of AIATSIS, the Australian Institute of Aboriginal and Torres Strait Islander Studies.

Photographed on Sunday 10th January, 1915, at the Great Pyramid of Khafre (Cheops) in Egypt are some of the 703 men of Western Australia's 11th Battalion, 65 of whom would die in action on the first day of the Gallipoli landings, as Anzacs.

The champion buckjump horse, Curio, being ridden for the first time in eight years, by Alan Woods, at Marrabel rodeo, SA.
Photo by Keith Stevens.

Curio, dropping the shoulder in her trademark style, won this round.

The notorious convict and escapee, Moondyne Joe, wearing a kangaroo-skin coat.

Laurie Sinclair and his brothers, of Hardy Norseman and gold fame.

16-year old heroine Grace Bussell, with Aboriginal stockman, Sam Isaacs, plunged their horses into raging seas for four hours to save 40 shipwrecked people from drowning.

A police patrol, per camels.

Author's painting, purchased Alice Springs Telegraph Station 2002

Camel train in foreground with Aborigines near Uluru sending smoke signals to tell of white men passing their way. Courtesy of the National Library.

A truckload of 3,600 koala pelts. In August, 1927, 600,000 koalas were killed for the demanding overseas fur trade and to generate income for the unemployed.

*Loading wool onto camels, Euston, on the Murray River, NSW, 1920.
Courtesy Victoria Museum, Melbourne.*

Australian soldiers marching through London, ANZAC Day Parade, 1916. Courtesy of Victoria Museum, Melbourne.

A 67 strong camel train. Looking at the ground cover it may be near Charlotte Waters.

Jim Hubbard, an indigenous Wangkumara man, with a white father, from Thargomindah, Qld, born 1879, was recognized as one of Australia's best horsemen. He volunteered for WW1, Service number 1726, and was assigned to purchase and deliver 500 horses to Rockhampton to be shipped to the Middle East. There he served with the 5th Light Horse Regiment's 2nd Remount Unit commanded by Major Banjo Patterson, as a Rough Rider breaking in many of the 700 horses that arrived nearly every week by steamer from Australia. He was described as perfect in riding as Bradman in batting. After four years he returned to Weilmoringle Station, Brewarrina, NSW, and was a renowned horse-breaker around the border districts, riding until age 80. Drawing by George Washington Lambert, official Australian war artist, in the Middle East during WW1.

Aborigines fishing at Chowilla Station, 94,000 hectares and 42 km north of Renmark on the Murray River, South Australia. Home of the historically important Charles Todd obelisk.

19th century fishermen at Hastings Jetty, Victoria. They would go to sea after attending football on Saturday and church services on Sunday and return on Thursday with their catch.

17

Woomera and Coober Pedy

We know South Australia did not receive one of the 162,000 convicts sent to Australia and it wasn't until 1829 that a white man even appeared in the colony, which then was still part of NSW. The first settlement was on Kangaroo Island, until Colonel Light determined what would become Adelaide was the place to be, with its proclamation on 28 December, 1836. For some reason SA was declared a province, not a colony. The copper at Kapunda, followed by the even bigger strike at Burra, helped SA's development but it later stalled. Then came the Broken Hill silver, lead and zinc ore, all of which had to be refined via a smelter. So, did NSW run a railway line out to Broken Hill to take advantage of that incredible wealth? No. There was a rail line to Dubbo in 1881, Nyngan 1883, Bourke 1885 and Cobar 1892 but despite earlier progress the Parkes to Broken Hill line was not completed until 1927.

The NSW Government would not let SA extend the rail line it had at Cockburn but private enterprise built a way around that and most of the Broken Hill ore was shipped, by rail, to the smelter in Port Pirie in SA. The outgoing trains from Port Pirie took coal and timber for the mines to Broken Hill and returned with the proceeds of the richest mine in the world. It is not hard to see who had the best of that deal and that includes Peterborough. Today a camel and wild horse export registered abattoir operates in Peterborough, producing high quality meat, offal, hides, meat and bone fertiliser and tallow. There are enough wild camels roaming Central Australia to provide sufficient stock.

We continued on and 36 km down the road we came to another delightful town; Orroroo. Much smaller with just 540 people the town has an open friendly feel about it. Like Peterborough it was a rail town but those days have passed and today it is a regular rural community, catering to the production of sheep and cattle along with wheat and oats farming. There is also a long-term well-established kangaroo meat processing works. We drove a little way out of town until we came to a collection of life-size figures of early settlers and their livestock along the side of the road. Nearby were plaques that depict the history of the area and they note that this place marks a section of Goyder's Line, the demarcation line that George Goyder used to determine safe and recommended areas for farming, south of the line, as against the too risky low rainfall area, to the north of the line.

The first white people who settled in the Orroroo district took up the *Pekina Run* of 80,000 hectares. After seventeen months and not receiving one drop of rain, they sold it for just £30.

Turning off a bush road, we followed a track that brought us to a 500-year-old river red gum tree. There are stands of river red gums around the country that are 700 years old but this one is easily accessible and lovely to observe. Like its brothers it is about 45 metres in height and has a full spread of heavy widow-maker branches endowed with a thick canopy of leaves. In pioneer days it was said these trees were sought as timber cutters could make 1,400 fence posts out of such a tree with its 10.4 metre circumference. In Traiguera, Spain, botanists claim local 1,700-year-old olive trees were planted by the Romans. They say olive circumferences of 10 metres indicate an age over 1,000 years. Some of those trees would have been planted in the days of the Roman Emperor Constantine.

As long as it has the water supply, the river red gum grows fast and what suits it most, apart from rainfall, is flood water as then the moisture goes deep into the subsoil and if that is clay soil, all the better. What nowadays goes against the tree are dams and irrigation as those practices do not provide the free-flowing recharging that the great tree is accustomed to. The seeds of the tree germinate keenly after floods but they need annual spring floods to ensure their continuing life flow. I am told the majority of the river red gums in the lower Murray River, lacking those flows, are under such pressure they are dying off but they are still numerous along the Macquarie River at Dubbo.

We stopped for a picnic lunch in Port Augusta, which was founded by Thomas Elder's elder brother, Alexander Elder in 1852. Sitting on the wharf's timber planks by the water's edge in the warm winter sunshine was a pleasure but after buying fresh fruit and vegetables for the track ahead we moved on. By the time we arrived in Woomera we had covered a steady 340 km for the day; not far but by taking it easy we did enjoy the drive. We opted to stay in the Eldo Hotel for the night as not only did the rain come down heavily but the temperature dropped like a guillotine blade. It was the wettest July day in Adelaide for seventy-five years and although Woomera is 486 km north of the 'City of Churches' we felt its frigid touch from afar and it didn't inspire us to camp out. However someone was doing that.

As we were checking over the Land Cruiser in the early morning chill, prior to departing, I fell into conversation with a forty-something bloke packing gear onto his motorbike. His name was Terry, from Merimbula, on the South Coast of NSW, and I mention him because we would meet up with him along the way. He told us that he was travelling with his mate, Nick. When I asked where was he?, Terry jerked the thumb of his right hand over his shoulder and said, 'out there'. The rain had stopped during the night but the air was still freezing and Terry told us that his friend Nick had stayed out in the rain last night. He added, 'He's like that. He's happy in the bush. He loves the challenge of it. The harder the better for him. I like my comfort but we'll meet up on the road today and ride together.'

Roger and I drove downtown and walked around the Missile Park. The air was brisk and although the sun came out, the wind was fresh and we put on our heavy coats. The town of Woomera is part of the Australian Defence Force base, RAAF Base Woomera, and all that is encompassed in the systems testing range which covers 127,000 square kilometres. The renowned Kidman cattle station *Anna Creek*, is one of twenty-seven rural properties that is wholly or partly within that area and for that apparent reason *Anna Creek* was excised from the sale of the whole Kidman conglomeration.

One of those other properties was the one million hectare *Commonwealth Hill Station* and in 1947 the government decided to expand the Woomera Test Range. This meant that various stations such as *Commonwealth Hill, Roxby Downs, Bulgunnia* and *Andamooka* lost some of their land and consequently their wool income from sheep. The station owners hired lawyers to argue that they would establish a working agreement to ensure the continuation of their livestock industry would not interfere with the long-range weapons activities. One outcome of this was that the Australian Government told the station owners that the government would pay for the installation of blast-proof bomb shelters. How about having one of those at your home?

Woomera is the largest land-based defence systems testing and evaluation facility in the world and it allows many approved countries to do their testing, away from prying eyes. There have been more than 4,000 rocket launches and nine atomic tests. A group from Norway had only just left Woomera before we arrived and many Americans are still living and working there.

The Missile Park contains a Black Arrow rocket, one of which put up a still orbiting satellite, a Meteor Mark 7 British jet aircraft, the Jindivik Australian designed and built pilotless target aircraft and many more weapons systems and the wrecks of numerous rockets that fell back to earth. It is a rare opportunity to see homing torpedoes, rockets, satellite launchers and the like even though they are out of date. The current ones were not available to our eyes.

We drove out of town to the gates of Camp Rapier, which used to be an immigration detention centre but that was as far as we were allowed to go. Today it is the secure garrison support and specialised training compound within the Woomera Prohibited Area. The gates were locked to the likes of us so we moved on to the cemetery.

There was no objection to us blending in with the deceased. We found the grave of Len Beadell, the man who achieved great things in Central Australia. Not only was he asked, due to his experience and knowledge of the terrain, to select the site for Woomera and within that, the atomic bomb testing site, but he and his crew surveyed and constructed thousands of kilometres of roads, such as his well named, 1,400 km, Gunbarrel Highway, through the outback. Needless to say, those men did the job in tough conditions and they did not have the machinery of today to work with. With his team of five men, a bulldozer, a grader, two big four-wheel drive trucks and his own specially modified short-wheel base Land Rover, they completed up to four miles of road every day, an enormous achievement. Their original Gunbarrel Highway crossed the harsh

Gibson Desert and went west to Carnegie Station, among few others. In those far-ranging days Carnegie Station's nearest station neighbour to the east was more than 800 miles or 1,280 km away. They carved out 6,000 kilometres of roads, most of them as straight as slate, from 1947 to 1963. He and his men are another mob we are indebted to. Ask a 4WD traveller.

Another easy drive of 388 km took us further north to Coober Pedy, famous for its opals. The first find was made in 1915 and when soldiers returned from the World War One trenches they introduced the technique of living in a dugout, underground. It was and still is a most appropriate form of habitation as the area is known for high temperatures.

We made our way to *Venus Hill*, the home of Mike Venus who came out from Austria in 1990 and like most residents dug in and stayed. Mike's place is at the base of a hill and he has dug out a good section of it and built a lovely home. The soil is compressed sandstone so it is not too hard to dig out a home area, although the sandstone does have soft patches and builders need to be mindful of that. He has diversified by providing accommodation for travellers. Alongside his home he has dug out a long tunnel into the hill and then extended on both sides to create bedrooms, living areas, kitchen and bathroom. We could have rented that for the night and the experience of living underground, even for one night, would have been enjoyable but we had not come there for that and it was far cheaper to rent an above ground transportable donga, such as is the custom in most mining camps. Mike had a basic donga to accommodate both of us so we moved in there. *Venus Hill* is out on the edge of the town and the beauty of that was that we had a top view over the surrounding terrain. It is plains country, flat as a blacksmith's anvil, highlighted by distant mesa-like hills and dusted with a windblown salmon-shaded crust that yields to the sand blasting sun. A good place to stay at this time of year. The annual long-term rainfall average for Coober Pedy is 156 millimetres.

Coober Pedy used to have thousands of opal miners in the 1970s and the 1980s. The numbers have lately fallen away dramatically, due to the high cost of mining, despite the rewards on offer. The town has transformed itself to being more of a tourist centre. These days the shafts are put down by machinery and it can cost from $800 to $1,000 to have the first shaft drilled but the three-month licence fee is a reasonable $35 or the yearly fee is $130 although Mike's two-month electricity bill is sometimes $1,000.

In 1916 water carriers brought in water to Coober Pedy, their camels each carrying two 110-litre barrels of water and walking 64 km to do so. In 1921, the government provided the materials to build a 2,250,000-litre water tank and everything, including the cement, was carried on five wagons, each hauled by a team of fourteen camels, from William Creek.

Due to the low rainfall, which in some years is virtually non-existent, the tank took years to fill. Today water comes from a sub-artesian bore, 25 km away, is put through a desalination plant and then reticulated through the town. The desalination plant can produce 1,400,000 litres per day but the end result is expensive. The fixed charge is $170 with the water itself costing $6.80 per kilolitre; expensive but still less than the price of water in Cockburn. The cost of electricity in Coober Pedy is subsidised by the SA Government, otherwise there would most likely be more people leaving town. Water is always an issue in the bush, as it is and will be, in too many places around this world.

Coober Pedy has a school, a hospital and an increasing number of people from Asia. Last year, 2015, twenty-four Sri Lankans arrived to spend two years in the outback as part of their qualification for receiving Australian residency. I gather this happens often. Excluding the odd exception, blocks of land in the town cost from $5,000 to $40,000, depending on any work already done such as face cutting a hill block and /or commencing to dig out tunnels. Not all houses are underground. The area around the main street with above ground houses looks like any other town. One thing to be aware of is the land title as the locals say leasehold land is worthless. They claim such land can be and has been, taken from owners and transferred to Aboriginal people while freehold land is still sacrosanct.

Many individuals have made their fortune from finding opals at Coober Pedy and some small groups of partners have had amazing success. One such group of miners from Eastern Europe had a claim over a patch of ground that measured 50 metres by 50 metres. It was found to be all opal, not just everyday opal but precious black opal, all of it. Not only that but instead of going down and working the claim over the usual two or three levels, they dug out ten levels, all of which produced staggering amounts of black opal. I am assured they made so much money they could afford to buy an entire suburb of Adelaide. Another group, of Greeks and Yugoslavs, who struck similar riches, hired an aeroplane to fly to their homelands and return with women and alcohol, to their tastes, to celebrate their good fortune. Some of the ladies married, stayed on and are still in Coober Pedy.

That evening we were walking across the main street when a 4WD utility seemed to swerve in towards me and brushed me by. I was thinking that was close, why would he drive like that, when a voice called out, 'Bill, hey Bill.' I stopped as the ute pulled in and parked by me as I reached the footpath and looked at the driver who had called out to me. It was a friend, David, from my home town of Dubbo, with his wife and daughter. It was good to see them and we had a yarn before they headed out of town to find a place to pitch their tent for the night. With the long-range fuel tanks in that dual-cab ute they could drive for 1,400 km and they hadn't stopped for fuel until they reached Port Augusta which is 1,200 km from Dubbo.

Roger and I had a look around the *Desert Cave Hotel*, with its multi levels and first-rate restaurants and accommodation. It was a surprise to find such a resort out there but as was suggested, Coober Pedy is becoming more and more a town with tourist appeal. John's Pizza Restaurant was recommended and according to reviewers was rated the fifth best pizza place in all of Australia. That's a big wrap so we went in and had pizza. It was good but so was our lovely waitress with the equally enticing name of Desiree. A beautiful young woman, and I couldn't help myself but ask what she was doing in Coober Pedy? She said she had just returned from two years in Canada but she was born and raised in Coober Pedy and there is no place like home. Home is where the heart is. Good for her.

In the morning we opened the door of our donga and stepped outside. I then moved back inside and reached for my camera, for directly ahead of us, in the eastern sky was the most colourful of sunrises. The initial golden glow was now turning red and I do mean a bold red, with the gold dissolving to faint slivers amongst that overpowering and brilliant red. I've seen a few good ones and this sunrise was on par with the best of them, and the sky was so big.

That made for a great start to the new day and we continued on our way north-north-west to Marla. As we drove out of Coober Pedy and along the road, I was stunned by the number of mounds of earth brought up by the miners as they dug down in search of opal. They continued for 20 km on both sides of the road and spasmodically after that for another 20 km. In the days of my youth I was a jackaroo for two years at *Wingadee Station*, south of Walgett, NSW, and on its northern side is Lightning Ridge. On our one day a month off work we would occasionally go the Ridge and scratch around for a bit of opal. I thought the Ridge was big but it is a grain of sand on Manly beach compared to Coober Pedy. In 1999, it was calculated there were more than 250,000 mine shafts around Coober Pedy.

Along the track, Roger and I stopped for a cup of morning tea from the thermos we always carried when Terry from Merimbula came by on his motorbike and said hello. A few minutes later my Dubbo mate, David, roared past, blowing the horn. We passed through the small town of Marla, the town at the northern end of the Oodnadatta Track, and went on to the South Australia/Northern Territory border. A couple of km later we turned off to the left, on to the Mulga Park road and past *Victory Downs Station*. We could have kept on heading north in the direction of Alice Springs and then turned left on to the sealed Lasseter Highway but we wanted to be on the dirt so we took the first of the two roads. I had driven 402 km for the morning run and when we were nicely on the Mulga Park road we stopped for lunch by the roadside. As we were having a bite to eat, Dubbo David went past us, again. He must have stopped somewhere, probably in Marla, and he was on the move once more.

Roger drove on until we found a decent place well in from the road to camp for the night. We put up our tents where we could briefly see any vehicles passing by but they could not see us. There was no rush in the late afternoon sunshine and we relaxed around the camp fire before cooking our dinner. The air was warmer and we slept well, until 4.00 a.m. I was woken by the sound of rain on the tent. Every drop could be heard, so distinctly, and in the still of the night it was loud, like a drumbeat at a funeral procession. Rain, pure and life-sustaining water, but the one thing we didn't need on this trip. It was not the inconvenience of being cold or uncomfortable but it doesn't take much rain to close these dirt roads and 2016 was turning in to the second wettest winter in Australia's recorded history. I went over to Roger's tent and we discussed driving the Land Cruiser out while we could and leaving it by the side of the road. If it really did rain at least we could carry the tents and gear out and then have a chance of getting underway but if we were truly bogged off-road, that could just be awkward. We decided to wait a while. We must have pulled the right rein because the rain left. It lightened off and as it drifted away so did I, sleeping in until 6.00 a.m.

We had dug a pit for last night's fire and the ashes were thick enough to survive the rain so I stoked them up and soon had the fire underway. It was not light enough until 7.00 a.m. but in that hour we packed up and put our gear away before having our breakfast of porridge, bananas and billy tea. Since we made camp at 4.00 p.m. yesterday only one vehicle came by. While giving the Land Cruiser its morning check, Roger discovered a bolt had become loose from the lower shock absorber and fallen out. He replaced it and we hit the road.

Mid-morning when we pulled over for smoko Roger did another check and found that his replacement bolt had also disappeared. It was a puzzle as to how it had worked its way out so soon, but for the time being it didn't affect us. The Mulga Park dirt eventually joined up with the Lasseter Highway with its solid surface and we turned on to that. *Curtin Springs Station* has a lot of road frontage amongst its 404,000 hectares and has established a roadhouse with other facilities to entice the traveller. It looked as though they had a good set-up but we stopped only briefly. I did manage to talk with two of the stockmen and they told me the station normally runs 4,000 head of cattle. Due to the season being so good and cattle prices so high, they sold this year's sale stock and had nothing left to sell for the rest of the year, without disrupting their regular breeding program.

The property was once known as Mt. Connor Station and is 85 km east of Uluru and south-west of Alice Springs. In the early 1950s the name was changed to Curtin Springs in honour of Australia's renowned 14th Prime Minister, John Curtin, the man who guided the nation through the traumas of World War Two, only to die weeks prior to the war ending. He is one of three Prime Ministers to die in office. Mt. Connor is still within the station's substantial boundaries and its enticing mesa formation and outback colours inspired Albert Namatjira to produce another of his famous watercolours. In colonial days the property was owned by the Andrews family and a faded photograph, in the book, shows a woman taking a wagon from Curtin Springs to Alice springs to collect supplies. The wagon was pulled along by twenty six donkeys and the distance was 360 km, each way.

It was not only pioneering settlers and explorers who did it hard in colonial Australia. By 1903 there were but seven European women living in the Alice Springs area. Another photo shows six of those redoubtable heroines who overcame the lack of necessities and infrastructure such as are taken for granted today. An additional burden at that time was the introduction of the Marriage Bar, which was intended to keep women Australia-wide from taking men's jobs and to boost the birth rate. Many women kept their marriage a secret. The Marriage Bar meant that women working in education were not permitted to teach after marriage until 1956 when the Temporary Teachers' Club was successful in its lobbying but it was 1966 before the Marriage Bar was lifted in the Australian Public service.

One might think that travelling aboard the Oodnadatta to Alice Springs mail coach would have been an opportunity to sit back and relax for a few hours but there were times when even that was a feat of endurance. On sections of the journey the horses refused to pull a full load and the passengers were required to get out and push or follow the coach over rough terrain in searing heat. They walked alongside the coach struggling to keep up the pace, all the time listening to the abusive language of the coach driver urging his horses on. In 1909 the Alice Springs Central Advocate reported a passenger's lament as 'after about three hours we came through the ordeal and, to our gladness we came upon more level country. By this time man and beast were exhausted. I will remember walking miles that day, following behind the mailman; at times I thought we would never catch up again'.

We had obviously bypassed Alice Springs, even though Mills had discovered and named it and now came to Yulara, the village or town established to service nearby Uluru (Ayers Rock). If you like your comfort I don't think you will be disappointed with the resorts and other accommodation to be found today at Yulara but Roger and I set up our tents in the local camping ground and there wasn't much bare ground around. It was school holiday time and a popular place for families to bring their children and to avoid the blistering summer heat. At times it truly is a small world. Terry walked by and said hello. His tent was only 30 metres from ours and he said, 'Nick's here.'

Well I just had to meet this bloke so I went over and introduced myself and I'm glad I did for Nick is a very likeable feller. Probably in his late thirties, average height and weight, a good-looking man I guess but nothing about him that seemingly makes him different to many others. He had been out in the scrub alright and whilst Roger and I were warm and dry in Woomera, Nick had been out in that horrible night of freezing rain. That's part of camping and what he loved to do, and possibly what he lives for, but despite his experience, his motorbike became bogged, good and proper. He dug it out and continued to ride across country to Yulara and this was when and where he had caught up with Terry, as he said he would.

Nick's bike was an Austrian KTM 1,000 cc which he told me can go anywhere in the rough and yet had great power for road travelling. He was pleased that the Australian rider Toby Price had earlier in the year won the annual Dakar off-road race on a KTM and in the process become the first Australian to win that prestigious world event. I asked him what was the hardest part of such competition and he instantly replied, 'concentration'. He said, on a motorbike, ridden at high speed, the failure to see in time, let alone take account of, one stone up ahead, one wheel rut that beats you, it can be the difference between winning and losing.

As you drive into Yulara there is a large sign that says, 'Mechanical Repairs'. I imagine a lot of people find that reassuring and we were no different. We found the workshop on the edge of town and it is a big set up so it must be well in demand. Even though it was a hive of activity we were immediately asked what do we need? Roger explained the missing bolt situation and within minutes the Land Cruiser was up on a hoist. They didn't have the exact same bolt in stock but took one from another vehicle, I presume one of theirs, and fitted it. The mechanic was from north Queensland and, like many people out in the Centre, utilising the flexibility of his trade to literally work his way around Australia. He could not have been more helpful or pleasant and he made an absolute certainty of that bolt, guaranteeing his life on it that the new bolt will never come out. I wouldn't have minded if he was my mechanic. You didn't hear that, Mick.

In the evening Roger and I finally met up with David and Margaret Hewitt of Alice Springs. David would be our guide to Skirmish Hill and our passport into Aboriginal territory. Margaret would travel with us part of the way. They took us to the home of friends of theirs, Rod and Marianne, who have lived at Yulara for many years and work in airport security. The six of us went out to dinner and Roger and I learned a bit about what happens at airports. Rod told us there are only two people in the world who do not have to be scanned in Australian airports. They are Queen Elizabeth II and the Pope and there are no exceptions for anyone else. We were equally fascinated to learn that there were still people who make a joke about a bomb at an airport. Once those words are picked up the person who spoke them is taken away and interviewed, or interrogated, and the Captain of their flight informed. Even though the words were most likely uttered in jest they are not treated that way and when the offender has been made to see the error of their ways it was up to the Captain to decide if the joker could go aboard his plane. Invariably, according to Rod, the Captain will refuse to allow the person on board and he or she has to wait overnight and if possible be allowed on another flight the following day. So, the old adage still prevails, 'least said, soonest mended'.

18

Ways of the Aborigines

We filled up with fuel and followed David and Margaret out of town to a turn-off road just before Ayers Rock. It was a good spot for a photo of the monolith in the clear early morning light. The explorer William Gosse saw and named it after Sir Henry Ayers, the Chief Secretary of South Australia. For almost 50 years Ayers was in control of the 'Monster' copper mine at Burra, north of Kapunda, where he and the state of South Australia both prospered. Roger, David and Margaret have seen the Rock many times and I was able to climb it in 2002 so we moved on and turned off at that point, onto the road to Western Australia. Shortly after we stopped and climbed a low hill which has a viewing platform that looks over The Olgas.

The Olgas are a collection of thirty-six substantial sized red rocks or domes that are formed up in a natural circular group, with the highest rock reaching 546 metres above ground, about 200 metres higher than Ayers Rock. Collectively they are a most attractive formation and intriguing to walk amongst as the wind sometimes wafts between them and sings to you.

The Olgas are also known by their Aboriginal name, *Kata Tjuta*. When the explorer Ernest Giles came upon Lake Amadeus and The Olgas he wanted to name them Lake Mueller and Mt Ferdinand, after his benefactor Ferdinand Mueller but the good botanist insisted Giles name them Lake Amadeus, after King Amadeus of Spain and Mt Olga, after Queen Olga of Wurttemberg. Olga Nikolaevna was the second daughter of Nicholas I, Emperor of Russia from 1825 to 1855, and the Empress Alexandra of Russia. Olga married Prince Karl of Wurttemberg and when he ascended to the throne and became King, she was crowned Queen of Wurttemberg. They never had children and Karl was reputedly of a homosexual nature. So they became a pair, a queen and a queen.

We drove on. It was a lovely day and I would like to say Ayers Rock was looking its best. Before we are too far away, I might mention the ownership of the Rock as it came up in discussions while we were in Yulara. On solid local information it appears there are more than 200 traditional owners, those people who have lived there, and the number is growing. People want to be included in the ownership and therefore share in the spoils, the money that the Rock brings in. That's fair enough but I am assured the following is gospel. A few years ago a convoy of cars containing Aborigines from another tribe was going past Ayers Rock when one of the cars, in which there was a husband and wife, broke down. The wife was on the point of giving birth and when no one could get their car started again, she had the baby then and there.

The years rolled by and the baby boy grew to manhood. He put in an application to be included amongst the owners of Ayers Rock on the basis that he was born in its shadow, or thereabouts. Even though he and his family are of another tribe and a distant one at that, his application was successful and he was added to the list of traditional owners, which some say is now nearer to 300 than 200.

When we stopped for a cup of tea along the track I noticed a low-lying green plant with long succulent stems. It was the parakeelya plant and traditional Aborigines like the fleshy leaves and the roots and eat them steamed although some eat the leaves raw. The plant has bright pink/purple flowers and the Aborigines also grind the seeds and eat them in the form of a paste. David told us an interesting but sorry and well-known story. Cattle also have a liking for the plant as they gain so much moisture from it they do not need to drink water. A mob of cattle found a large area of the plant and ate it as they followed the fresh food forward. Eventually the cattle ran out of parakeelya and found themselves in an area devoid of water. The owner realised his cattle were missing and sent up a helicopter to find them. The pilot found the cattle dead, of thirst, all 260 of them.

Driving on we passed the turn-off to the Mannanana Range cave, where Lewis Harold Bell Lasseter had sought sanctuary after his camels broke away from him and he was left stranded, bar receiving assistance from some Aborigines who for a while gave him food and water. Lasseter stayed in the cave for twenty-five days in January, 1931, and then attempted to walk to Ayers Rock but tragically perished. Lasseter was of course, and I suppose still is, known for his claims of having found a massive reef of gold out here, which neither he nor anyone else has since seen. Roger and I did not visit the cave as we had both, on different occasions, been there previously.

When I visited Lasseter's cave with a few friends, we afterwards made our camp for the night nearby. We had the fire settling down and the tents up when a bloke on a motorbike arrived and seeing us there he asked would we mind if he camped with us. We said he was most welcome and invited him to have dinner with us, which he did. Someone asked him where he was heading and he said he had just felt like going for a ride on his bike and that was what he was doing. It turned out he lives in Melbourne and his ride had taken him a little more than 3,000 km to be there. He was a professional racing motorbike mechanic and didn't think anything of the ride, distance-wise. To him it was just that, a ride on his motorbike.

After a comfortable drive of 230 km, the next morning we crossed the Docker River on the border of the Northern Territory and Western Australia. An Aboriginal community of 240 people live there and we followed David and Margaret to the Health Care Centre. It was obvious by the welcome they received from the three white women who managed the Centre and from several of the residents, that they are popular with all. There is a high mesh fence around the grounds and the gate is locked, until one of those three ladies allow people in. Despite that, someone had come in earlier that morning and stolen a few items from the room of one of the residents, who was now making a noise about it. Only some people don't see it as theft.

It transpired that a family member had been admitted through the gate, gone to the then unoccupied room and helped himself to some electrical items. Their society or social structure permits that, because in their eyes, everything is said to be shared. There were a few old-timers sitting back in their rocking chairs in front of their rooms and basking in the winter sunshine. I talked to a couple of them and then went across the rather dusty ground to where a woman was sitting cross-legged in front of a fire. She was hitting a solid piece of wood into the shape of a club with an axe and when I asked her what she was doing, she replied, 'I'm making a nulla nulla'. Well, *nulla nullas* are of course, Aboriginal clubs, of mulga wood, and heavy enough by all accounts to split a shield, let alone someone's head. They are used not only for fighting but for enforcing Aboriginal laws. That reminds me that in 1936 the Education Act of Western Australia empowered white parents to object to any Aboriginal child attending the same school as their white children. In the Northern Territory prior to 1939, Aborigines were banned from entering towns during daylight hours without written approval, i.e. medical. If later found in town without permission, between 8.00 p.m. and 5.00 a.m., they incurred a penalty of one month's imprisonment.

Central Australian Aborigines had interesting burial procedures. Generally speaking if a man died he was buried in a tree, on a platform in the treetops. But if he was an old man with little flesh left he was considered to have lost his corroboree and was put straight into the ground. The young lubras, i.e. young women, and boys and girls were also placed in trees but not young men who had done the wrong thing, such as marrying a woman of the wrong class. Old women were put straight into the ground because, so it is said, people were not sorry enough to put her in a tree. Little children were put in trees so that their spirits may come out again and re-enter their mothers and be reborn.

Widows in some tribes were/are required to enter into a period of silence after their husband died. They were ordered to cut their hair and not allowed to remarry for one year, although in some tribes the widows were allowed to remarry after six months because unattached women tended to cause trouble in the community. Probably for that reason the brother of the deceased husband was the preferred spouse. That aside, in certain tribes the widows covered their bodies with a mixture of fat, mud and excrement. They camped separately, not surprisingly. They also wailed a high-pitched keening from dawn to dusk. After burial the widows kept on lamenting and mourning the departed, chanting all his good deeds, burning their hair and scratching their face with their fingernails. Bodies that were burnt in cremation were smoked, not as ashes to go into the air but back into the ground.

A widow would be fed because to do otherwise would be disrespectful to her deceased husband and might cause her to come into contact with other men before the period of mourning was over. Widowers on the other hand were expected to feed themselves. A woman seeking her own food constituted a danger that was qualitatively far different from that of a man. According to Tindale, 1931, the Ramindjeri tribe had a special club with a poisoned head for punishing wayward women.

Neither were they permitted to speak to anyone for months, and in some instances, not for years. This was known as Koymainjil, the Ban of Silence. One widow who was banned from speaking for three years passed that mark and then she never spoke again for twenty years. In a sense that was not the hardship we may think it would be. Sign language was a regular and alternative way of communication amongst many tribes, certainly amongst the Arrernte of Central Australia and more so the neighbouring tribe to the north-west, the Warlpiri. Amongst the Warlpiri the custom was for widows to live away from their families, with other widows or young single women. The Warlpiri sign language was in constant use and the women knew it far better than the men. I once drove from Halls Creek down the Tanami Track to Alice and along the way stopped at the Warlpiri community of Yuendumu. I bought a woman's painting there and found the sign language is still prominent. The ban of silence was not restricted to women for I know of a time when a man answered a newly-met woman who had asked him a question. He replied by placing his hand on his nose, indicating he was bound to silence.

If one man casually met another he might say, nungyardil — who are you? But if they were strangers wary of each other a most revealing sign was usually transmitted. The elder man of the two would raise his index finger, which was not so much to ask the name of the other but to enquire of his Skin, meaning his place in the relationship system. A simple gesture but a complicated matter to understand for those not raised as an Aboriginal child. There are eight Skin groups in the land or at least in Central Australia, and they provide everlasting identity with the Dream Time, guide one's behaviour to others, determine whom one can marry, and, so I am told, whom one's off-spring may marry. As I once found amongst the people of the Trobriand Islands to the east of Papua New

Guinea, the Aborigines of times gone by did not believe babies arrived by way of copulating but that a spirit entered the woman. I apologise if in error but I feel it is too worthy to ignore as in both groups, that, along with magic in both peoples' traditional customs, is among the last of the age-old adherences to be overcome.

There are Aboriginal customs that prevent a person from talking directly to their mother-in-law, or even seeing her. A mother-in-law eats apart from her son-in-law or daughter-in-law and their spouse and if they are both present at a ceremony they sit with their backs to each other. They can communicate via the wife or the husband, as the case may be. Girls often marry at puberty but a man in most areas may not marry until he is in his late twenties, even older. This can result in the man being of similar age to his mother-in-law. Brothers and sisters may play together until initiation. These restrictions are means of trying to avoid incest in small groups of closely related people.

From Ion Idriess talking of Aboriginal lore I am led to believe that in numerous tribes the young men were unmarried for another reason. The older men, having served the community and paid their dues to the well-being of the tribe, put pressure on the chief and his council of elders to ensure that the young women were made available only to them. Some men took two, three and even four wives for themselves and used their tribal positions to dominate any discussions and to suppress dissent. Young men had not yet earned the right to speak.

At a particular campsite a man had died on the far side of a creek. The tribe's Kunki, medicine man, said he had deliberately defied tribal custom and this charge laid him open to an attack of evil magic. The people who had been camped on the same side of the creek as the deceased crossed over to the near side as they were fearful of meeting the Ungwulan, which is the spirit of the man. The camp on the far side was destroyed and it remained deserted for many months. No one would then live there.

Despite that unsettling death, the tribe as always was required to display the correct mourning etiquette for otherwise the dead man's spirit would be offended by the lack of respect. One of the procedures required men who were associated with the deceased to harm themselves and in this instance several men severely cut themselves on their thigh. For healing treatment they simply bound the wounds and lay down on their side, for an indeterminate time. The deep scars on one man, who must have had many past friends, had no less than twenty-three self-inflicted wounds. He had done his duty.

All Aboriginal men had to pass through a series of initiation ceremonies. In Central Australia they began when a boy was judged ready to live and hunt with the men, at ten to twelve years of age, and lasted well into adulthood. Of the 68 Aborigine tribes in NSW in the 19th century, the largest tribe was and still is the Wiradjuri, which includes the Dubbo district and narrows as it extends south to the Victorian border. The second biggest, the Kamilaroi, joins the north-east corner of the Wiradjuri and goes north to part of the Queensland border. I was interested to learn that a tribal elder said, when his people had first seen white men, 'We thought white men were black men who had died and returned to the place where they had died long ago.' I probably took that with the white man's usual grain of salt and did not pay it enough respect. Later I was told of Wunda, an Aboriginal spirit with a white skin. According to Ion Idriess, buffalo shooter, author of more than fifty books, boundary rider, dingo scalper, shearer, gold prospector, spotter to the Anzac sniper Billy Sing, Bulletin journalist, wounded at Gallipoli and Beersheba, a man who later lived with an Aborigine tribe on Cape York Peninsular, belief in Wunda existed for virtually every Aborigine tribe, varying by name only in distance and location. They saw the white man as the white-skinned Wunda in reincarnated form. Wunda stood for good but just sometimes for bad and when the white man attacked the black man the Aborigines believed Wunda was angry and they retaliated with their weapons. Their superstitious fear of Wunda was boosted by their trepidation of the white man's horses, otherwise Australia may not have been settled as relatively easily as it was.

When the young men of these tribes completed their tests of initiation, which in many tribes included having a tooth knocked out, they gained the bor, the belt of manhood and they became kubara, an initiated warrior. According to the Deborrah custom it was the bi-cuspid tooth i.e. the canine or eye tooth, that was hammered out with a rock and a bone chisel. Each tribe had a chief or king who was usually a strong leader but the person most feared by all Australian Aborigines was the witchdoctor or Kadaitcha man. As Hamilton Hume observed that man had only to point the bone at his intended victim and his power of reputation and mind over matter assured the man's death. The most valuable man in the tribe was not necessarily the best fighter but the best hunter.

Each initiated man carried three war spears, two hunting spears, two war boomerangs, one hunting boomerang, a nulla-nulla or fighting club, a throwing stick for breaking the legs of game or flying birds at close quarters, his shield, his stone knife and a short-handled stone tomahawk that was tied with strips of hide to his belt made of human hair, or where possible, of twisted possum fur, around his waist, and held at the small of his back. The belt also contained two feather-weight fire-making sticks.

From the Docker River we followed David as usual, and after a while he turned off the road and headed in to some deep country; long grass, small trees and mulga. The rough track deteriorated and it seemed as though it is rarely used. I would describe it to you as it turned out to be something special, which is what David generously had in mind for Roger and I, but I will have someone else who came this way relate his story for he is again worthy of mention and has superior description.

Ernest Giles, that relentless explorer, with his good companion, W.H. Tietkens, from the Gibson Desert incident, when Alfred Gibson so tragically lost his way and died a cruel and lonely death, was here on 10th March, 1874. In his 1880 book, *The Journal of a Forgotten Exploration*, Giles wrote: *From hence we had a good view of the country farther east. A curved line of abrupt-faced hills traversed the northern horizon; they had a peculiar and wall-like appearance, and seemed to end at a singular-looking pinnacle 34 or 35 miles away, and lying nearly east. This abrupt-faced range swept around in a half circle, northwards, and thence to the pinnacle. From Weld Pass to the pinnacle was a difficult traverse over very rough ground and through dense mulga and occasionally harried by the Aboriginals who set fire to the spinifex.*

The following morning the explorers were in the vicinity of the pinnacle, cutting their way through thick scrub when they emerged on the banks of a creek and, always searching for water, they travelled upstream and *soon saw some green bushes in the bed. A little further up we saw more, brighter and greener, and amongst them a fine little pond of water. Farther up, the rocks rose in walls, and underneath them we found a splendid basin of overflowing water, which filled several smaller ones below. We could hear the sound of splashing and rushing waters, but could not see from whence those sounds proceeded. This was such an excellent place that we decided to remain for the rest of the day.*

Ernest Giles named the water Gordon Springs, (see below) and Bob Buck, who years later went searching for Lasseter, spoke with an Aborigine who knew where Lasseter had been prospecting for gold. He said, *and after lunch we went out and inspected the place. We could see no signs of workings but the native stated he had been working on a watercourse and had put in a peg which had since been washed out. A reef ran a short distance along the side of the creek but knapping failed to show any gold.*

It's quite possible that Lasseter did visit Gordon Springs, he left ample evidence of his travels further west and there are the often-quoted lines from one of his last letters, 'I photographed the datum post on the quartz blow. The post is sticking in a waterhole and the photo faces north.' Lasseter added, 'the blacks have a sacred place nearby and will pull the peg up for sure.'

Giles left a lurid description of the Aboriginal ceremonial ground that he found at Gordon Springs, describing one large bare rock in the creek bed as a kind of teocallis, a terraced pyramid with a temple on the top, such as has been found in Mexico in several places and he imagined the gory rites that took place. He concluded: *There is very poor grazing around this water. It is only valuable as a wayside inn, or out. I called the singular feature which points this water to the wanderer in these western wilds, Gill's Pinnacle, after my brother-in-law, and the water, Gordon Springs, after his son. In the middle of the night, rumblings of thunder were heard, and lightning illuminated the glen. When we were starting on the following morning, some Aborigines made their appearance, and vented their delight at our appearance here by the emission of several howls, yells, gesticulations and indecent actions, and, to hem us in with a circle of fire, to frighten us out, or to roast us to death, they set fire to the triodia, dry spinifex, all around. We rode through the flames and away. 12/03/1874.*

The good rains extended out to the Centre this year and our vehicles almost disappeared amongst the tall, uneaten grasses as we bounced along a winding and rarely used trail. We passed through flowering trees and surprisingly rich, green vegetation which flowed up nearby hills like lava in reverse to meet the bold red rocks that showed through on the slopes. A miniature mountain off to our right is known as Gill's Pinnacle and as the track vanished, we edged as close to its base as even a 4WD would permit, the countryside under foot was dotted with red rocks of all sizes.

In years past David had climbed to the top of the Gill's Pinnacle, not to be confused with The Pinnacles on the other, coastal, side of Western Australia, but today we followed him on foot through the bush towards those red rock walls directly in front of us and which now appeared to block our way forward. To reach whatever it was up ahead we threaded our way between tall white gum trees at the base of which a small stream meandered on its indifferent course, in its own timeless manner. Since leaving Yulara and with the exception of the Docker River we had seen no one. I wondered where and to what David was leading us. Fallen timber, and sometimes the water, slowed us for a while but then we stepped into a clearing. Our way forward was stopped by a magnificent red rock wall that rose up for the best part of 75 metres and if not at 90 degrees then surely at 80 degrees. That slight differential allowed for shallow ridges, like lips, to occur and the water that was falling from the very top of the rock face, cascaded down and bounced off them. Miniature waterfalls.

At the bottom and now at our feet, was a rock pool of that crystal-clear water, that Giles saw, and it was so pure that the fallen water created new lines across the surface of which every droplet could be clearly seen, like a spider's web on a rose bush of a sunny but frosted winter morning. The overflow of water which escaped the rock pool went on to become the stream we had followed. We arched our backs to see the top of the wide section of rock wall where trees on either side were pillars of support and down which the water ran. Roger and I were gob-smacked. I wish everyone could witness such beauty of nature. How could it be? David said that up above, beyond the crest of the wall, were a series of waterholes leading this way and whenever he had come here, water runs down the wall. It was not making an appearance due solely to this year's rains. We were now in the eastern reaches of the Gibson Desert and this is totally unexpected. We departed through the long grass, the seeds descended from those with which the Aborigines attempted to burn Ernest Giles and W.H. Tietkens.

Perhaps it was in keeping with that attitude, I don't know, but several times as we drove on that day, we passed large signboards by the side of the road which in heavy black print on yellow backing, boldly stated, 'Aboriginal Freehold Land. No Entry. Penalty $1,000'.

Back on the track we turned south-west and the further we went, the harsher the countryside became, more as expected. The trees were mulga and desert oaks. Fortunately the road surface had been well maintained, as we found they invariably were in Aboriginal territory. For the most part their dirt roads were in far better condition, courtesy of a regular grader or two, than the many dirt roads that abound in western NSW.

Eventually we made a hard left-hand turn, one that cuts back to the left so severely that if you weren't looking for the turn-off, you would drive right past it. There was no road sign to say the turn-off was there so perhaps it was meant to be all but concealed. We followed it. After several kilometres we could see in the distance a collection of buildings amongst the trees atop a low hill. We drove up to it and in amongst the buildings, where six vehicles were parked side by side, all of them having reverse parked.

This ensured each vehicle was facing out and if need be, could get away as quickly as possible, for any reason. We were in a mining camp.

Metals X, headquartered in Perth, Western Australia, is one of the country's Top Ten gold companies with operations at South Kalgoorlie; Higginsville, between Norseman and Coolgardie; and on the Murchison, all in WA, while there is a development project in the Northern Territory. This camp is working on developing up a nickel mine and there are just two employees here for two weeks when they are replaced by two others, for their two weeks and so on in turn. Due to its remote location they have to fly from Perth to Sydney, then another flight to Ayers Rock and from there they take a charter plane to the camp, ending up in the state they started from. The charter flight takes the two who are departing, into Alice and from there they are then able to fly to Adelaide and back to Perth.

Fran, the cook from Perth and Zaan, the young Maori, showed us around. There were two rows of single men's quarters that join in an L shape, although realistically you can be married or female if you wish to stay there, e.g. David and Margaret. These are typical dongas with a single bed and they house just enough space for one's personal items. People who know about the camp and are passing by can arrange to stay here, such as the men who come out from Perth to oversee the installation and operation of solar power, electricity, water and building construction and maintenance in Aboriginal communities and to keep those roads so well graded, as they do. We were each allocated a donga and not long after, Roger and I took the opportunity to have a shave with hot water and of course a shower. We washed our clothes and felt so refreshed it was as though we were just about to start out. Better still, it was time for dinner.

In her younger days Fran was one of the very first women to drive a haul-pak truck, as we used to call them but nowadays they are known as dump trucks, in the mining camps. She was a damn good-looking grandmother with a lovely personality and a dab hand in the kitchen, as good as any shearer's cook I ever met or even heard about. She served up a fabulous meal of barramundi with all the trimmings on the plate with a help-yourself philosophy. The dessert was to die for and afterwards I suffered bloat like a poisoned pup.

19

Skirmish Hill

Saturday 9th July, 2016. This was to be the big day. I awoke, fully refreshed and after breakfast in the camp kitchen we made sandwiches to take with us for lunch before David, Roger and I hit the road, to find the explorers' tree on Skirmish Hill. Margaret stayed in the camp with Fran and Zaan. I had gone for a walk before breakfast and found Zaan working out in the open air at a set of homemade weights he had built himself using cast-off iron, wheels, bars, even a pulley etc. He was a pleasant young man, well-spoken and polite. A willing worker, I could soon understand why Fran liked to have him around to do the heavy lifting and to help out generally in the camp.

We drove back to the main track and took the road that runs from Wingellina, west towards Blackstone. The tribal elders who had initially said they would come with us failed to turn up so David drove on by himself and we followed him. Roger and I had brought gifts of shirts, knives, leather belts and hatbands for them and David later passed them on as a gesture of our appreciation for being allowed access to their land. When we were nearly halfway along that road, David turned left onto a lesser, unmarked track that we followed pretty much due south for 60 km. Due to recent rains the track was soft and in places it had a soup-like appearance that induced us, with some apprehension, to drive off-road to get around the soggy conditions. David was bogged once on the track itself but after a few minutes and with his decades of experience he drove out of it. We saw no sign of human life and precious little of animal life, bar many groups of wild camels. If we became seriously bogged down here it could be a problem. The track is mostly red sand and that should be okay but in places it is heavy, thick sand and it grabs at the wheels like glue, the moisture content no doubt adding to its weight, as though trying to prevent us from moving on. Where there were sections of track that were underwater for 60 metres or so we had no difficulty as it was a firm base below that held that water. Other times we slipped and slid through the mix, hoping it didn't rain on the track before we returned.

Red sand is predominant and for the most part covered in that rather ghastly spinifex, amongst prickly mallee and mulga with she-oaks, quandongs, acacias or wattles and the occasional gum tree. The Blackstone area is well known for its Aboriginal bush tucker and the quandong is one of the best. Quandongs grow well in soil that is poor in nutrients, frequently in drought and they are salt-tolerant. Greedy but practical, they latch onto acacias, casuarinas and she-oaks, sometimes growing from their base, to add to their own supply of water and nutrients. Even so they are slow growers and the resultant wood from the 4-metre to 6-metre high trees are, or were, highly sought by the Aborigines for the making of traditional bowls or coolamons. The quandong fruit is known as the desert peach.

I cannot say the track we were on was the one that Mills took but knowing the direction he came from we must certainly have crossed his path the nearer we came to Skirmish Hill and may well have been on it. He and other explorers would certainly have been eating the quandongs, when in season, as they have twice the vitamin C content of oranges and it protected them and others such as pastoralists, stockmen, prospectors and miners from the dreaded scurvy. When game was in short supply Aboriginal men substituted it for meat while the Pitjantjatjara women made the gathering and preparing of the quandong, women's business. The fruit, which is red when ripe, can be eaten raw or dried for future use. The women separate the edible fruit from the pitted stone and roll it into a ball.

The quandong ball would then be shared for eating by the tribal group. I am also told they knew how to make a type of tea from the fruit which they would drink as a purgative. That puzzled me a little for when Mills and others came across Aborigines for the first time and would boil the billy for their tea, the Aborigines had not before seen boiling water, which they then called, in their tongue, 'laughing water'. They could make fire but as far as I know did not have suitable containers for the boiling of water. Perhaps they had cold tea.

The Aborigines ground the roots of the quandong tree and used that as an infusion for the treatment of rheumatism. When they mixed the crushed leaves with saliva they were able to produce an ointment for skin sores and boils. And if they were ever short of stock they knew the fruit was a favourite of the emu, which provided a ready supply of seeds via their droppings, if that takes your fancy. White women used the peeled quandong fruit to make chutney and jams, even quandong pie while their men folk, stockmen and prospectors, out in the bush, added the leaves when baking their damper, for flavour and freshness.

Off to the right we saw what we believed to be Mt Maria in the distance, but for the life of me I do not know which wanderer named that one. Breaking up the otherwise flat landscape was the Bell Rock Range which approached us from the left or to the east of us. Its remarkably straight and narrow 15 km length almost reached us. It expired no more than a kilometre from the track and Roger suggested we should walk over to it and test it. We would have to walk because apart from the risk of becoming bogged we ran the other distinct possibility of staking the tyres in that country. Anxious to reach Skirmish Hill we pressed on, hoping there would be a better opportunity on our return. The attraction of the Bell Rock Range was that if you strike the rocks therein with a hammer they resonate with the sound of a bell. In desert country that should be fascinating.

After 50 km we saw an even fainter track running off to the right and a sheet of galvanised iron on which was scrawled, in now faded paint, the words *Kunmarnara Bore*. We knew of its existence and that we were now close. We soon came over the top of a sandhill and ahead of us and marginally off to the right was a low but widespread hill, it was Skirmish Hill. I had not expected it to be so spread out and that concerned me a little as its gross area would seemingly make it harder to find the tree, even though we had a latitude reading. According to the explorers' journals Moses Creek begins its life somewhere up there in the folds of the hill and runs down a gully or two before forming into a creek that we should soon come to. We passed over a depression of insignificant size and kept going. Despite the recent rain there was no water in it and it just didn't look right. A few minutes later we stopped in the bed of a substantial creek as it crossed our path. We had come 60 km on this track, which, looking at various maps, we had estimated would be the distance from the Wingellina-Blackstone road turn-off. It felt right.

We still couldn't risk driving off the track so we turned to the immediate right, into the dry creek bed, one with a good sand base. We hurriedly ate our sandwiches for an early lunch and then put items such as a water bottle, torch, camera, toilet paper, fruit and maps into our day packs and set off with great expectations. The latitude bearings taken in 1873, 1874 and 1882 may not have been too accurate but we held high hopes for the later 1891 reading, taken by the Elder Exploration Expedition.

The earlier of those explorers, Forrest, Gosse and Mills, described the tree as being near a waterhole of the creek and we had a later photo of the tree, taken in 1891, but no one said which side of the creek. They all camped by the tree and one of them did say that he afterwards rode from the camp to the top of Skirmish Hill, a distance of two miles. Again, that made us a little uneasy as looking at it, the distance didn't seem that great, unless the tree was off to the left-hand side of the track we had just come along and not as we believed, off to the right, somewhere in front of us. We might have to eliminate a few possibilities. We foolishly thought that shouldn't be too difficult.

Our thoughts were so concentrated with the matter in hand that we had not been considering the immediate weather. David and Roger were already walking up the bed of the creek as I finished doing up the straps of my day pack and I set off after them. Then it happened. I couldn't believe it. Rain fell, completely out of the blue and it fell heavily and without let up. I actually thought that the other two would turn back, especially as we had only just set off but neither man slackened stride. So I followed suit and I am prone to being as wet as the next person. Within fifteen minutes we were soaked to the skin and believing it could hardly be worse we continued on.

David stayed in the creek bed, looking for what would be a waterhole in times of good rain. I thought he wouldn't have long to wait. Roger and I stepped up onto the bank and spread out a little, looking for a tree that should be at least as big as any other and quite possibly the biggest. We had seen in the Elder photo that the tree was of substantial size and because we were searching along a creek, we assumed that would be a natural occurrence. As it happened infrequent moisture over the years has supported various trees to come forth but few of the size we sought. Away from the creek the land was relatively bare but as it rose up the slope of the hill, it became covered in small, red rocks.

For three hours we trekked through relentless rain. I noticed the water was no longer disappearing into the soil but was running across the ground and the slope of the same was definitely carrying it to the creek. Like Roger and David, I could not be any wetter but I called out to them, and when we came together, I suggested we get back to the vehicles before the creek fills up and floods them in, or away. They agreed and we started back. David again went back into the creek searching for the waterhole while Roger and I tramped out in the open, without sighting the tree. When we arrived back David's Land Rover and Roger's Land Cruiser were still standing in the creek bed without a care in the world and neither was the creek as yet filling up with water; but we had no doubt it would.

We immediately reversed the vehicles out of the creek bed and set them up on the road facing back the way we had come. There seemed to be little point in going on ahead as we didn't know what the lay of the land was; better the devil you know than the one you don't. We sat in the Land Cruiser, water collecting in a pool at our feet, and discussed our options. If the rain continued for the rest of the day and night we would almost definitely be trapped here for days and possibly weeks. We had no communication with the nearest people, at the mining camp and had to make a definite decision.

If we attempted to drive back to the mining camp the going would be tediously slow through the slush and waterlogged track. We would be driving through the night and the darkness would increase the chances of being well and truly bogged, quite possibly both vehicles. If we got through and reached the camp it would also mean our little expedition was over, we would have failed as David had, understandably, set a time limit on our venture, of three days. By going back that night the two vehicles would so carve up the track there would be no more travelling on it for a long, long time. This was becoming the year of the Big Wet.

On the other hand there was no point in staying there, sitting in a cold vehicle all night and as wet as a water rat. Neither could we get out and camp as it was too late to make that arrangement. Perhaps if we had set up our tents before we struck out on foot but this rain storm had taken us completely unawares. Why had the weather gods decreed we should be so punished? Is this why the tribal elders did not accompany us? No, it was simply the luck of the draw and we had to overcome it. The more we discussed it, the more resolve Roger and I developed. We had come this far, 3,000 km, for a one-off reason, to find that tree, and we were not going back beforehand, no matter how much it rained.

I remembered that sign referring to the *Kunmarnara Bore* and said that is only 10 km away. If we could get back there we could then turn down that track, which should not be cut up by any vehicles and it would be only eight km on an unused surface. With a bit of luck there may be the remnants of some workings etc, of the bore or even the airstrip which was still marked on the map, although we knew it had not been used for decades. Way back when, someone went out there and tried mining for something but it was not successful and whatever had been there was abandoned. That was the agreed plan so we set off with David once more in the lead as he had decades experience of driving out there although I doubt he would have encountered such wet conditions too often. Of course that also meant he had the better of the circumstances but Roger handled them superbly. Both drivers took it steady as one mistake would cost us dearly and although it seemed like an eternity, we covered the 18 km of both tracks without stopping.

By the time we reached *Kunmarnara Bore* the rain had eased off, thank goodness, but conversely the sky was darkening. We only knew we were there because we saw an old but large concrete water tank. On foot we followed a pipe from the tank back to where it originated at the top of an equally old bore but realistically it did nothing for us. I was disappointed there were no buildings. That surprised me as I thought surely something would have survived the passage of the years. Roger and David thought maybe, just maybe, they could see the outline of where a bush landing strip once was but my imagination didn't match theirs on that occasion, not amongst all the spinifex and mulga that covered most of the sodden sand.

We spread out in different directions, each of us taking one of the four main points of the compass, in an attempt to find some salvation for the night ahead. The disruptive rain was then replaced by an equally unfriendly wind which fairly ripped into us. It was a two-edged sword as whilst it was incredibly cold it did perversely help to dry us out, and to a degree, some of the mulga, which we began collecting for a fire. After fifteen to twenty minutes or so I saw, in the distance, the dull glint of faded galvanised iron through low hanging branches.

I hurried ahead and sure enough there was a palace. Well, a place. Built soon after the Ark it was a small, simple two-room affair with a lean-to on both the western and the eastern sides. Inside, the frame of a dividing wall was in place but no one ever got around to putting in the wall cladding so effectively it was a one room hut. The floor was red dirt and any first ideas we had of sleeping on it were instantly put aside. It looked as though no less than hordes of pigs had used it for farrowing, for many generations of litters. I happily called to Roger and David and they brought the vehicles close to the hut. The bitter wind seemed to be coming from the south-west, via Antarctica, so that ruled out using the lean-to on the western side. David wasn't travelling with a tent. He was so used to sleeping out in this country he packed his swag and if that wasn't good enough, he just put up with the elements. So we told him that he could have the lean-to on the eastern side while Roger and I put up our tents. By the time David laid out his swag, Roger and I, motivated by the freeze factor, had managed to have a fire going under that lean-to. There was barely enough room for the three of us to later sit around the fire, let alone sleep there. But that was fine. When the time came, Roger and I were as happy as Larry to have a tent to crawl into later that night.

We had to help each other put up the tents as the rain may have passed over but the wind was trying to do as much damage as its brethren at Cape Horn. Never have I welcomed a fire as I did that night. It was one of the joys of my life, as simple as that probably sounds. It served us so much. We were able to cook a proper meal courtesy of that fire, it thawed us out and it took a while but it dried out our soaking clothes. Rarely has such a simple thing been so appreciated. I shudder to think what we would otherwise have done that night.

I had put my tent pegs firmly in the ground and during the night that wind did howl. It verily shook the tent and I often felt it would be blown down. It also served to keep me awake but in due course sleep came. When I stepped outside in the early morning light the wind had gone but taken two of my tent pegs part of the way with it. The morning broke fine and clear, I found the pegs and we had our breakfast, giving thanks that order had been restored. We had a clear blue sky and soft sunshine that would help to dry the ground out. We felt encouraged to go back to Moses Creek and patted ourselves on the back for not attempting to totally retreat last night. We were still in the hunt. It was tempting to leave the tents up and return to *Kunmarnara Bore* tonight but then we reasoned that if the rain returned or we incurred some other form of setback, we did not want to find ourselves up the creek without our tents. So we packed everything up and carefully, ever so carefully, drove the 18 km back to the creek. I say that because by then the road was well and truly under water.

On arriving at the spot where we had parked yesterday we found the creek running a banker. Whereas the entire creek was bone dry the previous day, now it was full, with 1.7 metres of water flowing through it. I venture to suggest few people would have seen Moses Creek as such. Fortunately the road is higher where it crosses the creek and we were able to drive over to the far side as that was the area we now wanted to search. The previous day the creek had been so dry David could not discern where a definite waterhole might be. Today it was all under water. As we had followed the creek yesterday we now took a latitude bearing that indicated we should cut across the adjoining flat plain and intersect the creek where it turned to the left. From that point we would follow it up the lower slopes of Skirmish Hill.

With renewed hope and vigour we crossed the little plain, a walk of just 700 metres or so. On reaching the creek again Roger found a section that was considerably wider and the water not as deep so he crossed over in order that we could explore both sides at the one time. We began to find signs of fires that had come through but many decades ago. Quite a few of the trees had been burned, some of them completely and in other places were the faded, blackened remains of ancient camp fires. Both of us picked up sharp edged pieces of quartz rock that would have been used by the Aborigines for cutting and skinning purposes.

Probably feeling a little discouraged we continued on and as we followed the creek up the slope and presumably to its source, those red rocks came more and more into prominence. As we edged higher, they grew larger until Roger made the point that William Gosse, who made the original camp by the tree, presumably only weeks after he had discovered Ayers Rock, could never have come this way with his dray. No one would have deliberately put the wheels of the dray at risk by bouncing it over those rocks, as any damage would surely be too awkward to rectify out here. It did not make sense. We were on the wrong track. John Forrest had come from the west, as in travelling from Western Australia, and it was possible he came around the slopes of Skirmish Hill, to be on the eastern side, where the latitude clearly showed the tree to be, but again why would he be so far up the rough slope. Something was wrong. We should have found the tree by now and as we hadn't we would have to start again. We spent the day out there and perhaps it was one of those times when no matter how hard you try it is just not meant to be.

So we made it our night. We decided we wouldn't go back to *Kunmarnara Bore*. We would camp right there, at Skirmish Hill. That helped on two fronts. By not driving back there we would not be making a mess of the track and considering what we came here for, what better place, historically and emotionally, could there be than to camp as near as we know to where Mills, Forrest and Gosse, those early explorers, camped, so many years ago. Perhaps some nomadic spirit from another century will find us here and lead us to the tree.

We had time to have a good look around and we found cleared space without that ghastly spinifex not far from the creek and the track. We carried our gear and put up our tents and then got to work on a good fire out in the open. It wasn't hard to tell it was going to be a typical cold winter night in desert country, especially following on from rain. It did seem as though the previous night t we had been caught in a cold front blowing up from the Bight but this time we would be prepared. We broke off enough mulga wood to build and sustain a fire well into the night. I gathered up the dried-out inner core of several old spinifex and laid that at the base of the wood and when I lit a match it took off like a rabbit that had wandered on to the dog track.

David was well satisfied to have his dinner by the fire but Roger and I thought we would dine in style. We set up our collapsible table and chairs and did the cooking in the last of the daylight, so that we could eat as darkness enveloped us. We positioned the table so that Skirmish Hill formed a lovely backdrop and we sat up at the table like two toffs. There was no red wine to drink as we abided by the laws of the Aboriginal land and did not have any alcohol with us. For Roger and I, for reasons of personal and Australian history, this country and Skirmish Hill in particular, has much significance.

After dinner we kept the fire stoked and talked for a few hours into the night. One of the great joys of life has to be a good camp fire, more so in the company of endearing friends. Afterwards I was a little cold in my tent but I should not have been surprised. As mentioned, the scientific Elder Exploration Expedition camped here on 20th July, 1891, and its leader, David Lindsay, wrote that the overnight temperature dropped to 19 degrees Fahrenheit or 13 degrees below freezing. We camped here on 10th July, 2016, and it wasn't much warmer. I was woken at 5.00 the next morning to the clear sound of a dingo howl and a little later I heard the mournful far-off reply. When all is said and done I wouldn't swap that experience of camping along Moses Creek at the base of Skirmish Hill for a year's accommodation in a luxury hotel. Some things just have their own unique value. The explorer William Christie Gosse named Moses Creek after Moses, the Aboriginal boy who was in his group at Skirmish Hill. The Aboriginal name for the creek is mawutja or Devil's Creek.

The next morning and another day. David was expected to be at Wingellina that day to tend to an Aboriginal grave but agreed to continue the search for the tree until 11.30 a.m. Then we would have to depart. So as usual we were up an hour before the sun and we didn't know it at the time but as we would hear later, there was a cold weather snap that was unleashing itself on Tasmania, Victoria, South Australia and even up to the Northern Territory. I think some of it crossed the western border. At 6.00 a.m. we were dressed, had the tents down and away and having breakfast. By 7.00 a.m. when we could see by the light of day we were back in the field, with a more definite plan.

Now we would go by the latitude the Elder Exploration Expedition recorded.

That would keep us on the eastern side of the hill but on the southern arm of Moses Creek and within minutes we noticed that there were three trees there of substantial size, commensurate with the tree in the Elders photo. From afar, the trees on the northern arm looked big enough but when we reached them they were all found to be lacking in size. After a while I came closer to the third substantial tree, on the southern arm. We would have walked past this tree early on the Saturday afternoon, not long after setting off along the creek but didn't notice it because of the rain and because it was mostly obscured by no less than eight suckers that had sprung from the base of its trunk and reached almost the same height as the original tree, covering it in a green mantle. Now it could be clearly seen that it was the apparent correct height and size and better still, that its latitude was only two seconds or 55 metres from the reading as recorded by the Elder Exploration Expedition.

As soon as I saw that tree I was drawn to it and I called out to David and Roger, 'That's it, that's the tree.' I hurried over to it and after pushing through the green growing suckers I discovered why the few exposed branches up high appeared dead. The tree had been burnt. It had been badly burnt at the base and upwards for a metre and a half but it still stood and I was sure the reason it stood was because of its great girth. The section of tree 1.6 metres above ground level was the worst as two thirds of the trunk of the tree had been eaten away by fire and unfortunately, perhaps even tragically, the blaze that William Whitfield Mills had cut deep into that side of the trunk had been burnt away. That was the one crucial element that was missing and although everything else appeared to be as it should, we had enough doubt to be hesitant in claiming this tree was the true one, the holy grail.

The three of us peered and measured, examined the fire and burn marks, their height, the fact that the suckers all but enclosed the tree, as though to hide it deliberately and they were evenly spaced around the base of the dead father figure from which they had sprung. We measured the distance from the tree to the creek, which was 40 yards as stated in the explorers' reports, the ground in between was cleared and all but level as they had selected for their camp site and as in the photo and although the creek was full, the bank edged inwards to the land as it might in dry times so as to allow eager hands to reach down to a waterhole, the one which tenacious David had keenly sought.

We stepped back and gazed over the green coating to the raised dead arms that protruded at the highest level. It was not as we had expected but that is not an unusual result in many aspects of life. At least it was there and still fighting for its existence. Like the others, I took photos of the tree and of the tree with us around and in front of it, but it was David who took the most important photo, the correct photo, the one that would soon settle the matter of identity. I asked the others for their opinion as to the probability of this being THE TREE and each of us gave the same assessment, eight out of ten. I know we wanted to rate it higher but a joint conservative instinct held the three of us back.

I bent down at the base of the tree and carefully removed three new growth, green, shoots about one-third of a metre in length and packed them away, to take home. It was an anticlimax after that, especially when we realised how close we had been to the tree in the beginning but every moment was worthwhile and we had covered interesting ground, with the Aboriginal cutting and skinning stones. Roger made the valid point the one thing we missed out on was to climb to the top of Skirmish Hill as the explorers had done but then they were not pressured by time. They did not exactly request Aboriginal permits.

That raised another interesting point. Whilst it seemed certain that no one has been in this region for decades the fact is that wherever the Aborigines lived in those days, in their bark gunyahs or similar, they did not wear clothes and as we had just experienced, the weather can be bitterly cold in winter and we all know it is ferociously hot every summer. They might have lacked what to us are the necessities of life but they must have had a resilience of the highest order just to survive.

I have a friend who lives at Stanthorpe, south-eastern Queensland, just above the border with NSW. The town has an altitude of 900 metres and can have several falls of snow during the winter. She told me the Aborigines of that area had a particular way of keeping warm in the winter. Curious to know what clothing or structures they used I asked her how did they survive such a cold climate? She said every winter they packed up and moved to what we know as Queensland's Gold Coast.

19 Skirmish Hill

Apart from the Emu War of 1932 when the Australian Army was called in to keep an army of 20,000 emus from attacking the Western Australian wheat crops, the greatest predator of the emu was the dingo. Aborigines tended to kill emus only out of necessity and in doing so they utilised every component of the big bird. In my jackaroo days we only needed one emu egg to make an omelette that would otherwise require ten hen eggs. The emu's oil-rich meat ensured the coats of our working dogs shone with a lustrous glow. Today the emu is a deserved protected species and there are as many as when the First Fleet arrived, except in Tasmania.

In lands which were enriched by the presence of numerous emus there were tribes which believed in certain seasons the people could strengthen themselves courtesy of the noble bird. While the emu has only one point five per cent fat it was enough for the Aborigines to mix it with the fine ashes of acacia wood and rub it thoroughly onto their bodies to keep the rain and cold at bay. Apparently it also kept the people supple and enabled them to resist the sickness that could, and still can, rise up out of damp earth.

David was anxious to be underway so we drove steadily for the 60 km back to the Blackstone/Wingellina Road. In the forty-eight hours since the rain, the track was still waterlogged but it had dried out somewhat and by taking it steady we got through. Once back on the regularly graded road we had no trouble in reaching the mining camp again. We were in time for one of Fran's lunches and after that David and Roger took both vehicles to the Aboriginal community at Wingellina, where they refuelled. As we were still in Western Australia and not returning by the same route but via South Australia, our next available fuel would be at Marla, 675 km to the east. David and Roger then drove to Surveyor General's Corner, which marks where the boundaries of the Northern Territory, South Australia and Western Australia meet. Because they represent three time zones there are three different times for New Year's Eve, if you just happen to be in the vicinity, at that time. David attended the grave of an Aboriginal friend at Surveyor General's Corner. The man had recently died and David added a collection of white stones to the grave.

I later queried how someone could be buried at Surveyor General's Corner and he simply said the man had owned land there. I was given much the same answer some years ago in Israel on finding that a few people were buried almost alongside where Jesus Christ was first placed and wanted to be with Him. I stayed in the camp to have a hot shower, to shave and to wash my clothes but most importantly, to me, to write up my notes as the recent camping and rain had not allowed time nor daylight for that. I also wanted to talk with people of interest in the camp before they were gone.

The camp is a convenient stopover for the men and women who work amongst Aboriginal communities and they were happy to relate what they encounter, and to verify that. At Warburton, 200 km to the west, one of the community men had died in the street. A number of 200 litre drums were placed at either end of that street, so as to block it off and prevent anyone driving along it for the next twelve months. This was done as a mark of respect for that Aborigine and such an action is a common occurrence out there but is usually done for a shorter time period. It is also forbidden to speak the dead man's name.

In the Jameson Aborigine community, 125 km on from Warburton, contractors have built houses, roads and other infrastructure for the locals, including a pump for a sub-artesian bore. Water was pumped via a pipe to a storage tank on a hill. That water exercise cost in excess of a million dollars. The day came when the local men decided to burn off the surrounding grass as there were too many snakes. The fire burnt through the pipe, cutting of the water supply. Rather than repair the pipe the people abandoned the whole project and, as well as the grass, sent one million dollars up in smoke.

In another community many of the elderly women have the talent to produce worthy Aboriginal paintings that sell for an average price of $8,000. They take about fourteen days to paint and as we learned at the Docker River the art money is shared, or taken. The community as a whole receives payments for mineral rights and owns the distribution rights for the sale of fuel in the area and somewhat beyond and they receive dividends from that. All up, every man, woman and child in that community had an average income of $56,000. The rub is that the aged adults also receive the Age Pension and as Aborigines they are exempted from being assessed under the Incomes and Assets Test. A favourite reputed ploy amongst the young is to register for unemployment and other benefits under numerous names, their nominal 'white' names and their Aboriginal names, which are said to confuse authorities, and so receive multiple payments.

On one occasion David, with permission, entered an Aboriginal home and asked the lady of the house if all the children gathered there were hers. 'Yes,' she replied. 'Shouldn't they be in school?' he asked. 'They don't have to go to school,' was her response. David calculated that no more than 50 per cent of Aboriginal children, in the outback, go to school and on any one day when a group of them is in attendance, the percentage may well be similar the next day or next week but it will be another group of children.

On the other hand, an Aboriginal family from Yiriya, a remote outstation north of the Warburton Ranges and an hour from Warakurna, walked 230 km from there to Warburton, to take their son, Bernard, to school, and leave him there. The family then walked home.

Warburton is well known to some because in 2008 when Prime Minister Rudd gave an apology to the Aboriginal people re the stolen generations, a local man, when asked what he had to say about it, replied, 'All I want is a new gearbox for me Falcon.' It is said the Aborigines out there had no interest in the apology but, and this is just my thought, possibly because they didn't understand it. In some areas only nine per cent of them speak English.

Another community, further west, goes by the name of Cosmo Newberry, which I thought rather odd, until I was told it was named after an industrial chemist of that name. After an existence as a cattle station, a penal colony and a church mission, the area was abandoned. In 1989, four Aboriginal families moved there with the intent of bringing the community back to life. They were able to establish a fuel station, a shop, health clinic and as other families joined them, a school. I talked with a man from Perth who has been working there to improve the quality of their water, using the process of reverse osmosis, a water purification technique. Applied pressure removes bacteria and dissolved and suspended species from the water, specifically if it is brackish as in the bush or saltwater for coastal areas. In fact this man assured me that the process he uses takes out everything and leaves just pure water, which is not so good.

Therefore the next step he and his co-workers take is to put in the water the minerals required to make it, as he said, the best water in the world. He was adamant the cost of this is near to one million dollars per community and it is to be done for every Aboriginal community. Such water is better than what his family has in Perth.

The men who build community housing say it costs $390,000 on average to build one house while houses that reach four years of age are assessed for repairs. They cost, average again, $165,000 to be brought back up to where they were initially. The usual requirements for repair, replacement or additions are in-roof insulation, evaporative air-conditioning, new stoves, hot plates, new outside lights and new fences. Some houses, even after four years, are not worth the cost of repair as they have been destroyed. The government is said to be at last starting to make the residents take responsibility for their actions, if they expect the constant infrastructure and repairs to be provided.

Health and alcohol are, as might be expected, major issues in the communities. Alcohol is said to be banned in all Aboriginal communities in the Northern Territory, South Australia and Western Australia and that may be the case but it is known young people have access to several drugs. Bans have been requested and imposed by the Aboriginal people themselves but both still cause problems. Few cars out here are insured, registered or licensed and we all too often saw wrecked and abandoned cars by the roadside. At one stage Sims Metal brought a crusher to Blackstone and cleaned up a lot of those eyesores. However they did not return nor did they go to any other community because the locals demanded payment. The profit margin was already slim for the operator and so the company never came back.

*Many of the following items are courtesy of the
Old Timers Traeger Museum, Alice Springs*

Sulky transport on Federal Station, Bloods Creek, south of Alice Springs

Unloading a wagon from Oodnadatta, at Bloods Creek

The Cameleer.

Butchers of the Outback

Alice Springs township 1894, a classic photo, courtesy of the Horn Expedition.

Alice Springs waterhole, found and named by W.W. Mills, 11th March, 1871.

Drover's gear including branding irons

The rest of his working gear

The baskets holding the (beer) bottles of cattle dip concentrate were woven by blind people. Right, packhorse water containers, courtesy of Indiana Station, east of Alice Springs.

Charlie Myers' saddlery in Todd Street, Alice Springs

Cues, as described by William Whitfield Mills, to go on a bullock's split hoof

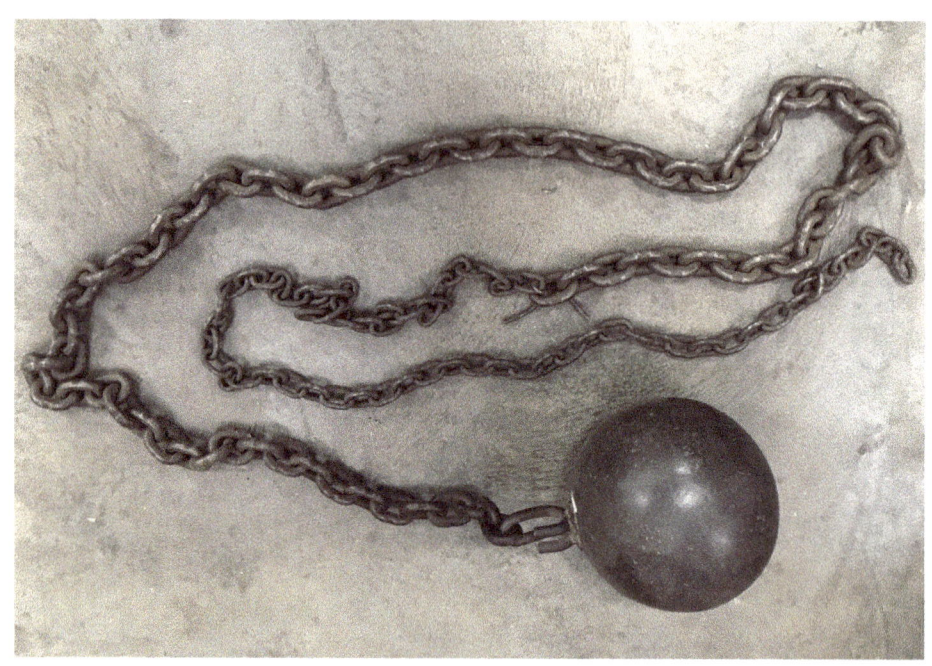
Prisoner's ball and chain, surprisingly heavy weight makes it difficult to lift with one hand

Dingo and fox traps

First gaol in Central Australia, built of timber, 1904, at Heavitree Gap, Alice Springs

Described as '1895 First crossing from South to North by pushbike'

First cars into Alice Springs.

1925 Dodge, from the Dodge Brothers, Detroit, Michigan, exact same model as owned by John Flynn of the Royal Flying Doctor Service. Flynn's original Dodge ended up at Rockhampton with a butcher who used it to deliver salted beef

Aboriginal woman's digging stick, longer and much heavier than the author expected. Magnificent timber, smooth but solid, for digging, hunting and fighting

Poster of the 1956 film, *A Town like Alice*

A goose-neck spur handmade by a blacksmith on Wave Hill Station, which once carried 58,000 head of cattle. It adjoins Victoria River Downs, Northern Territory

The 26 donkey-drawn wagon travelling from Curtin Springs Station to Alice Springs, for supplies and 360 km of hardship each way. Donkey teams were used in making roads and the workmen lived off the land.

Home-made nails from Muckaty Station, usually known as Muckaty, 110 km north of Tennant Creek and some 800 km south of Darwin, NT. In remote areas one needed to improvise to survive and the development of nails around the world is a clue as to how buildings and construction progressed. In colonial days when people needed to move they would sometimes burn their house to the ground and retrieve the valuable nails from the ashes in order to build a new house.

Construction of the Oodnadatta to Alice Springs railway

The left-hand side of the handcuffs was deliberately smaller so as to give more control over the prisoner

*A backscratcher rests above a genuine horsehide leather strop.
After using a sharpening stone, men used a strop to polish the edge of a
cut-throat razor's thin blade to obtain a mirror-like finish.*

Six of the seven pioneer women who lived in the Alice Springs area in 1903

The commemorative plaque to William Whitfield Mills at the Telegraph Station, Alice Springs

The Alice Springs waterhole, in dry times it is still a sight to behold

20

Alice Springs

Whilst I was interviewing and writing, two men drove into the camp and Fran and Zaan took their place in the vehicle and drove to the camp's airstrip to catch the charter flight back to Alice Springs. I said goodbye to them and in their place met the men. One was Tony, who would be doing the cooking, and the other was Max Maczurad, the senior project geologist for Metals X Limited at the Metals X Nickel Project, Wingellina mineral exploration camp.

When Roger and David returned we had a get-together with Max and filled him in on what we had been doing and expressed our reluctant uncertainty about the tree. Max is a lifelong geologist and has been out in this part of WA for the past eleven years. He knows every type of rock, tree, plant and soil particle out there. We cleared a table and showed him the original Elder Exploration Expedition photo of the tree and then some of the photos we had taken. When Max saw the particular photo of the tree that David had taken with the slope of Skirmish Hill in the background, he said, 'What's wrong with you blokes? That's the same tree. Look at it.'

Sure enough, David must have taken his photo on the very spot that someone in the David Lindsay group did. Max did add that the worst winds hereabouts come from the south-east and that was the side of the tree most burnt, where Mills and others had blazed the tree. He studied the old photos of the tree, taken as they were from the south-east and the north-west. And when he pointed out the similarity of the top branches of the tree, the few dead but exposed branches, he emphasised the similarity in their position and shape as compared to how they were in 1891. The physical position of the tree and the ever so slight rise of the ground from the creek to the tree were the clinchers but thank goodness David had the common sense, which I didn't, to photograph that particular angle and position. When Max said, 'This is the same tree,' and he gave it ten out of ten, we were ecstatic.

David has many friends among the Aborigine tribes and one of the elders of the APY, as they are known, short for; Anangu Pitjantjatjara Yankunytjatjara, passed away some years ago and last year his wife died. David attended her funeral, at her family home, and he now had written permission to go back there and place a plaque on her grave. White men are not allowed to enter that land and permits are not known to be handed out. In fact Roger, who I earlier mentioned has been travelling in the Centre for the past ten years, has, like others, often applied for such a permit and had always been refused. Only the trust and respect that David and Margaret have garnered over the past four decades allows them to pass that way.

Now I am more than satisfied with having, finally, been allowed to reach Skirmish Hill but as we were travelling with David and Margaret, we were also granted permission to enter those rare lands. I think for Roger this was a totally unexpected privilege and he was thrilled at the prospect of seeing that country. I share his feelings as I have heard it has a beauty of its own but it also appeals, as it does for Roger, because renowned explorers such as William Gosse and Ernest Giles rode through there, and of course so did Mills.

The following morning we said goodbye to Max and Tony and set off, not north to the Docker River via the way we had come, but soon due east, into that sacred off-limits land of the north-west country of South Australia. It was a glorious morning, it felt exciting and as I was driving, on a good dried-out road, I thought to myself, 'What more could I ask for?'

We crossed the border from Western Australia into South Australia and immediately were on a flat plain, perhaps 10 to 15 km wide, with the Tomkinson Ranges on our right, to the south, and the Mann Ranges that initially have Surveyor General's Corner behind them, on our left, to the north. It wasn't so deep that you would call it a valley but it was equally attractive.

The well-graded road allowed for fast driving but that would have been a waste, a sacrilege. The red soil plain was complemented by dark ranges on either side where warming winter sunlight brought out shadows and shades in the folds and ridges of hills that channelled us through this silent and enchanting land. It was a painting such as rarely seen let alone produced and I am being selfish but if caravans of people were to be allowed in, it would not be the same timeless landscape. Only the tracks of the grader blade reveal the interloper.

The Pitjantjatjara, (pronounced by some as the shorter Pitjanjara, for convenience no doubt) which I much prefer to use than the APY, do refer to themselves as the Anangu. In 1981 the Pitjantjatjara Land Rights Act granted freehold title to 103,000 square km of this country to the Pitjantjatjara, making it the largest freehold Aboriginal province in Australia and no modern mineral exploration has been allowed since 1980.

After 15 km we turned off to the right and drove into the community of Kalka. We stopped so David could let the people know we were passing through and why. About seventy people live there and some of them came over to see the plaque we were to place on the grave. There were 110 people a few years or more ago. It is a pretty basic set-up but the authorities back then did build them a health clinic, an aged care centre and a TAFE training centre. Nowadays none of those are in use, they are all wasted. I have little doubt that David and Margaret who have done so much for the Aboriginal people are heartbroken that they have not taken up many of the opportunities and the assistance given to them. It is sad to relate but some of the people, such as this community which has a truckload of food delivered to them every fortnight, do not eat well let alone have sufficient exercise.

As David pointed out, some of them are so overweight that an echocardiogram, which is used for the diagnosis, care and follow up for those people who have or are suspected of having heart disease, has no apparent effect on them, but he and Margaret do their best for them. When they do not eat the available western food they still eat kangaroo although we have yet to see one. Now that their land is freehold they do whatever they like and I was often told they have shot all the 'roos and whatever else takes their eye. Speaking of which the eye of the 'roo is regarded as the most delicious part to eat, because of its salt content. Kangaroo, which the Pitjantjatjara call *malu*, has less than two per cent fat, a high supply of protein and is a good source of vitamins B6 and B12 plus thiamine, riboflavin and niacin. The older people are given the soft intestines because they are out of teeth.

From what we heard, they are not averse to calling people, black, white or in between, as they please. There is no political correctness out there. To them, a person born of one black parent and one white parent is not so well regarded and they are not averse to calling such people 'yellow man' or 'half-a-caster'.

We continued on along this remarkable road until we stopped at a roadside plaque to that quite unique man, Len Beadell, the road builder. We parked amongst a group of desert oak trees, as distinct from the she-oaks, trees that provide a memorial in themselves.

The desert oak is a beautiful tree and in its element in this normally dry environment, having long ago worked out how to successfully pass through the ages to maturity. Whilst the tree is virtually fireproof, which is a good start for any one and everything, the dropped seedling is brought to life by fire. It grows slowly, generally amongst that sharp spinifex and takes on the appearance of a bottlebrush as a mass of spiky tangles protrude from ground level to the top of its trunk. This defensive array prevents it from being grazed and all the while it is slowly but surely expending the bulk of its energy on ensuring its tap root goes as deep as it has to until it strikes water. When that happens, the spiky matter and side branches wither away and the trunk becomes strong, tall and clear. The crown then develops and fills out with a grey/green canopy, the ends of which tend to drape down like a cloak and they present a handsome sight, a prince of a tree in the dry desert country.

I drove past a magnificent specimen of a dingo no more than 30 metres from the road but before I could stop he was gone. I regretted that because he was the first I had seen and he was superb with his head raised in the air and as still as a statue, until he bolted. Late in the morning David punctured a tyre and we stopped to change it. Up ahead was a narrow pool of water, about 25 metres length, by the road. Minutes later I happened to lift my head and I was happily surprised to see a dingo drinking from the water. He hadn't been there when we stopped but there was no mistaking his lovely light red coat and those superb ears. Asking Roger and David not to make a sound, I took my camera from the Land

Cruiser and as quietly as possible began to walk up the road towards the dog.

Initially he was 100 metres from me and I took my first photo from that distance. I gained 20 metres before he took off and I thought that's torn it, but he trotted, steadily, and moved, not in the opposite direction but towards my left-hand side, at a 45-degree angle. He passed between bushes and small trees and stepped out of them 60 metres from me. I took the opportunity for a photo before he was on the move again, in the same direction. I had nothing to lose so I stepped off to my left to somehow intercept him for he definitely had his mind set on proceeding in that direction. It must have been my lucky day for a few moments later he stepped out into the open, stopped and looked me in the eye, about 35 metres from where I stood. He remained perfectly still and beautifully balanced on his rather long legs with his ears standing equally upright. He was a most handsome dog, young but verging on being full grown and with an unusual but to-die-for light red coat. When I slowly raised my hands with the camera he stood stock still. It was as if he knew I just wanted that one good photo and he allowed me that. Then he was gone. Dingoes rarely bark, they howl.

Studies suggest the first dingoes were brought to Australia about 3,500 years ago by south Asian seafarers and most likely they came from Indonesia's island of Sulawesi, where Janice and I so fortunately travelled up into the island's highlands. The colour of a dingo's coat is affected by where he or she lives but usually the three main colours are a ginger-yellow, black and tan and creamy white. Unlike the domestic dog which has nine genes the dingo has but three that affect coat colour. Our red dingo's colour may therefore be unusual as in desert country he tends to have a more golden yellow coat. Perhaps this particular dingo's colour is brought on by the heavy red soil of that country.

Dingoes generally eat rabbits, kangaroos, wombats and wallabies and when they are scarce they turn to domestic animals. The dingo is a solitary hunter but when large game is afoot he will form packs. It is probably just as well the dingo never made his way into beautiful and mountainous Tasmania. He is known for being cunning and for his strategy but rarely fights unless cornered. Hunters who have cut dingo litters out of logs, which contained numerous bones and feathers, said the bitches ran away, always. They never attempted to defend their cubs and on occasions they did not return at all. When the mother stays with her pups she weans them at just two months of age. Other attributes of the dingo with its lean, hardy body that is designed for speed, agility and stamina are its excellent eyesight, a sharp ear and a keen sense of smell, befitting its proven connection to a south Asian variety of the grey wolf.

We were underway but before long David stopped again, just for a look, where a side road runs off to the right and keeps going south for a long, long way into pure desert. It has the unusual name of Kintore Avenue. I don't know the significance of it apart from the fact that it is initially lined by desert oaks and is typically dead straight. It might be named after the Earl of Kintore, a former Governor of South Australia. The turnoff is also marked by one Len Beadell's grader tyres.

We had driven about 200 km through the ranges when David turned to the right and kept going, for another 15 km. This brought us to Harry Creek. Mills had named Harry Creek, no doubt after his younger brother, who also came to Australia, and the reason why David, and Roger and I, are allowed into Pitjantjatjara land lay there. By the look of its undisturbed surface the road had not been driven on since the burial of the tribal elder's wife the previous year.

The fact that we saw no one but the few people at Kalka added to the attraction of the land but as we drove down that last side road of 15 km it had the feel of 'now you're really on your own, boy', about it. The countryside was big, wide open and flat with a vastness about it, another land. I think what raised that sensation was the ground itself. Apart from the odd tree there was nothing but a sea of buffel grass. No, make that an ocean of buffel.

If you happen to be a Queensland cattleman/woman you will no doubt be pleased to hear of its presence as in that state and much of northern Australia, the ever-spreading buffel is planted as a pasture grass and well accepted as cattle feed. It is popular there because of its ease of establishment, rapid growth rate, prolific seed production, tolerance of drought and grazing. Here at Harry Creek the buffel grass is knee high with a similar width that joins it all together like a carpet and it is as dry as a skinflint's wallet. The first thought that came into my mind on seeing it was 'Fire'. Obviously there are no herds of cattle out here to eat if off, due to the lack of water, and if this grass so much as smelt the head of a fire stick I think the whole countryside would go up in flames, for while the buffel is said to have some initial fire resistance it does burn and when the conditions suit, it burns with intensity.

In South Australia the buffel is now classified as a weed and the sale and movement of the grass in that state is banned as it takes nutrients out of the ground and is displacing native grasses. Before its arrival, sandy creek beds acted as firebreaks but with the build-up of buffel along water courses the grassy streams now aid the spread and speed of fire. The grass is believed to have come to Australia via the grass-packed saddles brought in by the cameleers from Pakistan, Afghanistan and elsewhere. The heaviest infestations in South Australia are in the north-west, in the land of the Pitjantjatjara and I would suggest this is the heart of it. Most arid or semiarid ecosystems are relatively resistant to alien invasions but buffel appears to be the exception. When established it is difficult to remove and the only chance of halting its spread is to hopefully hold it at bay when it first arises, otherwise it replaces native species. Aboriginal women in this region find the buffel to be so widespread they say they can no longer find their bush tucker as in days past. Today they sing about the 'bad grass'.

We came to the home of the deceased lady. It consisted of two substantial houses, of close to 400 square metres each with verandahs included, and one about half that size. They were all for the one family. After her husband died in 1997 the compound was abandoned. The lady's husband and their son are buried nearby and her grave now lies alongside theirs. Her grave was outlined by a rim of concrete with a larger, broader section at the head of the grave, which itself was covered with twenty or more bunches of bright, artificial flowers. Judging by the weeds that had sprung up on the ground around the three graves, it seemed no one had been back since, so in this instance it may be fortunate plastic survives as well as it does.

After David had the plaque professionally made, he then had it securely attached to a steel or star post, one that has three sides or edges to the post. When the concrete base at the head of the grave was put down a carefully arranged and fitting slot was inserted so that in the future a post such as this could pass into and through the concrete. Our first job was to dig out the soil below that concrete, without disturbing the actual grave, a fine line indeed, and to then pass the post through the concrete and compact the soil back in.

Roger took a long-handled shovel and started digging. The deeper he went the more the angle narrowed and each time a little less soil came up. I relieved him and found it so but the deep red soil was relatively soft. The earth is so red hereabouts that when I later looked at our photographs of the completed work the bright plastic flowers were all but put in the shade by the brilliant colour of the soil. We did a dummy run with the post by marking it off against the length of the shovel and thought we had the hole deep enough. David eased the post into the concrete slot and fortunately it passed through, ever so neatly, and it then dropped down into the hole. He then did some minute adjusting to ensure the lady's plaque was the exact height above the ground as those of her husband and son, alongside her. If you are going to travel so far and go to such lengths to pay your respects you may as well go the extra effort and make it perfect. Well satisfied, David nodded to Roger and I and we took up a conveniently found wooden pole and used it to ram the soil back into place.

A rather rustic netting and plain wire fence surrounded the little burial ground and much of it had fallen in to a state of disrepair, so we repaired it. We dug out and straightened the corner posts before setting them right, pulled up the wire and used our pliers to strain them and twitched the netting back on to them. Then we used the two shovels, we had one for each vehicle, to dig out the hundreds, and I do not exaggerate, of weeds that littered that bright red burial ground soil. Neither Roger nor I knew the lady in question but if that was what David felt he should do, we happily did it alongside him. That took a good two hours and then we moved up to the houses. There were enough for David and Margaret, Roger, and me, each.

David and Margaret took one house, putting their swags on the ground outside the front door but under the cover of the overhead verandah roof. I did the same outside the other big house while Roger camped in one of the interior rooms. I found the outside to be colder but cleaner. Considering the houses have been abandoned for nineteen years I couldn't expect it to be clean but each to his own. The structure of all three buildings was excellent and no apparent cost had been spared in that endeavour. They must have been grand homes when lived in although every window has a protective covering of heavy mesh.

Built mostly of metal construction with perspex windows they had survived the high risks of termites, fires and intruders. There were thirty-two solar panels on the roofs for electricity plus two large ones for water heating, floodlights under the eaves, double garages, steel water tanks, evaporative air-conditioning, three bedrooms, large kitchen, living rooms, even wheelie bins, would you believe. Who on earth would pay for and run such a service for one family out here in the never-never? You and I. The toilets out the back are long drops and I guarantee you won't find better. You could drop a wobbly wallaby down there and not touch the sides which are cylindrically perfect and descend to the depths of the devil. The air vent on top extends so high in the sky it would worry the Flying Doctor and alongside the base of it, on the roof, is a solar panel that provides light in the night.

The three houses are on the one side of the street and just in case someone couldn't remember which house is theirs, there were solar powered street lights out the front. Telstra had come to the party and supplied twelve solar panels, a power box the size of a large refrigerator and a satellite dish so that everyone can watch the latest Prime Minister. Off in the distance was a 90,000-litre concrete tank, and a bore, from which water is pumped to the house. We were suitably impressed by the workmanship of the builders who must have come from Alice Springs or Adelaide and the consensus of opinion is that it would cost, in 2016 currency, $1.65 million to build the three homes in this remote land, for the one family, before they were abandoned.

Roger and I were relieved from putting up our tents, but the rather cold desert air that night reminded me I was somewhere special, another place where Mills had camped. I was glad about that. I was up early in the morning and went for a quiet walk before breakfast. Along the track that brought us here the previous night, I found fresh dingo prints in the red soil. The paw prints were so large I took photos of them alongside a torch and a 20-cent coin.

We drove back to the main track through the ranges and turned to the right, still heading due east, until we came to another Pitjantjatjara community, Amata. This was a bigger grouping of some 500 people. David strongly advised me not to even show a camera let alone attempt a photo. He and Margaret, who was a nurse, had some locals to catch up with, so Roger and I waited while they met up with their acquaintances and presented them with tennis, football and soccer balls, I gather out of the goodness of their hearts and wallets. The town was at the western end of the Musgrave Ranges so our journey through these lands was drawing to a close. We did have a drive around the town and it was interesting to note that almost every house has two satellite dishes on the roof, except for those with three satellite dishes. I don't have one, too time consuming, distracting. Most houses had a few cars but I couldn't help notice the home with nine cars and two motorbikes. Perhaps they had early morning visitors. A few years ago, a swimming pool was built in the town and it seemed to be Olympic size. So that it remained in good order, a prison grade security fence was constructed around the complex to ensure no one broke in, unlike a prison where they generally break out. It hardly mattered which way they went. Within forty-eight hours, the local villains had broken in and pleased themselves.

Leaving Amata, we turned north-east on to the Giles road which leads in to the Mulga Park road, *Mulga Park Station* being at the junction of the two roads. When I was out here in 2002 the total wild camel population was estimated at one million. A few years later, I think in 2009, an official reduction campaign was introduced and over the next four years the numbers might have dropped by 400,000. Perhaps they have built up again because we kept hearing of mass shootings to reduce the overwhelming numbers, such as at *Mulga Park* where 2,000 camels had been shot.

Having reached *Mulga Park Station*, we were back in the Northern Territory and we followed that road, still tracking east, to the Stuart Highway. We stopped there for a cup of tea by the side of the road before saying farewell to David and Margaret and thanked them for their assistance and company. They turned left, heading north and after 300 km would be back in Alice Springs.

It is hard to go to the Centre without having something to do with the Alice so now that the years have passed I will recount an incident that affected my life, and sadly those of others, and I doubt the passing of time has eased the pain for those who lost their loved ones. If that be the case I apologise for this reminder but as death is in life, so did it happen.

This is a story within the main story. In 1971 I was a drilling rig operator on Koolan Island, 140 km north of Derby in Western Australia's Kimberley. Koolan Island is in Yampi Sound which constitutes part of the Buccaneer Archipelago and is or was one of the richest and purest iron ore deposits in Australia or the world for that matter. The iron ore which makes up most of the island is 67 per cent pure and much of that is what we called fines. Sometimes the black ore is so fine it does not need to be crushed, although the trucks drop their entire loads into the crusher and those include large slabs of solid ore which require crushing so as to save space and enable fine ore to be fed along the conveyor belts straight into the ships which then came from Japan and tied up alongside the island, so deep is the water. To get there I flew the 2,000 km from Perth, all through the night. Planes were slower back then and it was really a mail run with stops along the way. After 1,200 km and in the dark of the night we saw the flares and lights of BHP's Mt. Newman iron ore mine below us.

Thirty years later, in 2001, Mt. Newman would set the record for having the longest and heaviest trains in all the world. In June of that year, a 7.3-km-long train weighing 99,734 tonnes and consisting of 682 rail wagons hauled by eight engines, carried 82,000 tonnes of iron ore from Yandi to Port Hedland, a distance of 275 km. Back to 1971. Just before our plane began its descent into Derby, we saw the sunrise. We landed and a fellow passenger and I were asked to wait in the terminal for our next flight, out to the island. A few minutes later we saw the morning sunrise, this time from the ground level. For the only day in my lifetime I thus saw the sun rise twice in the one morning.

We boarded a small plane and headed out to sea, out into the Indian Ocean. Being seated behind the pilot I had an absorbing view when he dropped the plane towards the top of a sheer black, iron ore cliff which rose dramatically out of the turquoise water for 160 metres, as vertical as a flag pole but many hundreds of metres wide. The edge of the cliff was the start of the island's runway and if he put down too soon I'm sure you can imagine the plane would be splattered against the cliff face. While it is a long runway the plane came in and over the edge of the cliff at what seemed like close quarters. Men worked on that remote and testing island for the high wages and rarely took a day off but there were times when you could play the homemade golf course. I recall the 6th hole, a par 7, was 800 metres long. It was the longest golf hole in the world and also a major part of the runway.

When I left Koolan Island I didn't fly out. In those days the State Steamship Company had ships that sailed from Perth to Darwin and many places in between, delivering people and supplies for difficult to otherwise reach areas. For instance, after picking me up at Koolan Island our ship stopped at Wyndham. This on, off, on, off and on-again town was founded by the great WA explorer and Premier John Forrest as a result of Charles Hall finding gold at Halls Creek. Wyndham is 3,200 km from Perth and important to the state for its physical position as a port, for its meatworks and the development of the Ord River, as is the town of Kununurra. Wyndham was bombed, several times, by the Japanese, in World War Two.

It was recently reported that the maximum daily average temperature for the 365 days of 2016 in Wyndham was 37.5 degrees, Celsius, and I have little doubt that the humidity is just as intense and draining as I found it to be. From Darwin I took a bus to Alice Springs and along the way stopped for a while in the little town of Elliott, population about 400 people, 763 km north of Alice. I don't know the temperature that day but it is without a doubt the hottest place I have encountered on the planet although Marble Bar in the north-west of Western Australia is said to be the country's hottest town. The only salvation in Elliott was a lovely dry heat devoid of humidity. After arriving in Alice Springs I visited the old telegraph station. It is four km from Alice and built on a rise just above the springs that Mills named after Alice Todd. It was constructed in 1872 as a repeater station and incorporates the substantial stone buildings such as the actual telegraph office, the station master's residence, a kitchen, blacksmith's premises, harness room and wagon shed.

I was entranced on seeing it and taken aback by the soft, green grass that slopes down from the buildings to the body of water, edged by large rocks on the banks and firm dry riverbed sand on either side of the water. Tall trees surround the area and it is picturesque, too good to be true but it was more than that. I sensed an aura all around me as though this indeed is a special place, a sacred place. I could understand why the Alice Springs telegraph station is generally acknowledged as the most scenic of them all and whilst I am a realist I think I experienced something spiritual then and there.

As I walked down to the water I came to a monument and stopped to read it. It was in honour of Mills and the thought crossed my mind that such recognition would not have occurred to him at the time or afterwards, while he and his men pressed on towards Darwin and the eventual completion of the Overland Telegraph Line. Not only were the water and the OTL of significance but no one then could possibly have considered that those two simple words, Alice Springs, would become and forever be, entrenched in the minds of all Australians as representing an iconic part of their heritage. Was ever a town so well-named?

The Aborigines who live in the Central Australia/Alice Springs area are of the Arrernte tribe. One of the Arrernte men told me their name for Alice Springs is Mparntwe, which is pronounced Embungla.

The waterholes themselves are not springs in the usual sense as the water sits on top of slabs of granite rock and while it evaporates it does not soak away through the rock. Mills selected that site above the water, in the Todd River and it would become the OTL's most important repeater station. The Alice Springs telegraph station, being in the Centre of Australia, became a father figure and source of supplies to the repeater stations that carried the OTL further to the north. As I left a calm wave of contentment and serenity washed over and came with me.

Alice Springs residents later told me that on 11th March, 1971, a centenary celebration of Mills finding and naming the site was attended by 3,000 citizens, all of whom were dressed in period clothing of the 1870s. That evening an open-air dinner for 1,200 people was held at the Alice Springs Telegraph Station. That must have been a stupendous day and night celebration in the Centre of Australia.

The next morning I was up early and waiting outside the boarding house where I was staying for a few days. A taxi picked me up and then stopped to collect two

American visitors, a U.S. Senator and his wife, before taking us to the Alice airport for the flight to Ayers Rock. The other passengers on the 10-seater Beechcraft Queen Air were a couple with their baby son and an older gentleman, plus the sole pilot. In those days, 1972, the 470-kilometre-long road was corrugated and nothing like today's smooth, convenient surface for travellers. Normally I would have taken the bus but my accumulated miner's pay afforded a one-off luxury. At about 7.20 a.m. we were all but aboard the plane when I turned around and walked back through the terminal and outside, to the front of the building. I can only tell you what happened in the simplest of terms for that is all I know. Some things I cannot explain.

I wasn't hearing voices as such but as I had moved towards the plane there was a repetitive message permeating my head and it told me to leave the airport, to get away from the plane. With the rare and rather odd feeling of being in a trance, I spoke only to a taxi driver whom I asked to take me back to the boarding house. I silently made my way into the lounge room and sat in a chair, where I experienced what I have heard some people describe as looking at themselves from outside their body. It was only three minutes later that I was disturbed from my blank mind when I heard the phone on the wall ring. I didn't lift my head to it until I realised the lady of the house had entered the room and was now talking to someone. As I looked up she was staring at me in a slow, surprised manner and saying, 'Yes, he's here.'

She finished her conversation and came over to me. Rather gently she asked why I didn't go on the plane as planned. I wasn't quite sure how to answer that. I later calculated I had previously flown on about forty planes and never thought twice about any of them, except that I seem to have a preferred liking for small planes. As I recall, I simply told her I was not able to go on that flight, something inside me forbade it. My total flights now number in the hundreds and that day's foretelling and internal refusal to fly have not been repeated.

I later learned that a main bearing in one of the plane's engines was slipping. That slippage caused the keeper to stop and when it seized it broke the crankshaft. That resulted in half of the engine not running and consequently it was pouring fuel into the augmenter tubes, of which I gather four of them extracted exhaust gases and the remaining two allowed fresh air to enter and keep the engine cool. My understanding as a layman may be inaccurate. Consequently the engine became hotter and fire broke out. When the flames reached the flaps they ignited the magnesium component therein and magnesium fire is extremely difficult to extinguish. Any amount of water cannot do that. Subsequent investigation showed the unfortunate pilot had used two relevant fire extinguishers but it is generally accepted that under such circumstances a pilot has no more than three minutes to put his plane on the ground, a near impossible manoeuvre.

From what the lady initially told me the plane took off with the pilot and six other passengers. It was still in sight from the Alice Springs airport tower when the end of the starboard wing along with the starboard engine caught fire and fell off. The plane crashed to the ground and all aboard died instantly. On the occasions when I reflect on it, I naturally think of those who died and then wonder why I did not. I have not gone on to develop a medical cure or necessarily make life better for others. I dare say other people have had similar experiences but that apparent haphazard aspect of our time on earth makes me curious as to why it sometimes evolves in such a Russian roulette manner. At times I feel a little guilty still being here.

The phone began to ring frequently with strangers, media perhaps, requesting to talk to me. I had nothing worthy to say and declined them all. Taking my leave of the good lady I walked down town to escape the unwanted attention but within minutes, I noticed people pointing at me and heard some of them making remarks about myself to others. They weren't unpleasant or pushy but they made me the centre of attention and I was uncomfortable with that. In the current circumstances where people had died there was nothing positive I could add and I certainly did not want to talk about myself.

As I walked along Todd Street I came to the John Flynn Church and I quickly stepped inside. No one followed me in and so it was my sanctuary for the next two hours as I tried to make some sense of what had happened. It was cool in the great man's building as I seated myself in an empty pew and I began to mentally absorb my situation. Nevertheless, no revelations flashed before me and although my head cleared I was none the wiser, bar one thing. Until I thought back to the previous day at the Alice Springs telegraph station, when and where I had been enamoured by the setting as had never occurred to me before. I felt affected by that and now it entered my head that the subliminal warning I had received to abandon the airport and the plane had come from there. In fact, I could feel the direct connection although at that stage of my life I knew little of Alice Springs and nothing of Mills.

Yet the reality was my conviction, that Mills, as absurd as it may sound at this point, or later, had communicated that ethereal bond from himself, across intervening years to my unplanned physical presence, such as a supposed genie might do for a fortunate wanderer. Rather ridiculous, isn't it? But for whatever reason, it, or he, saved me from an early demise.

21
Birdsville Races and Bloods Creek

Having farewelled David and Margaret off to Alice Springs, we turned south and had an easy 180 km drive to Marla, S.A. Marla is the town at the top of the Oodnadatta Track. Roger and I stayed overnight in the roadhouse and first thing the next morning we set off down the Oodnadatta Track. Even along the Track the good season continues, with one exception. Gibber country appeared, that harshest of land where winds have blown away not only what grass and vegetation once existed but then they have removed soil, sand and dust. The stones that remain are then varnished by the searing winds and being so dry and bare, the surface becomes exceedingly hard. The Aboriginal word for stone is gibber. With their hooves, sheep, cattle and horses are not suited to gibber country, but the pads of emus, kangaroos, dingoes and camels can traverse it with comparative ease.

Nothing was growing on that country but it soon passed and once more the bountiful season in most of Australia for 2016 came to the fore. Sheep and cattle fed on green grasses and herbage and we saw our first kangaroo on this trip. It was hard to believe but we had driven 3,920 km before that first sighting and as if to make up for that lapse there were now hundreds of them. They didn't bother to come to the roadside for feed, there was more than enough all around. It is of course a dirt track and we were a little surprised when a keen cyclist came towards us. We stopped for a talk and he told us he had cycled from Coober Pedy, which is a distance of 234 km. To overcome the tough road he had outsize tyres and said he would take the bus from Marla to Alice and cycle on from there.

We drove by the now unused Algebuckina Bridge, which was part of the Old Ghan railway line. The bridge was of interest because it was constructed in Scotland and transported out there where 350 men toiled in the heat to put it together, one dying of heat exhaustion. The Sturt desert pea is one of the most attractive of Australia's wild flowers, with its standout blood-red flowers surrounding a jet-black centre. Like several other people we stopped to photograph them while they were in superb bloom.

Mound Springs have long been part of the Aboriginal way of life in the Centre and in the north of South Australia there are some 5,000 such springs. We drove off road to have a close look at some. Mound Springs are natural outlets for water of the Great Artesian Basin which lies under 22 per cent of Australia, mostly in Queensland with the edges taking in portions of the Northern Territory, South Australia and New South Wales. Water is forced through fractures and faults to the surface where it generally and over time meets with windblown sediments, minerals and of course, salt. These form a mound and the water accumulates inside that, sometimes overflowing to enable wetlands to occur. A fringe often occurs around the mound resulting in emerald green vegetation, such as we saw, and it is said the early explorers, such as Gosse, Stuart, Warburton and Babbage who passed this way, along with pioneers and cattlemen, were able to make good tea from it. We had our thermos. It may be that the Aborigines derived their tea from that hot water but they still did not have the containers.

When news of the readily available water got about, pastoralists took up land leases and moved into the area while explorers such as Ernest Giles used it as a base for his forays into the far interior. In keeping with the mounds we stopped at Coward Springs for the night. This was a well-known camping ground with an open-air spa, full of happy campers when we saw it. Nearby were the heritage Engine Drivers Cabin and the Stationmasters House. Roger and I set up our tents amongst the shady tamarisk trees and then paid $10 for an old ironbark sleeper and a blockbuster to split it up into firewood. Coward Springs was formerly a railway station on the Old Ghan rail line. We cooked our dinner and came across interesting people, all of whom were very relaxed and enjoying their time at one of the best camping grounds in many a day's drive. We had enough firewood to kickstart the fire in the morning and soon after breakfast and the light of day we made an early start.

It wasn't long before we came to Oodnadatta. The town of 250 to 300 people has a pink roadhouse but just the name is enticing and we had to stop. I was walking around with my camera and came upon an Aboriginal stockman, dressed in black and with a black hat atop his snow-white hair. With his dark brown skin and deep-set eyes his firm facial features must have made him a favourite character for photographers. He didn't object to my taking his photo. Our next stop was at William Creek.

William Creek has a population of six people, give or take the odd couple, and is situated 210 km north of Marree and 165 km east of Coober Pedy. The town is known for its iconic William Creek Hotel, the twice weekly mail run from Coober Pedy to William Creek and on to Oodnadatta and for scenic flights over Lake Eyre. A few months ago a friend of mine was in William Creek and he met the manager of nearby *Anna Creek Station*. My friend is a lifelong livestock buyer for the meat industry, for NSW and overseas markets, and being accepted as a knowledgeable man of the land the manager regarded him with equal respect. The manager confirmed that when his area receives good rains, such as in 2016, the cattle fatten on the natural grasses quicker than they would otherwise do in a feedlot where they are fed intensively and expensively, for sixty to ninety days, on grain.

I don't believe that lot-feeding cattle was a major enterprise in Kidman's day but I have no doubt that the man was well versed in the beneficial nature of the outback country when the gods dispensed their favours. Neither do I believe that Kidman went around talking about the inherent and intrinsic values to be uncovered in the back of beyond. He played such knowledge to his advantage.

Alongside the town was *Anna Creek Station*, proclaimed as the largest cattle station in Australia. As we drove through *Anna Creek Station* a man landed his plane on the road and gave instructions to three stockmen waiting there on their motorbikes. Part of that *Anna Creek Station* land is on the Woomera testing grounds and whilst technically and physically that is in South Australia, Woomera is Federal land, owned by the Commonwealth of Australia.

We left William Creek behind and came around a bend in the road to see a great body of water ahead. It was Lake Eyre South and due to the good rains of 2016 it was still filling up and in so doing, drawing thousands of people who wished to see it as such. It may not be deep and high levels of evaporation soon dilute the widespread body of water but the basin area itself occupies close to one-sixth of Australia. In places, the lake is 15 metres below sea level. We indulged in a little more photography.

Then it was on to my favourite town along the Track, Marree. I have only been there once before but it has an intangible pull about it, I guess it has character. It just feels good. Marree sits at the junction of the Oodnadatta Track and the Birdsville Track. Tom Kruse, the outback mailman, lived here when he wasn't out serving the community. In 1936, Harry Ding bought the Marree to Birdsville mail run and Tom Kruse worked for Harry from then until 1947 when he took over the run himself. He delivered not just mail but medicine, fuel and general goods, as required, in his Leyland truck that, like himself, had to contend with becoming bogged in sand dunes and just sometimes, flooded creeks, often travelling off the Track to reach far away stations and people in need. From Marree it is a testing 520 km north to Birdsville, just over the Queensland border, and the journey would invariably take Tom fourteen days to complete and there were times when his good old truck would break down. He had to fix it. He kept doing this until 1963 and the efforts didn't kill him off. They probably strengthened him for he lived until he was 96. A real bushman.

Birdsville has always been a hard place, remote, hot and too often dry. As one stockman said to his mate, 'it's a hard town to get out of, with your money. It has a pub at each end of the town'. There was only one street then but it was straight and wide enough for twelve horses to race abreast. In keeping with tradition the Birdsville races are now an annual two days of horseracing held at the beginning of September and renowned for everyone having a good time in the outback. The meeting has been conducted since 1882 and these days such is its popularity that hundreds of planes convey some of the 6,000 to 7,000 visitors to Birdsville. As there are only 140 permanent residents there is a severe shortage of accommodation and a tent city rapidly arises. Most of the planes have a tent erected under a wing, while other revellers drive from far and wide to be there and to let their hair down.

Back in the Kidman and colonial era, Birdsville was popular because it is on the Diamantina River and then three stock routes converged on it from all over that corner of south-west Queensland. That part of Queensland was then known to one and all as 'the corner'. One of the pubs was Dingo Charlie's and the other the Royal. The Birdsville gaol did exist until a former prisoner destroyed it with two sticks of dynamite and it was never replaced. Prisoners were then handcuffed to a verandah post of the police station. When one raucous offender began to loudly sing he so annoyed the policeman that he was transferred to the cart-shed, further away. He was chained to the wheel of a big table-top wagon, belonging to the Queensland Government Rabbit Fence Board. Left to his own devices the prisoner found the usual jack in the boot of the wagon. He jacked up the wheel, unscrewed the hub cap with a large spanner and, still chained to it, trundled the wagon wheel to one of the pubs. He crashed his way inside, leaned the wheel against the counter and called for drinks all-round. His fellow drinkers were so impressed they paid on his behalf.

Apart from horseracing there were gambling schools where men wagered extraordinary amounts of money on the spin of a coin or the roll of the dice. When they won big, the doors were locked and they were allowed the traditional five minutes head start. For some men that wasn't enough.

A century and more ago, people came to Birdsville races from Marree, 500 km to the south, from Aidavale 700 km to the east and from Boulia, another 500 km wagon or horse ride to the north on the Georgina River. Such was the quality of the outback station horses that one of them, *Bullawarra* by name, was sent to England to run in the Grand National at Aintree.

The program for the 1912 Birdsville races shows prize or stake money of £500, which today, on the most conservative of measures, equates to $100,000. After the last race, which could be days later, the winning owners collected the stakes money and handed it, all £500, over the bar of the hotel. The owners kept the money they won on bets with the bookmakers but not the stakes money. It was then used to buy drinks, beer and, so they say, Champagne (which I imagine was chilled in the waters of the Diamantina River which flows, usually, through Birdsville) for everyone. Sometimes added money increased the stakes but whatever the extra it was all spent on drinks for everyone. Melbourne currently has nineteen horse races with prize money of $1 million or more and a spring carnival of $27 million but take Sydney's Epsom Handicap with total prizemoney of $1 million as an example. Can you possibly imagine the owners putting their one million on the counter and shouting all round? We were egalitarian in the colonial days, at least in the bush.

A neighbouring cattle station, a mere 50 km to the west of Birdsville was the 6,667 square kilometre *Annandale Station*, the first property bought by Kidman in Queensland. In addition to his cattle, *Annandale Station* carried 2,000 head of horses with more on his adjoining property, *Glengyle Station*. At one point two brothers were contracted to break in 600 horses. Some of these had never been handled before and were now five to six years of age. These were not brumbies, the ownerless and truly wild horses, but station horses which had been running free on unfenced land, until they were rounded up in a muster.

To gain an insight to some of Kidman's thinking I might mention *Innamincka Station*, which is usually referred to as simply *Innamincka*. It is 240 km south, maybe south-east, of Birdsville and Kidman bought that when it had an area of 10,360 square kilometres. By buying up surrounding properties he acquired a total of 20,000 plus square kilometres or 12,000 square miles as it was then. He paid leasehold rent that ranged in cost from a shilling to 18 pence per square mile per year. If we say Kidman paid the top 18 pence per square mile for the entire amount of land his total cost for one year would have been a maximum of a quite affordable, for him, £900.

This was part of Kidman's Channel country strategy as it was situated on the Cooper River, one of the three rivers, along with the Diamantina and the Georgina that produced flooding rains and overflowing rivers, sometimes. If the Cooper aggregation was dry Kidman could de-stock and sit it out, while still paying the £900. When it rained and filled his Koongi Lakes property it provided 2,500 square kilometres of clover. Clover that was about a metre high. On that alone, Kidman could run 60,000 head of cattle and permanent clover will exceed that. A stockman out there was once ambushed by cattle thieves, the bullet striking him between the knee and the thigh. He survived, grateful that being alone he was not hit in the thigh proper but was adamant he heard the shot coming strangely a full second after he was hit.

It might also be worthwhile mentioning the Georgina River, for beside its value when the good rains fell, it had another benefit, for the area's Aborigines. A narcotic weed grew along the Georgina. Known as pitchory or more recently as pituri, the *Duboisia hopwoodii* plant was cured and crushed to produce a type of drug substance. Tribes from most parts of the continent sent travellers to secure their supplies. The narcotic had many uses but most often was used to ward off fatigue and hunger on long walkabouts. At other times it served to induce increased courage or it was simply used as a means of exchange. The Aborigines chewed it and passed the same wad or quid around and around until such times as they had had enough and it ended up being placed behind someone's ear, to be used yet again, later. Aborigines were always surprised that when the white men smoked their tobacco, they burned it, wastefully.

The Marree Hotel caters to the town population of about 600. The number varies as some people pull up stumps when the summer heat arrives. We went to see one of those gypsies, a bloke from Melbourne who travels up in the cooler months every year, to run his business, the Lake Eyre Yacht Club. He is the Commodore of the Yacht Club and when it rains people come out of the woodwork to put their preferred mode of boating out on the water and enjoy themselves in the unusual. Today when the lake is full, about noon the surface is flat and reflects the sky so the horizon and water surface are virtually impossible to discern, as in my photo. The Commodore stated sailing during this time has the appearance of sailing in the sky. Wave-built terraces provide evidence that in the 9th and 10th centuries Lake Eyre was permanently full.

Leaving Marree our course became south-east to Farina. In its prime, the 1880s to 1890s, Farina was a hive of activity, with nigh on 600 people choosing to live here. It was a railway town but many chose to try their hand at farming, despite the dry surrounds. The elements won out but then others dug for copper and silver but success did not match their enthusiasm. Despite that the town had two hotels, two breweries, a store, a church, a school, a brothel and last but not least, a swag of blacksmiths; five in fact. Not only were horses in demand but also camels and in addition to the Afghan cameleers who found they could ply their trade here, so did our old friend, Mills. For some years he was established here with his Camel Carrying Company. The Ghan railway line brought in freight from Adelaide to the railhead at Farina and Mills carried it on from there. On the recommendation of Postmaster-General Charles Todd, the South Australian Government had awarded Mills the contract to carry freight from Farina to The Peake at £20 per ton as well as from Farina to Charlotte Waters at £32 per ton. Freight carried by camels went as far north as Innamincka, which as we have seen is just short of the Queensland border and whilst I don't have proof that Mills went that far I have little doubt such a journey was well within his capabilities, knowing his skill with camels and his rather extraordinary endurance.

Thomas Elder bought *Cordillo Downs Station* which is the far side of Innamincka and as Mills had taken Thomas Elder's thirty camels under contract to Western Australia, I am even more confident he did other jobs for Mr. Elder. One of those occurred when Thomas Elder built an enormous stone vaulted-roofed woolshed and outbuildings. The wool scouring machinery was carried from Farina on the backs of camels and then they returned to the railhead at Farina with the station's wool, carrying four bales per camel. One report from there said the bigger bull camels carried a quarter of one ton on each side and therefore half a ton, or 509 kilograms, all up. Peter Waite, who from 1869 was a supervisor for Thomas Elder's *Beltana Station* took over *Cordillo Downs*. He was an innovative and renowned sheep man and known for his generosity to the arts, science and education, in addition to owning thirty-one Arthur Streeton paintings. After more than a century of ownership *Beltana* sold *Cordillo Downs* in 1981 to Bill Brook, who had been a stockman on the station in 1918, when and where he earned £1/10/0 a week. He purchased *Cordillo Downs* for $1.2 million.

From 1878, a fortnightly stagecoach ran from Farina to Innamincka, with six horse change stations along the way. In addition to carrying freight Mills's camels were sometimes required to pull the coaches through the sand dunes and the loose sand which occasionally built up on the track. Rabbits had ringbarked the precious trees and eaten every vestige of herbage and vegetation. There were times when drought caused dust storms that blew for three, sometimes four days. One dune that had to be crossed, called Cobblers, was seven km in length and only teams of camels and mules could cross it when under load. Some outback stations bred mules and if you think herding cats is nigh on impossible, they say mustering or droving wild mules is similar. The way of controlling those mules was to individually break them in to make them pliable but their toughness was equally undeniable.

Mills also spoke of having to cue bullocks. He was referring to bullocks that were used in bullock wagon teams and the times they had to be shod, such as the horses were. The difference of course is that the bullock has a divided hoof and the farrier had to nail a pair of half shoes to the beast's hoof. Sometimes that would have been a most trying exercise. I have a photo of a wagon at Boorowa, NSW, typically loaded to an impossible height, as was usually the cost-conscious case, with bales of wool. Standing in front of the wagon is the engine required to pull that load, a team of twenty-four bullocks. In the background of the photo is a second such bullock team and wool wagon, tailing off in the distance. The bullocks were yoked as oxen had been when they were used in building the Egyptian Pyramids, with a log across their shoulders held in place by an iron bow coming up under their necks and through the log. All the yokes were hitched to a heavy chain from the end of the wagon pole. Mills doesn't say how many camels he maintained but in Central Australia where he operated, it was not unusual for there to be sixty camels in a camel train.

Constantly being out in the open air was mostly healthy but at times it made men subject to dangers that office workers were not liable to. One bullocky was suddenly overtaken by a thunderstorm directly above him. A flash of lightning struck his team, killing twelve of his hardy sixteen bullocks in an instant. He was knocked to the ground, his clothes singed and one of his boots split open but he did survive. In the 1890s a bullocky with fourteen beasts in his team delivered a load of 14.5 tons of wheat to Temora and in 1898 Dick Turbot took 18 tons of Edgeroi wool into Narrabri in a single load, most likely an Australian record weight although I don't know how many bullocks he had in his team on the day. Those men called their line of work, bullock punching. Some boundary riders gave bullockies a hard time because they forced them to move along quickly when passing through their land. Where possible, on far-inland trips, bullockies took their family with them, along with hens and goats. Sometimes there were up to eight bullock wagons and families in convoy. At the end of the day the men relaxed by the wagons, the women under the cool trees and barelegged children played, giving the bullocky some pleasure in life. During the day the women rode on top of the load or walked while the barefoot children drove the goats and spare bullocks. The chicken coops swung underneath the wagon. If the wagons were late the bullockies paid £1 per ton per day penalty. That broke some men.

When Mills was making his way from Oodnadatta to Charlotte Waters he came to Bloods Creek which is just 30 km below the SA/NT border, with Charlotte Waters a little further, on the NT side. Owing to his surveying that area in 1871 Mills knew the area better than the three men who a few months later came up from Adelaide to take charge of the new telegraph stations. They rashly left their experienced guide behind, hurried on and ran into water trouble in what to them was unknown territory. Two of the three men survived by backtracking the way they had come and by drinking the blood of one of their horses. The third man perished of thirst and was found at the foot of a telegraph post, where he was buried. Bloods Creek, with no apostrophe, was not named after the men drinking horse blood but after J.H.S. Blood, the stationmaster of The Peake Telegraph Station and the son of the good Dr. M.H.S. Blood, of Kapunda, no less.

At some point a government employee decided it was too cumbersome to have apostrophes in place names and that is how that spelling eventuated. It was then decreed that the 's' should be deleted so that the name would be Blood Creek but that is a sinister sounding step too far for some of us.

Thirty years later, in 1901, those intrepid anthropologist/photographers, Baldwin Spencer and Frank Gillen, came to Bloods Creek where they found, *'a miserable little store and eating house and grog shanty. Kept by a man named Harvey. Found half a dozen men there including the proprietor all more or less drunk—principally more. We moved on to the creek and camped there.'* The same year an unknown traveller died at Bloods Creek. The local men rounded up the empty whisky crates and thoughtfully made a coffin out of them. Despite their good intentions they were one crate short of a coffin and when they buried the fellow his legs were sticking out the end of his final resting place.

The consumption of alcohol at these grog shanties was so prolific that in 1873 the Chief Secretary requested troops be stationed at The Peake and Charlotte Waters. As they were Mills's main freight destinations they would have added to his trials and tribulations but life was hard if not brutal for all in the outback. Water was always an issue as was having a regular supply of adequate food, and heaven help those in need of medical or dental services. Blacksmiths more often than not took care of the latter. Spencer and Gillen filled their water casks at Charlotte Waters and said that for quite some time afterwards it tasted distinctly of goat. Mills said that the area was known for its stony surrounds which was why horses and bullocks had to be shod but his camels with their large padded feet took the rough terrain in their stride.

Mills's freight journeys from Farina took him up the Oodnadatta Track to Marree, to Curdimurka which is a little way west of Lake Eyre South, then on to Strangways, William Creek, Anna Creek, Mount Dutton and to Oodnadatta before arriving at The Peake, in a straight line a distance of some 320 km. It was then 258 km of rather arduous country from The Peake to Charlotte Waters. This was pretty much the line of the Overland Telegraph Line and it in turn was later followed by the Old Ghan Railway Line. Tenders for the railway construction stipulated the engine be of horsepower or steam engine but either way it must be capable of doing at least 13 km per hour. It did not reach Alice Springs until 1927 and in 1980 the Old Ghan was moved 160 km to the west to avoid the times when the railway was washed out by rare heavy rains. It then became the Ghan Railway that we know today.

Mills would have seen and experienced at first-hand the challenges and the less numerous rewards that awaited those who took on Mother Nature in such parlous areas. The area was and still is known for cattle stations the likes of Clifton Hills, New Crown and Horseshoe Bend. The Peake was the most northerly telegraph station in South Australia and Mills might have felt some trepidation for it was widely acknowledged, in his time, that everyone who went north from The Peake needed to carry firearms. In the same era, from 1870 to 1910, in the more settled areas of NSW, South Australia and Queensland some Aborigines had re-established themselves on country and through a combination of traditional methods of subsistence and European farming had become successful on the land. They prospered on 16 to 20-hectare blocks of land which they cleared, fenced, cropped, grazed livestock and built homes on. Records indicate that Aboriginal people were winning blue ribbons in local agricultural shows and in many instances were clearing in excess of £100 annually from their labour.

The freedom, movement and enterprise of Aboriginal people in this period was far greater than many of us probably realise or give credit to. In 1880 and 1881 and more so from 1899–1902 the Boer War in South Africa saw a surge in the numbers of Aborigines who wanted to participate on Australia's behalf. It may sound slightly odd but the Boer War was then described as a *man's war* and many Aborigines paraphrased the cry, 'Let us go … it's a blackfellow's war.' To many observers of the day, there was a mindset that the role of Aborigines within their families and the broader Aboriginal communities had been denied, displaced and even destroyed by the state. Numbers of Aborigines wanted to prove they could ride and shoot as well as any white man and they could certainly track better, which was an invaluable attribute against the home-based Boer. Analysts have found it difficult to determine how many Aborigines served in South Africa as some did not proclaim their heritage, to ensure their being accepted by the military, while others used different names. After the Boer War ended, the Aborigines' role in society apparently reverted to where it had been prior and then the official White Australia policy came into being after Federation.

It is interesting to note that in Victoria from the 1860s until 1901 Aborigines were included in the Census count. In South Australia Aboriginal women were granted the right to vote (1894 law) before women in any of the major cities of the western world had the vote. The 1910 Defence Act exempted from war service, persons who were not substantially of European origin or descent. This recruitment policy was relaxed after heavy losses in World War One but it was not repealed until 1951. The 1912, Maternity Allowance Act declared Aboriginal natives of Australia were ineligible to receive benefits and the 1918 Aboriginals Ordinance Act widened the definition of Aborigine and increased the powers of the Protector of Aborigines and police. There were various numbers of Protectors of Aborigines in the states to do the work of their title. A Protector was to watch over the wellbeing and interest of the Aborigines, ensure there was no intrusion on or mistreatment of their property, speak to the government on their behalf, learn their language and assist them in creating cultivation, buildings and general good conduct. He would see to their education, clothing, promotion of the Christian religion and conduct an Aboriginal census. In 1926, David Unaipon, the distinguished Ngarrindjeri Aboriginal writer, speaker, preacher and inventor campaigned for Aboriginal Territory. His campaign may have contributed to being arrested, on a charge of vagrancy.

David Unaipon was fifteen years of age when a mentor stated, 'I only wish the majority of white boys were as bright, intelligent, well-instructed and well-mannered, as the little fellow I am now taking charge of.' Over the years Unaipon took out nineteen patents for his varied inventions such as a pre-World War One helicopter, the polarisation of light, ballistics, ahead of his time sheepshearing machines and perpetual motion. He became known as the Leonardo da Vinci of Australia and he attended the coronation of Queen Elizabeth II in London. He was the first Aboriginal author to be published in English and he often wrote articles for the *Sydney Daily Telegraph*, with his strong penchant for correct English. Despite all his achievements and his popularity as a public speaker he all too often found accommodation difficult to procure, due to his race.

Some of us are in touch with David Unaipon every day for he is the man on the Australian $50 bank note. Somewhat disappointingly, the honour was clouded when a man said to be his great-nephew claimed that the woman who gave permission for using his image in that fashion was not a member of the family. The fellow took umbrage and sued the Reserve Bank of Australia for a mere $30 million in compensation, ten years of legal fees and for good measure some non-monetary items. He lost.

Another danger in Central Australia was the all too frequent dust storm. There is an interesting account of a catastrophic dust storm in that area in the 1890s. Elder Smith sold 500 bullocks account of *Warrenda Station* in Queensland to Sidney Kidman, for delivery at Birdsville. Drover Jack Clarke brought the cattle down the Georgina River, which rises in the Barkly Tablelands, to *Glengyle Station*, that much favoured property that Kidman would later buy, and on to Birdsville, where Jack Clarke thought he had completed his good work. He then received a letter from Kidman's agent requesting him to take the cattle south to Andrewilla waterhole. When the rains come and the rivers flow, the Diamantina, which starts near Longreach, Queensland, makes its way down to Birdsville and from there to Goyder Lagoon and along that waterway is Andrewilla. When it has been filled that most helpful waterhole can last for two seasons as it is then 20 kilometres in length and six metres deep. The Diamantina, like the Georgina, is named after a lady of Queensland and on its overall 1,000-kilometre journey to Lake Eyre, its gradient falls by an average of 27 centimetres every kilometre. It enters Lake Eyre at 15 metres below sea level, the lowest point in Australia.

Jack Clarke took the cattle on as requested but he had two problems to overcome. Crossing the border from Queensland to South Australia would be expensive. Prior to Federation, customs duties were payable when crossing from one colony to another along the stock routes. Customs stations, officials and police were then part of the drover's life. Mr. Clarke negotiated with the customs officers for a fee of £1,000, to be paid as duty on the 500 cattle. Other colonies charged £1 for cattle and one shilling for sheep. He didn't have it with him but he was allowed to proceed. By now he probably wasn't surprised when on arriving at Andrewilla he found Kidman's agent had again failed to arrive. He then received a letter, the mail service of the day must have been coincidental or brilliant, from Kidman saying he would refuse to take delivery of the cattle unless they were delivered to Marree.

Those cattle could already have been expensive as in the droving days cattle coming from north of Tennant Creek were invariably infected with cattle tick and in order to cross into Queensland for sale purposes they had to be tick free. Stock inspectors supervised the dipping and the recharging of the dip water with dip concentrate. A regular sample was sent, in two twenty six ounce beer bottles, held securely in tightly enclosed wicker baskets to the branch laboratory in Alice Springs. This was necessary to keep the dip water up to full strength in order to eradicate the tick. A twenty six fluid ounce beer bottle was the equivalent of 770 millilitres. A drover's gear was vast and just his night camp usually consisted of two pack saddles, a riding saddle, a set of water canteens, horse bells, a pair of spurs, his stockman's whip, axe and pouch, billies and pouch, a pair of horse hobbles, a neck water bag, three saddle bags, one pack bag, a bridle, his leggings, a Bedourie oven, quart pots and quart pannikins.

Jack Clarke reasoned it was too far to go back but the way ahead along the Birdsville Track was in the grip of another major drought with little or no feed and unreliable water supplies. He pushed the cattle south along the Birdsville Track for 310 kilometres to *Mungerannie*, the cattle station and the hotel, where they all rested up. He had another 200 kilometres to cover to reach Marree. To avoid the day's heat he waited until midnight and then set off, droving the cattle until nine o'clock in the morning when men and cattle alike disappeared in a dust storm of great magnitude. For the next day they had to weather the storm, unable to do anything about the smothering dust and sand. Of the 500 head, only seventy-two survived the all-encompassing life-choking combination of a lack of air and surfeit of sand that caused the cattle to perish in gasping agony.

Kidman refused to accept the cattle and Elder Smith lost £4,000 on the deal. Jack Clarke had given his word on making the customs payment but Elder Smith stepped up and paid the £1,000. The only positive to emerge from the disaster was that Mr. Clarke earned the respect of people who had experienced such storms and droughts and understood how the drover had stood the test.

Cordilla Downs consisted of 10,000 square km, situated between *Innamincka Station* and Birdsville, and with two neighbouring stations, made up a total of 18,000 square km and carried 80,000 sheep. That is 4.5 sheep to the square km which would have made a clean muster difficult. An Aboriginal stockman would go out early in the morning, usually before sunrise, on the night-horse, to bring in the regular horses for his companions to ride that day. The white stockmen said that the Aborigines could determine one set of hoofprints from another and not only could they recognise their horses' tracks but they could say, with accuracy, if sheep were missing from the mob.

Another bushman told of an Aboriginal hunting expedition during which one man ran ahead of the others. A common thing for that man was to indicate to his mates if he was going to change direction. He would go straight on for a short distance, then turn through the segment of a circle, thus crossing his previous track and thereby forming a loop in the trail, then go on in the new direction. The purpose of the loop was to indicate there is a change of direction and prevent them overrunning. Likewise an Aborigine might come to a river in the evening and camp on the far side. In the morning he would send up signalling smoke and drive a stake in the ground near the fire. He would then plant his foot close to the stake with the toes pointed in the direction he intended to travel and leave beside the camp fire the footprint which indicates his course.

When out hunting it was traditional that Aborigines would tell their companions of their success by making sand pictures on the ground or beside the trail. If a snake, goanna, wallaby, kangaroo or emu had been captured the picture of the prize told those following that they had no need to continue the hunt and to return to the camp. As children they quickly learned to draw pictures in the sand that were not only of animals but of animal footprints including camel pads as well as human footprints. They would do their artwork courtesy of their fingers, the palm of the hand, elbows, knees and with sticks. It seems there was much merriment, rivalry and excitement to produce the best artwork.

By the turn of the century, white stockmen earned £1 pound per week for basic stockwork, with no mention of the pay for the Aboriginal stockmen. On the even more remote properties the pay was higher when and where it involved longer hours, particularly with cattle which lacked the infrastructure to yard them overnight. The men generally received a food allowance by the name of eight-ten-two-and-a-quarter, which was the conventional eight pounds of flour, ten pounds of meat, two pounds of sugar and a quarter-pound of tea. This was one week's supply and if the men were lucky they could also have a little pepper, some salt and tomato sauce.

We drove into a town full of remains or perhaps, ruins, from days long gone. In the past Farina, originally known as Government Gums, had a bakery and some well-intentioned and dedicated people are taking it in turns to run a recently established bakery, out there, where otherwise I doubt you would see a soul. It was amazing and pleasing at how the word gets around because like us there were other people detouring off the track to buy freshly baked bread, fabulous meat pies, tasty rolls and more. I couldn't try them all but there were definitely other temptations. We sampled some as we strolled through the remains of an historically interesting building. It was being restored as from 1878 to 1928 it was the Transcontinental Hotel, from 1928 to 1945 a Bush Nursing Hospital and from 1945 to 1955 a boarding house. The walls, and I mean the original ones, were exceedingly thick, no doubt to ward off the excessive heat. Although others, all volunteers, were doing the work, it was gratifying to see Farina come back to life. In the earlier days, of 1893, Farina had the only doctor between Port Augusta and Darwin. Farina had a hospital constructed of iron and Kidman bought it to dismantle and rebuild as shearers' quarters for his men. In turn he also bought the Transcontinental Hotel, in 1928, and he donated it to be used as a hospital for the Bush Nurses, as it was a much cooler building, for nurses and patients alike.

Not surprisingly mutton sheep and rabbits formed a major part of the basic diet, and vegetables, other than potatoes and onions, were a rarity. At a bush hotel, the menu was, 'Mutton Broth with Roast Mutton, Boiled Mutton or Mutton Pie, and mashed potatoes.' The Victorian goldfields had been known for mutton and damper for breakfast, lunch and dinner. At that time there were scores of hotels in the cities, they proliferated, and the competition amongst them to entice the drinkers was intense. Then as now the pubs publicised their counter lunches and the working man knew full well their culinary differences. One that I know of, albeit a century and more ago, allowed patrons to arm themselves with the hotel's carving knives and help themselves to as much as they liked from a baron of beef or ham, supplemented by bread by the loaf, butter on ice, pickles and plates of salad. All those pub counter lunches were free, for drinkers. Try asking for one today, with your drink. A baron of beef is thought to have been so-named when King Henry VIII was served a spit-roasted double sirloin of beef. Henry was so enraptured he called it Sir Loin, the Baron of Beef.

Those who had goats used them for milk and meat. Refrigeration for houses was the time honoured 'Coolgardie safe' which is essentially a box shape construction with a galvanised iron tray on top and hessian bags or strips hanging down from the tray, which is full of water. The wet fibres expand to hold the water which eventually makes its way down and along the hessian. A passing breeze cools the air, as in the 'safe' and enables meat, butter and milk to be preserved. Aborigines carried water in kangaroo skins and in my younger days we hung canvas waterbags on the front of the vehicle to 'air-condition' the water. The canvas waterbag is an Australian invention.

Farina was the first refuelling stop, in 1927, on the flight from Adelaide to Darwin with Guinea Airways. The airstrip was out on nearby Lake Farina. It was usually dry. The storekeeper brought out tins of fuel while his wife took tea and sandwiches to the passengers. The plane left Adelaide at 10.15 a.m. on Friday and arrived in Darwin at 4.15 p.m. on Saturday. Weekly baths were with shared water. The girls went first and afterwards the water was poured on to any gardens, while outside toilets were often blown away in storms. When the sun went down you stayed up with a kerosene lamp or went to sleep. By the 1950s you could drive the 620 km to Adelaide in the family car in three days.

From Marree south to Lyndhurst is 83 kilometres and once we left Marree, all that land on the left-hand side of the road belongs to one family, out to the dog fence, the dingo fence. They have owned the first two stations for many years and a couple of months ago bought the third. The first one, the most northerly and nearest to Marree, is *Mundowdna Station* and that has history. It was bought by Kidman in 1906 and while he passed on in 1935, it stayed within the Kidman portfolio for fifty years, until 1956. The present owners have been there since and that consistency of ownership over the past 110 years suggests it is good country. In 1873 a *Mundowdna* station hand placed this advertisement in an Adelaide newspaper. 'Wanted, a WIFE, by a young Gentleman twenty-five years of age. He is in a good position, is considered good looking, he would prefer one younger than himself. Money no object, beauty indispensable. Those matrimonially inclined please enclose carte. Address M.U.F. *Mundowdna Station*, North West.'

An Aboriginal woman who was later employed at the station had a son whose father was an Afghan who had served in the Indian Army at Kandahar,

Afghanistan and Karachi, Pakistan. The boy grew up on the station and when Kidman bought it, he worked for the cattleman. With the advent of World War One he joined the Australian Army and was in the landing at Gallipoli. He survived that but was captured by the Turks and detained for the duration of the War. He returned to South Australia and lived to an age well in excess of 100 years. Perhaps he should have written a book about his life.

Today *Mundowdna Station* consists of 2,200 square kilometres. The recently purchased, 8th April, 2016, third station in the family trifecta is the 3,400 square kilometre *Mt Lyndhurst Station*. The property is relatively well-watered as its watershed southern hills are fed from the Northern Flinders Ranges which supply the many creeks that spread out on to the north of the Station. There are seventeen bores and fifteen dams that support some 1,600 cattle and 10,000 sheep. Livestock were included in the purchase price of $7.05 million. The stock carrying capacity according to the SA Pastoral Board is 6,800 cattle or 34,000 sheep equivalent so the current stocking rate appears to be conservative. *Mt Lyndhurst Station* marks the beginning of the Strzelecki Track which takes one north-east to Innamincka.

Local cattlemen said to me the fourteen years up to 2009 were dry, they were hard years. The six years since then have been good but the average rainfall per annum is only 150 ml. To October, 2016, they have had 275 ml to 350 ml for the year, from one station to another. Some stations have been running Santa Gertrudis, which are a lovely breed of cattle. They look so good but the men said all too often they take too long to produce the first and second calves, at least out here, a situation which is loss-making, unproductive. After that they breed well. Today some Santa Gertrudis breeders are using different lines of bulls, such as the popular Angus and Murray Greys to put to their Santa Gertrudis cows and having excellent results.

There is strong demand from America for Australian organic products and with so many sheep farmers switching from Merinos to Dorpers, which do not need shearing, both sheep and cattle meat from South Australia are in high demand. Prime lambs at seven to eight months have sold for $150 and if grown out for eleven to twelve months, to 32 kilograms (kilos) net at $6.20 a kilo, have been selling for $200. In the cattle markets of late, organically-grown steers that weigh 500 kilos dressed have sold for $6 a kilo or $3,000 a head. Cattle producers who bypass the sale yards and sell direct have achieved those prices while I was assured that one beast, but one only, returned $3,500. So stock theft is on the rise again. The dingo is still a problem, with a sheep man saying that in 2014 they shot or poisoned seventy wild dogs on their place alone, despite being near the dog fence, or perhaps because of it.

Late Note. In some parts of Australia lamb prices have since soared. One of my former neighbours has sold lambs in the Dubbo saleyards for what was at the time, an Australian record price of $340 a head. It may still be but I did hear a farmer from Griffith sold lambs for $345. Who knows how high it goes? Now, just a little further down the track, heavy lambs have sold for $380. When I was finding my feet in Dubbo back in late 1974 and 1975 I bought first-cross ewes, to breed lambs from, in the Dubbo saleyards for the princely sum of $2 a head. That seems unbelievable today but I have kept most of my journals and cashbooks and similar sheep now bring 100 times that. Friends of ours were recently outbid at $330 for ewes. Australia-wide the top price for excellent, well-grown and superbly bred first-cross ewes is currently $413, each.

I was probably fortunate the markets were down for at the end of 1974 the cattle prices had collapsed due to the escalating cost of lot fed cattle in Europe and America eventually leading to a glut of beef held in overseas storage and a consequent downward price spiral. I picked up quality four-year-old Shorthorn cows with calves at foot for $90. (A fellow told me the other day that some cow and calf prices have now soared to $3,000.) That helped us get started in the livestock business but I well remember the outstanding pen of two-and-a-half-year-old *Bundemar*-blood Hereford heifers, pregnancy tested in calf. I have never seen a better presentation of heifers and they sold for a pittance of $85. Not so good for the vendor who deserved due credit and an appropriate price, but serendipitous for the purchaser. I mention this to suggest many things surprise with the years and will continue to do so, no matter what we think at the time.

22

Beltana and Wingadee

One of the advantages of running Dorpers is that the breed is much stronger in that they are not as susceptible to being ravaged by the dingo as the Merino is. It might sound odd but the Dorper, to a fair degree, will stand up to the wild dog. Sheepmen out here tell me they now have less than one tenth the losses of the Dorper as they did with the Merino, re dog attacks. The Dorper breed was developed in South Africa by crossing the British breed Dorset Horn with the Persian Blackhead sheep to produce a meat sheep that can sustain itself well in arid areas and not be encumbered by wool that is susceptible to fly strike and requires maintenance. The name Dorper was derived from taking the first three letters of each breed, although it appears that the Persian Blackhead sheep did in fact come from Somalia, in the Horn of Africa, and there aren't many places as dry and arid as there.

When my great-great grandfather Robert Kennedy was on *Wonnaminta*, the NSW Government dictated how many stock were to be run on leasehold country and a similar thing happened in SA where the stocking rate was also set way too high, at eighty sheep to the square km. I think it is generally accepted that the equivalent of ten sheep is one cow, in this case that would be eight cows per square km. Today the relevant government agency has determined that around here, up to Marree for instance, that cattlemen can run up to two cows per square km, which is much more conservative. Further north they are restricted to running one cow per square km. With ownership of the three stations from Marree to Lyndhurst that family now has the privilege and the responsibility of working and caring for 6,000 square km of land.

We refuelled at Lyndhurst as we would be going off-road on the further way home. You might recall, with surprise, that previously I said there had been 500 million rabbits in Australia. I might be in error here or there as one report quoted 300 million, unconfirmed, but I endeavour to keep this story strictly as it happened, non-fiction. Well, back in those earlier days there was a rabbit processing plant here at Lyndhurst to cater for the trade in rabbits. In just one year how many rabbits do you think, or believe, were delivered from *Innamincka Station*? Before I write the answer I should add that the total rabbit meat was more than that received from all the cattle that *Innamincka Station* sent to market that year. The answer for one year was 12 million rabbits and the information is courtesy of Historical Research Pty Ltd and Jim Vickery.

One station manager wrote, 'but where we could kill 500 or 600, as many would come to the funeral.' Till then, wild dogs had not been too plentiful but with an ample supply of rabbits they soon bred up. The Railways Commission of 1916 was shown the figures on the deaths of sheep in South Australia owing to dingoes and foxes. From 1908 until 1914, there were 651,933 sheep losses courtesy of the dingo and the fox. Unfortunately they all pale into insignificance when compared to the animal which causes the most financial loss in Australia. I asked one fellow if he knew of it and he suggested it was the wild camel. No it is not the camel. The feral cat, he then said. No, I replied. I know what it is, he told me, *women*. Not quite. The answer is the tiny, blind, defenceless termite. There are numerous types over most of the country but the worst of them is the Mastotermes Darwiniensis, found in Australia, north of the tropic of Capricorn.

Darwin in particular and the Territory in general has long suffered from various elements. Today many people refer to Darwin as the Gateway to Australia but back in the 19th century it was known as the Front Gate. Boats and ships incurred an unusual number of calamities in its harbour, people were speared by the locals or taken by crocodiles, floods and cyclones arrived with brute force, the Chinatown went up in accidental flames while a Chinese goldmining camp was burned to the ground by Aborigines, it was remote and isolated until the planes eventually delivered the first overseas travellers and after the wet season more than 50 per cent of deaths were due to fever. Other hazards were malaria, sandflies, leprosy, the termites, smoking opium, the all-encompassing jungle, nine-metre high tides, dry season thirst, yellow fever, cannibalism, snakes, buffalo flies, inadequate food and cattle ticks. In 1897 a cyclone, shades of 1974's Cyclone Tracy, hit Darwin so hard that every building bar six was totally destroyed and eighteen of the twenty-nine pearling luggers and ships in the harbour were wrecked. Nothing, not even a candlestick, remained of the Catholic church. Strongly constructed buildings collapsed like packs of cards, large houses were lifted off their foundations and deposited metres away, as 292 millimetres of rain deluged the city.

Despite the intense work undertaken by Goyder, Mills and others to survey and plan a future city there were said to be six attempts to create and populate Darwin. In frustration and despair the South Australian Government, which administered the Territory, tried but failed to sell it to one of the other states. So it was decided to virtually give it away.

The price of 500,000 square miles of agricultural land was reduced to sixpence for a square mile, for the first seven years. In England's Cornwall and Devon, citizens were offered free passage to the Territory with free and unconditional settlement. No one accepted the generous give-away terms.

Mennonites, the religious Protestant offshoot that had been persecuted in many countries, fleeing from Russia, rejected the Australian hospitality, preferring to take refuge in Canada. I once met Mennonites living in the jungle of English-speaking Belize, Central America, where they had carved out sections of the jungle to create their freedom and way of life, but not in the Northern Territory. Envoys were sent to India, offering Hindus the freedom of their faith along with their assured wellbeing and other benefits. They declined. There were more than enough Chinese of the lower class already in the north so the upper echelon were invited. At that stage they were not interested in any offers from Australia. Nor could the Japanese be enticed by any consideration, such as free passage to the Northern Territory, courtesy of the government of South Australia.

What a difference time makes. Now foreigners are buying Australia's agricultural land quicker than a brown snake strikes. In the past twelve months they purchased a nett 900,000 hectares and 410,000 of those are in the Northern Territory, where 15 million hectares are now under foreign control. To the nearest whole number here is the list of foreign ownership of

Australian agricultural land, expressed as a percentage of that state or territory's total agricultural land. In NSW foreigners own five per cent of our good land, Victoria six per cent, South Australia ten per cent, Queensland twelve per cent, Western Australia seventeen per cent, Tasmania twenty-six per cent and the Northern Territory twenty-six per cent. China holds the most of our leasehold agricultural land. Source, the Foreign Investment Review Board, which has overseen these transactions.

I suspect that those who know agriculture have long-held high regard for Tasmania. In the 19th century Tasmania grew the most cereal crops of all the Australian states, or colonies as they were known. Today Victoria produces thirty per cent of Australia's food but Tasmania was the early saviour. The island colony was exporting grain by 1812 and it supplied food to struggling Sydney and Melbourne for a long time, in fact until the inland railways of NSW and Victoria were finally constructed. Even in the 1850s NSW was also importing wheat from South Australia. Tasmanian wheat for milling bread flour was renowned for its keeping quality and Tasmania's excellent malting barley was disease resistant.

The road south took us past what for decades has been one of SA's main energy suppliers, the Leigh Creek coal mine. For no less than 20 km it was a nonstop collection of heaped mullock and other residue from the low-grade black coal seams and you wouldn't know, from the road, how far back it all goes. It had ceased production and when we were at Farina, in the bakery, an employee of the coal mine who had been kept on to do maintenance work, told me the mine had become too expensive to operate; wind and solar power being so competitive. He said that all the staff had lost their jobs, although, as we observed, there was a big job to be done in cleaning the place up and restoring the environment as it once was.

We came to the town of Beltana, with a population of twenty-four, rated these days as a ghost town. Once the railway came to the town in 1881, it was followed by shopkeepers, a post office, the usual brewery, saddlers – always a good sign – and even a mining exchange. Some 500 people gathered there and made a living, but after the Leigh Creek coal mine opened, its close proximity to Beltana sucked the life out of that town. In the 1960s, infrastructure such as a hospital, police station, schools and more, drew people to work and live at Leigh Creek. We drove slowly through the old town and shortly after turned off to our goal of *Beltana Station*. The road leading into historic *Beltana Station*, which Thomas Elder purchased and made his home, in 1862, winds around a hill and then takes you up to the top of a ridge on which sits the grand old homestead. Further on is the woolshed, numerous large machinery sheds and at the far end, the shearers quarters, which we were directed to.

Inside the main gates to *Beltana Station* is a large concrete enclosed well, alongside *Warrioota* Creek, the latter being where the Afghan cameleers set up their camp. The well became known as the Afghan Well. Nearby are lovingly preserved stone and slate water troughs for camels. *Beltana Station* became known while in the ownership of Thomas Elder, who, as noted earlier, had followed his brother Alexander out from Scotland and who with Robert Barr Smith established what is now known as the pastoral company Elders. In 1860 Elder and Samuel Stuckey were riding through the *Lake Hope* area, considering pastoral settlement, when they observed the explorer John McKinlay using four camels. Elder took the advent of the camel seriously and he sent Stuckey to Karachi from where he returned with 124 camels and thirty-one Afghan cameleers, men who came from various countries.

Thomas Elder had the camels carefully selected; the *Mekraua* breed was for fast riding, the *Scinde* camel was a general beast of burden and the *Kandahar* camel was a strong camel for the heavy work. No less than one hundred of Elder's camels were used in the building of the Overland Telegraph Line with their ability to relentlessly carry heavy loads and to thrive in the environment being crucial. They were far superior to horses and bullocks. The bullock drivers considered it cruel that such large loads were placed on the camels but when those proud and seemingly arrogant cameleers and their equally proud camels overtook a bullock team, each pretended not to see the other. Bias against Afghan camel drivers was evidenced by the horse and bullock teamsters but the feeling was engendered by economics and seldom seems to have degenerated into racial prejudice. Chinese communities at Wilcannia and Silverton were said to have remained on friendly terms with their neighbours.

I will relate a little story about the Chinese and as the reader might doubt me, let me say that it comes not from myself but from Ernestine Hill, the lady regarded by many as the best and most popular writer in Australia in the 1930s. Early in her career she was the secretary to the literary editor of the highly successful *Smith's Weekly* magazine in Sydney, managed by Robert Packer, the man who began the Packer dynasty. He and she were very close.

Ernestine's writing was said to be vivid, enthusiastic and involving although sometimes, perhaps, she was not always factually accurate. Writing of the days in 1881 when hard-pressed Darwin's population had again fallen, this time to 713 Europeans and 4,000 to 5,000 Chinese, she recounted the occasion when Aborigines were similar to bushrangers, holding up travellers for their food and tobacco, with dead men's rifles. She wrote, *Three wandering diggers found the remains of a gang of Chinese on a Roper River track. On the principle that the Chinese are always smuggling gold, they burnt the bodies and panned them out, and got fifteen ounces.* Ernestine Hill went on to become a commissioner of the ABC, the Australian Broadcasting Commission.

It is not surprising that Mills came here to take the thirty camels across the centre of Australia for Thomas Elder and that he rode camels himself, for many years. Well-known expeditions led by Peter Warburton, Ernest Giles and David Lindsay of the Elder sponsored scientific Elder Exploration Expedition, all came to *Beltana Station* and rode on Thomas Elder's camels. Elder not only bred and sold camels but he was known to lend them to genuine explorers. Generally a bull camel could carry a load of 273 kilograms although, as was noted earlier, there were recorded instances of some bulls conveying far heavier loads, of 509 kilograms. Camels were known to carry their loads while averaging 40 km per day for nine days without water and they held the teamsters' record of delivering beer, wine and spirits without breakages.

Thomas Elder also owned the recently mentioned *Mt. Lyndhurst Station* and other country in the northern Flinders Ranges. Stockmen of the day passing by, along with others riding that way, reported that when it was owned by Thomas Elder they could call in and receive a meal. They were good enough to describe the iron-roofed stone buildings, inside which the shade was so deep after the glare outside that it was minutes before the eye accustomed itself and discerned the meagre furnishings of rough-hewn tables and benches with naked rafters under the blistering iron overhead. Meals, though plentiful and sustaining, consisted of hot roast mutton and dry bread with rice, prunes and currant loaf, and were as spartan as the surroundings but free. While Marble Bar and other places are hotter, as I found in Elliott in the Northern Territory and Wyndham in the Kimberley of Western Australia, there was a period of six weeks after Christmas one year, at Innamincka, when the police station recorded the lowest overnight temperature was 43 degrees, Celsius. During the day the maximum varied from 50.5 to 52 degrees, for six weeks.

A diversion now occurs. In February, 1965, when I was a jackaroo on *Wingadee Station*, Coonamble, we did the annual sheep classing. The expert sheep classer was brought in and for two weeks we filled the race for him with the 60,000 sheep. The race was out in the open air with a narrow roof overhead to protect the sheep and the classer from the summer sun. For those fourteen consecutive February days the maximum daytime temperature was 47 Celsius. On the old scale, when I was there, that was 117 Fahrenheit, every day but it was a bearable dry heat.

As I have briefly referred to *Wingadee Station* (*Wingadee*) on three earlier occasions I might take the liberty of giving it further and hopefully justified mention here. The station, some 40 km north of Coonamble depending where one stood or rode upon that part of the wide, brown land, was taken up in 1840 and consisted of at least 122,000 hectares, (300,000 acres). The Castlereagh River runs through the western half of the property as does today's Castlereagh Highway which takes travellers further north to Walgett. When I began my time as a jackaroo, apprentice stockman for want of a quick description, in 1964, *Wingadee* was still fully engaged in running sheep and cattle on an area half that original size. Farming came later. We looked after 60,000 sheep and 5,000 head of cattle. I couldn't ride a horse when I arrived there but we rode every day and after two years I was content.

Wingadee Station, Coonamble. Ninety bales of wool were pressed every day during the three week annual shearing.

Mustering a day's shearing to the Wingadee woolshed during the 1965 drought

Boundary rider Ken Harvey, left and the author's fellow jackaroo, Malcolm Robertson

Wingadee calf marking and branding.

Wingadee Station cattle yards with jackaroos' quarters in the background

*Coonamble drover
Harry Whitehead*

I think it fair to say that *Wingadee* has long been regarded as a showpiece property of the district. In the early days the Local Government body was *Wingadee Shire* before amalgamating into the Coonamble Municipality. In August, 1891, 150,000 sheep were shorn on *Wingadee* and in the early 1890s it was reported that 260,000 sheep went through the famed woolshed, including neighbours' sheep. It held fifty-two shearers' stands, but when I was there it was down to twenty-six shearers in a straight line. It was said, many years ago, two strangers met in a Coonamble hotel and one asked the other where he was working. The man replied, somewhat proudly, 'I shear at *Wingadee*, on number three stand.' The first said, 'Well I'll be blowed, I'm on number 50.'

From 1890 to 1925 *Wingadee* used *Wanganella*-blood sheep from Tasmania, but by the end of that century, they were of *Haddon Rig*, Warren, blood. They were big sheep and thrived in the district. When I was there the paddocks were mostly of magnificent Mitchell grass with areas of blue saltbush which was handy in the hard, dry times to carry the sheep through. The gun shearers would shear 200 Merinos a day and earn big money but apart from them the biggest wages then went to the wool pressers. Four of them used two old-style two-box Koerstz wool presses, which were 2,810 mm tall and built of strong timber with iron bands and a long timber handle. A man had to be powerful to competently do that work all day long. The wool pressers in my time put out a minimum of ninety bales of wool per day to ensure ninety bales were loaded onto the truck every day for three weeks and despatched. The wool press designer was Christian Koerstz, of Denmark, and the presses were manufactured in Sydney. I later had an Ajax but it was on the small side, a basic one-man operation.

In World War One, the Coonamble district was reputed to have the honour of the highest enlistment, per head of population, in NSW, for military service. As a result, it was later recognised by a visit from His Royal Highness, Edward, Prince of Wales, who duly stayed at *Wingadee*, where he was given a guard of honour by the stockmen, jackaroos, Aborigines and neighbours. The prince was accompanied by his Aide-de Camp, Lord Louis Mountbatten, who was a second cousin once removed of Queen Elizabeth II, uncle of Prince Philip, the Duke of Edinburgh, and would later be an Admiral of the Fleet and the last Viceroy of India before he was assassinated by the IRA.

The dreaded rabbit appeared and *Wingadee* fought back. Not only were the vast boundary fences netted but so were the internal fences. Management then drove a determined and costly campaign to eliminate the pest paddock by paddock. In 1905, two million rabbits were destroyed on rabbit drives on *Wingadee*. The exercise was well worth the expense of £1/5/6 per acre as once the unnecessary timber and the ghastly warrens of the rabbits were gone, the station took on the appearance of parkland.

World War Two brought different visitors. I have seen photographs of American servicemen piled onto the back of station trucks and some on horseback as they held their rifles aloft in search of kangaroos and wild pigs on *Wingadee*. The Americans seemed fascinated to observe the bushmen use their pig-dogs to flush the pigs out of the lignum scrub or to run the wild pigs to ground in the open. When the pigs stopped, they turned to face the dogs, which in their turn were then in a state of feverish excitement, desperate to hear the command to get at their prey. An over-anxious or careless dog could be ripped open in an instant by the sudden lunge and slash of a pig's tusks but an experienced dog could anticipate and out-manoeuvre the beast at bay. The hunter would circle the distracted pig until he could leap onto its back, hold it by the ears and then kill it with his knife. Either for self-satisfaction or proof of his kill, he would cut off the snout and claim the government-sponsored bounty money. Other hunters would simply shoot the pig and claim the bounty.

I wasn't around to witness that of course but when we did the annual shearing in the 1960s, one of the wool pressers would stay on the station for the weekend. He would go down to the infamous Bullock Paddock, which was 5,260 hectares (13,000 acres) of heavy lignum and hunt pigs in the same manner. Lignum is a Latin name for wood and it is an Australian plant that thrives in wetlands, growing to 2.5 metres with a heavy growth of intertwined and tangled branches. The low-lying Bullock Paddock was regularly flooded by its neighbouring Castlereagh River and, along with the natural trees and grasses, it was difficult to ride through without becoming lost while mustering the fattening cattle who were quite content to stay hidden there, as were wild pigs and foxes. When we mustered that monster paddock, everyone on the station, including the cook, had to saddle up. We rode in a straight line, trying to flush out the cattle and for most of the day it was impossible to see the man either side of you if he was more than five to ten metres distant. That was what our pig-hunting wool presser encountered. The only difference between him and every other hunter was that he went in there barefoot. We all declared he was as mad as a cut snake but he always won out.

The favoured type of pig-dog was anything crossed with a bull terrier. Purebred dogs were deemed to be set in their own ways and accompanying faults, but one could breed a good pig-dog by mating a bull terrier, with its instinctive and in-built tolerance of pain or opponent, and its absolute fearlessness, with a dog of a lesser resilience but one that utilised a little more common sense. It took a dog of exceptional fortitude to be a genuine pig-dog and such an animal was highly valued and sought after.

On our farm, my wife Janice and I did not go into that side of breeding but we did have bull terriers. We bred them commercially as registered stud dogs for twenty seven years and owned them for thirty two years. To ourselves and other such breeders they were invariably raised like children. They were showered with love and affection while being instructed in necessary discipline. We never had a moment's problem with a single bull terrier. Maintaining five breeding bitches and a sire, Janice and I were always conscious of, and wary of, those people who appeared to want a pup for pigging and we never knowingly sold to them, especially not to those who wanted to buy three pups at a time.

I will concede there were times when cattle prices were once again on the low side and we were able to easily sell eight-week old pups for more money than was achieved by breeding and selling a twelve to fifteen-month old steer. In fact, all our pups for those twenty seven years were sold at eight weeks of age, such was the constant demand. We attended many a country show with our bull terriers and once gained second place at the Sydney Royal Easter Show. When we took them out to Bourke, a local policeman told us if we didn't keep a close eye and a tight lead on our dogs they would be stolen. The old pub where we stayed wasn't concerned about security in those days so I found the policeman and he kindly took care of the matter for us. Each night, he locked our dogs up in the Bourke police station cells. They were house trained.

Wingadee was so large that in my time we had five boundary riders spread around the perimeter. This saved a fortune in time and effort when sheep and cattle had to be mustered or moved over long distances. Each boundary rider was a product of his day, somewhat of a loner as he resided over his far-flung portion of the station but most capable and reliant in all aspects of animal husbandry. They were stockmen par excellence. One was a little different, of course. Andy had fifteen sheep, cattle and kangaroo dogs, a mob of horses, no TV, a wife and seventeen children. More children than dogs.

After I left *Wingadee*, it was split up into the central homestead block of 21,580 hectares, which was bought by Martin Ryan, and smaller outstations which were sold off to neighbours. This was in 1977 and Mr. Ryan worked on developing it into farming as well as livestock. Unfortunately, he died in a plane crash and in 1989 *Wingadee* was put up for sale. It wasn't so big as it had been nor as others are but it sold at public auction for $12.9 million, which was then an Australian record price for rural property.

Back to *Beltana Station*, which in 1878 hosted ninety shearers, still using blades in those days, many for their own 17,000 sheep but also for those of neighbours. This was hardly surprising, as by 1870, Australia was the number one wool producer and supplier in the world. Then sixty people worked on *Beltana Station*, as station hands, tank sinkers, fencers and doggers (trapping and scalping wild dogs).

The shearers' quarters have been reconfigured and renovated as eleven individual rooms, all in a row and were able to accommodate two, three or four guests. We were allocated a long, narrow, room in which two single beds lay head to toe with a little space on the other side of the room to place our gear. Opposite our entrance door was an undercover washroom, showers, toilet block. Other rooms were occupied by four men who were there in the school holidays to teach their combined group of young sons the finer points of riding motorbikes and there was plenty of room and encouragement to do that in these surrounds.

Before we saw them in action, we realised they took the activity seriously as the dozen or so motorbikes were in immaculate condition and the trailers they came on had been welded and constructed by craftsmen.

The old woolshed had been turned into a museum of rural and station life, and considering its size and history, it was easily the best of its type I had seen, not that I had seen any others as a museum. That aside, it was a walk through time and every step reeks of the life and events on this historic sheep, cattle, horse and camel station. Even the sheep pens were filled with memorabilia and the shearing board now had a stone floor and some of the best furniture I have ever had the pleasure of dining at. There were various tables for different seating arrangements with one being of six chairs on either side and one at each end. We asked for the square table with two chairs on all sides as we had met interesting people. All the furniture had been built by men who worked on the station and the timber likewise was homegrown, from *Beltana Station* river red gums. And I mean red, real redwood. It would be hard to find a more pleasing colour, it is beautiful timber.

We shared our table with two, forty-something, couples from Tasmania we had met when camping at Coward Springs. They were touring Australia, going right around and in and out. They had an exciting itinerary and a fabulous sense of humour. We enjoyed their company and also that of the fourth couple. They just looked a little different so when one of us asked how did they get there, we weren't completely surprised when they replied, 'we walked.'

Younger again, the Aussie man and his French-Canadian girlfriend, in their thirties, had walked 1,200 km from Alice Springs to *Beltana Station* with their camels. They set off from Alice with nine camels and were only a little surprised five days later when one camel gave birth on the track. That didn't particularly slow them down, as they weren't in a hurry, and after four months, they walked into the station. The owners not only permitted them to stay, but gave them a handy 180-hectare paddock to keep the camels in and all up they had eighteen camels. The station owners, Graham and Laura Ragless, had been generous to virtual strangers and both parties would no doubt benefit from the plan to organise camel treks from the station.

The eight of us had a happy, boisterous time over dinner in that marvellous old woolshed, which during the quiet of the day had the distinct aroma of lanolin adding to the nostalgia. The station staff prepared the dinner on the far side of the shearing board and I think it fair to say their talent in the kitchen matched their stockwork ability out in the vast paddocks.

Variety was on offer but we all had some of the ribs, cattle chops, with the meat on them between 50 to 75 millimetres thick. We had to hold them in our hands as though we were cavemen ripping into mammoth steaks, and this time we were able to indulge in a little red wine without offending anyone. The conversation was invariably of great interest and made for a memorable night. The company was good and topped off when I moved to another crowded table and took the liberty of introducing myself to Graham, the station owner.

He dressed like one of the station hands at the end of a good day's work. There were no airs or graces about the man who with his wife, Laura, ran this family-owned property which embraced not only rural country, but Australian history. When I asked him about the size of the place, he simply said 600, not in acres, neither in hectares, not in square km but as Kidman and the like would say, 600 square miles. He also owned the neighbouring *Puttapa*, 120 square miles. The total of 720 square miles equals 460,800 acres or 194,331 hectares.

I gained the impression he was proud to be the owner of such a famous property. He didn't say that but I could see the place in that light with its historical connection to Thomas Elder, one of the men who did so much to open up and develop the new nation. I was thinking along those lines when we turned in for the night and I was soon sleeping where station hands and shearers had lived and slept for more than 150 years.

I slept well but during the night I awoke, sensing something. There was no rain falling on the iron roof, no one calling out goodnight to his hard-of-hearing mates or carelessly slamming a door with the last of his day's energy, but something had happened. Other than opening my eyes, I did not move and thank goodness for that. There was a man standing by the end of my bed. A faint glow came from under the door behind my head where the outside light was turned on for those who needed the amenities block during the night. The light defined his form, enough for me to judge his height at about 6 feet or 180 cm, he wasn't heavy nor wide and I could discern, as his head was turned to mine and the soft light from behind me allowed, that he did have sideburns. Eerily, he uttered no sound nor did he make a single move. I closed my eyes, slowly, lest he noticed the movement, and when I opened them, he was still in front of me. Motionless. A moment of realisation overcame me, a portrait in the Mortlock wing of the South Australia State Library, and I shut them, uncertain of what to say. Again I opened my eyes, and my mouth, to now speak, but he was gone.

I knew I had not been dreaming, two glasses of good wine do not affect my judgement and I did not believe it was Roger who had stood there, but I called across the room to him. There was no answer. I left my bed and checked to see that he was in his. He was sleeping soundly.

Thomas Elder prospered from his actions but nothing was handed to him. He was fortunate that in his early days, he put money into copper deposits that came good. He was also, as were other men, able to take up leasehold country at little more than peppercorn rates.

On the other hand, those rates were so, in part, because much of the land was in low rainfall areas but he backed his judgement by putting a fortune into fencing the land and establishing water supplies, which in turn increased the stock carrying capacity of the land. It is said that at one time he owned a pastoral area greater in size than his native Scotland. The pastoral industry had no need for expensive clearing or the ploughing of land. At first such men were able to move unrestricted onto land they liked and while establishing themselves, the laws, well the rules, the rules were first come, first served. Up to 1842, governments didn't issue pastoral or other leases. After 1842, some governments did initially charge stock owners £5 per annum for their landholdings irrespective of the amount of land they held.

With his brother-in-law Robert Barr Smith, Elder later took up the leasehold of 20,000 acres of country at Black Range, in the Flinders Ranges, at the then cost of one farthing per acre, a total of £20/16/0, per year. At that price it may not have been as good as their other country. Until 1961 a farthing existed as one-quarter of one penny, or half a cent today. I was living at Mudgee in 1961 and the bloke who did our plumbing always signed his name Henry 1/4, for Henry Farthing. Robert Barr Smith went on to own *Bundaleer Station*, as did John Maslin and C.B. Fisher, near Jamestown, SA, regarded by good judges of the day as then the best rural land in Australia while Elder himself built up the ownership of a considerable number of quality properties. The men trusted each other implicitly and established a wide range of businesses including the Adelaide Steamship Company, the Bank of Adelaide and were directors of the AMP and other banks and businesses. My daughter and her husband have recently bought country near Wagga Wagga and changed its name to *Bundaleer*.

In the early 1880s, Elder and Barr Smith were shearing 1.5 million sheep on land they owned or leased, and producing 30,000 bales of wool annually. The big difference is that in the 1880s, a Merino sheep produced an average fleece weight of 1.5 kilograms, by 1901 it was 3 kilograms, whereas today it cuts 4.5 kilograms nett, and sometimes more. On that basis, the wool from 30,000 sheep, of good quality, can today return, as a wool buyer recently told me, a gross sale price of $51 million or more. And the price of wool is once more on the rise. Late Note: By March 2018 the Eastern Market Indicator showed an average price of 1,830 cents per kilogram clean. If those 1.5 million sheep were producing today's average of 4.5 kilograms of wool at the 2018 price the annual gross return would be $123 million. If.

By the end of that 1880s decade the wheel was turning. Along with drought came the pesty rabbit. So numerous were they that Elder and Barr Smith employed 120 rabbit trappers on just two of their properties at Wilcannia in western NSW. In six months, they caught 618,000 rabbits. They don't name the properties but they did own two near to Robert Kennedy's *Wonnaminta* and we know the rabbit was there in similar plague proportions. One of those was *Momba Station* and from the mid-1860s until 1872, a young man by the name of Edward Bulwer Lytton Dickens, known by his nickname, 'Plorn', worked there. He later managed *Mount Murchison Station* and was the son of the author Charles Dickens, regarded by many as the premier novelist of the 19th century. Thomas Elder is recorded as owning *Momba Station*, in a Wilcannia register of landowners in 1884 and it was then the biggest property in NSW. From Wilcannia it extended north for 139 km and from east to west it was 100 km wide. It consisted of 8,479 square km or 847,962 hectares with water from the Paroo Channel. I have no doubt nearby Robert Kennedy would have known Thomas Elder.

Momba Station has since been cut up and it is fascinating, but not so surprising, to see that it has been owned by such prominent men as Thomas Elder, Peter Waite, Sidney Kidman and the current owner Tom Brinkworth. The latter bought his first five acres of land, with money borrowed from a bank, at the age of nineteen on which he bred chickens and pigs. From that humble start in 1956 he now owns one hundred rural properties, buying one or two each year. Last month he purchased the prime *Kaladbro Station*, in western Victoria, for $24 million. He bought back the 2,632-hectare property from Qatar's Hassad company. In 2013 he bought 18,000 head of cattle, in north Queensland and walked them from Longreach to his *Uardry Station* in NSW. The $8 million purchase price for an average of $444 for each of those cattle would be two to three times that today.

Thomas Elder and Robert Barr Smith both gave and bequeathed enormous sums of money and buildings to charities, schools, art galleries, etc. The films *Gallipoli*, *Stealth*, *Rabbit Proof Fence* and *Tracks*, were filmed in part on *Beltana* and *Puttapa Stations*. As Roger and I were driving away from the shearers' quarters early in the morning, the owner was walking over from the homestead and stopped for a last talk. I hoped it was not final as *Beltana Station* has a wonderful history, and it is continuing its success and I like to think that its future is assured for it is, to myself, emblematic of Australian rural life. Once we were on the road I mentioned to Roger the incident of my late night-time visitor and asked if he had heard anything. He hadn't, but asked who it was? I told him, 'Mills.'

When Thomas Elder owned *Beltana Station* he not only bred camels but also horses. By all accounts they were good, hardy horses but they had a name for wildness. They could be hard to handle but to a good stockman they were well worth having. Thomas Elder made a point of not selling his horses locally, as a perceived counter to horse stealing, so they were often found in mustering camps and cattle stations over much of Australia and all were recognisable by the *Beltana Station* horse brand, TE, for Thomas Elder.

From *Beltana Station*, we continued south until we turned east in to the Flinders Ranges, on a dirt road for the start of a great day. From the flat country that we had constantly been on, we gained 100 metres or so of elevation and stopped by the side of the road at a series of large panels that describe how the geological formations and ages of the earth are exemplified in the Flinders Ranges. From where we stood, we looked down on a creek brilliantly lined with magnificent river red gums.

Nearby was a family from Adelaide and I spoke with the man, his wife and three daughters. He told me they regularly drove up to this part of the Flinders as the area is so beautiful and they never tire of it, or the long drive. I had not been there before and I was somewhat envious he had experienced such a wonder for much of his forty-odd years. The roadside panels describe the type and ages of the land ahead that we would pass through.

We entered the Brachina Gorge and the first area we came to consisted of grey limestone which is 520 million years old. After passing through time, we were in white quartzite with 550 million years of age. When we came to the Brachina formation we were amongst siltstone, shale and sandstone that has existed for 600 million years and we could see it all. But the real beauty is the way through the gorge itself. It is 20 km in length and for the first 10 km we needed to be in first gear as we came around bends in the pathway to see sheer rock walls dropping down beside us as we edged through pristine shallow water that flowed towards us over a flat rock base, handsome trees that greeted us at close quarters and then backed off to allow us to see the glorious red, white and orange variations of exposed rock walls that represent twelve time periods from 500 million years ago to 650 million years past. During that era the area was flooded and by driving through the gorge today we could see the revealed rock strata that provides one of the most complete sedimentary records to be found anywhere in the world for that 150 million-year time period. It is a magic drive.

It is history. I suppose you could say it is living history and cannot be denied but over and above that we were fortunate to have the clear, winter sunshine that encouraged each tree leaf to glisten and every ripple of running water to sparkle. The sheer beauty of Brachina Gorge on such a perfect day stamped it as the most beautiful part of Australia I have seen. I have not encountered it all, not by a long shot but if I see anything better it will be at big odds against.

After 10 km we were able to move up to second gear, not that we wanted to be away but that is how steady you need to drive through this wonderland and after 20 km we came out of the Brachina Gorge and into open grazing country. Apart from one group of campers in the gorge, we saw no one for hours, not that it mattered. But there is a soothing sensation to being there and while doing so one feels ownership of that pristine environment and aches for more. Later one truck came along while we were having a cup of tea on the side of the road and admiring a line of saw-tooth edged hills in the Flinders Ranges and I am sure that was the only vehicle that came our way all day.

We continued east and followed the road to the well-known stations, *Martin's Well*, *Erudina Woolshed* and *Curnamona*, where we then turned south and continued on until we reached the small town of Yunta, on the Adelaide–Broken Hill road. That was a lovely drive. That night we stayed in Broken Hill and the next morning stopped in Wilcannia.

Broken Hill is a great city and well known while Wilcannia has some social/racial issues that do not entice too many people to stop there other than for fuel, if that. Which is a little sad. So we did stop and found it to be much cleaner and better presented than it is usually given credit for. We drove down tidy streets with well-maintained houses and lawns, so obviously those people had pride in where they live. Aborigines from differing and conflicting tribes were ill-advised to be moved there. The lovely Wilcannia Hospital was built of locally quarried sandstone and was designed by the Colonial Government Architect for NSW, Edmund Blackett. Wilcannia Hospital was the first hospital outside Sydney to have X-Ray equipment. NSW needs towns in geographic areas such as Wilcannia to hold the widespread fabric of rural life together.

In 1816, Governor Lachlan Macquarie appointed the former convict, Francis Greenway, who was judged to be guilty of forgery and therefore fortunate not to have been executed, as the first Government Architect and this year, 2016, marks 200 years of that high office. Amongst the notable works that Edmund Blackett designed are Sydney University, St. Andrew's Cathedral in Sydney and St. Saviour's Cathedral in Goulburn and more than one hundred churches, including those at Patrick Plains, which today is known as Singleton and St. Marks Church, Darling Point. The latter is one of Sydney's high society churches and Elton Hercules John was married there in 1984.

As noted, 'Plorn' Dickens worked on *Momba Station* in the 1860s–1870s. In 1885, he was the Police Magistrate in Wilcannia whilst a prosecution witness was Frederick James Anthony Trollope, the son of another great novelist, Anthony Trollope.

From Wilcannia we drove home to Dubbo and to all intents and purposes our trip was over. However having found out that Mills had seemingly died in hard circumstances and was buried in an unmarked grave in the Western Australia goldfields had me thinking about something that had been on my mind for some time. Roger and I, with David's help, found the tree blazed by Mills and now I wanted to find his unmarked grave. That person who had come to me at *Beltana Station* in the night was Mills and I knew that when I recollected the portrait of him in the SA State Library. It shows he had long sideburns on both sides of his face, running down from his ears to his jawline and that was the defining feature of the man at *Beltana Station*. A group photo of the surveyors of the Overland Telegraph Line shows him as tall, of lean-to-good build with long sideburns. Believe me or not, it was the same man. It was not beyond reason that at the very least we slept in the room he had at *Beltana*. I recognised him.

The underground Commonwealth Savings Bank of Australia, Coober Pedy, 1925. Now closed, the nearest bank is 540 km away at Port Augusta. 848 km south to Adelaide, 690 km north to Alice.

Coober Pedy, SA, sunrise.

Helen Springs station, Northern Territory, with 17 trucks loading 2,865 prime cattle.

Helen Springs station, of 5,700 sq. km carrying 30,000 Brahman/ Charbay cattle. Peter Sherwin was the head stockman there in 1953 before later buying Victoria River Downs station for $12 million.

Curtin Springs station, Northern Territory.

An early morning photo of Lake Eyre South as Roger and the author returned from Skirmish Hill, reflecting a receding blend of salt lake, flood waters and sky.

Island of the Dead, Port Arthur penal colony, Tasmania.
Holding 1,000 plus graves of which 180 had tombstones for the non-convicts,
such as colony administrators, staff and miners.

Docker River country on WA side of the WA/NT border.

Wild camels, Skirmish Hill, WA.

A dry Moses Creek, Skirmish Hill.

Moses Creek, 14 hours later.

Skirmish Hill.

Author and the tree blazed, in 1882, by W.W. Mills, Skirmish Hill.

Pitjantjatjara land, in the north-west of South Australia, in a wet year, 2016.

Young dingo roaming the Pitjantjatjara land.

Oodnadatta man. The town's 204 residents proclaim it is, 'the driest town, the driest state, of the driest continent.'

Sturt's Desert Pea or Swainsona Formosa, from the Latin word formosa meaning beautiful. The state flower of SA, discovered by William Dampier in 1699, often associated with the explorer Captain Charles Sturt and known to the Aborigines as the Flower of Blood.

Section of the guest dining room in the old wool shed at Beltana Station, SA.

Shark's teeth-like jaws reveal ancient and now crumbling limestone rock at the ocean fringed d'Entrecasteaux National Park, WA.

The Desert Mounted Corps Memorial atop Mt. Clarence in the National Anzac Centre, Albany, WA. Two ANZAC soldiers, one New Zealander and one Australian. Brothers-in-arms.

On an avenue lined with NSW Swamp Mahogany trees on Mt Clarence rests a poignant memorial dedicated to a mother's son.

Winter surfing at the stunning white sand beaches and beautiful blue waters of Esperance, WA.

Entering gold country.

The eye-catching town of Coolgardie, the Mother of the Goldfields, has 23 magnificent buildings listed with the National Trust.

A new friend in Kalgoorlie.

More gold, at the Super Pit, Kalgoorlie. The combined area known as the Golden Mile was once considered the richest square mile on the planet. In total it has produced in excess of 60 million ounces of gold and is still going strong.

A standard 400-ounce gold bar from Kalgoorlie Refineries. On today's gold price, it is valued at one million dollars, plus.

A working room at a Kalgoorlie brothel.

This painting, 'Night Attack', depicting the bark hut of two settlers being attacked by Aborigines, is one of 19,000 paintings, sketches and cartoons created by the American-born artist Livingston York Yourtree Hopkins. In 1864 his Civil War regiment was reviewed by President Abraham Lincoln. He loved travelling outback Australia, worked at the Bulletin and stayed in Australia for his final 44 years.

The painting above, of the Bangarang tribe's 'Corroboree on the Goulburn River, Victoria' at what is now Murchison, and the painting below of 'Native Fight on the lower Goulburn River between the Bangarang and Oorilim Tribes', were witnessed and described by Albert Le Souef in 1842 and painted by his wife, Caroline Le Souef in 1895. Courtesy of Victoria Museum, Melbourne.

William Barak, (1824-1903), a Ngurungaeta or clan leader of the Wurundjeri and the last chief of the Yarra Yarra tribe painted this historical work of an Aborigine ceremony using brown ochre and charcoal, in the 1880s. In June, 2016, one of his paintings sold for $512,400. Barak was associated with the escaped convict William Buckley who lived with Aborigines for 32 years and John Batman who founded Melbourne while he also knew Alfred Howitt, who had searched for Burke and Wills and found their expedition's sole survivor, John King. Alfred Howitt was the first owner of the Western Lands country on which the author's great-great grandfather, Robert Henry Kennedy, would establish 'Wonnaminta Station', Packsaddle.

23
Dubbo to Manjimup

Having survived the rigours of sailing around Cape Horn a few months earlier, Janice had followed up by tripping on the concrete pavement just 150 metres from our Dubbo home and breaking her kneecap in four places. Such incidents necessitate a long recovery period and after having steel and titanium wires inserted, with hooks to hold her knee together, she had now advanced to a walking stick and was adamant that she was coming with me.

We flew to Perth, where a good friend picked us up at the airport and drove us into the city, as we had a hire car waiting for us. He had suggested we stay with him first but we wanted to be on our way and would see him on our return. By noon we were rolling down the road, heading south. Instead of driving east, out to the goldfields we would go south along the coast, east to Esperance and then north to the goldfields before turning west back to Perth.

An easy 224 km brought us to Busselton, an attractive tourist town of 34,000 people, a refurbished jetty that extends out to sea for 1.8 km and by all accounts, a good lifestyle. Whatever you do in life there always seems to be two sides to it and in our case, by virtue of passing this way in winter, we encountered shorter and cooler days. The trade-off was that we had the place to ourselves, with no queues and good accommodation at much reduced prices. It is no exaggeration to say that at every place we stayed on this most enjoyable trip, we received large discounts and often we did not have to enquire about them.

For the first night we stayed in a cabin at a caravan park for $69 as against the summer price of $104. It was spacious, comfortable and deathly quiet, until I heard Janice speaking in Burmese to someone. She remembered the manner of greeting people from our trip to Burma a few years ago and she had found out that the manager's wife was from Burma. They had a good talk and we learned that the first Australian medal, bronze, at the Rio de Janeiro Olympic Games had just been won by an archer, Taylor Worth, from Busselton.

Busselton, like other places of course, has thrown up people of note in addition to the good archer and the list includes one Grace Bussell. In 1876, an Aboriginal stockman, Sam Isaacs, saw the 210-ton steamship SS *Georgette* breaking up as she was being pounded by the sea a little way offshore, and her lifeboats filling with water as the waves broke over them. He went for help and found sixteen-year-old Grace Bussell who immediately saddled up. They set off and when Grace appeared on top of a nearby cliff, witnesses were amazed to see her put her horse over the edge and, like the Man from Snowy River, ride him faultlessly to the bottom, before plunging into the sea and swimming her horse out to a lifeboat that was being swamped by sea water. The sixteen-year-old girl encouraged people to hang onto her or her horse and the two of them conveyed crew and passengers alike onto the shore. Over four hours, Sam Isaacs and Grace Bussell saved forty people. Courageous Grace Bussell married and had seven fortunate children. She received the Royal Humane Society Silver Medal and several places were named after her, including the nearby coastal village of Gracetown. By coincidence, Arthur Ashwin had sailed on the SS *Georgette* in 1874, and when the ship stopped in Albany he heard news of Mr. Burt, Mills's offsider in 1871, arriving at Roeburne.

In the morning we drove on to the picturesque town of Cowaramup, which is in the heart of excellent dairy country. Like most of Australia this year the rural scene rarely looked better on such a widespread landscape. Taking advantage of its mainstream activity there were statues, fibreglass it seems, of Friesian cows and calves dotted throughout the town. Cowaramup is a little difficult to pronounce so most people refer to it, nicely, as cow-town. One of the locals took the time to tell me about the Cowaramup Bombora. I hadn't heard of it but when I used to surf at Manly/North Steyne beach, the next beach up was Queenscliff and now and again it would produce exceptionally large winter waves, up to 15 metres high, some 1,700 metres offshore and known as the Queenscliff Bombora. I certainly didn't go out there but a few blokes did. This fellow was telling me about the local version that derives from large sea swells from the

Southern Ocean and that Tom Carroll was here to ride it, back in the 80s. I well remember Tom Carroll for his goofy (left) foot surfing ability. One business thought so much of him they gave him the first one-million-dollar contract ever awarded to a surfer. The local was still impressed after some thirty years, but I was interested to learn that the Cowaramup Bombora is two km offshore from Grace Bussell's Gracetown. In June last year Felicity Palmateer became the first Aussie girl to ride the Cowaramup Bombora; I'm told about nine metres high at the time, pretty good.

Another 12 km and we were in the wine town of Margaret River. As we cooked most of our evening meals, we stopped in the local Woolworths to pick up some fruit and vegetables. Now that has nothing to do with the history of the country or anything to do with our travels but I feel the need to say that neither Janice nor I have ever seen a better presented supermarket. For space, layout and cleanliness I would suggest it is a model for everyone else in the retail food business.

Margaret River, of course, is the centre of a great wine-growing district, with 212 vineyards encompassing 5,000 hectares growing grapes. We drove out to the recommended 'Leeuwin Estate' and that is impressive as is the next winery we walked around, the 'Voyager Estate', where Asian visitors were paying $35 each for a lecture on the finer points of winemaking. Advanced lessons cost up to $60, each. We chanced a little buying on our own assessments.

The daytime temperature was only 16 degrees but with no cold winds the weather was simply pleasant and we were absolutely loving the serenity of the richly endowed countryside and having it virtually to ourselves. We drove to Augusta, a town that we were told was expensive. Well maybe it is, in the summer, but like the thermometer, the prices are much lower in August. We checked into an excellent motel and motored on to see Cape Leeuwin, where there was no accommodation but a lighthouse of importance. Along with Cape Horn and the Cape of Good Hope, Cape Leeuwin constitutes for navigators and sailors the three capes of the Southern Hemisphere. I sailed from Cape Horn to the Cape of Good Hope but have not seen Cape Leeuwin as I sailed west to east. The first known sighting was by that far-sailing Frenchman, Vice-Admiral Bruni d'

Entrecasteaux and later by Matthew Flinders when he surveyed it. I think the Dutch name, Leeuwin, means lioness. We were told that only yesterday a white whale had been sighted there. I hoped it would stay awhile for we couldn't see it that day. Matthew Flinders of course came up with the name of Australia for the country and there are more statues of him in the land than of anyone else. Even his constant companion, Trim, the cat, has many statues.

Back at the motel the manager told me that at 3.30 p.m. the day before, a Chinese gentleman had phoned and reserved a room for later that night. He told the motel manager he might be a little late as he was coming from Albany. The manager told him, it was a seven or eight hour drive and to leave it until the next morning. 'No, no,' said the Chinese man, ' I want to see the whales at Cape Leeuwin.' 'You can see them at Albany,' responded the manager. 'No, no, I go to Cape Leeuwin, now,' said the Chinese man. The manager added, 'Do not do that. It's a long, hard drive in the dark, wait till the morning.'

At 10.50 that night the Chinese gent arrived at the motel. He rushed inside, yelling to the manager, 'come outside, come outside, see this, you must see this.' The unimpressed manager said, 'It's cold out there. I was just going to bed.' 'No, no, you see this, see this,' repeated the Chinese man as he led the protesting manager outside. The Chinese fellow had a rented car and the passenger door and side was a total wreck. There were two things about that. First it was surprising that the car could still be driven and second the man's wife and children were huddled in the back seat, seemingly safe and sound. 'Something hit my car, it was bigger than my car, bigger than my car,' he constantly said.

The manager nonchalantly told him, 'That's a kangaroo mate, you hit a kangaroo.' The Chinese man did not care about the damage to the car, far from it. In fact, he was excited about it and the next morning loaded his wife and kids into the mangled car and rattled off. The manager said most people become distraught but not this bloke. Which reminds me of a sign I saw in the town. 'You're in safe hands with Martin Danger, your mobile solicitor.'

In the morning we met the only other people staying in the motel, a couple from Sydney. We had a talk and the husband told me they used to live in Dubbo, three streets from where we now live. Small world again. I stopped at a service

23 Dubbo to Manjimup

station to fill up with petrol and a lady came outside and did it for me, just like it was done in the old days. She checked the oil, tyres and windscreen so we had a time for a talk. She said that she used to live on the Scotland–England border and the town's hotel, with two bars, was literally on the border. The liquor laws being different in the two countries meant that when the English bar closed for the night the hotel's drinkers moved to the Scottish bar, for a later closing time.

The motel manager showed me a day-old email he had received saying two white whales, a mother and calf, were at a nearby marina so we went there but only found a few dolphins. We set off for Pemberton but as it was not far, decided to take a detour by way of Manjimup. I was glad we did for we passed through endless stands of magnificent jarrah and karri timber, which grow straight and strong, the jarrah to 40 metres tall and the karri to 50 metres. Their finished timber ranges in colour from pink to red and red-brown. When the jarrah is fresh it can be worked but as it becomes seasoned it develops a hardness that renders woodworking tools ineffective. The completed jarrah products are used as household and outdoor furniture and flooring, boat building and structural assets such as bridges and wharves. Jarrah is durable and termite and water resistant. I have always heard of these trees so it was gratifying to at last see them. We stopped amongst them for our morning tea and found the setting and the chance to be among them in nature's peaceful backyard a privilege.

I read a traveller's account from ninety years ago. He said that he was escorted by a sawmill manager through the karri. He told of watching two axemen, of the perfect combination, one left-handed, the other right-handed and both, he said, beautiful men, not tall but broad-shouldered and deep-chested, superbly muscled and as lissom as cats. Each wore a slouch hat, trousers tucked into heavy boots and a seamless coat of 'Tasmanian bluey', cut low around the neck and under the arms. They swung in turn, steadily, unerringly; the chips flew from the scarf, red, like blood. The axemen would cut out a shallow wedge or scarf in the trunk of the tree to determine which way it would fall. It breaks the hinge wood at the right time to prevent the wood splintering and to give the axemen maximum control over the fall. For hardwood trees the angle of the scarf is cut from between 30 to 45 degrees. When the giant tree was toppled the manager proclaimed, 'She's a good 120 feet to the first branch.' The roots of the karri are known to descend for 50 metres. Many karri trees grow to 60 metres but some are known to have attained 90 metres and not for nothing is the tree known as King Karri. Such hardwood trees cannot be cut from ground level as there is too much strength within the tree that holds it deep into the soil. Axemen cut slots up the side of the trunk and insert planks from which to work.

If karri is put in the ground the termites will eat it within twelve months, whereas jarrah has extraordinary resistance to rot and is used in the making of hot tubs. It also burns well in slow combustion stoves. Rather unfortunately, for our history, far too much jarrah was exported to England and as the French-Canadian convicts constructed Parramatta Road in Sydney, so the English cut jarrah into blocks and covered them with asphalt for their roads. The roots of the jarrah tree often extend down into the earth for 30 metres and another difference between the two trees that does determine their identity, apart from height, is that if burnt the karri turns to white ash while the jarrah when burnt becomes valuable charcoal.

The same observer stated he saw a team of eighteen yoked bullocks hauling and manoeuvring a 20-ton log. They toiled to the bullocky's command, obeying one word or many and when their work was done, the brown, dappled and black beasts stood as rocks, immovable rocks, bar their nostrils blowing steam. He was advised that horses can suffice for the jarrah but karri commands the bullock, subject to having one or two good leaders.

After a lovely drive through the great trees we arrived in Manjimup. For a town of about 5,000 people there was much to do. Not surprisingly timber production is the main industry and locals told us the jarrah trees take 400 years to mature while the karri is somewhat less. Old growth logging is banned in WA but recently some of those carbon dated superb 400-year-old jarrah trees have been cut down. Not surprisingly new forests of trees have been planted but not of the famed jarrah or karri species. People don't have the time to wait or consider the future. Everyone is busy planting Tasmanian blue gums as they are quick growing hardwoods.

With their cool, wet winters and dry, warm summers, Manjimup farmers grow a variety of fruit and vegetables, grain crops, all manner of dairy products, wool, grapes, apples and especially, cherries. I have to mention the apples because years ago the WA Department of Agriculture had the wisdom to invite an English horticulturalist to work with them. Thank goodness John Cripps accepted the offer because in Manjimup he created the 'pink lady', which to Janice and me is one of the best apples in the world. Nowadays the 'pink lady' is exported to India while Manjimup spring water goes to India, Singapore and Saudi Arabia.

While its climate is quite different to what I am used to, it is apparently similar to the truffle-producing areas of France and consequently Manjimup is the leading mainland grower of Australian truffles. Growers plant oak or hazelnut trees which are inoculated with spores of the French black Périgord truffle. Below the base of the tree a network of fine white filaments constitutes a fungus which attaches itself to the root of the tree and feeds from its nutrients. The search for truffles runs from early June to the end of August and while most people use particular dogs to scent out the truffles I was told some do use pigs.

Manjimup shares some of its characteristics with the Shizuoka area of Japan; the fertile and clean soils, rainfall and temperature being so similar to that green tea growing area that the Japanese tea is undergoing tests to see if it will be introduced here in Manjimup. Pemberton was our stop for the night and we were given top accommodation at the Karri Forest Motel along with a $50 reduction in price, for a self-contained suite, to entice us to stay on a winter's night. Due to stopping in Manjimup, we arrived late but by 7.30 the following morning were on our way to Northcliffe, from where we turned due south.

24

Convoy of the First Anzacs

The road south from Northcliffe took us for 27 km through the d'Entrecasteaux National Park to Windy Harbour and then up to nearby Point d'Entrecasteaux, which is the high point of the coastline with views to the west extending for 70 to 80 km and to the east it must be 100 km, on a clear day such as we experienced. We detoured there because we had an interest in the French Vice-Admiral, d'Entrecasteaux, who came ever so close to making Australia a French colony, having come across his wake in Adventure Bay, Tasmania and the d'Entrecasteaux Channel, east of Papua New Guinea.

On the point there are several viewing spots, but once again, because there was not one other person to be seen all that morning, I made my way, carefully, over the broken limestone that leads to the edge of the cliff. There are signs that say to be aware of crumbling limestone and collapsing caves, that can break your bones or drop you into the ocean below and I understand that but sometimes I become a little tired of being told what to do in Australia. Expressing that simple opinion hopefully allows me to mention Dr. Thomas Wood, who was sent from England to Australia, in 1930, for two years. His work took him to every Australian state where he met Australians from all walks of life. They interested him so intently that when his official medical duties were finished, he stayed on for another year in order to see and learn more of the relatively new nation and its people.

The good doctor was overall full of praise for both the country and its people although in essence he said that while he had received nothing but courtesy wherever he went he found Australia to be bound tight within a spider web of rules. Whilst some are sound and designed for the better many are irksome. He said what he wants to press home is the conviction of the stranger: *This country is over governed. Not everywhere: I repeat, there are two Australias. In the outback, a man is free to do what he likes, provided he is not committing the grosser sins. But in the cities he is hampered or coddled at every turn by authorities who can never have been born of daredevil carefree pioneer stock. They are descended from a long line of maiden aunts and Australia must be a great country to keep going ahead in spite of them.*

He determined that opinion and wrote such words in 1930 and whilst I am marginally surprised that he found Australia to be so controlled back then, I wonder how he would react to the heavier layers of political correctness that stifle and restrict Australians' freedom and businesses today.

Janice could not come with me on account of her healing broken kneecap so I cautiously reached the edge and looked down. Relentless rolling waves became broken white frustrations as they hurled themselves at the rock wall at the base of the cliff, wearing it away at an infinitesimal rate. Along the cliff edge are holes in the limestone that form a jagged circle, reminiscent of a set of the open jaws of a shark but twice the size. Looking down through them to the relentless ocean adds extra depth to the rugged nature of this headland.

We returned to Northcliffe and took time to walk around another charming town in the hardwood country of south-west WA. In the olden-day but warm and friendly Post Office, we stood in the shadows of time as locals organised their fundraising, bought bags of stored fertiliser, went outside en masse to joyfully inspect someone's new car and then put up posters for the town's annual ball. They had until 5 p.m. to post their day's mail.

Another scenic drive brought us to the coastal town of Denmark and we stayed in a motel set amongst karri and jarrah trees beside a river, its beauty augmented even more by enticing gardens. I don't know the formula for becoming such a sea-change environment but I imagine Denmark does. It was charming and appeared to be a relaxed and easy-going town. I had earlier made contact with a lady who lives in Denmark and who was a keen, probably fanatical 4WD off-road explorer. She is the only person I have come across who has been to the island where Mills was buried and she kindly gave me general directions over the phone as to how to find it. I had hoped to meet her in person but she was away so I went downtown to meet her husband in his office.

He was just as helpful as her but not into 4WDs. We had a long talk about many things and I was glad he gave me so much time. He said the town of 5,000 easily doubles in the summer and is attractive to people wishing to escape the seasonal heat in Perth. He told me when the first settlers came here they were each given 100 acres of land, a tent, a bag of flour and an axe or two. Unfortunately many of them were from large cities in England such as York and Birmingham and had no idea of rural life, so they struggled to survive. When they were finally getting on their feet they discovered their cattle were dying. The area is deficient in cobalt and knowing that today the farmers put out annual applications of fertilisers that rectify the shortcoming. The land is also lacking lime and because of the roots of those superb trees the ground water is acidic.

These matters can be overcome but they require losses and learning, as usual in general life. The countryside looks fabulous but obviously all that is green is not necessarily correct. Housing is becoming expensive as there is rising demand from people wishing to live in this idyllic town and to pay for it by commuting the 53 km to the much bigger Albany to work. To build a new house here, in August, 2016, costs $1,800 per square metre; a high price for a small, country, seaside town but he did add that the few local builders have the game sewn up and the land of course is extra.

As our conversation flowed he told me that the great-great grandson of the famous explorer and first Premier of Western Australia, John Forrest, lived there. As John Forrest and Mills blazed the same tree, the one we found at Skirmish Hill, I was rather excited. He gave me the gentleman's phone number and I phoned him that night. Whilst we got along famously, courtesy I imagine of that common link, he was in Perth at the time and we were not able to meet, just yet.

The following morning we drove the short connection to Albany, the first settlement in Western Australia and 418 km south-south-east of Perth. Being early, we detoured to the popular spots of Emu Point, Emu Beach and the striking Middleton Beach, which is 4 km long and yet just 4 km from the city centre. Albany had a 2016 population of 34,000 and maintained a whaling station until 1978, the same year the railway from Perth, also ceased operation. Another sad rail loss.

Everyone praised the National Anzac Centre and we drove out along Marine Drive, which is regarded by some as the most beautiful drive in Australia; contentious but worthy of claim. King George Sound is the 8 km-wide ocean entrance to Albany, with Middleton Beach being 10 km inside that. King George Sound has a surface area of 90 square km and within that are the entrances to Oyster Harbour and Princess Royal Harbour, which is the port area of Albany. It would hardly be possible to have more protected waters and Albany has two such harbours. The entrance to Princess Royal Harbour is narrow, only 200 metres wide, and yet it is one of only six significant harbours in the world that has not needed to be dredged. What I find amazing is that there is so much foreshore and with only 34,000 residents most of it is untouched. Although I wasn't around at the time, all that bushland reminds me of photographs of what Sydney looked like before the Harbour Bridge was built and most of the northern and north-eastern land from North Sydney to Palm Beach and across to the Hawkesbury was virgin country.

We entered the vast National Anzac Centre and followed a winding road up to the top of Mt. Clarence. The ascending avenue is lined on both sides by NSW swamp mahogany trees and each tree has a plaque that gives the name, rank, age and death details of ANZAC soldiers killed in action. I left the car and walked among them and was, as usual in such circumstances, saddened by my thoughts of those who paid the supreme sacrifice. One in particular affected me. It was a plaque to a twenty-one year old from his mother. At the top of the mountain is the Desert Mounted Corps Memorial sculpture of two ANZAC horsemen, a New Zealander and an Australian, side by side. There were about forty people present and I was surprised and pleased to see many were Asian visitors, here to view our history.

Next on our agenda were the barracks of the military base established by Major Edmund Lockyer in 1826, with twenty soldiers and twenty-three convicts sent from Sydney, to formally take the territory for Great Britain. There was a fear the French may still try to plant their flag. Major Lockyer named the site Frederick Town and only later did it become Albany. Edmund Lockyer was born in Plymouth, where Mills was born and raised. Mills's uncle was

Edmund Lockyer Whitfield and it is believed that Mills was inspired to go to Australia partly on account of Edmund Lockyer's success there. Nine mayors of Plymouth have been Lockyers and in Australia Edmund Lockyer accumulated 4,779 hectares of land.

Today the barracks buildings are in excellent, restored, order. An old soldier took Janice and I into the original guard house and he showed us around. He had served in the Irish Guards but transferred to the Scots Guards. Sometimes it is hard to distinguish the truth from the blarney with old Irish and I rather had the impression this bloke, at least in his younger days, had been a bit of a rogue. He took a shine to Janice and perhaps in view of her still injured leg, bundled us on to his electric cart and drove us up to the highest point on the mountain so that we could see out over most of King George Sound and Princess Royal Harbour. That view is worth a long day's drive and dare I say it, is pristine.

The next morning saw us at the Boathouse Markets, a change from the farmers' markets. We bought fillets of harpuka, a red and white flesh fish, which was well worth the effort of the fisherman who told me he goes to a shelf 43 km out to sea, to catch them. We could hardly ask for a better day, warm and sunny, 18 degrees and light breezes coming off the water. The near-full marina hinted of the good life as did the neatly kept homes that enticingly rise from the harbour up the nearby hills. The maximum forty-two passengers on the whale-watching boat pulled out of its nearby berth and headed out to King George Sound. The three-hour voyage costs $95, or $88 for seniors, and whether you see whales or not, you are allowed back at any time in the next fourteen days to enjoy another three-hour trip searching for whales. I think it is an easy and clever promotion to keep visitors in Albany, for longer. To help ensure you do see whales there are two men with powerful binoculars stationed on top of high hills. They continually scan the waters for any sign of whales and inform the skipper accordingly.

Although the city does not have cobblestone streets it reminded me of Hobart with the mainly low-level housing spread around the waterways and interspersed by ample trees. Of the sea-change and tree-change regions I have seen I would say I could comfortably live in Albany. Now that I say that, I recall my captain on the Dutch Tall Ship, *Europa*, saying that he believes Albany has the freshest, cleanest air in the world, due to the uninterrupted winds from the west and its geographical location. Albany has a wind farm which produces 80 per cent of the city's electricity consumption.

And only after seeing Albany for myself did I read of another impartial review, from a century ago. That English author was stunned by the spectacular harbours of Albany and the pure air. I quote him, *This is the Albany of the future; Albany as it deserves to become. The Albany of today is a small port whose harbour on its own account would nearly repay a voyage to Australia. (But not quite) Cliffs run up straight from the edge of two landlocked basins, each of which would hold the Royal Navy, the Royal Navy of 1918. That glorious air may bring health, but apparently it has not brought business, and business we had nothing to do with. Our gain was quiet and happiness and a new friend or two. Albany is full of them, and what can any town give you better than this?* – Dr. Thomas Wood.

We walked from the Boathouse around the harbour foreshore to the full-size replica of the *Amity*, the ship which Major Lockyer, his troops and convicts, sailed from Sydney to Albany, to begin life in Western Australia. Back to the car and we drove around the harbour for 20 km to the site of the old whaling station. A whale-catcher ship was beached for people to inspect, along with good grounds and restaurants. Many visitors were there from Japan and India and I wondered why even more people didn't come at this time of year. It is so easy and the winter weather is superb.

After lunch of corn-on-the-cob by the water it was back to the National Anzac Centre, to the building that houses the military records and heritage. If you have been to Sydney's Taronga Zoo you would know the fabulous views to be had when looking over the harbour or towards the city. This is similar but without another building to be seen and yet so close to the city of Albany. As we walked inside the Anzac Centre a stirring sound came to our ears, the tramp-tramp-tramp of hundreds of feet in heavy boots. Then we saw on the tall white walls black and white film of endless legions of Australian soldiers from World War One marching in ranks towards us with rifles over their shoulders, slouch hats on proud heads. Many men looked the camera in the eye as they passed by and their quiet resolve could be seen and possibly understood. They are inspirational and make for moist eyes. Initially the men, all volunteers, recruited for that war, were selected on the highest standards of physical and medical assessments. In that sense they were the best of the best, the pride of the fledgling nation.

Every person entering the Centre is given a card with the name and photo of a serving soldier from the War. Mine was of Bugler Otto Siefken, who was of a German family settled in Western Australia. Even though Otto was in the Australian Army, his father Carl was classed as an enemy alien and had to report to the local police station every week. Otto sailed from Albany and went ashore at Gallipoli, Turkey, on 25th April, 1915, in the second wave. The first wave having alerted the Turks, the second wave came under heavier fire. Otto later wrote a letter to his mother from Gallipoli in which he said, 'a terrific row but we were having good sport knocking them … it was like a play watching them come up and get in our barbwire and all singing out 'Allah, Allah, Mohamed; and dropping like sheep. They had over three thousand … dead in front of our trenches. The stink was awful in a few days and millions of flies came round'. Otto survived that campaign and like many others was then sent to the Western Front, fighting in Belgium and France. After transferring to a machine-gun company he was captured by German troops in 1917 and placed in a rather brutal prisoner-of-war camp. He died just three weeks before the Armistice.

Perhaps the National Anzac Centre was designed to pull at the heartstrings. There are other reminders to be seen and whatever it cost, not in human lives but in dollars, to put it together, it emotionally succeeds. In addition, there are the high windows that allow the most wonderful views out over the surrounding bush and down on to King George Sound. One looks out over the Sound where on 1st November, 1914, the first convoy of ANZACs sailed off to war. One hundred years later, on 1st November, 2014, the National Anzac Centre was opened. A few politicians wanted it to be in Canberra, as a National Memorial but this was where the first of those virtually hand-picked troops gathered and from whence they sailed. For all too many of those men the heights of Mt. Clarence was their last sight of Australia.

In late October, 1914, a convoy of fourteen troopships carrying soldiers from Victoria and New Zealand and escorted by one cruiser, sailed into Albany to join up with other contingents. Over the next few days more and more ships gathered in the Sound. On the 1st November, 38 troopships and three Navy escort ships sailed out of King George Sound, bound for Egypt and Gallipoli. It must have been an impressive sight and certainly the excitement ran high. Maori war cries were answered by stirring Australian cooees, both occurrences said to move a stoic. And the bands played Waltzing Matilda.

The ships carried some 30,000 soldiers and 7,600 horses and never had there been a convoy such as this, for the fourteen-year-old nation. Captains were more apprehensive about running into each other than encountering armed conflict. The ships' speed was controlled to a quarter turn of the screw but hampered by the pace of the slowest ship, the *Southern*, which at best could only average 10 knots. Ships had to be set distances between each other, day and night. Discipline of this high order was new but swiftly instilled.

The Australian transports sailed in three columns, the New Zealanders followed behind in two columns of their own. And there was a foreigner amongst them all, the Japanese battle cruiser *Ibuki*. Twenty years earlier Great Britain had refused to join the Triple Intervention of France, Germany and Russia against Japan and instead signed the Anglo-Japanese Treaty, because it was wary of Russia. The Japanese *Ibuki* escorted a convoy of ten New Zealand troopships to Melbourne and on to Albany and then set sail with the entire convoy, to guard the Australians and New Zealanders. What a strange world evolves at times.

When World War One commenced, Australia was fearful that with its mother country of Great Britain engaged in European warfare, Japan might take advantage of that to attack Australia. There was a certain relief in 1914 when Japan announced it would honour its treaty with Great Britain. 23,000 Japanese soldiers, along with a small detachment of 1,500 English forces, defeated German troops at the Siege of Tsingtao, China, in November, 1914.

Even in those early days of World War One the German Navy was a serious threat to the convoy. On 21 September, 1914, the armoured cruisers *Gneisenau* and *Scharnhorst* bombarded Papeete in France's Tahitian paradise, although on 8

December the British would destroy both those cruisers and more in the decisive Battle of the Falkland Islands. The light cruiser *Konisberg* was away off the coast of Africa but on 8 October the *Emden* had entered Malaysia's deep-water port at Penang where it sank a Russian cruiser and a French destroyer. Now she had disappeared but was somewhere ahead of the Anzac troopships.

The Japanese were serious about their role. When the German Navy ship *Emden* was sighted off WA's Cocos Islands, the commander of the *Ibuki* requested the honour of engaging the German raider. The Japanese battlecruiser was superior to the Australian light cruiser HMAS *Sydney* but the home ship was ordered to take on the enemy and did so, destroying the German ship by gunfire and running her aground. In response, for years afterwards, up to 1939 but no longer, the Royal Australian Navy celebrated the samurai spirit of the *Ibuki* whenever Imperial Japanese ships visited Australia.

In the Gallipoli campaign 8,709 Australians died and approximately 16,300 were injured.

'When I speak of our boys I mean the Aus and us, for when you're hard pressed and you look to your left and find an Aus – telling you, "it is alright cobber, I'm here to help you" and the same on the right, I can tell you it makes you think of them as more than brothers.' – Trooper Garry Clunie, Wellington, NZ, Mounted Rifles Regiment, 1 September, 1915.

The body of only one Australian soldier was returned during World War One, that being of Major-General Sir William Bridges, Commander of the Australian 1st Division. He died at sea after wounds received at Gallipoli. Of the 136,000 horses Australia sent to war, his horse Sandy, was the only horse to return, in 1918. Fighting troops as a percentage of various Commonwealth country's population were Australia 11.2, Canada 8.9, New Zealand 6.8, U.K. 5.0, South Africa 2.0, India 0.4 per cent.

25

Hardy Norseman

Another day and we rather reluctantly left Albany astern. We cast off at 7.00 a.m. and covered the 480 km to Esperance arriving there at 1 p.m. I took it easy and noticed that in the first 255 km, I passed no one and only a single car overtook us. That winter effect, perhaps. For the first 80 to 90 km I was driving directly into the rising sun, the road is easterly the whole way, and therefore I slowed down, which was just as well when a brute of a kangaroo put in one of those last moment appearances and jumped out right at me. I was able to back off just enough for his tail to flick the front bumper as he asked if I had insurance. There weren't too many at that daylight hour but the numerous roadkill revealed several as large as this one. After that first 80 km the bushland and the blue gum plantations gave way to open paddocks of golden canola and wheat crops, for all of the next 400 km. Those wheat crops were tremendous, after the wet winter. If the season finishes off they should produce several tonnes to the hectare, quite probably more. I can't determine canola but it also looked substantial.

After 325 km we saw a large mining operation off to our right, and 155 km from Esperance. This is the Ravensthorpe nickel mine and hydrometallurgical processing plant and it has a chequered history. BHP spent $3 billion on establishing the complex and local people were greatly heartened by its development, apparently buying land and housing for their own ends and investing for the anticipated needs of the workforce. The global financial crisis of 2008–2009 saw the price of nickel collapse from $50,000 a tonne to $11,000 a tonne and the whole exercise became futile, untenable. After a mere nine months of operating but incurring a $3.6 billion writedown in the process, BHP shut Ravensthorpe down in January, 2009.

We heard local people still lamenting their losses, bitterly, but of course the outcome was not intended. In December of 2009, BHP sold the business for $340 million and as the new ownership started operating in December of 2011 hopefully that was better late than never. In 2012, the Canadian owned operation produced 32,000 tonnes of nickel from the mine which by then had overcome technical difficulties that were previously hampering production and now the mine has a life expectancy of more than thirty years. The Esperance Port can handle ships of 200,000 tonnes and is the largest nickel concentrate exporting port in the Southern Hemisphere. Other nickel producers in the area include Poseidon Nickel which recently bought the Lake Johnston operation from the world's biggest producer of nickel, the Russian company, Norilsk.

About 100 km before we came to Esperance we stopped at the little town of Mangilup. We drove around the town and were amazed at the high quality of the roads. This seems to be the norm in WA, wherever we turn. Perhaps the state government invested in road infrastructure while the mining boom was on. However it happened, they have good roads to carry them through for a long time. At Mangilup and two other flyspecks on the map between Albany and Esperance are wheat silo depots, as big as I have seen anywhere. It appears the state caters to farmers. Perhaps that is why the Chinese are now buying large areas of Western Australian broadacre farmland.

I had expected Esperance, which took its name from the French ship *L'Esperance* and translates as hope, to be a country town but it is more than that. Having driven through the uncrowded outer reaches we soon found ourselves looking out over a vast waterfront with sparkling ocean waters, a port for loading 200 ships annually, eight more massive grain silos, a marina, a yacht club, Arts centre, three National Parks with coastal scenery, and many quality motels and hotels along the esplanade, which is lined with perfectly shaped Norfolk pine trees. Tourism, agriculture and fishing are prominent activities in the town of 10,000 people, with more in the rural region, 720 km from Perth. That soil also needs fertiliser, particularly superphosphate but this is applied and contributes substantially to WA's wheat and barley crops. WA produces 80 per cent of Australian barley.

Accommodation on the esplanade is predictably higher priced but just a street back we found a peaceful caravan park with spacious cabins at half those prices and far more room. For no extra cost the lady owner gave us a cabin the size of a house with two bedrooms. That night I cooked dinner on the barbecue and in the morning she allowed us to use their commercial washing machines to do our laundry and again at no cost. It was a wonderful place, with or without that generosity.

When the French ship *Recherche* lost its mainmast near there the crew replaced it with timber cut from a Norfolk pine. So impressed were they that they planted as many Norfolk pines, presumably from fallen pine cones, as they could. Today locals and visitors alike are impressed with the results of the French foresight and I am still surprised we are not French. It is a fact that Britain despatched four explorers to survey Australia and France sent seven.

Determined to find Mills's grave and to mark it in his memory I had a plaque made in Dubbo. The local funeral directors and stonemasons assured me they could come up with a nice one but they all said it would be made of granite and there was no way I was going to attempt to carry a heavy headstone to the other side of Australia. Then it was suggested I try a sign-writer and that turned out brilliantly. The fellow produced two sheets of aluminium, cut to size, with a compound filler in between them that he guaranteed would last fifty years and expected that it would comfortably be in good shape after one hundred years. It was lightweight but had the strength of an anvil. It had a white background and at the top in red were the dates 19.11.1844–18.08.1916. In the middle in black was the name WILLIAM WHITFIELD MILLS and below that, once more in red, are the words SURVEYOR EXPLORER PROSPECTOR.

I went to Bunnings in Esperance to get some timber on which to place the board and a post on which to put the whole thing. I mention Bunnings by name because of the exceptional assistance I received. I couldn't find the timber backing I thought I needed so I was referred to Willi, an Indian-Australian. I told him what I was after and he said if I use timber it will only move or buckle over time and put stress on the plaque. He added I would then have to paint the timber and that would also fade away. He suggested the best thing to use was steel and I said well, that may be so but where am I going to find some of that? Here, he said, and took me to a selection. By some whim of the gods Willi produced a steel panel that was the exact size required for neat and sufficient backing. With a small drill bit followed by a larger version he drilled through the steel plate plus the plaque and then added the lot to a star post. After he put the bolts in place he then used a hammer and chisel to chip at the nuts, deliberately damaging them so they can never be undone, (should someone choose to do so and we all know there are enough strange people out there). Willi's manager had given him permission to assist me and whilst I paid for the parts I did not incur a charge for Willi's expertise and time. I now had an impeccable mounted and virtually unbreakable plaque. I simply had to find where to place it.

We went for a drive and found ourselves following the coastline out of town. We topped a hill and looked down on a white sand beach with beautiful blue water; it was a stunning colour, such as is seen in the Whitsundays or the Caribbean. Light blue water occupied the first 60 metres out to sea and it was brilliantly blue all the way out into the ocean. It was remarkable and it continued on for many km as each beach came to a headland and after we drove over or around that, the white sand and brilliant blue ocean was simply endless. About five km further on we came to a long beach with two groups of surfboard riders having the time of their lives in three-metre-high waves that held their shape and offered up glorious surfing conditions. I stopped in a parking bay above the beach and from a distance took a lot of action photos. Janice did not share my enthusiasm and although she was happy with the scenery I drove back into town and dropped her off at the Esperance Museum.

I went back to the surf and as I had hoped the board riders were now coming ashore. I showed them my photos, and what pleased them, or surprised them the most, was the fabulous blue of the water. It was as if they couldn't see the forest for the trees, being in the water, rather than standing back from it as I was. They had all come from Margaret River and would normally be surfing in Indonesia at this time of year but so many Australians are over there for the winter, they stayed home this year.

I returned to the museum and after having a good look around I was not surprised to hear several men saying amongst themselves they have never seen a better museum of Australiana. There were freight wagons, brewery wagons, saddlery, blacksmiths' tools, wool presses, shearing gear, wood lathes, printing presses, chaff cutters, seed graders, ploughs, a grain grister, radial arm saw, 19th century furniture, large sections of Skylab, barbers' chairs, Aboriginal weapons, trucks and tractors, a pilot boat, even a train and more and more. What caught my eye was the headstone of Tommy Windich, the Aboriginal guide/tracker who accompanied the Western Australian explorer John Forrest on several expeditions. It was not a copy but the 140-year-old original although at first I doubted that due to its superb condition. It had indeed fallen into a state of disrepair but a grant was given to have it restored. After the money ran out, the young restorer completed it for free.

The French ship *L'Esperance* came here in company with the *Recherche* in 1792 and nearby is the *Recherche Archipelago*. Matthew Flinders explored its 105 islands in 1802 and charted them so accurately his maps were used for more than one hundred years. In 1826, an American whaler reached Albany's King George Sound and when the crew were ashore a fight broke out between the men. A crew man was killed and Black Jack Anderson, an African-American, held accountable for murder. With a few followers he stole a smaller boat and escaped to the *Recherche Archipelago*, from where he and his men set about robbing passing ships of their sealskins, which were worth a hefty six shillings each, robbing other ships' passengers and being a law unto themselves, an illegal one.

The *Perth Gazette* reported that Jack Anderson and others were killing Aboriginal men by shooting or clubbing them and taking their women. The *Recherche Archipelago* has good soil and vegetation along with supplies of fresh water. Anderson, often referred to as Australia's only pirate, carried on regardless for ten years until finally he was killed by his own men.

Seal hunting boats around southern Australia, particularly working the Bass Strait and Kangaroo Island areas, had European, American, Aboriginal and Polynesian crew members. They forcibly kidnapped women from Tasmania, South Australia and Western Australia to become domestic workers, wives and sealing gang members.

In 1973, America's NASA launched Skylab, the country's first space station.

It orbited Earth until 1979 when it was returned with the intention of landing in the ocean 1,300 km south-east of Cape Town. It went a little off course and also began disintegrating at a much lower height than had been intended. Consequently a fair portion of Skylab, in varying sizes, landed on Esperance. NASA offered a reward of US $10,000 to the first person to bring in a piece of Skylab. A resident of Esperance climbed on to his roof, collected one of several pieces and took the first plane he could to San Francisco. He collected the US $10,000. Meanwhile the town of Esperance submitted a bill to NASA of $400, for the clean-up costs of Skylab. Even though President Jimmy Carter sent a letter of apology, NASA ignored the invoice but thirty years later listeners to an American radio station chipped in and paid the bill.

Our next stop was at 'Mermaid Leather'. No doubt you have various leather items around the house that are made from cowhide or kangaroo. Now you can have leather goods tanned from snapper, barramundi and shark, even a groper if you are so inclined. We had been told of this tannery with a difference, started in 1989 by two local fishermen, so we went to see it for ourselves. We watched a video on the business, saw some processing and marvelled at the end product. Usually fish skins are thrown away but these fellows have developed a fine art, using natural bark from the karri tree for the tannin. Shark leather has six times the strength of most land leather and is said to have been used by the Vikings for wrapping armour and grips for weapons. Later it was used by Japanese Samurai, English cavalry and the Australian Light Horse. The highest-ranking Samurai had access to sharkskin and stingray leather while in Europe it was used as sandpaper for 800 years and assisted in French polishing, gemstone and ivory workings. Some people use it as the grips of golf clubs and cricket bats.

Our guide said the most suitable marine life for leather making are blue groper, queen snapper, pink snapper, breaksea, saltwater barramundi, Tasmanian salmon, harpuka, boar fish, shark and nor-west snapper. He put a number of skins through a roller machine that pounds the skin and gives it a lovely touch so that the finished product is said to have a sexual feel about it. It seemed remarkable that there are so many end uses for the tanned fish leather but it is as attractive as any other and definitely different. We did buy some.

25 Hardy Norseman

The next morning we left Esperance as we did Albany, with a lot of regret. Anyway, for the first time on this little road trip I turned the wheel to the north and we headed off to Norseman, to the gold country. An official road sign amused us. It showed pictures of a cow and calf on the left-hand side and a kangaroo on the right. In between were the words, in large print, *Stray Animals*. Someone with a good sense of humour about how some of us pronounce the word Australia, by leaving out the L, had changed the wording by simply adding an A, so that the sign now said Straya Animals. Well, it appealed to me. For the first 150 km the countryside consisted of those thick, heavy bearing, grain crops. I recently heard the Esperance barley crops yielded seven dryland tonnes to the hectare for the 2016 crop. Fabulous for farmers. We had not seen a town but after 70 of those km we passed through the district of Patch of Grass, which hosts more wheat silos and bunkers.

At the Esperance Museum I had seen mention of Tom Starcevich, who lived here, at Patch of Grass. In World War Two he fought the German Army at El Alamein, where he was shot in the thigh, and then against the Japanese Army. While serving in Borneo he was a Bren gunner when the Australians came under fire from two Japanese machine-gun positions. He went ahead and took out both machine-gun emplacements. Later that day he destroyed two more, inflicting heavy casualties on the Japanese on all four occasions. He was awarded the Victoria Cross, remained a private for the rest of the war and died in Esperance aged seventy-one.

The 205 km road from Esperance is dead straight to Norseman and we were soon in the gold town. Norseman, the last town in WA before one heads out to the Nullarbor Plain, has life-size corrugated-iron camels around the wide streets that enabled live camel trains to turn around and has produced more than 100 tonnes of gold. In 1894, Laurie Sinclair, a man who had come to WA from the Shetland Islands, north of Scotland, was prospecting in the area. Being from the Shetlands he was proud of his Viking/Norse heritage and because, like his ancestors, he lived a hard life, he called his horse Hardy Norseman. One morning he found his horse to be lame. On lifting the horse's foot he saw a lump of gold was caught in the hoof. From there, he and his two brothers and another man discovered a substantial reef of gold, which he named after his horse. Today the town has a statue of the horse, Hardy Norseman.

I stopped off in Norseman decades ago on my way to work in a mining camp in the Kimberley and checked out the main hotel as it then had the longest bar in Australia. When Janice and I went to have a look, it was closed, still early in the morning, and a local told me that there aren't near as many drinkers as there used to be, so half the bar has been sealed off. There is still a gold mine in operation, on the actual edge of the town.

We earlier looked at the great gold rush in Victoria's Ballarat, but nearby Bendigo was also significant, not so much in area but what was below ground. The Bendigo goldfields covered no more than 200 hectares but the deepest shafts extended down between 1,200 metres and 1,500 metres. From 1850 to 1903 Bendigo produced over £70 million worth of gold. Today that equates to billions of dollars if not trillions of dollars. It is a difficult calculation for several reasons. Up to 1932, the price of gold was set at US $20.67 per ounce. Today it is on the variable open market at US$1,732 or about A$2,500 per ounce. It has been as high as US $2,000. In the 1850s Victoria produced forty-three per cent of the world's gold, today worth many billions of dollars. Australian gold exported to Britain from 1851 to 1880 is said to have paid off Britain's foreign debt. In 1856 annual Victorian gold production peaked at 94,982 kilograms and more gold was found at Bendigo from 1851 to 1900 than anywhere else on earth. By the 1880s Bendigo was assessed as the richest city in the world, as reflected in its magnificent buildings. Over the past 170 years Victoria has mined 2,400 tonnes of gold which equates to thirty-two per cent of Australia's and two per cent of the world's total gold production.

In 1903, Bendigo still produced seven tonnes of gold but today Western Australia produces 70 per cent of Australia's gold. A century ago if prospectors in Western Australia had found gold but suspected they might be robbed, some men would dig a grave by the side of the road and place their gold in the heaped up burial mound. They then placed a cross on the grave with brief words such as, 'In Memoriam. David Tucker, prospector. Thirst. Aged 47'. A good many David Tuckers died that way.

We continued on to Coolgardie, which was the centre of the goldfields. Kalgoorlie is better known today, but in the gold rush days, Coolgardie was a thriving gold field and town. Along the road from Norseman to Coolgardie we passed goldmine after goldmine, big and small, on both sides of the road and in operation. The current price of gold in Australian dollars is enticing many players to open up new and old mines alike, even the small ones. When the price of gold spikes for long enough prudent and organised gold miners turn to mining their lower grade or remote gold at peak prices. This sometimes lowers gold production by about 12 per cent but extends the life of the mine while still delivering expected margins for the shareholders and retaining the best gold still to come.

Coolgardie is coming back to life and that is a blessing for if you haven't seen it, hopefully you will. The buildings in the main street are sensational for they are grand and on a large scale. Just to look at the intricate brickwork gives rise to the standards of the 1890s and to be able to see it as it truly was is a revelation worth travelling a long, long way to witness. In those days a string of 70 or 80 loaded camels filing down the road was an interesting spectacle which people soon became used to. The camels were quicker and cheaper to operate than horse and bullock teams and there was no danger of a woolclip or other valuable commodities being left for months in the middle of a desert for want of grass and water. Coolgardie Day, 17th September, now attracts 10,000 people to the town.

It began in 1892 when Arthur Bayley and William Ford rode into Southern Cross with 554 ounces of gold they had discovered at Fly Flat (Coolgardie). They could hardly ride into Coolgardie as until then it did not exist, but quicker than a summer bushfire the news spread far and wide. Men walked the 188 km from Southern Cross to Coolgardie as others had walked a similar distance from Esperance to Norseman. The Bayley's Reward claim alone produced 500,000 ounces of gold over seventy years. It is recorded that after the gold was first found, Coolgardie saw the biggest movement of people in Australia's history. Coolgardie is often referred to as the Mother of the Goldfields.

26

Coolgardie and the Afghans

Albert Gaston recalled his trek to Coolgardie thus; 'My swag consisted of one 6 x 8 tent, one pair of blankets, one spare shirt, a small billy and the best friend I ever had on the goldfields, a gallon water bag. I have gone for days without my pipe and often without food, but never without my waterbag.'

Gaston may be an unusual name but surely what is more unlikely is the full name of a man who rests in the Laverton goldfields cemetery, Melbourne Perth Gaston.

Southern Cross, which Janice and I later drove to, is of interest because it is on the western side of WA's Eastern goldfields and was the site and start of the Eastern goldfields 'rush'. Thomas Risley wrote:

Myself, Toomey and Charlie Crossland started out from our camp at Barcoyton. After prospecting the belt for some days our water gave out. Our blackboy, whom I call Wheelbarrow, said he knew plenty of water at Koorkoordine. When we got to Koorkoordine we found one of Hunt's dry wells, just as dry as we were. We decided to start back through the night and return to our camp, distance about 40 miles, and we travelled by the Southern Cross, taken to stars to the north, thanks to Charlie Crossland's knowledge of the stars. Or our bones would be bleaching in the scrub now, as we were two days without water at this time. We had to remain at our camp until rains came, then myself and Mick Toomey set out again. We discovered gold four miles from Koorkoordine. I named the place Southern Cross.

Hugh Fraser found the biggest lode of gold at Southern Cross. There was so much gold there alone that the town as a whole prospered from it, yet Hugh Fraser died penniless and the mayor paid out of his own pocket to have him buried as a citizen, rather than as a pauper. From 1891 to 1898 there were 256 people buried in the town's Pioneer Cemetery and of all those people, ninety-four were buried in 1895, testimony to typhoid.

I can't help but notice the year 1895 crops up more so than any other in this history.

The main street of Coolgardie is Bayley Street, named after the young Canadian who made that initial gold strike. Those grand buildings, which housed twenty-three hotels, banks, two stock exchanges and all the other trappings of success, are on the widest streets I have seen in Australia and the single and important reason for that was the humble camel. The streets were made wide enough for camel trains to completely turn around, unhindered, and unlike other Councils which beautify their streets and take away precious space, these still exist. There were sometimes seventy camels in the one camel train. Camels were known to Afghans as the blessed animal. There are twenty-three buildings in the centre of Coolgardie that are listed with the National Trust and we had the pleasure of exploring several of them. We also went to one that is on Montana Hill, on a ridge on the edge of town. Along the way we passed the Gaol Tree. Prisoners were chained to this tree until the gaol was built for their trial.

Then we came to the residence for Coolgardie's first Resident Magistrate and Mining Warden. It was built in 1895 of local stone with high windows shaded by louvered shutters and surrounded by wide verandahs, at a cost of £2,800. The lovely and fortunately well-maintained residence was constructed by the Bunning Brothers. They had arrived in Fremantle in 1886 and established themselves as building contractors. After they had built additions to the Fremantle Lunatic Asylum they were up and away. The boom in jarrah timber suited them and they established sawmills in WA for which they imported modern machinery and equipment. They founded the firm Bunnings in 1887 and in 1952 it became a public company, one that today has a 20% share of the Australian retail hardware industry and, in 2016, revenue of $12 billion annually.

The Coolgardie Museum is an eye-opener and although there are only two remaining hotels, the Denver City and the Railway, they are a sight to behold, being expansive and prominent. I had been surprised to notice that the Railway had a large sign out the front saying that the hotel was for sale and giving details including that the hotel was not licensed. I then discovered that the Denver City was also for sale. Both hotels were once owned by the Kalgoorlie Brewing

Company, which was taken over by the Swan Brewery. For some reason, as part of the sale process, the Kalgoorlie Brewing Company registered a caveat on the title of the Railway Hotel that prevented it from holding a liquor licence, of any kind and in perpetuity. I imagine that suited the Denver City as according to its recent accounts for one year it had a turnover of $571,266 for a gross profit of $308,541 with nett profit of $134,454. If it hasn't sold by now, you might still be able to pick it up for $489,000. Not bad in a town of about 1,000 people.

A hotel that was popular in Coolgardie was the Marble Bar which was known for its good but cheap meals. If a prospector was down on his luck he could count on the Marble Bar owners providing him with a free meal and everyone, no matter how they were dressed, was made to feel welcome.

At the peak of its fame, 700 mining companies based in Coolgardie were registered with the London Stock Exchange. One of those was the *Esmerelda* goldmine that was floated by the Australian poet and journalist, Dryblower Murphy, who, after being a singer in the J. C. Williamson Opera Company, walked from Perth to Coolgardie. After his mine failed, Dryblower Murphy returned to writing. Perhaps it is not so surprising then that Mills walked 370 km from Great Eastern to Cue, to find those missing camels.

That most determined of men, Ernest Giles, who made five significant expeditions in Central and Western Australia, saw out his days in Coolgardie, employed as a clerk in a government department in a manner far removed from the hardships he had put himself through for much of his intrepid life. He succumbed to pneumonia and passed away in his nephew's house at Coolgardie in 1897. H.L. Finlayson wrote of the man:

All who have worked in that country since Giles' time have felt both admiration by the splendid horse-craft, the endurance, and the unwavering determination with which these explorations were carried through. To read Giles' simple account of those terrible rides into the unknown on dying horses with an unrelieved diet of dried horse for weeks at a time, with the waters behind him dried out and those ahead still to find, is to marvel at the character and strength of the motive which could hold a man constant in such a course.

Janice and I went to the Coolgardie Cemetery where, of the first sixty-one people buried there, twenty-nine had no identification. In the frantic rush to find gold before someone else did, little time was spared for those past caring. We found, at the extreme end, tucked away in the far left-hand corner of the cemetery, the Afghan section, seemingly as far away as possible from others. When Thomas Elder brought his camels to *Beltana Station* he also had cameleers accompany them and two of those were Faiz Mahomet, from Kandahar, and his younger brother, Tagh Mahomet. That was in 1862 and the previous year the first mosque in Australia was built at Marree in 1861. After twenty years, the brothers had set themselves up as camel importers with money borrowed from Thomas Elder. In 1883, they were at Marree, which became the centre of the freight business using camels, and ten years later they moved to Coolgardie, to cash in on the need for freight haulage due to that gold rush.

In 1896, Tagh Mahomet had just entered the Coolgardie mosque when an Afghan from another tribe shot him in the back while he was praying. He died; the deadly act being the continuation of a feud that had been festering between two tribes in their homeland, for hundreds of years. That continues today, as in Sydney. The murderer was hanged in Fremantle gaol. As an aside to that, Peshawar and Karachi were once Afghan cities but nowadays both are part of Pakistan.

Decades ago, a friend and I were camping in a forest in Yugoslavia when a fight broke out 60 metres from us. When peace had been restored we wandered over to the people then gathered around their fire to see what the fight was about. A family had a beautiful full-length coat which another group claimed was owned by their family. They had been arguing over the coat's ownership for 300 years.

Nearby was the grave of a prominent Muslim, Hadji Mullah Mehrban. According to his headstone he was the High Priest of the Muhammadan community in Australia. He died at the age of ninety-six as he was about to be married, again, this time to a twelve-year-old girl. She was saved.

In 1904, in Marree, an Afghan by the name of Sher Khan paid a £100 deposit on the agreed price of £150 to the father of a fourteen-year-old girl. He went up the Birdsville Track to earn the balance of £50 and while he was earnestly doing so an older Afghan with ready money made a higher offer to the girl's father, who immediately accepted the late proposal and just as quickly oversaw the marriage. Sher Khan shot and wounded the older man and headed off to seek refuge in the Ghantown in Farina. The code of his fellow tribesmen decreed that his actions were required to offset the insult to him. The Australian authorities saw it otherwise and gaoled him.

For quite some time the cameleers who came to Australia were without women. In time, some of them married Aboriginal or even Australian white women. They invariably lived in the marginalised Ghantowns and kept to themselves as the whites rarely mixed with them. In some towns there were three separate groupings, of Europeans/Australians, Aborigines and Afghans. Initially the cameleers came to Australia on three-year contracts and arguably the most successful was Abdul (Waid) Wade. From Kunar in Afghanistan he arrived in Australia in 1879 and began working for the brothers, Faiz and Tagh Mahomet. In 1895, he was the manager and overseer of the Bourke Camel Carrying Company and making trips to Karachi to procure camels and cameleers. In one year, he imported 750 camels to Port Augusta and supplied camels to various copper mines, no doubt to carry heavy ore. Financially successful, he took to riding a white camel and dressing like an Englishman, for which he was derided. Undeterred he married an Irish girl and purchased *Wangamanna Station*, 56 km east of Wanaaring and 134 km west of Bourke, where he bred camels. When droughts struck the Bourke district, Cobb and Co. used Abdul Wade's camels to haul their coaches. At one time, local cameleers were keeping 2,000 camels south of the town.

Several Afghans, Pathans, Pakistanis and other Muslims kept strings of camels, which they sold on hire purchase to men of their kin scattered across Australia, from Wyndham to Halls Creek in the Kimberley, from Port Augusta up to Newcastle Waters in the Centre and from Broken Hill to the Gulf of Carpentaria, to name but several. They transacted large amounts of money.

The Australian Workers Union, via shearers, shed-hands and other union members, did not allow pastoralists to use the Bourke Camel Carrying Company to convey their wool, saying that: 'the union will not consider Afghans as members, will not allow unionists to work in conjunction with the Afghans.' I imagine that bias unfairly assisted Mills, who was based at Farina with his Camel Carrying Company, and other carriers, through no fault of their own, to gain some of that freight business.

Abdul Wade was a long-time horseracing aficionado and he once challenged any European on a horse to race against himself on a camel, from Bourke to Wanaaring and back. He clearly won the race when his opponent's horse died of exhaustion at the halfway mark.

In 1902, Abdul Wade was naturalised and the following year he bought Northwood House, which included 17 hectares of land on the peninsula of Sydney's Lane Cove River. The two-storey sandstone residence was designed by that renowned architect, Edmund Blackett, and was long regarded as a prestigious residence. Today it is on the NSW State Heritage Register. At the apogee of his success Abdul Wade had 500 camels in work and sixty men working for him. He sent his son to the King's School, Parramatta, and his daughters to private schools. In 1917, he had to sell his Lane Cove land after he lost Northwood House in a game of poker. He had property at Redfern, Sydney and he owned the Adelaide Mosque from 1890 to 1920.

In 1914–15 he had offered his camels in Australia and his contacts in Afghanistan to the Australian Government for service in the Imperial Camel Corps to fight the Turks. The offer was taken up for only six camels, otherwise no sincere acknowledgement appears to have been made to Abdul Wade. The Imperial Camel Corps was of brigade size, consisting of 4,150 men and 4,800 camels in four battalions of camel-mounted infantry. The troops were two battalions from Australia, one from New Zealand and one from Great Britain. The Australians were drawn from men who had served at Gallipoli and gave the brigade a certain standing. Australian battalion commanders used the formation of the Imperial Camel Corps to transfer some of their more difficult troops and consequently the Imperial Camel Corps had a rough reputation. Their first action was at the Battle of Magdhaba in the Sinai Peninsula of Egypt in 1916 where they advanced against entrenched Turkish troops by riding as close as possible to six redoubts and made bayonet charges on camels, and then on foot, to win the day. The wounded soldiers were put on cacolets or structures that were fitted to both sides of a camel, in the form of a bed, so that two men could be transported, one either side, sitting up or even lying down. The Imperial Camel Corps also fought the Turks, and their German allies, at Gaza and Beersheba, amongst other battles and 246 of those soldiers died. Abdul Wade endeavoured to enlist his son into the Australian Army but once again his patriotism to his adopted country was refused. As he told the newspapers:

> *I am guilty of the unpardonable sin of having been born in Asia and although I have spent practically all my life in this country, I am denied the right of an ordinary citizen. I have made money here and if a loyal heart or a willing hand should be required to defend the country mine would be one of the first. But when my son, who is an Australian native, applies for entrance to a Military College, his application is rejected for no other reason than that of colour. I was prepared, and could afford, to pay all expenses and made personal application to the Minister of Defence, but was told that the blood of an Asiatic flowed through the veins of my son. His mother was a European, the boy was physically and intellectually fit but to my great disappointment my request was refused.*
>
> *Still, I am loyal to Australia, and the Defence Department has my offer of the use of 500 camels, and some horses, as well as my own experience. I have suffered a number of hardships under the White Australia policy but I am now quite independent. I, of course, would not like to see this beautiful country flooded with cheap labour, but rather than block a man from entering the country, because he happens to be a different colour, I would enquire into his qualifications and if he was worthy admit him, with full rights of citizenship.*

I have a cousin whose father, in Scotland in 1915, saw a young man crying his heart out in the street. He asked, 'What has happened, what's wrong?' The distraught man showed him his identification papers, marked by a red line. The young man had just been rejected by the Army, for World War One, as the red line in his identity papers, for prospective employers and certain other persons to see, indicated he was illegitimate. My cousin states Scotland was more conservative than England but as in Australia and elsewhere the stigma then attached to illegitimacy was all pervading and induced great shame. Today

40 per cent of Australian children are born out of wedlock and in Colombia, 74 per cent but in Japan just one per cent and in Israel only three per cent are born illegitimately.

After World War One and the further development of cars, trucks and aeroplanes the demand for the services of camels quickly declined, which meant a surplus of the animals began to wander the land, and in the eyes of many, knocking down fences and becoming another nuisance. In 1925, the Camel Destruction Act was introduced and this permitted anyone who found camels trespassing on their land, to gain permission for the next three months to destroy the animals, before gaining approval for another three months. The Act also made it illegal to possess unlicensed camels, which forced Abdul Wade to sell his breeding properties. His beloved camels were shot or mostly turned out into the bush.

Abdul Wade handed in his Australian passport and left Australia, disappointed if not broken-hearted. His son, Hamid, served in the Royal Australian Navy in World War Two.

It is estimated that from 1870 to 1900, 2,000 cameleers and 17,000 camels entered Australia. Would-be gold prospectors paid cameleers a shilling a day to carry their mining equipment and essential goods, including their daily ration of one gallon of invaluable water. The more experienced men employed Aborigines to lead them to water. Those who could afford it would buy their mates a bath, instead of a beer, such was the value of water.

The Afghan cameleers were physically suited to their work in the hot Australian climate and sometimes resentment arose from the non-indigenous Australians, even though they were essential in transporting goods to mining camps and returning with wool and, in fact, undertaking whatever was asked of them. White people feared the turbaned immigrants would marry local women, spread diseases and rule the commercial market by way of cheap labour.

The *Kalgoorlie Miner* of June, 1897, said of The Afghan Nuisance:

As a place of residence Kalgoorlie has luckily never appeared in the past to meet with great favour from Afghans. In Coolgardie their ragged tents can be counted almost in hundreds in one part of the suburbs. The associations of their camp are obnoxious in the extreme. Tins, old bones, filth and swarthy faces are the most prominent features. The settlement is indeed one of the very few blots on a clean and fair city. In the early days the Afghans of the goldfields made Coolgardie their headquarters and there they remained. The other centres were only favoured by their presence occasionally, when they visited them with their camels as carriers. Since the extension of the railway from Coolgardie, and more especially of late, Afghans have been more in evidence in Kalgoorlie and recently public attention was drawn by Mr. T.W. Child in the columns of this journal to the health of the community, occasioned by the state of their camp at the end of Piccadilly Street in the vicinity of the railway siding. The filthy habits and absence of sanitary arrangements render them objectionable to those residing in their neighbourhood. The advisableness of checking the immigration of coloured races and of introducing special legislation affecting Asiatics now in the colony will in all probability be discussed at an early stage during the next session of Parliament. The unanimity of feeling in favour of a white Australia does not permit of the question being ignored in the face of the increase of the number of alien arrivals and the fact that the difficulties of coping with the danger are made greater by delay. Pending the action of the Legislature, it is unquestionably the duty of the local Boards of Health within whose jurisdiction Afghan camps are situated to ensure they comply with the sanitary regulations.

Records show that there were 300 Afghans in Coolgardie in 1898. They were obviously cameleers because in 1895, Afghans had been barred from working in the goldfields of Western Australia as miners. In 1903 they were specifically barred from holding a Miner's Right on the WA goldfields, could not travel from state to state in search of work except under the most stringent conditions, were denied re-entry to Australia after going overseas and were not allowed to be naturalised.

In those days the Afghans were referred to, not so much as Muslims, but as Muhammadans. From their point of view; *The Australians were loud and undisciplined, given to swearing and drinking enormous quantities of beer after which they kicked up a ruckus and fell down drunk. They gambled and they smelt because, as everyone knew, they hardly ever bathed or maybe it was because of the swine flesh they enjoyed eating. Also they were not a very God-fearing people; you often heard them calling out for their lord at the most odd times. 'Jesus Christ!' they yelled if they hit their thumb with a hammer or if they got angry with you. Religiously speaking, they were a peculiar lot of kafirs (unbelievers) who worshipped idols in their church. How could you warm to such a race of people? But then you were not in Australia to make friends. Remember the old saying about white foreigners, 'the Feringhi (white foreigner) in their religion and we in ours'. Stick to your own kind, make as much money as possible and return home a hero.*

The Immigration Act 1901 was an Act of the Parliament of Australia which limited immigration to Australia and formed the basis of the White Australia policy which was intended to exclude all non-Europeans from Australia. A camel tax as outlined in the 1902 Roads Act, restricted movement and trade interstate and was perceived as extremely unfair. In 1903, the Naturalisation Act disqualified Afghans who were in Australia at the time, from becoming citizens.

All up, the Afghans, and others, more than ever found themselves on the wrong side of the tracks. And yet in 1902 the Attorney-General received a letter from John Edwards stating: 'It is no exaggeration to say that if it had not been for the Afghan and his camels; Wilcannia, White Cliffs, Tibooburra, Milparinka and other towns, each of considerable population, would have practically ceased to exist.' White Cliffs came to light in 1889 courtesy of two kangaroo shooters, G.J. Hooley and Alf Richardson. Hooley was tracking a wounded kangaroo when he came upon the enticing colours on the Momba Run. The value of the miners' opals today may be an enigma to the Tax Office but the town is well regarded as the birthplace of that great cricketer, Bill O'Reilly, and for its leadership in being the first town in Australia to utilise solar power for part of its electricity requirements. Years earlier Governor Richard MacDonnell said to Charles Sturt: 'I despair of much being achieved even with horses and I certainly think we have never given explorers fair play in not equipping them with camels or dromedaries and waterskins, which in Africa I found the best methods of carrying liquid.'

The Act now required anyone seeking entry to Australia to write out a passage of fifty words dictated to them in any European language, not necessarily English, at the discretion of the immigration officer. The test was not one that allowed the immigration officer to test applicants regarding their language skills, rather the nominated language was invariably one known in advance that the person would fail. They also barred immigrants with infectious diseases, who had been recently imprisoned, who were prostitutes or were 'idiots'. From 1902 until 1909, 59 people out of 1,359 did pass the test but only because the immigration officer in question was not fully aware of his intended role or was unable to choose a language other than English. After 1909, no one passed that strict language test. 'Any person who when asked to do so by an officer fails to write out at dictation and sign in the presence of the officer a passage of fifty words in length in a European language directed by the officer would be a "prohibited immigrant" and was to be prevented from landing.'

Before we come to the penultimate chapter I would like to remind you that Arthur Phillip and James Cook joined the Royal Navy in the same year. I wrote somewhat of the former but barely touched on the latter, who would surely also have been an admiral had he lived longer. I do not wish to repeat the history scribes but to acknowledge James Cook via the American Gene Roddenberry, who flew 89 combat missions in World War Two before becoming a police officer and then a writer and producer. He admired James Cook immensely and the following transpired.

James Cook was the son of a Yorkshire farmer, the captain of the *Endeavour* to Australia, and later of the *Resolution* to Antarctica. He wrote in his logbook that *ambition leads me not only farther than any man has gone before me but as far as I think it possible for man to go.* I have only now learned that 200 years later Gene Roddenberry created Star Trek with James Kirk as the son of an Iowa farmer and captain of the starship USS *Enterprise* who stated his intention *to explore strange new worlds, to seek out new life and civilisations, to boldly go where no man has gone before.* Captain Cook's right-hand man was Sir Joseph Banks, naturalist, botanist and President of the scientific Royal Society for 41 years. Joseph Banks was Roddenberry's inspiration for creating James Kirk's right-hand man, the half man/half Vulcan, the emotionless science officer Mr. Spock. The role of Spock was played by Leonard Nimoy whose parents lived in Iziaslav, Ukraine. Until recently the Star Trek television series, eight films, books and games have generated $10.6 billion of revenue, principally based the achievements of Captain James Cook as crafted by Gene Roddenberry.

Last resting place of W.W. Mills, on an island in a salt-lake in the goldfields of WA.

Vale W.W. Mills.

27

Vale W.W. Mills

From Coolgardie we came to Kalgoorlie and as much as I have a lot of time for historical Coolgardie, I have long wanted to see something of Kalgoorlie, like most Australians would. The name has an enticing ring to it, as do the likes of Wallabadah, Toowoomba, Longreach, Coonabarabran, Marble Bar, Cootamundra, Mungindi, Mooloolaba, Woolloomooloo and Goonoo Goonoo, near Tamworth. In my day Goonoo Goonoo was usually pronounced Gunny G' Noo but today I hear some say Gunna G' Noo. Janice and I did the round of the interesting museums and the grand hotels which are maintained so that travellers can see what they looked like in yesteryear. They are all good but what I have a mind to mention, are those that have been there the longest; goldmines and brothels.

Having my priorities sorted out I made my way to the recommended brothel, the Questa Casa. Driving a marked rental car, I stopped 80 metres short of the address and walked to the premises, to check it out. I arrived while two women were leaving. As I approached they turned to me, laughing, and said, 'Sorry, we're not working today.' I thought to myself, thank goodness for that, for they were nearly my age but I merely replied, 'that's alright, I'll come back later.' I returned a few minutes before 3 p.m. The Madame met me at the door and escorted me inside, then seated me in her waiting room.

I took the last empty chair in the room, the other fourteen being occupied by people of several ages but mostly mine and half of them women. These days the brothel does more business with tourists such as myself than with the regular trade. Janice did not feel inclined to come with me but she was quite okay with my enquiries. She supported my research. There used to be eighteen brothels in Kalgoorlie but today there are two, so it didn't take me too long to have a look around. The Madame started our tour by relating the history of the brothel which had been in operation since 1906, making it the longest running brothel in Australia. There were interesting tales to be told, notably about the man who died on the premises.

Then she showed us the working girls' rooms, which were mostly adorned with red and purple bedding, articles of clothing and other necessities, including whips and bondage aids. Aids being one of the reasons for a slump in trade. She told us that Asian girls have flooded the market, working alone and undermining the regular brothels, but the occupation for them is dangerous. The lady told us that sexual diseases are rampant, news of which rather deflated the mood. The girls used to split the takings 50/50 with the house but nowadays it was more like 60/40 to the girls. The prices are $120 for 15 minutes, $150 for 30 minutes, $220 for 45 minutes and for stayers, $280 per hour. No local girls can work in the Kalgoorlie brothels.

In the early days of Kalgoorlie, even after some men had married, there were still twenty men to one woman. This brothel had ten workrooms, but nowadays only three were being used. Most girls worked for three to four months, then went away and do their own thing before returning. A certain Dutch woman worked here for four months every year, for twenty-five years, from the age of twenty-five to fifty. For the rest of the year, she travelled first class back to and around Europe where her friends believed she had an administrative job with a mining company in Kalgoorlie. The Madame believed the advent of social media today makes it virtually impossible to now get away with such a double life.

Each working room fronted the street but had a section that, whilst it can be entered from outside, only permits entry for a couple of metres, where stands another door, a grille door. This door allows viewing for each party from both sides and that area is called 'the stalls'. The stalls permit the gentleman to discuss his proposition with the lady with some discretion in that he is then off the street and cannot be seen by passers-by. It also allows the lady to sum him up and decide whether to refuse him in safety.

These days, business for authorised brothels has been hit hard by mobile phones as the working girl can place her advertisements in the local paper and operate from private premises, of her choice. Fly-in, fly-out girls have the world at their feet.

On the other hand, Kalgoorlie is one of the few places these days that has not permitted fly-in, fly-out miners. At least the biggest mine, the Super Pit, hasn't. With a population of 34,000 people in the town I assume the mine operators felt they could come up with sufficient, capable staff locally. I knew men who lived in Dubbo and who were flown to South Australia and back in a Lear jet to work in the mines, well they were when the commodity prices were sky high and there are still many who live in Dubbo and drive to Orange or Cobar mines to work during the week and are home for the weekend. The man who bought our farm a few years ago works at Gove in the Northern Territory, 3,882 km away. He does that flight every eight days. His family live on the farm and every sixteen days he is home for eight days, less two days travel, and he has been doing that for eight years. All the eights, Chinese good luck.

Paddy Hannan, Thomas Flanagan and Dan Shea found the first gold in Kalgoorlie and sparked another gold rush, in July, 1893. Ten years later there were forty-nine operating mines with 100 headframes and 3,000 km of below ground workings on what was called the Golden Mile. Up until the 1980s the area consisted of a host of relatively small mines. Then Alan Bond came along and convinced many of those owners to sell to him. His intention was to combine those mines into one formidable goldmine with significantly lower production costs. He didn't quite stay the course, as in 1989, Normandy Australia and Homestake Gold had control. In 2001, Homestake Gold merged with Barrick Gold, which has operations in the Lawlers area which Mills had suggested was gold-bearing, and Normandy Australia merged with Newmont. They in turn own KCGM, which manages the Super Pit.

Janice and I drove out to the Super Pit which has an excellent viewing platform, free of charge for the public. It is deep and wide and the ore-carrying trucks take a long time to make their way up from the Super Pit, which, even though it is a long way down, is now all open cut. KCGM is Australia's second biggest gold producer behind Newmont's Boddington mine, 130 km south-east of Perth. Kalgoorlie is 600 km east of Perth.

The Super Pit uses CAT 793 trucks to haul the ore. Each truck weighs 166 tonnes, has a fuel tank of 3,790 litres and can travel at 55 km per hour, but not when carrying loads of 225 tonnes up the long winding road to the top of the quarry. While South Africa has dominated world gold production for the past 120 years it is now slipping down the list. Today the biggest gold producer is China, pumping out 450 tonnes a year, followed by Australia, 290 tonnes, Russia, the United States, Canada, Peru, and South Africa. Ever since 1851 gold has helped Australia's personal and national income but it is fortunate that the country has long had a diversification of business and industry. In 1895, about the height of the gold rush in WA, that wonderful American author and social commentator Samuel Langhorne Clemens, otherwise known as Mark Twain, travelled around Australia, gathering his impressions of the country for his fifth and final travel narrative, entitled *Following the Equator*.

He had much to say about us and I find the following to be quite relevant: *Australian history is almost always picturesque. Indeed, it is so curious and strange, that it is itself the chiefest novelty the country has to offer, and so it pushes the other novelties into second and third place. It does not read like history, but like the most beautiful lies. And all of a fresh new sort, no mouldy old stale ones. It is full of surprises, and adventures, and incongruities, and contradictions, and incredibilities, but they are all true, they all happened.*

At that time, 1895, Mark Twain observed both Great Britain and China-ruled populations of 400,000,000 people. No other power came close to those figures, not even the large Russian Empire. The population of Australia was then four million, or one per cent of those people under Great Britain's influence. The value of Great Britain's annual exports and imports was stated at three billion dollars and it was claimed that more than one-tenth of this great aggregate represented Australasia's exports to England and imports from England. In addition, Australia was conducting trade with other countries of $100 million a year and also domestic inter-colonial trade of $150 million. In round numbers Twain said that Australia's four million people buy and sell close to $600 million of goods. Looking at production only, Australia's four million people produced $300 million of goods while India's 300 million people produced $500 million.

To put it another way, the annual product of an Indian was $1.75 while the annual product of an Australian, for export, was $75. To take it further, the Indian family of man, wife and three children sent away an annual result worth $8.75 while an Australian family sent away $375 worth.

It seems Mark Twain was impressed with Australia. When one considers those figures were achieved from nothing to start with and on that basis they do read pleasingly. It was often said at that time Australia did have the highest standard of living in the world. In the years 2015–2016 Sydney alone produced goods and services to the value of $400 billion.

Back in Kalgoorlie's early days the gaol was another tree, as we have seen in Derby, but not a tree in which prisoners could be placed. In Kalgoorlie, offenders were chained to the tree, by the leg. On a day of the Kalgoorlie races, there were two men chained to the tree, one of whom was incensed by such a restriction curtailing his pleasure of being at the racetrack. The desperate punter hoped to attract someone to his plight and thereby hopefully gain release, so he set fire to the surrounding grass. That didn't exactly work in his favour for when would-be rescuers arrived he and his companion had been burnt alive, becoming ashes.

Janice and I had an interesting talk at the Kalgoorlie Museum with a man who worked there but for more than twenty years prior to that he had lived out in the bush. He said that last year a man who was visiting the museum told him that he has killed 50,000 camels in Western Australia. Now at first hearing I would doubt that but my museum man believed him. He seemed genuine. A few years before that, in 2009, the Federal Government allocated $19 million to have 390,000 camels eradicated. I don't know if this man's 50,000 camels were included in that quota or one since but I deem it to be possible overall. A camel breeder from Qatar heard about this and as the deaths upset him, he came to Australia to see if there was another way to solve the problem of uncontrollable surplus camels. He met camel breeders in Australia and he encountered slaughterhouse operators, who process fifty camels a day. At one Australian camel abattoir, the meat is sent under contract to the Army in Morocco while a breeder sends live camels to Muslim communities in Canada, his biggest market. Cattlemen who do not have the infrastructure to control camels told him they don't go hunting for them but they shoot them on sight. When he objected, they pointed out that in one recent six-week period, camels knocked down and destroyed 140 km of cattle fences. It then cost between $1,800 and $2,000 to put up one km of cattle-proof fence. The man from Qatar said that in the holy Koran the camel is mentioned before the mountains, the sky and the earth and that the Prophet Muhammad ate camel meat. He added that camel racing was big business in his country and that a champion racing camel is worth US $20 million. These days, feral cats cause more environmental damage than camels, in Australia.

I am assured by professional feral cat trappers and those who have carried out surveys of the matter that there are eight million feral cats roaming around Australia, along with two and a half million domestic cats. Each feral cat kills an average of three native Australian animals every day or night, or one thousand per year. Whilst domestic cat owners might not admit or know it, a good many of their cats are doing the same thing, to some extent. Feral cats have contributed to the extinction of twenty eight species of mammals in Australia. Some of these wild hunters have been caught and found to weigh seven kilograms. Their speed, strength and determination regularly kills pygmy possums, geckos, long-necked turtles, fairy penguins, sugar gliders, quolls, numbats, honey eaters, bush rats, the southern brown bandicoot, wallaby joeys, willy wagtails, western brown parrots, echidnas, the greater bilby and even the tiger snake, to name a few. The lesser bilby became extinct in the 1950s. It seems surprising that some feral cats kill the aggressive tiger snake with its toxic venom but they do. Butcherbirds, ibis and kookaburras also seek out tiger snakes for food, sometimes blinding the ones that get away. Due to the feral cat, survival is a serious issue for the wellbeing of the nation's remaining native animals and millions of birds.

That evening, in Kalgoorlie, I met an Aboriginal man of rather exceptional appearance and a wonderful grasp of the English language. He asked me where I was from and I, straight away, cheekily said, the Wiradjuri tribe, which is strong in the Dubbo area. He didn't blink an eyelid and said he was from the Wudjari tribe, in WA, as though he and I are long-lost relations. In case you are wondering, I am as white as he is black. His brother told me he is an actor and as I discovered, a well-known and a good one.

I just had to ask him if I could take his photo and fortunately he instantly and happily agreed. The next morning we were leaving very early and no one else was up and about until he walked by, with his mother. He introduced Janice and I to her and she was as fascinating as he. Obviously older but with striking good looks she was an interpreter in the law courts. Besides her impeccable English, she spoke five Aboriginal languages fluently and others partially. She appeared in court to assist those who were not so blessed. I could have talked with them both for hours but we all had different rows to hoe.

Mills died on 18th August, 1916. We had to find that grave today, so we turned around and headed south to Widgiemooltha, a goldmining area where Mills saw out his final days. Nearby was Lake Lefroy, a salt lake that was discovered by Henry Lefroy in 1863. Gold was found by the lake in 1896. I stopped at the Widgiemooltha roadhouse, parked and went inside. I hadn't been there before and so I found myself walking through the bar, where five men were each enjoying a heart-starter beer. One of them called out to me, asking what would my reaction be on finding that my Thai girlfriend in Bangkok was actually a boy? I didn't want to be caught up with that and gave an answer I thought would satisfy them. As they laughed heartily I thought I had succeeded.

I continued on to the kitchen and found the manager. I explained my reason for being there and asked if I could borrow a hammer for a few hours. He agreed to that without hesitation and returned a few minutes later with it. I walked back through the bar, hammer in hand, and attracted another question or two, but I did not answer the men this time and continued out to the car. I probably shouldn't have walked through the bar.

I had hardly reached the car when three of the five men, in their mid-thirties, appeared before me with beer in their tattooed hands. One immediately and brusquely asked me, 'What are you doing here, mate?' Before I could answer another one opened the front passenger door of our car, and said, 'there's someone in here,' and on seeing Janice grabbed the hat from her head. She immediately lunged at him and took it back, which surprised him. She shut the door on him and they turned to me, in a semicircle. I let the hammer in my hand slide, so that I only held it between no more than my thumb and forefinger, and

I let it slowly swing to and fro. I didn't lower my eyes but they dropped theirs to see the movement of the hammer.

I deliberately looked the hat grabber in the eye and slowly said, 'I'm here to bury someone.' That may have made him uneasy for he then changed the subject and said, 'What's in the boot?' Taking a deliberate firm grip on the hammer I said to him, 'I'll show you,' and moved towards it, knowing there was only our luggage in there. He immediately raised both his hands into the air, still holding his beer and backed off, saying, 'I'm not into that.' 'Well then, I'll show you this,' I said and took the Mills plaque out from the backseat of the car.

The third man, who hadn't spoken as yet but appeared to be in control of himself, and of the others, asked me what it was for and I told him. Following his lead, the aggressive attitude of the other two changed and all three of them became genuinely interested. I briefly explained what Mills and others like him had done to set this country up to be enjoyed by the likes of us today and they almost broke down. The leader took me by the hand, shook it and said, 'I hope you find what you're looking for.' He said they were goldminers and that they had been out there for four years. He suggested where I might find those graves, having heard of them.

Back in the car Janice and I continued on to the salt lake. I had a mud map that one person had sent me and notes that another had given me over the phone. The goldminer's advice married up with one of them, but I had the choice of two tracks to follow from the road, both by way of the bush and then down to the salt lake. Rather than go with the lady from Denmark, I decided on the advice which was supported by what the miner had said.

The first thing I had to do was to find the track that led down to the lake. I drove past it twice before I thought I had it right. With no one having been there for a long time it was all but overgrown and there were certainly no signposts. The lady from Denmark who told me she had been out to the graves, had said I would not be able to drive on the track in a basic car without staking the tyres and that the track was 7 km long. She had driven a 4WD and still staked one tyre and suggested I park the car and walk. I was conscious of the fact that hire cars were not covered for insurance unless they were driven only on a sealed road.

However the surface of the track was relatively bare and I couldn't see anything dangerous for the tyres. I wanted to get as close as possible to the lake because Janice couldn't walk far at the time. I drove on. After 3 km the track ended and I could go no further. I stopped at a solid wall of trees.

I walked on for 400 metres and breaking through the trees stepped out into the open. The now bare ground sloped down for another 100 metres to the edge of the lake and directly ahead of me, about 300 metres out in the lake, was an island. That had to be it but I had thought if there were only thirteen graves out there it must be a small island. One end of the island was directly ahead of me but it extended off to my right for the best part of 500 metres and I could not tell how far back it went.

I was certainly looking at 240 hectares and probably more. That took me by surprise and I wondered how on earth was I going to find thirteen graves in amongst that heavily timbered area, today? And there was something else. As I looked out over the lake, it shimmered in the early morning sunlight. Water. I had heard of people in the past who had gone out to the island by rowing boat but surely that was unusual. It didn't rain here too often but it must have rained recently and I thought it didn't look too bad. The water didn't start for 200 metres out but from then on it reached the island, completely encircled it and covered the rest of the lake as far as the eye could see.

I returned to the car and told Janice I was positive that this is the island but it was much bigger than anyone had suggested and covered in trees. I took a bright yellow CWA (Country Women's Association) bag from the boot of the car and suggested to Janice that she be patient and to please stay in the car and that I would be as quick as I possibly could. With the hammer, fruit and a bottle of water in my day pack and with plaque in-hand, I set off. I made my way to the far edge of the trees and after finding a fallen branch with a curved end on the ground, I reached up into the air with it and after several attempts, was able to pull a branch of a tree down to me. Holding it firmly I tied the yellow CWA bag around the branch and gently released it. I stepped back and looked up. The yellow bag was three metres off the ground and would be my marker for making my way back should I become lost.

I walked out towards the salt lake. It was firm, no doubt about that now but what would it be like under water? I walked rather slowly, carefully I suppose, and when I was halfway across I stopped and turned around. It only took a few seconds and then I could see the yellow bag, hanging in the tree. That made me feel good. Then as I was just about to turn back to the island, a movement caught my eye. I looked intently and yes, for the distance of 300 metres, could see there was a person by that tree. Who on earth could that be?

Then I recognised her, of course, it was Janice. I hurried back and couldn't help myself. I asked her, 'What are you doing? You said you would stay in the car.'

'I only said that to keep you quiet. I have come this far and there is no way I am not going with you to see that grave,' she responded. I told her it would probably be hard going and she would have to be so careful.

We headed off across the salt pan, one sure step at a time. Eventually we came to the section that was under water and I wondered what would happen if the salt become boggy or worse, gave way? We had nothing to be concerned about. The white salt pan underwater turned brown and was soft on top but we had a firm footing beneath it, and apart from our boots being under water, all was well. We went even slower, just in case. When we reached the shore of the island, I looked at it from one end to the other, trying to decide which way to go. If we went off to the far right-hand end and in from there, we could work our way back but that would be hard on Janice. She had steel and titanium wires with attached hooks still holding her kneecap together six months after it was shattered. She suffered daily pain.

We could start at the near left-hand end or split the difference and go to the middle. I reasoned that if the Denmark lady hadn't seen fit to tell me whereabouts on the island the graves were it might be because they were at the near end and she would have assumed that's the way we would go.

I looked again and noticed that the left-hand end of the island land sloped up at a lower angle, one that would be better for Janice. We went to the left. We could only go at her pace and her walking stick sank into the heavy red sand, but she progressed. We passed through a lot of mulga and the trees became more prominent but she made it to the top of the first ridge. Then off to my left I saw white stones. Now the ground on the mainland leading down to the salt lake was covered in quartz rocks, big ones as we came out of the trees, and running down to small stones by the edge of the lake. On the island there was not one natural rock to be seen, so what were the white stones doing here? Then I knew. They were grave stones, markers used to outline the grave. I left Janice and scrambled over for a closer look. It was a grave for a child. I went back, took Janice by the arm and helped her along. Then we saw a second grave, that of another child. We spread out, pushing aside old tangled mulga as we saw graves overgrown with bushes and mulga. It took time. I don't know how long, time did not matter now. We found the thirteen graves of which there were three unmarked adult graves. One identified grave was of E.J.A. Spence, a swagman, who died of thirst in 1899.

Which one was Mills's? All bar one were outlined by those white stones and one of the adult graves was wide enough at the top half but then the bottom half was not outlined by stones. I imagined the sands of time had blown over and covered them. As respectfully as I could, I knelt down by the grave and carefully dug down into the sand where the stones should have been. I couldn't detect a single one. It was a bit of a mystery but I couldn't believe whoever buried Mills here would have done only half the job. I deleted that grave, in my mind. Of the other two the one not outlined by stone was edged by strips of timber. Before I had arrived, I had heard of that and gave some credence to it being the one. However while the timber has aged it didn't look as though it had been there for one hundred years.

That left one other unmarked adult grave and the more I looked at it and the surrounds the more positive I felt. The grave was heaped by large quartz rocks and while some had been covered over partially or completely, enough of them showed through to see that originally they had covered the entire body area. Now I know that Mills had established a camp and that Knuckey, one of his fellow surveyors on the Overland Telegraph Line, had been there. On 18 April, 1871, while still on the OTL, Knuckey, of Kapunda, had been speared in the right elbow and in return shot his attacker in the shoulder. I had little doubt that there would have been a few old gold prospectors who would have welcomed the opportunity to join in and see out their days there in good company.

I also knew of other cemeteries closer to towns and wondered why some people had buried their family and friends on an island. In those days and with all those trees, the body would have to be carried, through the timber, over the salt lake and up the slope. While the digging was easy it was another matter carrying rocks from the mainland, to place on the grave. I am sure those old-timers would have chosen to do that as a way of showing respect and goodbye to their old friend. No doubt they had more time than money to say goodbye.

There was one more qualifier. The grave was placed on the higher part of the ridge so that, despite the surrounding mulga and trees, if we looked in one direction we could see, in part, the mainland and if we looked in the exact opposite direction there was a clear view of the lake on the far side of the island. That positioning may have been unintended but on the other hand it could have been deliberately thoughtful and if it was the latter, it seemed right.

Janice was in agreement and as a decision had to be made, this was it. I placed the plaque at the head of the grave, took the hammer out of the daypack and proceeded to drive the post deep into the ground. At the foot of the grave, the branches of a large mulga covered the ground, which at that point sloped slightly away. I crawled in, on my stomach, amongst the lower branches and cleared a space at the foot of the grave. There I planted one of the three new growth suckers from the tree at Skirmish Hill, that Mills had blazed. At home, I had planted the other two in the garden and every night kept this one in soil and well-watered. It might not live, I thought, but I dug out a narrow trench on either side of the grave, so that any rain would see the water furrowed down to the sapling and hopefully sustain its life.

I crawled out backwards, stood up and moved to the head of the grave. Without meaning to be dramatic I said a few words of regard to Mills, albeit a century late, but to the very day of his death. He might not have lived a perfect life but he had done it as he saw it and they were hard enough times. Unfortunately, he could not stay home in Kapunda or elsewhere, to earn his living and raise his daughters, as his work was invariably out in the bush. Not too many of us today would survive what such men went through, as did a 19th century Australian surveyor, explorer and gold prospector.

There's a legion that never was listed,
That carries no colour or crest
But, still in a thousand detachments,
Is breaking a road for the rest.
Our fathers they left us their blessing
They taught us and groomed us and crammed
But we've shaken the Clubs and the Messes
To go and find out and be damned.
Rudyard Kipling 1895

I went to find out and be damned, but I had it easy, in relative modern-day comfort, unlike Mills who had proven himself many times over by way of his fortitude and leadership on the Overland Telegraph Line, taking thirty camels on his epic ride across the western half of some of Australia's most arid and unchartered country and prospecting for gold where, just to stay alive, was an achievement for many.

You might wonder why I would go to the trouble for someone I never met. Apart from an interest in history and other aspects of the matter, I had driven, walked and flown 16,700 kilometres just for the two trips to Western Australia, by the time we returned to Dubbo. Thank you Roger, thank you Janice.

I have no doubt it was Mills who appeared to me at *Beltana Station* and who told me to leave the plane at Alice Springs. He saved my life, fifty-six years after he died, and he gave me another forty-four years, nowadays more. I owe him.

Today is 18th August, 2016. One hundred years ago, to the day that William Whitfield Mills died. He was my father's mother's father.

He is my paternal great-grandfather.

Suum Cuique: To each his own.

27 Vale W.W. Mills

The tree at Skirmish Hill blazed by W. W. Mills on the 46th day of his journey by camel from Beltana Station, S.A. to Northampton, W.A.

To be ignorant of what occurred before you were born is to remain a child. For what is the worth of human life, unless it is woven into the life of our ancestors by the records of history.
— Cicero.

William Whitfield Mills.

"W. W. Mills came into the camp tonight. The best shot in the Territory and a great companion around the fire,"

Bibliography

1) Allan, l., Batty, P., Morton, J. *The Photographs of Baldwin Spencer*, text only. Miegunyah Press and Melbourne University Press, Melbourne. 2005.
2) Bowen, J. *Kidman the Forgotten King*. Angus and Robertson, Australia. 1987.
3) Dickson, R. *HMS Guardian and the Island of Ice*. Hesperian Press, Perth, Western Australia 2012.
4) Hatfield, W. *I Find Australia*. Oxford University Press, London. 1937.
5) Idriess, I. *The Red Chief*, Angus and Robertson, Sydney, Australia 1953.
6) Jones, Philip. *Images of the Interior*—text and photographs. Wakefield Press, Adelaide, South Australia. 2011.
7) *Keith Brougham Reminiscences*, 1940, Archives of State Library of South Australia.
8) Lloyd, H. *Boorowa over 160 years of White Settlement*. Toveloam Pty Ltd, 6 Leeton Crescent, Panania, NSW. 1990.
9) MacDougal, J. *Beyond the Borders*. Jennifer Hume MacDougal and Prudence Grieve, 1991.
10) Magarey, A.T. Australian Aboriginal Tracking, Water Finding, Smoke Signalling. Hesperian Press. 2015.
11) McKenzie, J. *Wingadee A Great Australian Station*. Clyde Agriculture. 2003.
12) Mills, E.W. William Whitfield Mills Experiences with Darwin Survey and Overland Telegraph Parties. E.W. Mills 8b Holton street, Glenside South Australia 1993.
13) O'Grady, F. *No Boundary Fence*. Angus and Robertson. Sydney, Australia. 1960
14) *Royal Society of Western Australia*, journal article re. Bayley, marked 82.17-25 (1999).
15) Taylor, P. *An End to Silence*. Methuen Australia Pty Ltd. Sydney, Australia. 1980.
16) White, M.R. *Beyond the Western Rivers, From That Day to This*. Rigby Limited, Adelaide, South Australia.1961
17) Wood. T. Dr. Oxford University Press. London. 1934.

The author has exercised best endeavours in seeking permissions to use extracts from referenced titles.

Index

A

Abdullah, Mullah Pathan – 301-302
Albany – 462-465
Alice Springs – 262-264, 367. 239, 371-372, 377-378, 390-394
Anderson, Julius – 228
Andrews, Jimmy – 109
Anlaby Station – 216-217
Anna Creek Station – 64, 103, **397**
Annandal – 164, 400
Antill, , Captain – 17
Appin – 139, 288
Arrai-iga – 265
Ashburton Ranges – 84
Ashwin, Arthur – 94, 71, 73-75, 230
Aspinall, Butler Cole – 93
Atalanta – 47
Attack Creek – 83
Aunger, Murray – 216-220, 310
Ayers Rock (Uluru) – 335, 338

B

Bacon, Harleyy – 65
Bagot, Charles – 95
Baillieu, Sunday – 267
Ballarat – 91-93
Bangaroo – 27
Barrier Ranges – 188
Barron, Duncan – 213
Barry, Judge Redmon – 252
Barton, Sir Edmund – 100
Bateman, J. and W. – 101
Bayley, Arthur – 477
Beadell, Len – 328
Beckwith, J. 58-59, 63-64
Beltana Station – 61, 63, 101, 103, 111, 226, 402, 418-419, 428, 433
Bendiigo – 476

Benelong – 26-27
Best, Sarah – 139
BHP (Broken Hill Propriety – 117, 139, 143, 151, 157, 181, 187, 303, 389, 469-470
Birdsville/Track – 398-399
Blanchwater Station – 173-174
Blackstone – 349
Bligh, Captain William – 6, 29, 210-212
Blood, Matthew, Henry Smyth – 207-208
Bloods, Creek – 404
Boer War – 270-280
Boyoolee - 55
Brachina Gorge – 434
Brinkworth, Tom – 177
Broken Hill – 124, 188, 300-303, 435
Broome – 287
Brougham, Jack - 152
Brougham, John – 151
Brougham, Keith - 152
Buchanan, Nat – 81-82
Bulloo Downs – 164, 225
Burke, Robert O'Hara and Wills, William – 147
Burra – 99
Bussell, Grace – 319, 454
Busselton – 453-454
Byramine Hoestead - 41
Byrne, Matilda – 139
Byrne, Patrick – 139

C

Cape Leeuwin – 455-456
Castlesteads – 135, 146
Catapodi, Caroline – 133, 139
Catapodi, Peter – 139
Charley, Philip – 179-181, 185
Charlotte Waters – 65
Clarkke, Jack – 48-409

Clifton Hills - 405
Cloncurry – 61
Cobb & Co – 192-194, 196-197, 307
Cobb, Freeman – 192, 195
Cobhham Lake Station - 55
Cochons Island – 7
Cockburn (Coburn) – 302-303
Collingwood – 33, 145
Cooby Pedy – 329-332, 437
Cook, Captain James – 209, 488
Coolgardie – 477-481, 485-486, 488
Cordillo Downs – 402, 409
Corona – 190, 221
Coulson, Isabella (Tyson) – 287
Cowan, James – 117-118
Cowpasture, Jack – 15, 20-21, 30-31, 34
Cowpasture, Womga – 31
Cox. Alfred – 180
Croker, Sam
Crown Point Station – 117-118, 259
Crozet Islands – 6-7
Crozet, Julien-Marie – 6
Curtin Springs Station – 333-334

D

D'Entrecasteaux, Vice-Admiral Brui – 460
Dagworth Station – 251-252, 255-256
Dalglish, James – 186
Dangalong - 136
Darwin (Port Darwin) – 115
De Grey Station – 111-112
De Kerrilleau, Gabriel Marie Louis Huon – 140-141
Deakin, Prime Minister – 223

Index

Denmark – 461
Diamantina Lakes - 164
Dickens, Edward Bulwer Lytton – 432
Dight, Elizabeth – 27
Djabuganjdji tribe – 51
Docker River – 339, 344
Douro – 28, 30-31, 34
Drought, Phoebe – 252
Duke of Edinburgh – 143
Durham Downs - 164
Dutton, Francis Stacker – 95, 99, 216
Dutton, Frederick – 216-220
Dutton, Harry Hampden – 216-221, 310

E

Elder, Alexander – 60
Elder, Thomas – 60-61, 101, 103, 174, 226, 419-420, 431-433
Elder Exploration Expedition – 226-227
Erle, Judge William – 121
Eringa – 285, 287
Esperance – 469-475
Everard Ranges – 103
Eyre, Edward John – 59

F

Farm Cove – 22
Felton Station - 291
Fisher, Charles – 193
Fisher, Frank – 248-249
Flanagan, Thomas – 492
Flinders, Matthew – 456, 473
Flynn, Errol – 209, 212
Flynn, John – 61, 63, 149, 171, 373
Ford, William – 479
Forrest, John – 101, 122-123, 197, 232
Fort McKellar – 110
Fort Mueller – 109
Foreaux, Joseph – 15
Fremantle – 7-8

G

Gardiner, Frank – 32
Gibson, Alfred – 109-110
Gigson Desert – 110
Gilbert, Johnny – 32
Giles, Ernest – 65=66, 69-70, 101, 108-110
Gilmore, Mary – 189
Glengyle – 164
Gosse, George – 105
Gosse, William – 105-106, 108, 123
Goyder, George Woodroffe – 52-54, 58, 115, 326
Groongal – 288-289
Guardian – 3-6, 11, 13
Gul, Badsha Mahomed Pathan – 301-302
Gulnare – 53, 57
Gunnedah – 162-163

H

Hall, Ben – 32
Hall, Charles – 228
Halls Creek – 62, 228-229
Ham, David – 253
Ham, David Jordan – 266-273, 280, 282
Ham, Dr. Headly – 128, 132, 253-254, 266
Hamilton, Ann – 2
Hancock, Lang – 197
Hannan, Paddy – 492
Harvey, W. – 58
Heffernan, Ned – 228
Helen Springs Station - 438
Hewitt, David – 295, 297-298, 336-3389 346, 349, 352-53, 355, 358-61, 379-381, 384-388
Hewitt, Margaret – 295, 336-337, 388
Hill, John – 208
HMAS Sydney – 469
HMS Bounty – 210
HMS Buffalo – 208
HMS Resolution – 4
Holland, Dr. – 62
Horseshoe Bend - 404

Hovel, William – 27. 145
Howitt, Alfred – 147
Hubbard, Jim - 323
Hume, Andrew Hamilton – 1-3, 14-21, 27, 29-30, 36, 40-41, 140, 145
Hume, Elizabeth – 14-15, 30, 38, 41-43, 145
Hume, Emma – 135
Hume, Hamilton – 140
Hume, Isabel – 14
Hume, Jessie – 41
Hume John, 14, 21, 33, 38, 145
Hume, Mary Bozzom – 411
Humewood - 34
Hunt, Charles – 121
Hunter, Govenor – 14
Huon, Elizabeth – 110

I

Idress, Ian – 72, 248
Immigration Act 1901 – 487
Indispensable – 141, 287
Innamincka – 164, 168, 400, 402
Isaacs, Sir Isaac – 100

J

James, David – 179, 182-186

K

Kadaitcha – 21, 169
Kalgoorlie – 449-450, 490-492, 494-495
Kapunda – 94-99, 198, 207, 213-215
Karakais – 20-21
Kelly, Mary – 94
Kelly, Ned – 252
Kennedy, Amy - 150
Kennedy, Edith – 150
Kennedy, Elizabeth – 14
Kennedy, Emma – 144, 148
Kennedy, Frank – 144, 150
Kennedy, Fred – 173
Kennedy, George 0 173
Kennedy, James Raworth – 139
Kennedy, Jamie - 132

Kennedy, Mary (nee Bozzom) – 131, 144, 147-148, 151
Kennedy, May – 128, 130, 140
Kennedy, Madge – 130
Kennedy, Millie – 146
Kennedy, Robert Henry – 41, 131, 139-140, 144-145, 148, 151, 153, 155
Kennedy, Robert Henry Jr. – 41, 131, 139, 144-145, 159
Khan, Sher – 481
Kidman, Sackville – 172-173l 186
Kidman, Sir Sidney – 62, 96, 99, 139, 151, 163-164, 172-173, 196-197, 214, 223-225, 237-260, 284-287
King, John – 147
King, Lieutenant Governor Phillip Gidley – 13-15
Knuuckey, R.R. (Richard) – 58, 293, 500
Kruse, Tom – 398
Kunmarnara Bore – 354, 356-347

L
Lady Juliana – 10-11, 13
Lake Eyre – 497, 501
Lambert, George Washington – 136
Lambour, John – 192
Lasseter, Lewis, Harold Bell – 338-339, 345
Lawson, Henry – 189, 250
Le Mascarin – 6
Le Sage, Louisa – 140-141, 287
:eFroy, Henry – 496
Lind, George – 179-180
Lindsay, David – 226-227
Lockyer, Major Edmund – 463-464

M
MacArthur, Elizabeth – 141
MacArthur, John – 16, 18, 37, 140-141

MacDonnell Ranges – 51, 63, 65-67, 82
MacPherson, Christina – 255, 256
MacPherson family – 251-252
Macquarie, Lachlan – 16-17, 27, 37
Maczuard, Max – 379
Mahomet, Faiz and Tagh – 481
Manjimpu – 45-459
Marree – 398, 401
Margaret River – 455
Marla – 395
Marsden, Rev. Samuel – 136, 141
Mawson, Douglas – 153
McCulloch George – 179-180, 186
McMinn, G.R. – 58, 65, 83
Meehan, James – 17
Mehrban Hadj, Mulah – 481
Middleton, Albert and Francis – 41
Middleton, Rawdon Hume 42—43
Mills, Ada – 124, 185
Mills, Alice Thornton – 100, 124
Mills, Annie, 124
Mills, Ethel May – 123-124, 185
Mills, William Whitfield – 1, 47-49, 52, 55, 257-59, 61, 63-67, 70, 83, 85, 96, 100-107, 111-112, 115-116, 120, 123-124, 338, 230, 264-265, 293-294, 378, 404-405, 471, 489, 496-497, 500-504
Milner, Ralph and John – 59, 70, 74-75, 83
Mitchell, Emma 41, 140
Moira, Earl – 2
Moondyne, Joe – 121, 318
Moonta – 53
Momba Station – 432-433
Morant, Henry – 280, 282-283
Morgan, Mad Dog – 252, 255

Mt. Crawford Station - 123
Mt. Gipps – 172, 178-179, 181, 190
Mt. Lyndhurst – 413
Mt. Murchison - 432
Mueller, Ferdinand – 108-109
Mulga Park Station - 388
Mullen, Ada (nee Mills) – 185, 226
Mullen, Annie (nee Mills) 226
Mullen, John – 85-87, 91, 94095, 97-99 123, 213
Mullen, Mary Jane (nee Mills) – 85, 94, 123, 185
Mundine, Warren – 298
Mundowdna Station – 71, 261, 412-413
Murrumbidgee – 27
Musgrave Ranges – 105

N
National Anzac Center – 463-466
Neptune – 11, 292
New Crown - 405
Nicholas, Jimmy – 196-197
Noland, Sidney - 267
Norseman – 473
Nundora – 130-131, 148, 150, 156, 225
Nuntherungie – 146-147

O
O'Brien, Henry (Black Harry) – 27, 30-32, 34-35
O'Connor, Charles Yelverton – 232-233
Olgas (Kata Tjuta) – 337
Oodnadatta – 395-396, 398
Overland Telegraph Line – 50-51, 56, 58-59, 6-69, 83-84, 103, 122-125
Owen Springs – 197, 259
Oxley, John – 37, 78

P
Patterson, Andrew – 144
Patterson, Banjo 144, 255-256
Peachey, A. – 85

Index

Peck, John Murray – 192
Peterborough – 304
Phillip, Governor Arthur – 13, 17, 22-27
Playford, Thomas – 70
Poole, James – 179, 181-182
Poolmacca – 151, 153, 190
Prince Alfred, Duke of Edinburgh – 93
Price of Wales (Edward) - 425
Puttepa - 430

R

Ragless, Graha and Laura – 429
Raines, Harry - 172
Rasp, Charles – 178-180, 186
Redford, Harry – 173-174
Reibey, Mary – 149
Rinehart, Gina – 197
Riou, Captain Edward – 4-6
Roberts, John - 139
Robertson, Malcom - 423
Ross, John – 63-66, 69
Roto Station - 144
Royal Flying Service – 61-62, 171
Ruby Plains – 62, 64, 163
Rudd, Kevin – 363
Ryan, Martin – 428

S

Sandringham Station (Downs) – 164, 186
Scarborough - 292
Shaw, James – 215-216
Shea, Dan – 493
Sheppard, Jack – 8
Short, Charles – 101, 113
Sinclair, Laurie – 318, 475
Sing, Billy – 47, 247-248
Sirius – 19
Skirmish Hill – 107-108, 226, 295-299, 336, 349-351, 358-360, 379, 442, 462, 501-502
Skylab – 473-474
Smith, Elder 197

Smith, Robert Barr – 60, 431-432
Smith, Sir Keith – 110-111
Smith, Sir Ross – 110-111
Soverign – 14
Spinx – 11
Stanford, J.S. – 136
Stanford family tree – 142
Strangeway Station/Springs - 64
Streeton, Arthur – 255
Sturt, Charles – 29, 59
Surprize – 13, 292
Swanton, James – 192
Sykes, William – 139

T

Tasman, Abel – 10
Tietkens, William – 109-110
Tobermory Station – 164
Todd, Alice – 67
Todd, Charles – 58-59, 64, 67, 70, 84-85
Tomkinson, Ranges – 107
Tomkinson, Samuel – 107
Torrens, Sir Robert – 187
Tuckett – 62
Twain, Mark – 493-494
Tyson, Isabella – 287
Tyson, James 'Hungry' – 288-291

U

Uaipon, David – 407
Uardry - 177
Urquhart, George – 179-180

V

Victoria River Downs – 82, 163, 260, 286

W

Wade, Abdul – 170, 482-483, 485
Wade, Hamid – 485
Wade, Mary Ann – 11, 13
Warburton, Peter – 111
Warburton/Warburton Ranges – 111, 362-363

Wells, L.A. -- 227
White, Con – 164
White Fleet – 222
White, Myrtle Rose – 154
Whitton, Thomas – 34-36
Wilcannia – 435
Wilks, Tim – 166-167
Williams, Reg (R.M.) – 214-215
Wilpena Station - 163
Windich Springs – 123
Windich, Tommy – 120-122
Wingadee – 55, 421-422, 425, 428
Wingellina – 349, 361
Wonga – 31-32
Wonnaminta Station, 41, 129, 132, 134, 136, 139, 147-148, 156, 159, 161, 164, 225
Wood, Thomas – 247
Woods, A.T. – 58, 65-6Woomera – 327-328
Wright, Isabel – 178, 185
Wunnamurra – 144
Wyndham – 390

Y

Yarrwonga – 38
Young, Ned - 212

www.ingramcontent.com/pod-product-compliance
Lightning Source LLC
Chambersburg PA
CBHW051533010526
44107CB00064B/2711